C0-AYK-283

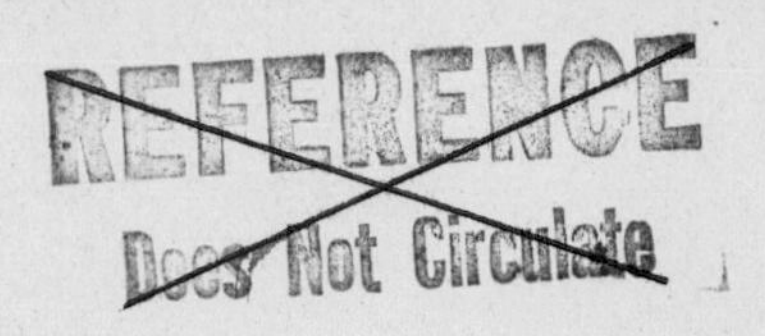
REFERENCE
Does Not Circulate

REFERENCE
Does Not Circulate

THE MYTHOLOGY OF ALL RACES

VOLUME X

NORTH AMERICAN

VOLUME I. *Greek and Roman*
WILLIAM SHERWOOD FOX, Ph.D., Princeton University.

VOLUME II. *Teutonic*
AXEL OLRIK, Ph.D., University of Copenhagen.

VOLUME III. *Celtic, Slavic*
CANON JOHN A. MACCULLOCH, D.D., Bridge of Allan, Scotland.
JAN MÁCHAL, Ph.D., Bohemian University, Prague.

VOLUME IV. *Finno-Ugric, Siberian*
UNO HOLMBERG, Ph.D., University of Finland, Helsingfors.

VOLUME V. *Semitic*
R. CAMPBELL THOMPSON, M.A., F.S.A., F.R.G.S., Oxford.

VOLUME VI. *Indian, Iranian*
A. BERRIEDALE KEITH, D.C.L., Edinburgh University.
ALBERT J. CARNOY, Ph.D., University of Louvain.

VOLUME VII. *Armenian, African*
MARDIROS ANANIKIAN, B.D., Kennedy School of Missions, Hartford, Connecticut.
GEORGE FOUCART, Docteur ès Lettres, French Institute of Oriental Archæology, Cairo.

VOLUME VIII. *Chinese, Japanese*
U. HATTORI, Litt.D., University of Tokyo.
(Japanese Exchange Professor at Harvard University, 1915–1916)
MASAHARU ANESAKI, Litt.D., University of Tokyo.
(Japanese Exchange Professor at Harvard University, 1913–1915)

VOLUME IX. *Oceanic*
ROLAND BURRAGE DIXON, Ph.D., Harvard University.

VOLUME X. *American (North of Mexico)*
HARTLEY BURR ALEXANDER, Ph.D., University of Nebraska.

VOLUME XI. *American (Latin)*
HARTLEY BURR ALEXANDER, Ph.D., University of Nebraska.

VOLUME XII. *Egypt, Far East*
W. MAX MÜLLER, Ph.D., University of Pennsylvania.
SIR (JAMES) GEORGE SCOTT, K.C.I.E., London.

VOLUME XIII. *Index*

1

2

PLATE I

Zuñi masks for ceremonial dances. Upper, all colours, mask of the Warrior of the Zenith; lower, black, mask of the Warrior of the Nadir. After *23 ARBE*, Plates LVI, LVII. See p. 189 and Note 65 (pp. 309–10).

THE MYTHOLOGY OF ALL RACES

IN THIRTEEN VOLUMES

LOUIS HERBERT GRAY, A.M., PH.D., Editor

GEORGE FOOT MOORE, A.M., D.D., LL.D., Consulting Editor

NORTH AMERICAN

BY

HARTLEY BURR ALEXANDER, PH.D.

PROFESSOR OF PHILOSOPHY

UNIVERSITY OF NEBRASKA

VOLUME X

BOSTON

MARSHALL JONES COMPANY

M DCCCC XVI

Entered at Stationers' Hall, London

Printed April, 1916

PRINTED IN THE UNITED STATES OF AMERICA BY THE UNIVERSITY PRESS
CAMBRIDGE, MASSACHUSETTS

BOUND BY THE BOSTON BOOKBINDING COMPANY

AUTHOR'S PREFACE

NO one can be more keenly aware of the sketchy nature of the study here undertaken than is the author. The literature of the subject, already very great, is being augmented at a rate hitherto unequalled; and it is needless to say that this fact alone renders any general analysis at present provisional. As far as possible the author has endeavoured to confine himself to a descriptive study and to base this study upon regional divisions. Criticism has been limited to the indication of suggestive analogies, to summaries in the shape of notes, and to the formulation of a general plan of selection (indicated in the Introduction), without which no book could be written. The time will certainly come for a closely analytical comparative study of North American myths, but at the present time a general description is surely the work which is needed.

Bibliographical references have been almost entirely relegated to the Notes, where the sources for each section will be found, thus avoiding the typographical disfigurement which footnotes entail. The plan, it is believed, will enable a ready identification of any passage desired, and at the same time will give a convenient key for the several treatments of related topics. The Bibliography gives the sources upon which the text is chiefly based, chapter for chapter. Other references, incidentally quoted, are given in the Notes. The critical reader's attention is called, in particular, to Note 1, dealing with the difficult question of nomenclature and spelling. The author has made no attempt to present a complete bibliography of American Indian mythology. For further references the literature given in the "Bibliographical Guides" should be consulted;

important works which have appeared since the publication of these "Guides" are, of course, duly mentioned.

For the form and spelling of the names of tribes and of linguistic stocks the usage of the *Handbook of American Indians* is followed, and the same form is used for both the singular and for the collective plural. Mythic names of Indian origin are capitalized, italics being employed for a few Indian words which are not names. The names of various objects regarded as persons or mythic beings — sun, moon, earth, various animals, etc. — are capitalized when the personified reference is clear; otherwise not. This rule is difficult to maintain consistently, and the usage in the volume doubtless varies somewhat.

The word "corn," occurring in proper names, must be understood in its distinctively American meaning of "maize." Maize being the one indigenous cereal of importance in American ritual and myth, "Spirits of the Corn" (to use Sir J. G. Frazer's classic phrase) are, properly speaking, in America "Spirits of the Maize." A like ambiguity attaches to "buffalo," which in America is almost universally applied to the bison.

The illustrations for the volume have been selected with a view to creating a clear impression of the art of the North American Indians, as well as for their pertinency to mythic ideas. This art varies in character in the several regions quite as much as does the thought which it reflects. It is interesting to note the variety in the treatment of similar themes or in the construction of similar ceremonial articles; for this reason representations of different modes of presenting like ideas have been chosen from diverse sources: thus, the Thunderbird conception appears in Plates III, VI, XVI, and Figure 1; the ceremonial pole in Plates XII, XVII, XXX; and masks from widely separate areas are shown in the Frontispiece and in Plates IV, VII, XXV, XXXI. In a few cases (as Plates II, VIII, IX, XI, XVIII, and probably XIX) the art is modified by white influence; in the majority of examples it is purely aboriginal. The motives which prompt the several treatments are interestingly various: thus, the impulse which lies behind Plates II, VIII, IX, XVIII, XIX is purely the desire for pictorial illustration of a mythic story; mnemonic, historical, or heraldic in character — prompted by the desire for record — are Plates V, X, XI, XVII, XX, XXI, XXX, XXXII, XXXIII; while the majority of the remaining examples are representations of cult-objects. Through all, however, is to be observed the keen aesthetic instinct which is so marked a trait of North American tribes.

The author desires to express his sense of obligation to the editor of this series, Dr. Louis H. Gray, for numerous and valuable emendations, and to Dr. Melvin R. Gilmore, recently of the Nebraska State Historical Society, now Curator of the State Historical Society of North Dakota, especially for the materials appearing in Note 58 and Plate XIV.

HARTLEY BURR ALEXANDER.

March 1, 1916.

CONTENTS

ILLUSTRATIONS

FULL PAGE ILLUSTRATIONS

ILLUSTRATIONS IN THE TEXT

MAP

INTRODUCTION

IF the term be understood as signifying a systematic and conscious arrangement of mythic characters and events, it is certainly a misnomer to speak of the stories of the North American Indians as "mythology." To be sure, certain tribes and groups (as the Iroquois, the Pawnee, the Zuñi, the Bella Coola, to mention widely separate examples) have attained to something like consistency and uniformity in their mythic beliefs (and it is significant that in just these groups the process of anthropomorphization has gone farthest); but nowhere on the continent can we find anything like the sense for system which in the Old World is in part evidenced and in part introduced by the epic literatures — Aryan, Babylonian, Greek, Norse.

Mythology in the classic acceptation, therefore, can scarcely be said to exist in North America; but in quite another sense — belief in more or less clearly personified nature-powers and the possession of stories narrating the deeds and adventures of these persons — the Indians own, not one, but many mythologies; for every tribe, and often, within the tribe, each clan and society, has its individual mythic lore. Here again the statement needs qualifying. Beliefs vary from tribe to tribe, even from clan to clan, and yet throughout, if one's attention be broadly directed, there are fundamental similarities and uniformities that afford a basis for a kind of critical reconstruction of a North American Indian mythology. No single tribe and no group of tribes has completely expressed this mythology — much less has any realized its form; but the student of Indian lore can scarcely fail to become conscious of a coherent system of myths, of which the Indians themselves might have become aware in course of time, if the intervention of Old-World ideas had not confused them.

A number of distinctions are the necessary introduction to any study of Indian myth. In the first place, in America, no more than in the Old World, are we to identify religion with mythology. The two are intimately related; every mythology is in some degree an effort to define a religion; and yet there is no profound parallelism between god and hero, no immutable relation between religious ceremony and mythic tale, even when the tale be told to explain the ceremony. No illustration could be better than is afforded by the fact that the greatest of Indian mythic heroes, the Trickster-Transformer, now Hare, now Coyote, now Raven, is nowhere important in ritual; while the powers which evoke the Indian's deepest veneration, Father Sky and Mother Earth, are of rare appearance in the tales.

The Indian's religion must be studied in his rites rather than in his myths; and it may be worth while here to designate the most significant and general of these rites. Foremost is the calumet ceremony, in which smoke-offering is made to the sky, the earth, and the rulers of earth's quarters, constituting a kind of ritualistic definition of the Indian's cosmos. Hardly second to this is the rite of the sweat-bath, which is not merely a means of healing disease, but a prayer for strength and purification addressed to the elements — earth, fire, water, air, in which resides the life-giving power of the universe. Third in order are ceremonies, such as fasting and vigil, for the purpose of inducing visions that shall direct the way of life; for among the Indian's deepest convictions is his belief that the whole environment of physical life is one of strength-imbuing powers only thinly veiled from sight and touch. Shamanistic or mediumistic rites, resting upon belief in the power of unseen beings to possess and inspire the mortal body, form a fourth group of ceremonies. A fifth is composed of the great communal ceremonies, commonly called "dances" by white men.

These are almost invariably in the form of dramatic prayers — combinations of sacrifice, song, and symbolic personation — addressed to the great nature-powers, to sun and earth, to the rain-bringers, and to the givers of food and game. A final group is formed of rites in honour of the dead or of ancestral tutelaries, ceremonies usually annual and varying in purpose from solicitude for the welfare of the departed to desire for their assistance and propitiation of their possible ill will.

In these rituals are defined the essential beings of the Indian's pagan religion. There is the Great Spirit, represented by Father Sky or by the sky's great incarnation, the Sun Father. There are Mother Earth and her daughter, the Corn Mother. There are the intermediaries between the powers below and those above, including the birds and the great mythic Thunderbird, the winds and the clouds and the celestial bodies. There are the Elders, or Guardians, of the animal kinds, who replenish the earth with game and come as helpers to the huntsmen; and there is the vast congeries of things potent, belonging both to the seen and to the unseen world, whose help may be won in the form of "medicine" by the man who knows the usages of Nature.

Inevitably these powers find a fluctuating representation in the varying imagery of myth. Consistency is not demanded, for the Indian's mode of thought is too deeply symbolic for him to regard his own stories as literal: they are neither allegory nor history; they are myth, with a truth midway between that of allegory and that of history. Myth can properly be defined only with reference to its sources and motives. Now the motives of Indian stories are in general not difficult to determine. The vast majority are obviously told for entertainment; they represent an art, the art of fiction; and they fall into the classes of fiction, satire and humour, romance, adventure. Again, not a few are moral allegories, or they are fables with obvious lessons, such as often appear in the story of the theft of fire when it details the kinds of wood from which fire can best be kindled. A third motive is our universally human curiosity: we desire to know the causes of things, whether they be the forces that underlie recurrent phenomena or the seeming purposes that mark the beginnings and govern the course of history. Myths that detail causes are science in infancy, and they are perhaps the only stories that may properly be called myths. They may be simply fanciful explanations of the origin of animal traits — telling why the dog's nose is cold or why the robin's breast is red; and then we have the beast fable. They may be no less fanciful accounts of the institution of some rite or custom whose sanction is deeper than reason; and we have the so-called aetiological myth. They may be semi-historical reminiscences of the inauguration of new ways of life, of the conquest of fire or the introduction of maize by mythical wise men; or they may portray recoverable tribal histories through the distorted perspective of legend. In the most significant group of all, they seek to conceptualize the beginnings of all things in those cosmogonic allegories of which the nebular hypothesis is only the most recently outgrown example.

Stories which satisfy curiosity about causes are true myths. With this criterion it should perhaps seem an easy task for the student to separate mythology from fiction, and to select or reject from his materials. But the thing is not so simple. Human motives, in whatever grade of society, are seldom unmixed; it is much easier to analyze them in kind than to distinguish them in example. Take such a theme as the well-nigh universally North American account of the origin of death. On the face of it, it is a causal explanation; but in very many examples it is a moral tale, while in not a few instances both the scientific and the moral interest disappear before the aesthetic. In a Wikeno story death came into the world by the will of a little bird, — "How should I nest me in your warm graves if ye men live forever?" — and however grim the fancy, it is difficult to see anything but art in its motive; but in the version known to the Arctic Highlanders, where the poignant choice is put, "Will ye have eternal darkness and eternal life, or light and death?" — art and morality and philosophy are all intermingled.

To perfect our criterion we must add to the analysis of motive the study of the sources of mythic conceptions. In a broad way, these are the suggestions of environing nature, the analogies of human nature both psychical and physiological, imagination, and borrowings. Probably the first of these is the most important, though the "nature-myth" is far from being the simple and inevitable thing an elder generation of students would make of it. Men's ideas necessarily reflect the world that they know, and even where the mythic incidents are the same the timbre of the tale will vary, say from the Yukon to the Mississippi, in the eastern forest, or on the western desert. There are physiographical boundaries within the continent which form a natural chart of the divisions in the complexion of aboriginal thought; and while there are numberless overlappings, outcroppings, and intrusions, none the less striking are the general conformities of the character of the several regions with the character of the mythic lore developed in them. The forests of the East, the Great Plains, the arid South-West, secluded California, the North-Western archipelago, each has its own traits of thought as it has its own traits of nature, and it is inevitable that we suppose the former to be in some degree a reflection of the latter. Beyond all this there are certain constancies of nature, the succession of darkness and light, the circle of the seasons, the motions of sun, moon, and stars, of rivers and winds, that affect men everywhere and everywhere colour their fancies; and it is not the least interesting feature of the study of a widespread mythic theme or incident to see the variety of natural phenomena for which it may, first and last, serve to account, since the myth-maker does not find his story in nature, but writes it there with her colouring.

The second great source of myth material is found in the analogies of human nature. Primarily these are psychical: the desires and purposes of men are assumed, quite unconsciously, to animate and to inspire the whole drama of nature's growth and change, and thus the universe becomes peopled with personalities, ranging in definition from the senselessly voracious appetites incarnated as monsters, to the self-possessed purpose and, not infrequently, the "sweet reasonableness" of man-beings and gods. Besides the psychical, however, there are the physical analogies of humankind. The most elementary are the physiological, which lead to a symbolism now gruesome, now poetic. The heart, the hair, and the breath are the most significant to the Indian, and their inner meaning could scarcely be better indicated than in the words of a Pawnee priest from whom Alice Fletcher obtained her report of the *Hako*. One act of this ceremony is the placing of a bit of white down in the hair of a consecrated child, and in explaining this rite the priest said: "The down is taken from under the wings of the white eagle. The down grew close to the heart of the eagle and moved as the eagle breathed. It represents the breath and life of the white eagle, the father of the child." Further, since the eagle is intermediary between man and Father Heaven, "the white, downy feather, which is ever moving as if it were breathing, represents Tirawa-atius, who dwells beyond the blue sky, which is above the soft, white clouds"; and it is placed in the child's hair "on the spot where a baby's skull is open, and you can see it breathe." This is the poetic side of the symbolism; the gruesome is represented by scalping, by the tearing out of the heart, and sometimes by the devouring of it for the sake of obtaining the strength of the slain. Another phase of physiological symbolism has to do with the barbarian's never-paling curiosity about matters of sex; there is little trace of phallic worship in North America, but the Indian's myths abound in incidents which are as unconsciously as they are unblushingly indecent. A strange and recurrent feature of Indian myth is the personification of members of the body, especially the genital and excretory organs, usually in connexion with divination. The final step in the use of the human body as a symbol is anthropomorphism — that complete anthropomorphism wherein mythic powers are given bodies, not part human and part animal, but wholly human; it marks the first clear sense of the dignity of man, and of the superiority of his wisdom to that of the brutes. Not many Indian groups have gone far in this direction, but among the more advanced it is a step clearly undertaken.

Imagination plays a part in the development of myth which is best realized by the aesthetic effect created by a body of tales or by a set of pictorial symbols. The total impression of Indian mythic emblems is undoubtedly one of *grotesquerie*, but it is difficult to point to any pagan religious art except the Greek that has outgrown the grotesque; and the Indian has a quality of its own. There is a wide difference, however, in the several regions, and indeed as between tribes of the same region. The art of the North-West and of the South-West are both highly developed, but even in such analogous objects as masks they represent distinct types of genius. The Navaho and the Apache are neighbours and relatives, but they are poles apart in their aesthetic expression. Some tribes, as the Pawnee, show great originality; others, as the northern Athapascans and most of the Salish, are colourless borrowers.

Borrowing is, indeed, the most difficult of problems to solve. In the abstract, it is easy to suppose that, with the main similarities of environment in North America and the general evenness of a civilization everywhere neolithic, the like conditions of a like human nature would give rise to like ideas and fancies. It is equally easy to suppose that in a territory permeable nearly everywhere, among tribes in constant intercourse, borrowing must be extensive. Both factors are significant, though in general the obvious borrowing is likely to seem the more impressive. Nevertheless, universal borrowing is a difficult hypothesis, for innumerable instances show an identity of Old-World and New-World ideas, where communication within thinkable time is incredible. Even in the New World there are wide separations for identical notions that seem to imply distinct origins. Thus the Arctic Highlanders, who have only recently learned that there are other peoples in the world, possess ideas identical with those of the Indians of the far South. When such an idea is simply that there is a cavernous underworld which is an abode of spirits, there is no need to assume communication, for the notion is world-wide; but when the two regions agree in asserting that there are *four* underworld caverns — an idea which is in no sense a natural inference — then the suspicion of communication becomes inevitable. Again, constellation-myths which see in Corona Borealis a circle of chieftains, in the Pleiades a group of dancers, in Ursa Major a quadruped pursued by three hunters, might have many independent origins; but when we encounter so curious a story as that of the incestuous relations of the Sun and the Moon told by Eskimo in the north and Cherokee in the south, communication is again suggested; and this suggestion becomes almost certainty when we find, further, that a special incident of this myth — the daubing of the secret lover with paint or ashes by which he is later identified — appears in another tale found in nearly every part of the continent, the story of the girl who bore children to a dog.

In the story just mentioned the children of the girl and the dog sometimes become stars, sometimes the ancestors of a tribe or clan of men; and this is a fair illustration of the manner in which incidents having all the character of fiction are made to serve as explanatory myths by their various users. The fundamental material of myth is rather a collection of incidents fitted into the scheme of things suggested by perception and habit than the stark invention of nature; and while the incidents must have an invention somewhere, the greater portion of them seem to be given by art and adopted by nature,— borrowing and adaptation being, for the savage as for the civilized man, more facile than new thinking.

In every considerable collection of Indian stories there are many adaptations of common ideas and incidents. In different regions this basic material comes to characteristic forms of expression. Finally, in the continent as a whole, viewed as one great region, there is a generally definable scheme, within which the mythic conceptions of the North American fall into place. It is in this sense, and with reference to this scheme, that we may speak of a North American Indian mythological system.

On the side of cosmology, the scheme has already been indicated. There is a world above, the home of the Sky Father and of the celestial powers; there is a world below, the embodiment of the Earth Mother and the abode of the dead; there is the central plane of the earth, and there are the genii of its Quarters. But cosmology serves only to define the theatre; it does not give the action. Cosmogony is the essential drama. In the Indian scheme the beginning is seldom absolute. A few tribes recognize a creator who makes or a procreator who generates the world and its inhabitants; but the usual conception is either of a pre-existent sky-world, peopled with the images of the beings of an earth-world yet to come into being, or else of a kind of cosmic womb from which the First People were to have their origin. In the former type of legend, the action begins with the descent of a heaven-born Titaness; in the latter, the first act portrays the ascent of the ancestral beings from the place of generation. Uniformly, the next act of the world drama details the deeds of a hero or of twin heroes who are the shapers and lawgivers of the habitable earth. They conquer the primitive monsters and set in order the furniture of creation; quite generally, one of them is slain, and passes to the underworld to become its Plutonian lord. The theft of fire, the origin of death, the liberation of the animals, the giving of the arts, the institution of rites are all themes that recur, once and again, and in forms that show surprisingly small variation. Universal, too, is the cataclysmic destruction of the earth by flood, or fire and flood, leaving a few survivors to repopulate the restored land. Usually this event marks the close of a First, or Antediluvian Age, in which the people were either animal in form or only abortively human. After the flood the animals are transformed once for all into the beings they now are, while the new race of men is created. It is not a little curious to find in many tribes tales of a confusion of tongues and dispersion of nations bringing to a close the cosmogonic period and leading into that of legendary history.

Such, in broad outline, is the chart of the Indian's cosmic perspective. It is with a view to its fuller illustration that the myths studied in the ensuing chapters have been chosen from the great body of American Indian lore.

NORTH AMERICAN MYTHOLOGY

NORTH AMERICAN MYTHOLOGY

CHAPTER I

THE FAR NORTH

I. NORSEMAN AND SKRAELING

IN the year of our Lord 982 Eric the Red, outlawed from Iceland, discovered Greenland, which shortly afterward was colonized by Icelanders. Eric's son, Leif the Lucky, the first Christian of the New World, voyaging from Norway to Greenland, came upon a region to the south of Greenland where "self-sown corn" and wild vines grew, and which, accordingly, he named Vinland. This was in the year 1000, the year in which all Mediaeval Europe was looking for the Second Advent and for earth's destruction, but which brought instead the first discovery of a New World.

As yet no people had been encountered by the Scandinavians in the new-found lands. But the news of Vinland stirred the heart of Thorfinn Karlsefni and of his wife Gudrid, and with a company of men and two ships they set out for the region which Leif had found. First they came to a land which they called Helluland, "the land of flat stones," which seemed to them a place of little worth. Next they visited a wooded land full of wild beasts, and this they named Markland. Finally they came to Vinland, and there they dwelt for three winters, Gudrid giving birth to Snorri, the first white child born on the Western Continent. It was in Vinland that the Norsemen first encountered the Skraelings: "They saw a number of skin canoes, and staves were brandished from their boats with a noise like flails, and they were revolved in the same direction in which the sun moves." Thorfinn's band was small, the Skraelings were a multitude; so the colony returned to Greenland in the year 1006.

Apparently no further attempt was made to settle the mainland, though from time to time voyages were made thither for cargoes of timber. But the Greenland colony continued, unmolested and flourishing. About the middle of the thirteenth century peoples from the north, short and swart, began to appear; encounters became unfriendly, and in 1341 the northernmost Scandinavian settlement was destroyed. Meanwhile, ships were coming from Norway less and less frequently, and the colony ceased to prosper, ceased to be heard from. At the time when Columbus discovered the Antilles there was a Bishop of Greenland, holding title from the Pope, but there is no evidence that he ever saw his diocese, and when, in 1585, John Davis sailed into the strait now bearing his name all trace of the Norsemen's colony was lost.

But the people of the Far North had not forgotten, and when the white men again came among them they still preserved legends of former Kablunait.[1] The story of the first meeting of the two peoples still survived, and of their mutual curiosity and fear, and of how an Eskimo and a white man became fast friends, each unable to outdo the other in feats of skill and strength, until at last the Eskimo won in a contest at archery, and the white man was cast down a precipice by his fellow-countrymen. There is the story of Eskimo men lying in wait and stealing the women of the Kablunait as they came to draw water. There are stories of blood feuds between the two peoples, and of the destruction of whole villages. At Ikat the Kablunait were taken by surprise; four fathers with their children fled out upon the ice and all were drowned; sometimes they are visible at the bottom of the sea, and then, say the Eskimo, one of our people will die.

Such are the memories of the lost colony which the Greenlanders have preserved. But far and wide among the Eskimo tribes there is the tradition of their former association with

PLATE II

Encounter of Eskimo and Kablunait, from a Greenlandic drawing. After H. Rink, *Tales and Traditions of the Eskimo.*

the Tornit, the Inlanders, from whom they were parted by feud and war. The Tornit were taller and stronger and swifter than the Eskimo, and most of them were blear-eyed; their dress and weapons were different, and they were not so skilful in boating and sealing or with the bow. Finally, an Eskimo youth quarrelled with one of the Tornit and slew him, boring a hole in his forehead with a drill of crystal. After that all the Tornit fled away for fear of the Eskimo and since then the Coast-People and the Inland-Dwellers have been enemies.

In the stories of the Tornit may be some vague recollections of the ancient Norsemen; more plausibly they represent the Indian neighbours of the Eskimoan tribes on the mainland, for to the Greenlanders the Indians had long become a fabulous and magical race. Sometimes, they say, the Tornit steal women who are lost in the fog, but withal are not very dangerous; they keep out of sight of men and are terribly afraid of dogs. Besides the Tornit there are in the Eskimo's uncanny Inland elves and cannibal giants, one-eyed people, shape-shifters, dog-men, and monsters, such as the Amarok, or giant wolf, or the horrid caterpillar that a woman nursed until it grew so huge that it devoured her baby — for it is a region where history and imagination mingle in nebulous marvel.[2]

II. THE ESKIMO'S WORLD

There is probably no people on the globe more isolated in their character and their life than are the Eskimo. Their natural home is to the greater part of mankind one of the least inviting regions of the earth, and they have held it for centuries with little rivalry from other races. It is the coastal region of the Arctic Ocean from Alaska to Labrador and from Labrador to the north of Greenland: inlandward it is bounded by frozen plains, where even the continuous day of Arctic summer frees only a few inches of soil; seaward it borders upon icy waters, solid during the long months of the Arctic night.

The caribou and more essentially the seal are the two animals upon which the whole economy of Eskimo life depends, both for food and for bodily covering; the caribou is hunted in summer, the seal is the main reliance for winter. But the provision of a hunting people is never certain; the seasonal supply of game is fluctuating; and the Eskimo is no stranger to starvation. His is not a green world, but a world of whites and greys, shot with the occasional splendours of the North. Night is more open to him than the day; he is acquainted with the stars and death is his familiar.

"Our country has wide borders; there is no man born has travelled round it; and it bears secrets in its bosom of which no white man dreams. Up here we live two different lives; in the Summer, under the torch of the Warm Sun; in the Winter, under the lash of the North Wind. But it is the dark and the cold that make us think most. And when the long Darkness spreads itself over the country, many hidden things are revealed, and men's thoughts travel along devious paths" (quoted from "Blind Ambrosius," a West Greenlander, by Rasmussen, *The People of the Polar North*, p. 219).

The religious and mythical ideas of the Eskimo wear the hues of their life. They are savages, easily cheered when food is plenty, and when disheartened oppressed rather by a blind helplessness than by any sense of ignorance or any depth of thought. Their social organization is loose; their law is strength; their differences are settled by blood feuds; a kind of unconscious indecency characterizes the relations of the sexes; but they have the crude virtues of a simply gregarious people — ready hospitality, willingness to share, a lively if fitful affectionateness, a sense of fun. They are given to singing and dancing and tale-telling; to magic and trance and spirit-journeys. Their adventures in real life are grim enough, but these are outmatched by their flights of fancy. As their life demands, they are rapacious and ingrained huntsmen; and perhaps the strongest trait of their tales is the succession of images reflecting the intimate habits of a people whose every member is a butcher — blubber and entrails and warm blood, bones and the foulness of parasites and decay: these replace the tenderer images suggested to the minds of peoples who dwell in flowered and verdured lands.

III. THE WORLD-POWERS

For the Eskimo, as for all savage people, the world is upheld by invisible powers. Everything in nature has its Inua,[3] its "owner" or "indweller"; stones and animals have their Inue, the air has an Inua, there is even an Inua of the strength or the appetite; the dead man is the Inua of his grave, the soul is the Inua of the lifeless body. Inue are separable from the objects of which they are the "owners"; normally they are invisible, but at times they appear in the form of a light or a fire — an ill-seen thing, foretokening death.

The "owners" of objects may become the helpers or guardians of men and then they are known as Tornait.[4] Especially potent are the Inue of stones and bears; if a bear "owner" becomes the Tornak of a man, the man may be eaten by the bear and vomited up again; he then becomes an Angakok, or shaman,[5] with the bear for his helper. Men or women with many or powerful Tornait are of the class of Angakut, endowed with magical and healing power and with eyes that see hidden things.

The Greenlanders had a vague belief in a being, Tornarsuk, the Great Tornak, or ruler of the Tornait, through whom the Angakut obtained their control over their helpers; but a like belief seems not to have been prevalent on the continent.[6] In the spiritual economy of the Eskimo, the chief place is held by a woman-being, the Old Woman of the Sea, — Nerrivik, the "Food Dish," the north Greenlanders call her, — while Sedna is a mainland name for her.[7] Once she was a mortal woman; a petrel wooed her with entrancing song and carried her to his home beyond the sea. Too late she found that he had deceived her. When her relatives tried to rescue her, the bird raised such a storm that they cast her into the sea to save themselves; she attempted to cling to the boat, but they cut off her hand, and she sank to the bottom, her severed fingers being transformed into whales and seals of the several kinds. In her house in the depths of the sea Nerrivik dwells, trimming her lamp, guarded by a terrible dog, and ruling over the animal life of the deep. Sometimes men catch no seals, and then the Angakut go down to her and force or persuade her to release the food animals; that is why she is called the "Food Dish." It is not difficult to perceive in this Woman of the Sea a kind of Mother of Wild Life — a hunter folk's goddess, but cruel and capricious as is the sea itself.

In the house of Sedna is a shadowy being, Anguta, her father. Some say that it was he who rescued her and then cast her overboard to save himself, and he is significantly surnamed "the Man with Something to Cut." Like his daughter, Anguta has a maimed hand, and it is with this that he seizes the dead and drags them down to the house of Sedna — for her sovereignty is over the souls of the dead as well as over the food of the living; she is Mistress of Life and of Death. According to the old Greenlandic tradition, when the Angakut go down to the Woman of the Sea they pass first through the region of the dead, then across an abyss where an icy wheel is forever revolving, next by a boiling cauldron with seals in it, and lastly, when the great dog at the door is evaded, within the very entrance there is a second abyss bridged only by a knifelike way. Such was the Eskimo's *descensus Averno.*[8]

IV. THE WORLD'S REGIONS

As the Eskimo's Inland is peopled with monstrous tribes, so is his Sea-Front populous with strange beings.[9] There are the Inue of the sea — a kind of mermen; there are the mirage-like Kayak-men who raise storms and foul weather; there are the phantom women's boats, the Umiarissat, whose crews, some say, are seals transformed into rowers. Strangest of all are the Fire-People, the Ingnersuit, dwelling in the cliffs, or, as it were, in the crevasse between land and sea. They are of two classes, the Pug-Nosed People and the Noseless People. The former are friendly to men, assisting the kayaker even when invisible to him; the Noseless Ones are men's enemies, and they drag the hapless kayaker to wretched captivity down beneath the black waters. An Angakok was once seal-hunting, far at sea; all at once he found himself surrounded by strange kayaks — the Fire-People coming to seize him. But a commotion arose among them, and he saw that they were pursued by a kayak whose prow was like a great mouth, opening and shutting, and slaying all that were in its path; and suddenly all of the Fire-People were gone from the surface of the sea. Such was the power of the shaman's helping spirit.

In the Eskimo's conception there are regions above and regions below man's visible abode, and the dead are to be found in each.[10] Accounts differ as to the desirability of the several abodes. The mainland people—or some of them—regard the lower world as a place of cold and storm and darkness and hunger, and those who have been unhappy or wicked in this life are bound thither; the region above is a land of plenty and song, and those who have been good and happy, and also those who perish by accident or violence, and women who die in child-birth, pass to this upper land. But there are others who deem the lower world the happier, and the upper the realm of cold and hunger; yet others maintain that the soul is full of joy in either realm.

The Angakut make soul-journeys to both the upper and the lower worlds.[11] The lower world is described as having a sky like our own, only the sky is darker and the sun paler; it is always winter there, but game is plentiful. Another tale tells of four cavernous underworlds, one beneath the other; the first three are low-roofed and uncomfortable, only the fourth and lowest is roomy and pleasant. The upper world is beyond the visible sky, which is a huge dome revolving about a mountain-top; it is a land with its own hills and valleys, duplicating Earth. Its "owners" are the Inue of the celestial bodies, who once were men, but who have been translated to the heavens and are now the celestial lights. The road to the upper world is not free from perils: on the way to the moon there is a person who tempts wayfarers to laughter, and if successful in making them laugh takes out their entrails.[8] Perhaps this is a kind of process of disembodying; for repeatedly in Eskimo myth occur spirit-beings which when seen face to face appear to be human beings, but when seen from behind are like skeletons.[12]

V. THE BEGINNINGS

The Sun and the Moon were sister and brother — mortals once. In a house where there was no light they lay together, and when the sister discovered who had been her companion, in her shame she tore off her breasts and threw them to her brother, saying, "Since my body pleaseth thee, taste these, too." Then she fled away, her brother pursuing, and each bearing the torches by means of which they had discovered one another. As they ran they rose up into the heavens; the sister's torch burned strong and bright, and she became the Sun; the brother's torch died to a mere ember, and he became the Moon.[13] When the Sun rises in the sky and summer is approaching, she is coming "to give warmth to orphans," say the Eskimo; for in the Far North, where many times in the winter starvation is near, the lot of the orphan is grimly uncertain.

The Greenlanders are alert to the stars, especially those that foretell the return of the summer sun; when Orion is seen toward dawn, summer is coming and hearts are joyous.

PLATE III

1

Example of gorget, or breast-ornament, of wood, used by the Eskimo of western Alaska in shamanistic dances, often in combination with a mask. On the original (now in the United States National Museum), the central figure of a man standing on a whale and holding fishes is painted in red, all the other figures being in black. The central figure represents a marine god or giant, probably the Food-Giver. See Note 9, (p. 274).

2

Harpoon-rest with sketch of a mythic bird capturing a whale. From Cape Prince of Wales. Now in United States National Museum. The bird is probably the Thunderbird, as in the similar motive in the art of the North-West Coast Indians.

The Eskimo tell how men with dogs once pursued a bear far out on the ice; suddenly the bear began to rise into the air, his pursuers followed, and this group became the constellation which we name Orion. A like story is sometimes told of the Great Bear (Ursa Major). Harsher is the tale which tells of the coming of Venus: "He who Stands and Listens" — for the sun's companion is a man to the Eskimo. An old man, so the story goes, was sealing near the shore; the noise of children playing in a cleft of rock frightened the seals away; and at last, in his anger, he ordered the cleft to close over them. When their parents returned from hunting, all they could do was to pour a little blood down a fissure which had been left, but the imprisoned children soon starved. They then pursued the old man, but he shot up into the sky and became the luminous planet which is seen low in the west when the light begins to return after the wintry dark.[14]

The Eskimo do not greatly trouble themselves with thoughts as to the beginnings of the world as a whole; rather they take it for granted, quite unspeculatively. There is, however, an odd Greenlandic tale of how earth dropped down from the heavens, soil and stones, forming the lands we know. Babies came forth — earth-born — and sprawled about among the dwarf willows; and there they were found by a man and a woman (none knows whence these came), and the woman made clothes for them, and so there were people; and the man stamped upon the earth, whence sprang, each from its tiny mound, the dogs that men need.[15] At first there was no death; neither was there any sun. Two old women debated, and one said, "Let us do without light, if so we can be without death"; but the other said, "Nay, let us have both light and death!" — and as she spoke, it was so.[16]

The Far North has also a widely repeated story of a deluge that destroyed most of the earth's life, as well as another widespread account of the birth of the different races of mankind — for at first all men were Eskimo — from the union of a girl with a dog:[17] the ancestors of the white men she put in the sole of a boot and sent them to find their own country, and when the white men's ships came again, lo, as seen from above, the body of each ship looked precisely like the sole of a boot!

VI. LIFE AND DEATH

Birth and death, in Eskimo conception, are less a beginning and an end than episodes of life. Bodies are only instruments of souls — the souls which are their "owners"; and what respect is shown for the bodies of the dead is based upon a very definite awe of the potencies of their Inue, which have been augmented rather than diminished by the last liberation. Souls may be born and reborn both as man and as beast, and some have been known to run the whole gamut of the animal kingdom before returning to human shape.[18] Ordinarily human souls are reborn as men. Monsters, too, are born of human parents: one of the most ghastly of the northern tales is the story of "the Baby who ate its parents"; it tore off its mother's breasts as she suckled it, it devoured her body and ate its father; and then, covered with its parents' blood and crying for meat, it crawled horribly toward the folk, who fled in terror.[19]

Besides the soul which is the body's "owner" the Eskimo believe in a name-soul.[20] The name of the dead man is not mentioned by his kinsfolk until a child has come into the world to bear it anew. Then, when the name has thus been reborn, the dead man's proper soul is free to leave the corpse and go to the land of the departed. An odd variant of this Greenlandic notion was encountered by Stefánsson among the western tribes: these people believe that the soul of the dead relative enters the body of the new-born child, guarding and protecting its life and uttering all its words until it reaches the age of discretion; then the child's own soul is supposed to assume sway, and it is called after a name of its own. If there have been a number of deaths previous to a birth, the child may have several such guardian spirits.

Sometimes a child had dire need of guardian spirits. Such a one was Qalanganguasê; his parents and his sister were dead; he had no kindred to care for him and he was paralysed in the lower part of his body. When his fellow-villagers went hunting, he was left alone; and then, in his solitude, the spirits came and whiled away the hours. Once, however, the spirit of his sister was slow in going (for Qalanganguasê had been looking after the little child she had left when she died), and the people, on their return, saw the shadow of her flitting feet. When Qalanganguasê told what had happened, the villagers challenged him to the terrible song-duel in which the Angakut try one another's strength;[21] and they bound him to the supports of the house and left him swinging to and fro. But the spirit of his mother came to him, and his father's spirit, saying, "Journey with us"; and so he departed with them, nor did his fellow-villagers ever find him again.[22]

Qalanganguasê was an orphaned child and a cripple; his rights to life — in the Polar North — were little enough. Mitsima was an old man. He was out seal-catching in midwinter; a storm came up, and he was lost to his companions. When the storm passed, his children saw him crawling like a dog over the ice, for his hands and feet were frozen — his children saw him, but they were afraid to go out to him, for he was near unto death. "He is an old man," they said, and so they let him die; for the aged, too, have little right to life in the Polar North.

Perhaps it is necessity rather than cruelty in a region where life is hard. Perhaps it is that death seems less final, more episodic, to men whose lives are always in peril. Perhaps it is the ancient custom of the world, which only civilized men have forgotten. "We observe our old customs," said a wise elder to Knud Rasmussen — and he was speaking of the observation of the rites for the dead — "in order to hold the world up, for the powers must not be offended. We observe our customs, in order to hold each other up. We are afraid of the great Evil. Men are so helpless in the face of illness. The people here do penance, because the dead are strong in their vital sap, and boundless in their might."

CHAPTER II

THE FOREST TRIBES

I. THE FOREST REGION

WHEN British and French and Dutch colonized North America in the seventeenth century, the region which they entered was a continuous forest extending northward to the tree line of Labrador and Hudson's Bay west, southward to the foot-hills of the mountains and the shores of the Gulf, and westward to about the longitude of the Mississippi River. This vast region was inhabited by numerous tribes of a race new to white men. The Norse, during their brief stay in Vinland, on the northern borders of the forest lands, had heard, through the Skraelings, of men who wore fringed garments, carried long spears, and whooped loudly; but they had not seen those people, whom it had remained for Columbus first to encounter. These men — "Indians" Columbus had called them — were, in respect to polity, organized into small tribal groups; but these groups, usually following relationship in speech and natural proximity, were, in turn, loosely bound together in "confederacies" or "nations." Even beyond these limits affinity of speech delimited certain major groups, or linguistic stocks, normally representing consanguineous races; and, indeed, the whole forest region, from the realm of the Eskimo in the north to the alluvial and coastal lands bordering on the Gulf, was dominated by two great linguistic stocks, the Algonquian and the Iroquoian, whose tribes were the first aborigines encountered by the white colonists.

The Algonquians, when the whites appeared, were by far the more numerous and wide-spread of the two peoples.

Their tribes included, along the Atlantic coast, the Micmac of New Brunswick and Nova Scotia, the Abnaki, Pennacook, Massachuset, Nauset, Narraganset, Pequot, etc., of New England, the Mahican and Montauk of New York, the Delaware of New Jersey, and the Nanticoke and Powhatan of Virginia and North Carolina. North of the St. Lawrence were the Montagnais and Algonquin tribes, while westward were the Chippewa and Cree, mainly between the Great Lakes and Hudson's Bay. The Potawatomi, Menominee, Sauk and Fox, Miami, Illinois, and Shawnee occupied territory extending from the western lakes southward to Tennessee and westward to the Mississippi. On the Great Plains the Arapaho and Cheyenne and in the Rocky Mountains the Siksika, or Blackfeet, were remote representatives of this vast family of tribes. In contrast, the Iroquoian peoples were compact and little divided. The two centres of their power were the region about Lakes Erie and Ontario and the upper St. Lawrence, southward through central New York and Pennsylvania, and the mountainous region of the Carolina and Virginia colonies. Of the northern tribes the Five Nations,[23] or Iroquois Confederacy, of New York, and the Canadian Huron, with whom they were perpetually at war, were the most important; of the southern, the Tuscarora and Cherokee. In all the wide territory occupied by these two great stocks the only considerable intrusion was that of the Catawba, an offshoot of the famed Siouan stock of the Plains, which had established itself between the Iroquoian Cherokee and the Algonquian Powhatan.

As the territories of the forest tribes were similar — heavily wooded, whether on mountain or plain, copiously watered, abounding in game and natural fruits — so were their modes of life and thought cast to the same pattern. Every man was a hunter; but, except in the Canadian north, agriculture was practised by the women, with maize for the principal crop,[24] and the villages were accordingly permanent. Industries were of

the Stone Age, though not without art, especially where the ceremonial of life was concerned. The tribes were organized for war as for peace, and indeed, if hunting was the vocation, war was the avocation of every Indian man: warlike prowess was his crowning glory, and stoical fortitude under the most terrible of tortures his supreme virtue; the cruelty of the North American Indian — and few peoples have been more consciously cruel — can be properly understood only as the reflection of his intense esteem for personal courage, to the proof of which his whole life was subjected. For the rest, a love of ritual song and dance, of oratory and the counsel of elders, a fine courtesy, a subtle code of honour, an impeccable pride, were all traits which the Forest Tribes had developed to the full, and which gave to the Indian that aloofness of mien and austerity of character which were the white man's first and most vivid impression of him. In the possession of these traits, as in their mode of life and the ideas to which it gave birth, the forest Indians were as one people; the Algonquians were perhaps the more poetical, the more given to song and prophecy, the Iroquoians the more politic and the better tacticians; but their differences were slight in contrast to an essential unity of character which was to form, during the first two centuries of the white men's contact with the new-found race, the European's indelible impression of the Red Man.

II. PRIEST AND PAGAN

Men's beliefs are their most precious possessions. The gold and the furs and the tobacco of the New World were bright allurements to the western adventure; but it was the desire to keep their faith unmolested that planted the first permanent English colony on American shores, and Spanish *conquistadores* and French *voyageurs* were not more zealous for wealth and war than were the Jesuit Fathers, who followed in their footsteps and outstayed their departure, for the Christianizing of the Red Man's pagan soul. It is to these missionary priests that we owe most of our knowledge of the Indian's native beliefs — at least, for the earlier period. They entered the wilderness to convert the savage, and accordingly it became their immediate interest to discover what religious ideas this child of nature already possessed. In their letters on the language, institutions, and ideas of the Indians, written for the enlightenment of those intending to enter the mission field, we have the first reliable accounts of Indian myth and religion.

To be sure, the Fathers did not immediately understand the aborigines. In one of the earliest of the *Relations* Père Lalemant wrote, of the Montagnais: "They have no form of divine worship nor any kind of prayers"; but such expressions mean simply that the missionaries found among the Indians nothing similar to their own religious practices. In the *Relation* of 1647–48 Père Raguenau said, writing of the Huron: "To speak truly, all the nations of these countries have received from their ancestors no knowledge of a God; and, before we set foot here, all that was related about the creation of the world consisted of nothing but myths. Nevertheless, though they were barbarians, there remained in their hearts a secret idea of the Divinity and of a first Principle, the author of all things, whom they invoked without knowing him. In the forests and during the chase, on the waters, and when in danger of shipwreck, they name him *Aireskouy Soutanditenr*,[25] and call him to their aid. In war, and in the midst of their battles, they give him the name of *Ondoutaete* and believe that he alone awards the victory.[59] Very frequently they address themselves to the Sky, paying it homage; and they call upon the Sun to be witness of their courage, of their misery, or of their innocence. But, above all, in treaties of peace and alliance with foreign Nations they invoke, as witnesses of their sincerity, the Sun and the Sky, which see into the depths of their hearts, and will wreak vengeance on the treachery of those who betray their trust and do not keep their word. So true is what Tertullian said of the most infidel Nations, that nature in the midst of perils makes them speak with a Christian voice, — *Exclamant vocem naturaliter Christianam*, — and have recourse to a God whom they invoke almost without knowing him, — *Ignoto Deo*." [6]

Exclamant vocem naturaliter Christianam! Two centuries later another Jesuit, Father De Smet, uses the same expression in describing the religious feeling of the Kansa tribe: "When we showed them an Ecce Homo and a statue of our Lady of the Seven Dolours, and the interpreter explained to them that that head crowned with thorns, and that countenance defiled with insults, were the true and real image of a God who had died for love of us, and that the heart they saw pierced with seven swords was the heart of his mother, we beheld an affecting illustration of the beautiful thought of Tertullian, that the soul of man is naturally Christian!"

It is not strange, therefore, that when these same Fathers found in America myths of a creation and a deluge, of a fall from heaven and of a sinful choice bringing death into the world, they conceived that in the new-found Americans they had discovered the lost tribes of Israel.

III. THE MANITOS[3]

"The definition of being is simply power," says a speaker in Plato's *Sophist;* and this is a statement to which every American Indian would accede. Each being in nature, the Indians believe, has an indwelling power by means of which this being maintains its particular character and in its own way affects other beings. Such powers may be little or great, weak or mighty; and of course it behooves a man to know which ones are great and mighty. Outward appearances are no sure sign of the strength of an indwelling potency; often a small animal or a lethargic stone may be the seat of a mighty power; but usually some peculiarity will indicate to the thoughtful observer the object of exceptional might, or it may be revealed in a dream or vision. To become the possessor of such an object is to have one's own powers proportionally increased; it is good "medicine" and will make one strong.

Every American language has its name for these indwelling powers of things. The Eskimo word is Inua, or "owner"; the Iroquois employ the word Orenda, and for maleficent powers, or "bad magic," Otgon; the Huron word is Oki;[26] the Siouan, Wakanda. But the term by which the idea has become most generally known to white men, doubtless because it was the word used by the Indians first encountered by the colonists, is the Algonquian Manitou, Manito, or Manido, as it is variously spelled. The customary translations are "power," "mystery," "magic," and, commoner yet, "spirit" and "medicine" — and the full meaning of the word would include all of these; for the powers of things include every gradation from the common and negligible to the mysterious and magical: when they pertain to the higher forces of nature they are intelligent spirits, able to hear and answer supplications; and wherever they may be appropriated to man's need they are medicine, spiritual and physical.

The Indian does not make, as we do, a sharp division between physical and spiritual powers; rather, he is concerned with the distinction between the weak and the strong: the sub-human he may neglect or conquer, the superhuman he must supplicate and appease. It is commonly to these latter, the mighty Manitos, that the word "spirit" is applied. Nor must we suppose that the Manitos always retain the same shape. Nature is constantly changing, constantly transforming herself in every part; she is full of energy, full of life; Manitos are everywhere effecting these transformations, presenting themselves now in this shape, now in that. Consequently, the Indian does not judge by the superficial gift of vision; he studies the effects of things, and in objects of humblest appearance he often finds evidences of the highest pow-

PLATE V.

Chippewa pictographic record of Midewiwin songs and rites. After Schoolcraft, *Indian Tribes*, part I, Plate LI. Two records are given: they are read from right to left, and upward. Following are interpretations of the figures, abridged from Schoolcraft.

Upper record: 1. Medicine lodge with winged figure representing the Great Spirit come to instruct the Indians. 2. Candidate for admission with pouch attached to his arm; wind gushes from the pouch. 3. Pause, indicating preparation of feast. 4. Arm holding a dish, representing hand of the master of ceremonies. 5. Sweat-lodge. 6. Arm of the priest who conducts the candidate. 7. Symbol for gifts, the admission fee of candidate. 8. Sacred tree, with medicine root. 9. Stuffed crane medicine-bag. 10. Arrow penetrating the circle of the sky. 11. A small high-flying hawk. 12. The sky, the Great Spirit above it, a manito's arm upraised beneath in supplication. 13. Pause. 14. Sacred or magic tree. 15. Drumstick. 16. Half of the sky with a man walking on it, symbol of midday. 17. The Great Spirit filling all space with his beams and halo. 18. Drum. 19. Tambourine with feather ornaments. 20. Crow. 21. An initiate or priest holding in one hand a drumstick, in the other the clouds of the celestial hemisphere.

Lower record: 1. A Wabeno's, or doctor's, hand. 2. Sacred tree or plant. 3. A Wabeno dog. 4. Sick man vomiting blood. 5. Pipe, here representing "bad medicine." 6. A worm that eats decaying wood. 7. A Wabeno spirit, addressed for aid. 8. A hunter with Wabeno powers. 9. The Great Spirit, filling the sky with his presence. 10. Sky with clouds. 11. Fabulous monster chasing the clouds. 12. Horned wolf. 13. The war eagle. 14. Bow and arrow, magically potent. 15. A Mide initiate, or doctor, holding the sky. 16. The sun. 17. Bow and arrow shooting power. 18. Man with drum, in ecstasy. Cf. Plate XX.

PLATE V

Chippewa pictographic record of Midewiwin songs and rites. After Schoolcraft, *Indian Tribes*, part i, Plate LI. Two records are given; they are read from right to left, and upward. Following are interpretations of the figures, abridged from Schoolcraft.

Upper record: 1. Medicine lodge with winged figure representing the Great Spirit come to instruct the Indians. 2. Candidate for admission with pouch attached to his arm; wind gushes from the pouch. 3. Pause, indicating preparation of feast. 4. Arm holding a dish, representing hand of the master of ceremonies. 5. Sweat-lodge. 6. Arm of the priest who conducts the candidate. 7. Symbol for gifts, the admission fee of candidate. 8. Sacred tree, with medicine root. 9. Stuffed crane medicine-bag. 10. Arrow penetrating the circle of the sky. 11. A small high-flying hawk. 12. The sky, the Great Spirit above it, a manito's arm upraised beneath in supplication. 13. Pause. 14. Sacred or magic tree. 15. Drumstick. 16. Half of the sky with a man walking on it, symbol of midday. 17. The Great Spirit filling all space with his beams and halo. 18. Drum. 19. Tambourine with feather ornaments. 20. Crow. 21. An initiate or priest holding in one hand a drumstick, in the other the clouds of the celestial hemisphere.

Lower record: 1. A Wabeno's, or doctor's, hand. 2. Sacred tree or plant. 3. A Wabeno dog. 4. Sick man vomiting blood. 5. Pipe, here representing "bad medicine." 6. A worm that eats decaying wood. 7. A Wabeno spirit, addressed for aid. 8. A hunter with Wabeno powers. 9. The Great Spirit, filling the sky with his presence. 10. Sky with clouds. 11. Fabulous monster chasing the clouds. 12. Horned wolf. 13. The war eagle. 14. Bow and arrow, magically potent. 15. A Mide initiate, or doctor, holding the sky. 16. The sun. 17. Bow and arrow shooting power. 18. Man with drum, in ecstasy. Cf. Plate XX.

N° I
N° II

ers. Stones do not seem to us likely objects of veneration, yet many strong Manitos dwell in them — perhaps it is the spark of fire in the impassive flint that appeals to the Red Man's imagination; perhaps it is an instinctive veneration for the ancient material out of which were hewn the tools that have lifted man above the brute; perhaps it is a sense of the age-long permanence and invulnerable reality of earth's rocky foundations[27]: —

> Ho! Aged One, eçka,
> At a time when there were gathered together seven persons,*
> You sat in the seventh place, it is said,
> And of the Seven you alone possessed knowledge of all things,
> Aged One, eçka.
> When in their longing for protection and guidance,
> The people sought in their minds for a way,
> They beheld you seated with assured permanency and endurance,
> In the center where converged the paths,
> There, exposed to the violence of the four winds, you sat,
> Possessed with power to receive supplications,
> Aged One, eçka.

It is thus that the Omaha began his invocation to the healing stones of his sweat lodge — a veritable omphalos, or centre of the world, symbolizing the invisible, pervasive, and enduring life of all things.

IV. THE GREAT SPIRIT[6]

The Algonquians of the north recognize as the chief of their Manitos, Gitche (or Kitshi) Manito, the Great Spirit, whom they also call the Master of Life.[28] It should not be inferred that a manlike personality is ascribed to the Great Spirit. He is invisible and immaterial; the author of life, but himself uncreated; he is the source of good to man, and is invoked with reverence: but he is not a definite personality about whom

* The spirits of the seven directions, above, below, here, and the four cardinal points. The passage is translated by Alice C. Fletcher, *27 ARBE*, p. 586. The word "eçka" may be roughly rendered "I desire," "I crave," "I implore," "I seek," etc., but has no exact equivalent in English.

myths are told; he is aloof from the world of sense; and he is perhaps best named, as some translators prefer, the Great Mystery of all things.

Yet the Great Spirit is not without proper names. Père Le Jeune wrote thus in 1633, concerning the Montagnais: "They say that there is a certain one whom they call *Atahocan*, who made all things. Talking one day of God, in a cabin, they asked me what this God was. I told them that it was he who could do everything, and who had made the Sky and Earth. They began to say to one another, 'Atahocan, Atahocan, it is Atahocan.'" Winslow, writing in 1622, mentions a similar spirit, Kiehtan, recognized by the Massachusetts Indians; and the early writers on the Virginia Indians tell of their belief "that there is one chiefe God that hath beene from all eternitie" who made the world and set the sun and moon and stars to be his ministers. The Iroquoian tribes have no precise equivalent for the Algonquian Kitshi Manito, but they believed in a similar spirit, known by the name of Areskoui or Agreskoui, to whom they offered the first-fruits of the chase and of victorious war. The terrible letter in which Père Isaac Jogues recounts his stay among the Iroquois, as a prisoner, tells of the sacrifice of a woman captive to this deity: "And as often as they applied the fire to that unhappy one with torches and burning brands, an old man cried in a loud voice: 'Aireskoi, we sacrifice to thee this victim that thou mayst satisfy thyself with her flesh, and give us victory over our enemies.'" [29]

The usual rite to the Great Spirit, however, is not of this horrible kind. From coast to coast the sacred Calumet is the Indian's altar, and its smoke is the proper offering to Heaven.[30] "The Sceptres of our Kings are not so much respected," wrote Marquette, "for the Savages have such a Deference for this Pipe, that one may call it *the God of Peace and War, and the Arbiter of Life and Death.*" "It was really a touching spectacle to see the calumet, the Indian emblem of peace, raised heavenward by the hand of a savage, presenting it to the Master of Life imploring his pity on all his children on earth and begging him to confirm the good resolutions which they had made." This is a comment of Father De Smet, who spent many years among many different tribes, and it is he who preserves for us the Delaware story of the gift of the Calumet to man: The peoples of the North had resolved upon a war of extermination against the Delaware, when, in the midst of their council, a dazzling white bird appeared among them and poised with outspread wings above the head of the only daughter of the head chief. The girl heard a voice speaking within her, which said: "Call all the warriors together; make known to them that the heart of the Great Spirit is sad, is covered with a dark and heavy cloud, because they seek to drink the blood of his first-born children, the Lenni-Lennapi, the eldest of all the tribes on earth. To appease the anger of the Master of Life, and to bring back happiness to his heart, all the warriors must wash their hands in the blood of a young fawn; then, loaded with presents, and the Hobowakan [calumet] in their hands, they must go all together and present themselves to their elder brothers; they must distribute their gifts, and smoke together the great calumet of peace and brotherhood, which is to make them one forever."

V. THE FRAME OF THE WORLD[11]

Herodotus said of the Persians: "It is their wont to perform sacrifices to Zeus, going up to the most lofty of the mountains; and the whole circle of the heavens they call Zeus; and they sacrifice to the Sun and the Moon and the Earth, to Fire and to Water and to the Winds; these are the only gods to whom they have sacrificed ever from the first." The ritual of the calumet [30] indicates identically the same conception of the world-powers among the American Indians. "On all great occasions," says De Smet, "in their religious and political ceremonies, and at their great feasts, the calumet presides; the savages send its first fruits, or its first puffs, to the Great Waconda, or Master of Life, to the Sun, which gives them light, and to the Earth and Water by which they are nourished; then they direct a puff to each point of the compass, begging of Heaven all the elements and favorable winds." And again: "They offer the Calumet to the Great Spirit, to the Four Winds, to the Sun, Fire, Earth and Water."

The ritual of the calumet defines for the Indian the frame of the world and the distribution of its indwelling powers. Above, in the remote and shining sky, is the Great Spirit, whose power is the breath of life that permeates all nature and whose manifestation is the light which reveals creation. As the spirit of light he shows himself in the sun, "the eye of the Great Spirit"; as the breath of life he penetrates all the world in the form of the moving Winds. Below is Mother Earth, giving forth the Water of Life, and nourishing in her bosom all organic beings, the Plant Forms and the Animal Forms. The birds are the intermediaries between the habitation of men and the Powers Above; serpents and the creatures of the waters are intermediaries communicating with the Powers Below.

Such, in broad definition, was the Indian's conception of the world-powers. But he was not unwilling to elaborate this simple scheme. The world, as he conceived it, is a storeyed world: above the flat earth is the realm of winds and clouds, haunted by spirits and traversed by the great Thunderbird; above this, the Sun and the Moon and the Stars have their course; while high over all is the circle of the upper sky, the abode of the Great Spirit. Commonly, the visible firmament is regarded as the roof of man's world, but it is also the floor of an archetypal heavenly world, containing the patterns of all things that exist in the world below: it is from this heaven above the heavens that the beings descend who create the visible universe. And as there are worlds above, so are there worlds beneath us; the earth is a floor for us, but a roof for those

PLATE VI

Chippewa side pouch of black dressed buckskin ornamented with red, blue, and yellow quill-work. The two large birds represented are Thunderbirds. Specimen in the Peabody Museum, Cambridge, Massachusetts. See Note 32 (pp. 287–88), and compare Plates III, XVI, and Figure 1.

below — the powers that send upward the fructifying springs and break forth as spirits of life in Earth's verdure. Further, both the realms above and the realms below are habitations for the souls of departed men; for to the Indian death is only a change of life.

The Chippewa believe that there are four "layers," or storeys, of the world above, and four of the world below. This is probably only a reflection in the overworld and the nether world of the fourfold structure of the cosmos, since four is everywhere the Indian's sacred number. The root of the idea is to be found in the conception of the four cardinal points or of the quarters of the world,[31] from which came the ministering genii when the Earth was made, and in which these spirits dwell, upholding the corners of the heavens. Potogojecs, a Potawatomi chief, told Father De Smet how Nanaboojoo (Manibozho) "placed four beneficial spirits at the four cardinal points of the earth, for the purpose of contributing to the happiness of the human race. That of the north procures for us ice and snow, in order to aid us in discovering and following the wild animals. That of the south gives us that which occasions the growth of our pumpkins, melons, maize and tobacco. The spirit placed at the west gives us rain, and that of the east gives us light, and commands the sun to make his daily walks around the globe." Frequently the Indians identify the Spirits of the Quarters with the four winds. Ga-oh is the Iroquoian Wind Giant, at the entrance to whose abode are a Bear and a Panther and a Moose and a Fawn: "When the north wind blows strong, the Iroquois say, 'The Bear is prowling in the sky'; if the west wind is violent, 'The Panther is whining.' When the east wind blows chill with its rain, 'The Moose is spreading his breath'; and when the south wind wafts soft breezes, 'The Fawn is returning to its Doe.'" Four is the magic number in all Indian lore; fundamentally it represents the square of the directions, by which the creator measured out his work.

VI. THE POWERS ABOVE

Even greater than the Wind Giant is the Thunderer,[32] whom the Iroquois deemed to be the guardian of the Heavens, armed with a mighty bow and flaming arrows, hater and destroyer of all things noxious, and especially to be revered as having slain the great Serpent of the waters, which was devouring mankind. Hino is the Thunderer's name, and his bride is the Rainbow; he has many assistants, the lesser Thunderers, and among them the boy Gunnodoyah, who was once a mortal. Hino caught this youth up into his domain, armed him with a celestial bow, and sent him to encounter the great Serpent; but the Serpent devoured Gunnodoyah, who communicated his plight to Hino in a dream, whereupon the Thunderer and his warriors slew the Serpent and bore Gunnodoyah, still living, back to the Skies. Commonly the Thunderer is a friend to man; but men must not encroach upon his domain. The Cherokee tell a tale of "the Man who married the Thunder's sister": [17] lured by the maiden to the Thunder's cave, he is there surrounded by shape-shifting horrors, and when he declines to mount a serpent-steed saddled with a living turtle, Thunder grows angry, lightning flashes from his eye, and a terrific crash stretches the young brave senseless; when he revives and makes his way home, though it seems to him that he has been gone but a day, he discovers that his people have long given him up for dead; and, indeed, after this he survives only seven days.[33]

One of Hino's assistants is Oshadagea, the great Dew Eagle, whose lodge is in the western sky and who carries a lake of dew in the hollow of his back. When the malevolent Fire Spirits are destroying Earth's verdure, Oshadagea flies abroad, and from his spreading wings falls the healing moisture. The Dew Eagle of the Iroquois is probably only the ghost of a Thunderbird spirit, which has been replaced, among them, by Hino the Heavenly Archer. The Thunderbird is an invisible spirit; the lightning is the flashing of his eye; the thunder is the noise of his wings. He is surrounded by assistants, the lesser Thunderers, especially birds of the hawk-kind and of the eagle-kind; Keneu, the Golden Eagle, is his chief representative. If it were not for the Thunderers, the Indians say, the earth would become parched and the grass would wither and die. Père Le Jeune tells how, when a new altar-piece was installed in the Montagnais mission, the Indians, "seeing the Holy Spirit pictured as a dove surrounded by rays of light, asked if the bird was not the thunder; for they believe that the thunder is a bird; and when they see beautiful plumes, they ask if they are not the feathers of the thunder."

The domain above the clouds is the heaven of the Sun and the Moon and the Stars. The Sun is a man-being, the Moon a woman-being; sometimes they are brother and sister, sometimes man and wife.[13] The Montagnais told Père Le Jeune that the Moon appeared to be dark at times because she held her son in her arms: "'If the Moon has a son, she is married, or has been?' 'Oh, yes, the Sun is her husband, who walks all day, and she all night; and if he be eclipsed or darkened, it is because he also sometimes takes the son which he has had by the Moon into his arms.' 'Yes, but neither the Sun nor the Moon has any arms.' 'Thou hast no sense; they always hold their drawn bows before them, and that is why their arms do not appear.'" Another Algonquian tribe, the Menominee, tell how the Sun, armed with bow and arrows, departed for a hunt; his sister, the Moon, alarmed by his long absence, went in search of him, and travelled twenty days before she found him. Ever since then the Moon has made twenty-day journeys through the sky. The Iroquois say that the Sun, Adekagagwaa, rests in the southern skies during the winter, leaving his "sleep spirit" to keep watch in his stead. On the eve of his departure, he addresses the Earth, promising his return: "Earth, Great Mother, holding your children close to your breast, hear my power! . . . I am Adekagagwaa!

I reign, and I rule all your lives! My field is broad where swift clouds race, and chase, and climb, and curl, and fall in rains to your rivers and streams. My shield is vast and covers your land with its yellow shine, or burns it brown with my hurrying flame. My eyes are wide, and search everywhere. My arrows are quick when I dip them in dews that nourish and breathe. My army is strong, when I sleep it watches my fields. When I come again my warriors will battle throughout the skies; Ga-oh will lock his fierce winds; Heno will soften his voice; Gohone [Winter] will fly, and tempests will war no more!"

The Indians know the poetry of the stars.[14] It is odd to find the Iroquois telling the story of the celestial bear, precisely as it is told by the Eskimo of northern Greenland: how a group of hunters, with their faithful dog, led onward by the excitement of the chase, pursued the great beast high into the heavens, and there became fixed as the polar constellation (Ursa Major). In the story of the hunter and the Sky Elk the sentiment of love mingles with the passion of the chase. Sosondowah ("Great Night"), the hunter, pursued the Sky Elk, which had wandered down to Earth, far up into the heaven which is above the heaven of the Sun. There Dawn made him her captive, and set him as watchman before the door of her lodge. Looking down, he beheld and loved a mortal maiden; in the spring he descended to her under the form of a bluebird; in the summer he wooed her under the semblance of a blackbird; in the autumn, under the guise of a giant nighthawk, he bore her to the skies. But Dawn, angered at his delay, bound him before her door, and transforming the maiden into a star set her above his forehead, where he must long for her throughout all time without attaining her. The name of the star-maiden, which is the Morning Star, is Gendenwitha, "It Brings the Day." The Pleiades are called the Dancing Stars. They were a group of brothers who were awakened in the night by singing voices, to which they began

PLATE VII

Secret society mask of the Seneca. The "Great Wind Mask," a medicine or doctor mask used in the ceremonies of the False Face Company. This society is said to have originated with the Stone Giants, who are represented in one of the masks used. Reproduced by courtesy of Arthur C. Parker, Archaeologist of the New York State Museum. See Note 65 (pp. 309–10), and compare Frontispiece and Plates IV, XXV, XXXI.

PLATE VII

Secret society mask of the Seneca. The "Great Wind Mask," a medicine or doctor mask, used in the ceremonies of the False Face Company. This society is said to have originated with the Stone Giants, who are represented in one of the masks used. Reproduced by courtesy of Arthur C. Parker, Archaeologist of the New York State Museum. See Note 65 (pp. 309–10), and compare Frontispiece and Plates IV, XXV, XXXI.

H. BIERCE

to dance. As they danced, the voices receded, and they, following, were led, little by little, into the sky, where the pitying Moon transformed them into a group of fixed stars, and bade them dance for ten days each year over the Red Man's council-house; that being the season of his New Year. One of the dancing brothers, however, hearing the lamentations of his mother, looked backward; and immediately he fell with such force that he was buried in the earth. For a year the mother mourned over his grave, when there appeared from it a tiny sprout, which grew into a heaven-aspiring tree; and so was born the Pine, tallest of trees, the guide of the forest, the watcher of the skies.

VII. THE POWERS BELOW

As there are Powers above so are there Powers below. Earth herself is the eldest and most potent of these.[34] Nokomis, "Grandmother," is her Algonquian name, but the Iroquois address her as Eithinoha, "Our Mother"; for, they say, "the earth is living matter, and the tender plantlet of the bean and the sprouting germ of the corn nestling therein receive through their delicate rootlets the life substance from the Earth. . . . Earth, indeed, feeds itself to them; since what is supplied to them is living matter, life in them is produced and conserved, and as food the ripened corn and bean and their kinds, thus produced, create and develop the life of man and of all living things."

Earth's daughter, in Iroquois legend, is Onatah, the Corn Spirit.[35] Once Onatah, who had gone in search of refreshing dews, was seized by the Spirit of Evil and imprisoned in his darkness under the Earth until the Sun found her and guided her back to the lost fields; never since has Onatah ventured abroad to look for the dews. The Iroquois story is thus a parallel of the Greek myth of Demeter and Persephone. The Chippewa, on the other hand, make of the Corn Spirit a heaven-sent youth, Mondamin, who is conquered and buried by a mortal hero: from his grave springs the gift of maize. Other food plants, such as the bean and the pumpkin, as well as wild plants and the various species of trees, have their several spirits, or Manitos; indeed, the world is alive with countless mysteries, of every strength and size, and the forest is all thronged with armies of Pukwudjies, the Indian's fairy folk.[36] "During a shower of rain thousands of them are sheltered in a flower. The Ojibwa, as he reclines beneath the shade of his forest trees, imagines these gods to be about him. He detects their tiny voices in the insect's hum. With half-closed eyes he beholds them sporting by thousands on a sun-ray."

The Iroquois recognize three tribes of Jogaoh, or Dwarf People: the Gahonga, of the rocks and rivers, whom the Indians call "Stone Throwers" because of their great strength and their fondness for playing with stones as with balls; [27] the Gandayah, who have a care for the fruitfulness not only of the land — for they fashion "dewcup charms" which attract the grains and fruits and cause them to sprout, — but also of the water, where they release captive fish from the trap when the fishermen too rapaciously pursue; and the Ohdowas, or underground people. The underworld where the Ohdowas live is a dim and sunless realm containing forests and plains, like the earth of man, peopled with many animals — all of which are ever desirous to ascend to the sunny realm above. It is the task of the Ohdowas to keep these underworld creatures in their proper place, especially since many of them are venomous and noxious beasts; and though the Ohdowas are small, they are sturdy and brave, and for the most part keep the monstrous beings imprisoned; rarely do the latter break through to devastate and defile the world above. As there are underearth people, so are there underwater people[9] who, like the Fire-People of the Eskimo, are divided into two tribes, one helpful, one hurtful to man. These underwater beings are human in form, and have houses, like those of men, beneath the waters; but they dress in snake's skins and wear horns. Sometimes their beautiful daughters lure mortal men down into the depths, to don the snake-skin costume and to be lost to their kindred forever.

Of monstrous beings, inhabiting partly the earth's surface, partly the underworld, the Iroquois recognize in particular the race of Great Heads [37] and the race of Stone Giants. The Great Heads are gifted with penetrating eyes and provided with abundant hair which serves them as wings; they ride on the tempest, and in their destructive and malevolent powers seem to be personifications of the storm, perhaps of the tornado. In one tale, which may be the detritus of an ancient and crude cosmogony, the Great Head obviously plays the *rôle* of a demiurge; and a curious story tells of the destruction of one of the tribe which pursued a young woman into her lodge and seeing her parching chestnuts concluded that coals of fire were good to eat; partaking of the coals, it died. These bizarre creatures are well calculated to spice a tale with terrors.

The Iroquoian Stone Giants,[38] as well as their congeners among the Algonquians (e. g. the Chenoo of the Abnaki and Micmac), belong to a wide-spread group of mythic beings of which the Eskimo Tornit are examples. They are powerful magicians, huge in stature, unacquainted with the bow, and employing stones for weapons. In awesome combats they fight one another, uprooting the tallest trees for weapons and rending the earth in their fury. Occasionally, they are tamed by men and, as they are mighty hunters, they become useful friends. Commonly they are depicted as cannibals; and it may well be that this far-remembered mythic people is a reminiscence, coloured by time, of backward tribes, unacquainted with the bow, and long since destroyed by the Indians of historic times.[2] Of course, if there be such an historic element in these myths, it is coloured and overlaid by wholly mythic conceptions of stone-armoured Titans or demiurges (see Ch. III, i, ii).

VIII. THE ELDERS OF THE KINDS[40]

The Onondaga story of the beginnings of things closes with these words: "Moreover, it is verily thus with all things that are contained in the earth here present, that they severally retransform or exchange their bodies. It is thus with all things that sprout and grow, and, in the next place, with all things that produce themselves and grow, and, in the next place, all the man-beings. All these are affected in the same manner, that they severally transform their bodies, and, in the next place, that they retransform their bodies, severally, without cessation" (Hewitt, *21 ARBE*, pp. 219–20).

Savages, and perhaps all people who live near to Nature, are first and inevitably Heracliteans: for them, as for the Greek philosopher, all things flow, the sensible world is a world of perpetual mutation; bodies, animate and inanimate, are but temporary manifestations — outward shadows of the multitude of shape-shifting Powers which govern the spectacle from behind the scene. Yet even the savage, conscious as he is of the impermanency of sensible things, detects certain constant forms, persistently reappearing, though in various individual embodiments. These forms are the natural *kinds* — the kindreds or species into which Nature is divided; they are the *Ideas* of things, as a greater Greek than Heraclitus would say; and the Indians all develop into Platonists, for they hold that each natural kind has its archetype, or Elder (as they prefer), dwelling in an invisible world and sustaining the temporary lives of all its earthly copies by the strength of its primal being.

The changing seasons themselves — which, for all peoples beyond the tropics, are the great facts governing the whole strategy of life — become fixed in a kind of constancy, and are eventually personified into such beings as we still fancifully form for Spring and Summer and Winter and Autumn.[39] To be sure, the seasons are not so many for peoples whose sus-

PLATE VIII

Iroquois drawing of a Great Head — a type of bodiless, man-eating monster (see Note 37, pp. 290–91). The picture, reproduced from Schoolcraft, *Indian Tribes*, part i, Plate LXXII, is an illustration of the story of the outwitting of the Great Head by an Indian woman, a story common to many of the Eastern tribes (see p. 29).

tenance is mainly obtained by the chase: for them, the open and closed, the green and the white, are the important divisions of the year. The Iroquois say that Winter is an old man of the woods, who raps the trees with his war-club: in very cold weather one can hear the sharp sound of his blows; while Spring is a lithe young warrior, with the sun in his countenance. The Montagnais were not sure whether the two Seasons were manlike, but they told Père Le Jeune that they were very sure that Nipin and Pipoun were living beings: they could even hear them talking and rustling, especially at their coming. "For their dwelling-place they share the world between them, the one keeping upon the one side, the other upon the other; and when the period of their stay at one end of the world has expired, each goes over to the locality of the other, reciprocally succeeding each other. Here we have, in part, the fable of Castor and Pollux," comments the good Father. "When *Nipinoukhe* returns, he brings back with him the heat, the birds, the verdure, and restores life and beauty to the world; but *Pipounoukhe* lays waste everything, being accompanied by the cold winds, ice, snows, and other phenomena of Winter. They call this succession of one to the other *Achitescatoueth;* meaning that they pass reciprocally to each other's places." Perhaps as charming a myth of the seasons as could be found is the Cherokee tale of "the Bride from the South." The North falls in love with the daughter of the South, and in response to his ardent wooings is allowed to carry her away to his Northland, where the people all live in ice houses. But the next day, when the sun rises, the houses begin to melt, and the people tell the North that he must send the daughter of the South to her native land, for her whole nature is warm and unfit for the North.

But it is especially in the world of animals that the spirits of the Kinds are important.[40] "They say," says Le Jeune, speaking of these same Montagnais (whose beliefs, in this respect, are typical), "that all animals, of every species, have an elder brother, who is, as it were, the source and origin of all individuals, and this elder brother is wonderfully great and powerful. The elder of the Beaver, they tell me, is perhaps as large as our cabin, although his Junior (I mean the ordinary Beaver) is not quite as large as our sheep. . . . If anyone, when asleep, sees the elder or progenitor of some animals, he will have a fortunate chase; if he sees the elder of the Beavers, he will take Beavers; if he sees the elder of the Elks, he will take Elks, possessing the juniors through the favor of their senior whom he has seen in the dream. I asked them where these elder brothers were. 'We are not sure,' they answered me, 'but we think the elders of the birds are in the sky, and that the elders of the other animals are in the water.'" In another connexion the Father tells the following story, which he had from a Montagnais: "A man, having traveled a long distance, at last reached the Cabin or house of God, as he named him who gave him something to eat. . . . All kinds of animals surround him [the god], he touches them, handles them as he wishes, and they do not fly from him; but he does them no harm, for, as he does not eat, he does not kill them. However, he asked this new guest what he would like to eat, and having learned that he would relish a beaver, he caught one without any trouble, and had him eat it; then asked him when he intended going away. 'In two nights,' was the answer. 'Good,' said he, 'you will remain two nights with me.' These two nights were two years; for what we call a year is only a day or a night in the reckoning of him who procures us food. And one is so contented with him that two winters, or two years, seem only like two nights. When he returned to his own country he was greatly astonished at the delay he had experienced." The god of the cabin is, no doubt, Messou (Manabozho), the Algonquian demiurge, for he is "elder brother to all beasts" and the ruler of animal life. Similarly, the Iroquoian demiurge Iouskeha is the bringer and namer of the primal animals: "They believe that animals were not at liberty from the beginning of the world, but that they were shut up in a great cavern where Iouskeha guarded them. Perhaps there may be in that some allusion to the fact that God brought all the animals to Adam," adds Père Brébeuf; and in the Seneca version of the Iroquoian genesis, the youth who brings the animals from the cavern of the Winds does, in fact, perform the office of Adam, giving them their several names.[41]

CHAPTER III

THE FOREST TRIBES

(Continued)

I. IROQUOIAN COSMOGONY[15]

THE Onondaga version of the genesis-myth of the Iroquois, as recorded by Hewitt, begins in this fashion: "He who was my grandfather was wont to relate that, verily, he had heard the legend as it was customarily told by five generations of grandsires, and this is what he himself was in the habit of telling. He customarily said: Man-beings dwell in the sky, on the farther side of the visible sky. The lodges they severally possess are customarily long [the Iroquoian "long house," or lodge]. In the end of the lodges there are spread out strips of rough bark whereon lie the several mats. There it is that, verily, all pass the night. Early in the morning the warriors are in the habit of going to hunt and, as is their custom, they return every evening."

This heaven above the visible heavens, which has existed from eternity, is the prototype of the world in which we dwell; and in it is set the first act of the cosmic drama. Sorrow and death were unknown there; it was a land of tranquil abundance. It came to pass that a girl-child was born of a celestial maid, her father having sickened and died — the first death in the universe — shortly before she was born. He had been placed, as he had directed, on a burial scaffold by the Ancient-Bodied One, grandmother to the child; and thither the girl-child was accustomed to go and converse with the dead parent. When she was grown, he directed her to take a certain journey through the heaven realm of Chief He-Holds-the-Earth, whom she was to marry, and beside whose lodge grew the great heaven tree.[42] The maiden crosses a river on a maple-log, avoids various tempters, and arrives at the lodge, where the chief subjects her to the ordeals of stirring scalding mush which spatters upon her naked body and of having her burns licked by rasp-tongued dogs. Having successfully endured these pains, he sends her, after three nights, to her own people, with the gift of maize and venison. She returns to her chief, and he, observing that she is pregnant, becomes ill with an unjustified jealousy of the Fire-Dragon. She gives birth to a daughter, Gusts-of-Wind; whereupon the chief receives visits from the Elders of the Kinds, which dwell in heaven, among them being the Deer, the Bear, the Beaver; Wind, Daylight, Night, Star; the Squash, the Maize, the Bean; the Turtle, the Otter, the Yellowhammer; Fire, Water, Medicine, — patterns of the whole furniture of creation. Aurora Borealis divines what is troubling his mind, and suggests the uprooting of the heaven tree. This is done, and an abyss is disclosed, looking down into a chaos of Wind and Thick Night — "the aspect was green and nothing else in color," says the Seneca version. Through this opening the Chief of Heaven casts his spouse and the child, who returns again into the body of her mother, first providing her with maize and venison and a faggot of wood, while the Fire-Dragon wraps around her a great ray of light.

Here ends the Upper World act of the drama. The name of the woman-being who is cast down from heaven is, as we know from the Jesuit *Relations*, Ataentsic or Ataensic,[43] who is to become the great Earth Mother. The Chief of Heaven is her spouse, — so that these two great actors in the world drama are Earth and Sky respectively; while their first-born is the Breath-of-Life.

The second act of the drama is set in the World Below. The Onondaga myth continues:

"So now, verily, her body continued to fall. Her body was

falling some time before it emerged. Now she was surprised, seemingly, that there was light below, of a blue color. She looked and there seemed to be a lake at the spot toward which she was falling. There was nowhere any earth. There she saw many ducks on the lake where they, being waterfowl of all their kinds, floated severally about. Without interruption the body of the woman-being continued to fall.

"Now at that time the waterfowl called the Loon shouted, saying: 'Do ye look, a woman-being is coming in the depths of the water, her body is floating up hither.' They said: 'Verily, it is even so.'

"Now in a short time the waterfowl called Bittern said: 'It is true that ye believe that her body is floating up from the depths of the water. Do ye, however, look upward.' All looked up, and all said: 'Verily, it is true.'

"One of the persons said: 'It seems, then, that there must be land in the depths of the water.' At that time the Loon said: 'Moreover, let us first seek to find some one who will be able to bear the earth on his back by means of the forehead pack strap.'"

All the animals volunteer. Otter and Turtle attempt the feat and fail; the Muskrat succeeds, placing the soil brought up from below on the back of the Turtle. "Now at this time the carapace began to grow and the earth with which they had covered it became the Solid Land." Upon this land Ataentsic alights, her fall being broken by the wings of the fowl which fly upward to meet her.[40]

On the growing Earth Gusts-of-Wind is reborn, and comes to maturity. She receives the visits of a nocturnal stranger, who is none other than the ruler of the winds, and gives birth to twins [44] — Sapling and Flint, the Yoskeha and Tawiscara of the *Relations* [45] — who show their enmity by a pre-natal quarrel, and cause their mother's death in being born. From the body of her daughter Ataentsic fashions the sun and the moon, though she does not raise them to the heavens. Sapling she casts out, for Flint falsely persuades her that it is Sapling who is responsible for their mother's death.

The third act of the drama details the creative acts of Sapling and Flint, and their enmities. Sapling (better known as Yoskeha, though his most ancient title seems to be Teharonhiawagon, He-Holds-the-Sky) is the demiurge and earth-shaper, and the spirit of life and summer. Flint, or Tawiscara, is an imitator and trickster, maker of malevolent beings, and spirit of wintry forces, but the favourite of Ataentsic.[38]

The act opens with the visit of Sapling to his father, the Wind-Ruler, who gives him presents of bow and arrows and of maize, symbolizing mastery over animal and vegetable food. The preparation of the maize is his first feat, Ataentsic rendering his work imperfect by casting ashes upon it: "The way in which thou hast done this is not good," says Sapling, "for I desire that the man-beings shall be exceedingly happy, who are about to dwell here on this earth." Next he brings forth the souls of the animal kinds, and moulds the traits of the different animals.[41] Flint, however, imprisons them in a cavern, and, although Sapling succeeds in releasing most of them, some remain behind to become transformed into the noxious creatures of the underworld. Afterward, in a trial of strength, Sapling overcomes the humpback Hadui, who is the cause of disease and decrepitude, but from whom Sapling wins the secret of medicine and of the ceremonial use of tobacco. The giving of their courses to the Sun and the Moon, fashioned from his mother's head and body by Ataentsic, was his next deed.[13] The grandmother and Flint had concealed these bodies and had left the earth in darkness; Sapling, aided by four animals, typifying the Four Quarters, steals back the Sun, which is passed from animal to animal (as in the Greek torch-race in honour of Selene) when they are pursued by Ataentsic and Flint. The creation of man, which Flint imitates only to produce monsters, and the banishment of Flint to the underworld complete the creative drama.

"Moreover, it is said that this Sapling, in the manner in which he has life, has this to befall him recurrently, that he becomes old in body, and that when, in fact, his body becomes ancient normally, he then retransforms his body in such wise that he becomes a new man-being again and again recovers his youth, so that one would think that he had just grown to the size which a man-being customarily has when he reaches the youth of man-beings, as manifested by the change of voice at puberty. Moreover, it is so that continuously the orenda immanent in his body — the orenda with which he suffuses his person, the orenda which he projects or exhibits, through which he is possessed of force and potency — is ever full, undiminished, and all-sufficient; and, in the next place, nothing that is otkon or deadly, nor, in the next place, even the Great Destroyer, otkon in itself and faceless, has any effect on him, he being perfectly immune to its orenda; and, in the next place, there is nothing that can bar his way or veil his faculties." [46]

In the *Relation* of 1636 Brébeuf says of the Hurons: "If they see their fields verdant in the spring, if they reap good and abundant harvests, and if their cabins are crammed with ears of corn, they owe it to Iouskeha. I do not know what God has in store for us this year; but . . . Iouskeha, it is reported has been seen quite dejected, and thin as a skeleton, with a poor ear of corn in his hand." [35]

II. ALGONQUIAN COSMOGONY [15]

As compared with the Iroquoian cosmogony, that of the Algonquian tribes is nebulous and confused: their gods are less anthropomorphic, more prone to animal form; the order of events is not so clearly defined. There is hardly a personage or event in the Iroquoian story that does not appear in Algonquian myth, and indeed the Algonquians would seem to have been the originators, or at least the earlier possessors, of these stories; yet the same power for organization which

PLATE IX

Iroquois drawing of Stone Giants. After Schoolcraft, *Indian Tribes*, part i, Plate LXXIII. The Stone Giants are related to such cosmogonical beings as Flint (Tawiscara) and Chakekenapok (see pp. 30, 41). They are generally malevolent in character. See Note 25 (pp. 291-92).

PLATE IX

Iroquois drawing of Stone Giants. After Schoolcraft, *Indian Tribes*, part i, Plate LXXIII. The Stone Giants are related to such cosmogonical beings as Flint (Tawiscara) and Chakekenapok (see pp. 36, 41). They are generally malevolent in character. See Note 38 (pp. 291–92).

is reflected in the Iroquoian Confederacy appears in the Iroquois's more masterful assimilation and depiction of the cosmic story which he seems to have borrowed from his Algonquian neighbours.

The central personage of Algonquian myth is Manabozho,[47] the Great Hare (also known by many other names and variants, as Nanibozho, Manabush, Michabo, Messou, Glooscap), who is the incarnation of vital energy: creator or restorer of the earth, the author of life, giver of animal food, lord of bird and beast. Brinton, by a dubious etymology, would make the original meaning of the name to be "the Great White One," identifying Manabozho with the creative light of day; but if we remember that the Algonquians are, by their own tradition, sons of the frigid North,[24] where the hare is one of the most prolific and staple of all food animals, and if we bear in mind the universal tendency of men whose sustenance is precarious to identify the source of life with their principal source of food, it is no longer plausible to question the identification, which the Indians themselves make, of their great demiurge with the Elder of the Hares, who is also the Elder Brother of Man and of all life.[48]

With Manabozho is intimately associated his grandmother, Nokomis, the Earth, and his younger brother, Chibiabos, who himself is customarily in animal form (e. g., the Micmac know the pair as Glooscap and the Marten; to the Montagnais they were Messou and the Lynx; to the Menominee, Manabush and the Wolf).[44] This younger brother is sometimes represented as a twin; and it is not difficult to see in Nokomis, Manabozho, and Chibiabos the Algonquian prototypes of the Huron Ataentsic, Iouskeha, and Tawiscara.

Various tales are told as to the origin of the Great Hare. The Micmac declare that Glooscap was one of twins, who quarrelled before being born; and that the second twin killed the mother in his birth, in revenge for which Glooscap slew him. The Menominee say: "The daughter of Nokomis, the

Earth, is the mother of Manabush, who is also the Fire. The Flint grew up out of Nokomis, and was alone. Then the Flint made a bowl and dipped it into the earth; slowly the bowlful of earth became blood, and it began to change its form. So the blood was changed into Wabus, the Rabbit. The Rabbit grew into human form, and in time became a man, and thus was Manabush formed." According to another version, the daughter of Nokomis gave birth to twins, one of whom died, as did the mother. Nokomis placed a wooden bowl (and we must remember that this is a symbol of the heavens) over the remaining child for its protection; upon removing the bowl, she beheld a white rabbit with quivering ears: "O my dear little Rabbit," she cried, "my Manabush!"

Other tribes tell how the Great Hare came to earth as a gift from the Great Spirit. The Chippewa recognize, high over all, Kitshi Manito, the Great Spirit, and next in rank Dzhe Manito, the Good Spirit, whose servant is Manabozho. The abode of all these is the Upper World. "When Minabozho, the servant of Dzhe Manido, looked down upon the earth he beheld human beings, the Anishinabeg, the ancestors of the Ojibwa. They occupied the four quarters of the earth — the northeast, the southeast, the southwest, and the northwest. He saw how helpless they were, and desiring to give them the means of warding off the diseases with which they were constantly afflicted, and to provide them with animals and plants to serve as food, Minabozho remained thoughtfully hovering over the center of the earth, endeavoring to devise some means of communicating with them." Beneath Minabozho was a lake of waters, wherein he beheld an Otter, which appeared at each of the cardinal points in succession and then approached the centre, where Minabozho descended (upon an island) to meet it and where he instructed it in the mysteries of the Midewiwin, the sacred Medicine Society.

According to the Potawatomi, also, the Great Hare appears as the founder of a sacred mystery and the giver of medicine.

The story is recorded by Father De Smet: "A great manitou came on earth, and chose a wife from among the children of men. He had four sons at a birth; the first-born was called Nanaboojoo, the friend of the human race, the mediator between man and the Great Spirit; the second was named Chipiapoos, the man of the dead, who presides over the country of the souls; the third, Wabasso, as soon as he saw the light, fled toward the north where he was changed into a white rabbit, and under that name is considered there as a great manitou; the fourth was Chakekenapok, the man of flint, or fire-stone. In coming into the world he caused the death of his mother." The tale goes on to tell the deeds of Nanaboojoo. (1) To avenge his mother he pursues Chakekenapok and slays him: "all fragments broken from the body of this man of stone then grew up into large rocks; his entrails were changed into vines of every species, and took deep root in all the forests; the flintstones scattered around the earth indicate where the different combats took place."[38] (2) Chipiapoos, the beloved brother of Nanaboojoo, venturing one day upon the ice, was dragged to the bottom by malignant manitos, whereupon Nanaboojoo hurled multitudes of these beings into the deepest abyss. For six years he mourned Chipiapoos, but at the end of that time four of the oldest and wisest of the manitos, by their medicine, healed him of his grief. "The manitous brought back the lost Chipiapoos, but it was forbidden him to enter the lodge; he received, through a chink, a burning coal, and was ordered to go and preside over the region of souls, and there, for the happiness of his uncles and aunts, that is, for all men and women, who should repair thither, kindle with this coal a fire which should never be extinguished." Nanaboojoo then initiated all his family into the mysteries of the medicine which the manitos had brought. (3) Afterward Nanaboojoo created the animals, put the earth, roots, and herbs in charge of his grandmother, and placed at the four cardinal points the spirits that control the seasons and the heavenly bodies, while in the clouds he set the Thunderbirds, his intermediaries.[31]

III. THE DELUGE[49]

The second of these episodes of the Potawatomi legend, in its more universal form, is the tale identified by the Jesuit Fathers as a reminiscence of the Biblical Deluge. In his *Relation* of 1633, Le Jeune gives the Montagnais version:

"They say that there is one named Messou, who restored the world when it was lost in the waters. . . . This Messou, going hunting with lynxes, instead of dogs, was warned that it would be dangerous for his lynxes (which he called his brothers) in a certain lake near the place where he was. One day as he was hunting an elk, his lynxes gave it chase even into the lake; and when they reached the middle of it, they were submerged in an instant. When he arrived there and sought his brothers everywhere, a bird told him that it had seen them at the bottom of the lake, and that certain animals or monsters held them there; but immediately the lake overflowed, and increased so prodigiously that it inundated and drowned the whole earth. The Messou, very much astonished, gave up all thought of his lynxes, to meditate on creating the world anew. He sent a raven to find a small piece of earth with which to build up another world. The raven was unable to find any, everything being covered with water. He made an otter dive down, but the depth of the water prevented it from going to the bottom. At last a muskrat descended, and brought back some earth. With this bit of earth, he restored everything to its condition. He remade the trunks of the trees, and shot arrows against them, which were changed into branches. It would be a long story to recount how he reestablished everything; how he took vengeance on the monsters that had taken his hunters, transforming himself into a thousand kinds of animals to circumvent them. In short, the great Restorer, having married a little muskrat, had children who repeopled the world."

The Menominee divide the story. They tell how Moqwaio, the Wolf, brother of Manabush, was pulled beneath the ice of a lake by the malignant Anamaqkiu and drowned; how Manabush mourned four days, and on the fifth day met the shade of his brother, whom he then sent to the place of the setting sun to have care of the dead, and to build there a fire to guide them thither. The account of the deluge, however, comes in connexion with the conflict of the Thunderers, under the direction of Manabush who is bent on avenging his brother, and the Anamaqkiu, led by two Bear chiefs. Manabush, by guile, succeeded in slaying the Bears, whereupon the Anamaqkiu pursued him with a great flood. He ascended a mountain, and then to the top of a gigantic pine; and as the waters increased he caused this tree to grow to twice its height. Four times the pine doubled in altitude, but still the flood rose to the armpits of Manabush, when the Great Spirit made the deluge to cease. Manabush causes the Otter, the Beaver, the Mink, and the Muskrat, in turn, to dive in search of a grain of earth with which he can restore the world. The first three rise to the top, belly uppermost, dead; but the Muskrat succeeds, and the earth is created anew.

A third version of the deluge-myth tells how the Great Hare, with the other animals, was on a raft in the midst of the waters. Nothing could be seen save waterfowl. The Beaver dived, seeking a grain of soil; for the Great Hare assured the animals that with even one grain he could create land. Nevertheless, almost dead, the Beaver returned unsuccessful. Then the Muskrat tried, and he was gone nearly a whole day. When he reappeared, apparently dead, his four feet were tight-clenched; but in one of them was a single grain of sand, and from this the earth was made, in the form of a mountain surrounded by water, the height ever increasing, even to this day, as the Great Hare courses around it.

It is obvious that in this chaotic flood we have an Indian equivalent of "the waters below the firmament" in the midst of which, according to the Hebrew genesis, the dry land appeared. And the Indians, like the Semites, conceived the world to be a mountain, rising from the waste of cosmic waters, and arched by the celestial dome. "They believe," says the author of the *Relation* of 1637, "that the earth is entirely flat, and that its ends are cut off perpendicularly; that souls go away to the end which is at the setting Sun and that they build their cabins upon the edge of the great precipice which the earth forms, at the base of which there is nothing but water."

IV. THE SLAYING OF THE DRAGON[50]

The deeds of the Great Hare include many contests with the giants, cannibals, and witches who people Algonquian folk-tales. In these he displays adept powers as a trickster and master of wile, as well as a stout warrior. The conflict with Flint turns, as in the Iroquois tradition, upon a tricky discovery of what substance is deadly to the Fire-Stone Man: Flint asks the Hare what can hurt him; he replies, the cat's-tail, or featherdown, or something of the sort, and, in turn, puts the question to Flint, who truthfully answers, "the horn of the stag"; and it is with stag's horn that the Hare fractures and flakes his body — a mythic reminiscence, we may suppose, of the great primitive industry of flint-flaking by aid of a horn implement.

The great feat of the Hare as a slayer, however, was his destruction of the monstrous Fish or Snake which oppressed and devoured men and animals. This creature like the Teutonic Grendel was a water monster, and ruler of the Powers of the Deep.[9] Sometimes, as in the Iroquoian myth, he is a horned serpent; commonly, among the Algonquians, he is a great fish — the sturgeon which swallows Hiawatha. The

Menominee tell how the people were greatly distressed by Mashenomak, the aquatic monster who devoured fishermen. Manabush allows himself to be swallowed by the gigantic creature, inside of which he finds his brothers, the Bear, the Deer, the Raven, the Pine-Squirrel, and many others. They all hold a war-dance in the monster's maw, and when Manabush circles past the heart he thrusts his knife into it, causing Mashenomak to have a convulsion; finally, he lies motionless, and Manabush cuts his way through to the day. In another version, Misikinebik, the monster who has destroyed the brother of Manabush, is slain by the hero in the same fashion. The Micmac, who live beside the sea, make the great fish to be a whale, who is a servant rather than a foe of Glooscap, and upon whose back he is carried when he goes in search of his stolen brother and grandmother. The Clams (surely tame substitutes for water demons!) sing to the Whale to drown Glooscap; but she fails to understand them, and is beached through his trickery. "Alas, my grandchild!" she lamented, "you have been my death. I can never get out of this." "Never you mind, Noogumee," said Glooscap, "I'll set you right." And with a push he sends her far out to sea. It is evident that the legend has passed through a long descent!

In his war against the underwater manitos, the assistants of the Great Hare are the Thunderbirds. In the Iroquoian version it is the Thunderboy who is swallowed by the horned water-snake, from whose maw he is rescued by Thunder and his warriors — as in the Hiawatha story it is the gulls who release the prisoner from the sturgeon's belly in which he has been engulfed as a consequence of his rash ambition to conquer the ruler of the depths. The myth has many variants however, and while it may sometimes represent the storm goading to fury the man-devouring waters, in a more universal mode it would seem to be but an American version of the world-old conception of the conquest of the watery Chaos by the creative genius of Light.

V. THE THEFT OF FIRE[51]

The conquest of fire by man deservedly ranks among the most impressive of all race-memories, for perhaps no one natural agency has done so much to exalt the potency of the human race as has that which gives us heat and light and power. Mythic imagination everywhere ascribes a divine origin to fire; the heaven, or some other remote region over which guardian powers preside, is the source of this great agency, from which — as in the Greek tale of Prometheus — it is "stolen in the pith" and borne among men to alleviate their estate.

In Algonquian myth the Great Hare, here as elsewhere, is "the benefactor of mankind." A Menominee version begins quite naïvely: "Manabush, when he was still a youth, once said to his grandmother Nokomis, 'Grandmother, it is cold here and we have no fire; let me go to get some.'" Nokomis endeavours to dissuade him, but the young hero, in his canoe, starts eastward across the waters to an island where dwells the old man who has fire. "This old man had two daughters, who, when they emerged from the sacred wigwam, saw a little Rabbit, wet and cold, and carefully taking it up they carried it into the sacred wigwam, where they set it down near the fire to warm." When the watchers are occupied, the Rabbit seizes a burning brand and scurries to his canoe, pursued by the old man and his daughters. "The velocity of the canoe caused such a current of air that the brand began to burn fiercely"; and thus fire is brought to Nokomis. "The Thunderers received the fire from Nokomis, and have had the care of it ever since."

It is not difficult to see in the old man across the Eastern waters a Sun-God, nor in the sacred wigwam with its maiden watchers a temple of fire with its Vestals. "Fire," says De Smet, "is, in all the Indian tribes that I have known, an emblem of happiness or good fortune." It is the emblem of life, too. Said a Chippewa prophet: "The fire must never be suffered to go out in your lodge. Summer and winter, day and night, in storm or when it is calm, you must remember that the life in your body and the fire in your lodge are the same and of the same date. If you suffer your fire to be extinguished, at that moment your life will be at its end." Even in the other world, fire is the source of life; there Chibiabos keeps the sacred fire that lights the dead thither; and, says De Smet, "to see a fire rising mysteriously, in their dreams or otherwise, is the symbol of the passage of a soul into the other world." He narrates, in this connexion, the fine Chippewa legend of a chief, arrow-stricken in the moment of victory, whose body was left, in all its war-panoply, facing the direction of the enemy's retreat. On the long homeward return of the war-party, the chief's spirit accompanies the warriors and tries to assure them that he is not dead, but present with them; even when the home village is reached and he hears his deeds lauded, he is unable to make his presence known; he cannot console his mourning father; his mother will not dress his wounds; and when he shouts in the ear of his wife, "I am thirsty! I am hungry!" she hears only a vague rumbling. Then he remembers having heard how the soul sometimes forsakes its body, and he retraces the long journey to the field of battle. As he nears it, a fire stands directly in his path. He changes his course, but the fire moves as he does; he goes to the right, to the left, but the spirit-fire still bars his way. At last, in desperate resolution, he cries out: "I also, I am a spirit; I am seeking to return to my body; I will accomplish my design. Thou wilt purify me, but thou shalt not hinder the realization of my project. I have always conquered my enemies, notwithstanding the greatest obstacles. This day I will triumph over thee, Spirit of Fire!" With an intense effort he darts through the mysterious flame, and his body, to which the soul is once more united, awakens from its long trance on the field of battle.[20]

VI. SUN-MYTHS

The Old Man and the Maids from whom Manabush steals the fire belong to the Wabanunaqsiwok, the Dawn-People, who dress in red; and, should a man or a woman dream of the Dawn-People, he or she must forthwith prepare a ball game. This, it is said, was instituted by Manabush in celebration of his victory over the malignant manitos; he made Kineun, the Golden Eagle and Chief of the Thunderers, leader of one side, and Owasse, the Bear and Chief of the Underground People, leader of the other; [52] but the Thunderers always win the game, even though the sky be darkened by cloud and rain.[33]

It is easy to recognize in the ball, which bears the colours of the East and the West, red and yellow, a symbol of the Sun; and in this myth (as in the Iroquois legend of the rape of the Sun) [51] to see a story of the ceaseless conflict of Day and Night, with Day the eternal conqueror. Sun-symbolism, also, seems to underlie the tale of Ball-Carrier,[13] the boy who was lured away by an old witch who possessed a magic ball that returned of itself to her wigwam when a child pursued it, and who was sent by her in search of the gold (Sunlight) and the magic bridge (Rainbow) in the lodge of a giant beyond the waters. Ball-Carrier, who is a kind of Indian Jack the Giant-Killer, steals the gold and the bridge, and after many amazing adventures and transformations returns to his home.

A similar, perhaps identical, character is the Tchakabech of Le Jeune's *Relation* of 1637.[42] Tchakabech is a Dwarf, whose parents have been devoured by a Bear (the Underworld Chief) and a Great Hare, the Genius of Light. He decided to ascend to the Sky and climbed upward on a tree, which grew as he breathed upon it, until he reached the heavens, where he found the loveliest country in the world. He returned to the lower world, building lodges at intervals in the branches of the tree, and induced his sister to mount with him to the Sky; but the little child of the sister broke off the end of the tree, just low enough so that no one could follow them to their destination. Tchakabech snared the Sun in a net; during its captivity there was no day below on earth; but by the aid of a mouse who sawed the strands with his sharp teeth, he was at last able to release the Sun and restore the day. In the Menominee version recorded by Hoffman, the snare is made by a noose of the sister's hair, and the Sun is set free by the unaided efforts of the Mouse.

In these shifting stories we see the image of changing Nature — Day and Night, Sunlight and Darkness, the Heavens above and the Earth beneath, coupled with a vague apprehension of the Life that is in all things, and a dim effort to grasp the origins of the world.

VII. THE VILLAGE OF SOULS[10]

The Great Hare, the Algonquians say, departed, after his labours, to the far West, where he dwells in the Village of Souls with his Grandmother and his Brother. Perrot tells of an Indian who had wandered far from his own country, encountering a man so tall that he could not descry his head. The trembling hunter hid himself, but the giant said: "My son, why art thou afraid? I am the Great Hare, he who has caused thee and many others to be born from the dead bodies of various animals. Now I will give thee a companion." Accordingly, he bestowed a wife on the man, and then continued, "Thou, man, shalt hunt, and make canoes, and do all things that a man must do; and thou, woman, shalt do the cooking for thy husband, make his shoes, dress the skins of animals, sew, and perform all the tasks that are proper for a woman." Le Jeune relates another tale: how "a certain savage had received from Messou the gift of immortality in a little package, with a strict injunction not to open it; while he kept it closed he was immortal, but his wife, being curious and incredulous, wished to see what was inside this present; and having opened it, it all flew away, and since then the savages have been subject to death." Thus, in the New World as in the Old, woman's curiosity is mankind's bane.[16]

A story which has many versions is that of the journey of a group of men — sometimes four, sometimes seven — to the abode of the Great Hare. He receives them courteously, entertains them after their long journey, and asks each his wish. One asks for skill in war, another for success in hunting, another for fame, another for love, and the Master of Life assures each of the granting of his request. But there is one man yet to be heard from, and his plea is for long life; whereupon he is transformed into a tree or, better, a stone: "You shall have your wish; here you shall always remain for future generations to look upon," says the Hare. An odd sequel to this story is that the returning warriors find their journey very short, or again that what has seemed only a brief period turns out to have been a stay of years — shifts of time which indicate that their travel has led them into the spirit-world.

In another tale, this time from the Huron country, the fateful journey to the Village of Souls is undertaken by a man who has lost his beloved sister. Her spirit appears to him from time to time as he travels, but he is unable to touch her. At last, after crossing an almost impassable river, he comes to the abode of one who directs him to the dancing-house of the spirits. There he is told to seize his sister's soul, imprison it in a pumpkin, and, thus secured, to take it back to the land of the living, where he will be able to reanimate it, provided that, during the ceremony, no one raises an eye to observe. This he does, and he feels the life returning to his sister's body, but at the last moment a curious person ventures to look, and the returning life flees away.[53] Here is the tale of Orpheus and Eurydice.

In both Algonquian and Iroquoian myth the path to the Village of Souls is guarded by dread watchers, ready to cast into the abyss beneath those whose wickedness has given them into the power of these guardians — for this path they find in the Milky Way, whose Indian name is the Pathway of Souls.[8]

VIII. HIAWATHA[54]

Tales recounting the deeds of Manabozho, collected and published by Schoolcraft, as the "myth of Hiawatha," were the primary materials from which Longfellow drew for his *Song of Hiawatha*. The fall of Nokomis from the sky; Hiawatha's journey to his father, the West Wind; the gift of maize, in the legend of Mondamin;[35] the conflict with the great Sturgeon, by which Hiawatha was swallowed; the rape and restoration of Chibiabos; the pursuit of the storm-sprite, Pau-Puk-Keewis; and the conflict of the upper and underworld powers, are all elements in the cosmogonic myths of the Algonquian tribes.

Quite another personage is the actual Hiawatha of Iroquoian tradition, certain of whose deeds and traits are incorporated in the poet's tale. Hiawatha was an Onondaga chieftain whose active years fell in the latter half of the sixteenth century. At that time the Iroquoian tribes of central New York were at constant war with one another and with their Algonquian neighbours, and Hiawatha conceived the great idea of a union which should ensure a universal peace. It was no ordinary confederacy that he planned, but an intertribal government whose affairs should be directed and whose disputes should be settled by a federal council containing representatives from each nation. This grandiose dream of a vast and peaceful Indian nation was never realized; but it was due to Hiawatha that the Iroquoian confederacy was formed, by means of which these tribes became the overlords of the forest region from the Connecticut to the Mississippi and from the St. Lawrence to the Susquehanna.

This great result was not, however, easily attained. The Iroquois preserve legends of Hiawatha's trials: how he was opposed among his own people by the magician and war-chief Atotarho; how his only daughter was slain at a council of the tribe by a great white bird, summoned, it is said, by the vengeful magician, which dashed downward from the skies and struck the maiden to earth; how Hiawatha then sadly departed from the people whom he had sought to benefit, and came to the villages of the Oneida in a white canoe, which moved without human aid. It was here that he made the acquaintance of the chief Dekanawida, who lent a willing ear to the apostle of peace, and who was to become the great lawgiver of the league. With the aid of this chieftain, Hiawatha's plan was carried to the Mohawk and Cayuga tribes, and once again to the Onondaga, where, it is told, Hiawatha and Dekanawida finally won the consent of Atotarho to the confederation. Morgan says, of Atotarho, that tradition "represents his head as covered with tangled serpents, and his look, when angry, as so terrible that whoever looked upon him fell dead. It relates that when the League was formed, the snakes were combed out of his hair by a Mohawk sachem, who was hence named Hayowentha, 'the man who combs,'"—which is doubtless a parable for the final conversion of the great war-chief by the mighty orator.[55] After the union had been perfected, tradition tells how Hiawatha departed for the land of the sunset, sailing across the great lake in his magic canoe. The Iroquois raised him in memory to the status of a demigod.

In these tales of the man who created a nation from a medley of tribes, we pass from the nature-myth to the plane of civilization in which the culture hero appears. Hiawatha is an historical personage invested with semi-divinity because of his great achievements for his fellow-men. Such an apotheosis is inevitable wherever, in the human race, the dream of peace out of men's divisions creates their more splendid unities.

PLATE XI

Iroquois drawing of Atotarho (1), receiving two Mohawk chieftains, perhaps Dekanawida (2) and Hiawatha (3). After Schoolcraft, *Indian Tribes*, part i, Plate LXX.

3
2
1

CHAPTER IV

THE GULF REGION

I. TRIBES AND LANDS

THE states bordering the northern shores of the Gulf of Mexico — the "Cotton Belt" — form a thoroughly characteristic physiographic region. Low-lying and deeply alluvial, abundantly watered both by rains and streams, and blessed with a warm, equable climate, this district is the natural support of a teeming life. At the time of its discovery it was inhabited by completely individuated peoples. While there were some intrusions of fragmentary representatives from the great stocks of other regional centres — Iroquoian and Siouan tribes from the north, and Arawak from the Bahamas — the Gulf-State lands were mainly in the possession of linguistic stocks not found elsewhere, and, therefore, to be regarded as aboriginals of the soil.

Of these stocks by far the largest and most important was the Muskhogean, occupying the greater part of what is now Georgia, Alabama, and Mississippi, as well as a large portion of Tennessee, and including among its chief tribes the Choctaw, Chickasaw, Creek (or Muskhogee), Alabama, Apalachee, and Seminole Indians. Probably the interesting Natchez of northern Louisiana were an offshoot of the same stock. Two other stocks or families of great territorial extent were the Timuquanan tribes, occupying the major portion of the Floridan peninsula, and the Caddoan tribes of Louisiana, Texas, Arkansas, and Oklahoma. Of the beliefs of few aboriginal peoples of North America is less known than of the Timuquanan Indians of Florida, so early and so entirely were they destroyed; while the southern Caddo, by habit and thought, are most properly to be regarded as a regional division of the Great Plains tribes. Minor stocks are the Uchean of South Carolina, early assimilated with the Muskhogean, and the highly localized groups of the Louisiana and Texas littoral, concerning whom our knowledge is slight. In the whole Gulf region, it is the institutions and thought of the Muskhogeans — with the culturally affiliated Cherokee — that are of dominant importance and interest.

Historically, the Muskhogean tribes, in company with the Cherokee of the Appalachian Mountain region, who were a southern branch of the Iroquoian stock, form a group hardly less important than the Confederacy of the north. The "Five Civilized Tribes" of the Indian Territory, so recognized by the United States Government, comprise the Cherokee, Chickasaw, Choctaw, Creek, and Seminole tribes, the major portion of whom removed from their eastern lands between the years 1832 and 1835 and established themselves in the Territory under treaty. In a series of patents to the several nations of this group, given by the United States (1838 to the Cherokee, 1842 to the Choctaw, from whom the Chickasaw derived their title, and 1852 to the Creek, who, in turn, conveyed rights to the Seminole), these tribes received inalienable titles to the lands into which they immigrated; and they advanced so rapidly in the direction of self-government and stable organization, building towns, and encouraging and developing industry, that they came to be known as "the five civilized tribes," in contrast to their less progressive brethren of other stocks. The separate government of these tribes, modelled upon that of the United States, but having only a treaty relation with it, continued until, as the result of the labours of a commission appointed by the United States Government, tribal rule was abolished. Accordingly, in 1906 and 1907, the Indians became citizens of the United States, and their territories part of the state of Oklahoma.

II. SUN-WORSHIP[13]

It is not extraordinary that the Gulf-State region should show throughout a predominance of solar worship. Everywhere in America the sun was one of the chief deities, and, in general, his relative importance in an Indian pantheon is a measure of civilization. In the forest and plains regions he is likely to be subordinated to a still loftier sky-god, whose minister he is; but as we go southward we find the sun assuming the royal prerogative of the celestial universe, and advancing to a place of supremacy among the world-powers. Possibly, this is in part due to the greater intensity of the southern sun, but a more likely reason is the relative advance in agriculture made by the southerly tribes. Hunting peoples are only vaguely dependent upon the yearly course of the sun for their food-supply, and hence they are only slightly observant of it. Agricultural peoples are directly and insistently followers of the sun's movements; the solar calendar is the key to their life; and consequently it is among them that the pre-eminence of solar worship early appears. Proficiency in agriculture is a mark of the Muskhogean and other southern Indians, and it is to be expected that among them the sun will have become an important world-power.

It is interesting to find that the Cherokee, an Iroquoian tribe, assimilated their beliefs to the southern type. There is little that is metaphysical in their pantheon. Above a horde of animal-powers and fantastic sprites appear the great spirits of the elements, Water, Fire, and the Sun, the chief of all. The sun is called Unelanuhi, "the Apportioner," in obvious reference to its position as ruler of the year. Curiously enough, the Cherokee sun is not a masculine, but, like the Eskimo sun, a feminine being. Indeed, the Cherokee tell the selfsame story which the Eskimo recount concerning the illicit relations of the sun-girl and her moon-brother: how the unknown lover visited the sun-girl every month, how she rubbed his face with ashes that she might recognize him, and how, when discovered, "he was so much ashamed to have her know it that he kept as far away as he could at the other end of the sky; ever since he tries to keep a long way behind the sun, and when he does sometimes have to come near her in the west he makes himself as thin as a ribbon so that he can hardly be seen." [17] The Cherokee myth of the raising of the sun by the animal elders, handbreadth by handbreadth, until it was just under the sky-arch, seven handbreadths high, is evidently akin to the similar legend of the Navaho of the South-West; while the story of the two boys who journeyed to the Sunrise, and the Cherokee version of the myth of Prometheus — in which, after various other animals have failed in their efforts to snatch fire from the sacred sycamore in which Thunder had concealed it, the Water-Spider succeeds — are both doublets of tales common in the far West. Thus legends from all parts of the continent are gathered in the one locality.

Like the Cherokee, the Yuchi Indians, who were closely associated with the Creek politically, regarded the sun as a female. She was the ancestress of the human race, or, according to another story, the Yuchi sprang from the blood trickling from the head of a wizard who was decapitated when he attempted to kill the sun at its rising — a tale in which the head would seem to be merely a doublet of the sun itself. Among the Muskhogean tribes generally the sun-cult seems to have been closely associated with fire-making festivals and fire-temples, in forms strikingly like those of the Incas of Peru. Perhaps the earliest account is that preserved, with respect to the Natchez, by Lafitau, in his *Mœurs des sauvages américquains*, i. 167–68:

"In Louisiana the Natchez have a temple wherein without cessation watch is kept of the perpetual fire, of which great care is taken that it be never extinguished. Three pointed sticks suffice to maintain it, which number is never either increased or diminished — which seems to indicate some mys-

PLATE XII

Florida Indians offering a stag to the Sun. The drawing is from Picart (*Ceremonies and religious Customs of the various Nations of the known World*, London, 1733–39, iii, Plate LXXIV [lower]), and represents a seventeenth century European conception of an American Indian rite. The pole is a symbol in the sun-worship of many Plains and Southern Indians.

tery. As they burn, they are advanced into the fire, until it becomes necessary to substitute others. It is in this temple that the bodies of their chiefs and their families are deposited. The chief goes every day at certain hours to the entrance of the temple, where, bending low and extending his arms in the form of a cross, he mutters confusedly without pronouncing any distinct word; this is the token of duty which he renders to the Sun as the author of his being. His subjects observe the same ceremony with respect to him and with respect to all the princes of his blood, whenever they speak to them, honouring in them, by this external sign of respect, the Sun from which they believe them to be descended. . . . It is singular that, while the huts of the Natchez are round, their temple is long — quite the opposite of those of Vesta. On the roof at its two extremities are to be seen two images of eagles, a bird consecrated to the Sun among the Orientals as it was to Jupiter in all the Occident.

"The Oumas and some peoples of Virginia and of Florida also have temples and almost the same religious observances. Those of Virginia have even an idol which they name Oki or Kiousa, which keeps watch of the dead. I have heard say, moreover, that the Oumas, since the arrival of the French who profaned their temple, have allowed it to fall into ruin and have not taken the trouble to restore it."

III. THE NEW MAIZE[39]

The most famous and interesting ceremony of the Muskhogean tribes is that which has come to be known in English as "the Busk" (a corruption of the Creek *puskita*, meaning "fast"). This was a celebration at the time of the first maturing of the maize, in July or August, according to locality, though it had the deeper significance of a New Year's feast, and hence of the rejuvenation of all life.

In the Creek towns, the Busk was held in the "great house,"

which consisted of four rectangular lodges, each divided into three compartments, and all open-faced toward a central square, or plaza, which they served to bound. The lodges were fitted with banks of seats, and each compartment was assigned to its own class of men. The place of honour (in some towns at least) was the western lodge, open to the morning sun, where was the seat of the head chief. In the centre of the square was kept burning a fire, made from four logs oriented to the four cardinal points. The structure is highly suggestive of a kind of temple of the year, the central fire being the symbol of the sun and of the four-square universe, and the twelve compartments of the lodges perhaps indicative of the year's lunations. Although the Busk was not a festival of the summer solstice, it came, none the less, at the season of the hottest sun, and so marked a natural change in the year.

The Busk occupies four days in the lesser towns, eight in the greater; and the ceremony seems to have four significant parts, the eight-day form being only a lengthening of the performance. On the first day, all the fires of the village having been previously extinguished, a new fire is kindled by friction, and fed by the four logs oriented to the cardinal points. Into this fire is cast a first-fruits' offering, consisting of four ears of the newly ripened maize and four branches of the cassine shrub. Dances and purificatory ceremonies occupy the day. On the second day the women prepare new maize for the coming feast, while the warriors purge themselves with "war physic," and bathe in running water. The third day is apparently a time of vigil for the older men, while the younger men hunt in preparation for the coming feast. During these preliminary days the sexes are tabu to one another, and all fast. The festival ends with a feast and merry-making, accompanied by certain curious ceremonies, such as the brewing of medicine from a great variety of plants, offerings of tobacco to the cardinal points, and a significant rite, described as follows:

"At the miko's cabin a cane having two white feathers on its end is stuck out. At the moment when the sun sets, a man of the fish gens takes it down, and walks, followed by all spectators, toward the river. Having gone half way, he utters the death-whoop, and repeats it four times before he reaches the water's edge. After the crowd has thickly congregated at the bank, each person places a grain of 'old man's tobacco' on the head and others in each ear. Then, at a signal repeated four times, they throw some of it into the river, and every man, at a like signal, plunges into the water to pick up four stones from the bottom. With these they cross themselves on their breasts four times, each time throwing one of the stones back into the river and uttering the death-whoop. Then they wash themselves, take up the cane with the feathers, return to the great house, where they stick it up, then walk through the town visiting."

In the opening ceremony (according to one authority) the fire-maker is said to converse with "the Master of Breath." Doubtless the cane tipped with white feathers is (as white feathers are elsewhere) a symbol of the breath of life, and the rite at the riverbank is thus to be interpreted as the death of the year throughout the world's quarters.

That the Indians regarded the Busk as a period of momentous change is clear from its attendant social consequences. The women burned or otherwise destroyed old vessels, mats, and the like, replacing them with new and unused ones; the town was cleansed; and all crimes, except murder, were forgiven. The new fire was the symbol of the new life of the new year, whose food was now for the first time taken; while the fasting and purgation were purificatory rites to prepare men for new undertakings. The usual date for the ceremony was in July or August, though it varied from town to town with the ripening of the maize. Ceremonies similar to the Creek Busk, though less elaborate, were observed by the Chickasaw, Seminole, and, doubtless, by other Muskhogean tribes.

IV. COSMOGONIES[15]

The Gulf States, representing a region into which tribes from both the north and the west had pressed, naturally show diverse and contradictory conceptions, even among neighbouring tribes. Perhaps most interesting is the contrast of cosmogonic ideas. The Forest tribes of the north commonly find the prototype of the created world in a heaven above the heavens, whose floor is the visible firmament; the tribes of the South-West very generally regard the habitable earth as an upper storey into which the ancestors of man ascended from their pristine underground abodes. Both of these types of cosmogony are to be found in the Gulf region.

Naturally the Cherokee share with their Iroquoian cousins the belief in an original upper world, though their version of the origin of things is by no means as rich and complicated as the Iroquois account. "The earth," they say, "is a great island floating in a sea, and suspended at each of the four cardinal points by a cord hanging down from the sky vault, which is of solid rock. When the world grows old and worn out, the people will die and the cords will break and let the earth sink down into the ocean, and all will be water again." Originally the animals were crowded into the sky-world; everything was flood below. The Water-Beetle was sent on an exploration, and after darting about on the surface of the waters and finding no rest, it dived to the depths, whence it brought up a bit of mud, from which Earth developed by accretion.[40] "When the earth was dry and the animals came down, it was still dark, so they got the sun and set it in a track to go every day across the island from east to west, just overhead. It was too hot this way, and Tsiskagili, the Red Crayfish, had his shell scorched a bright red, so that his meat was spoiled; and the Cherokee do not eat it. The conjurers put the sun another handbreadth higher in the air, but it was still too hot. They raised it another time, and another, until it was seven handbreadths high and just under the sky arch. Then it was right, and they left it so. This is why the conjurers call the highest place 'the seventh height,' because it is seven handbreadths above the earth. Every day the sun goes along under this arch, and returns at night on the upper side to the starting place." [13]

The primeval sky-world and the chaos of waters, the episode of the diving for earth, and the descent of life from heaven all indicate a northern origin; but there are many features of this myth suggestive of the far South-West, such as the crowding of the animals in their original home, the seven heights of heaven, and the raising of the sun. Furthermore, the Cherokee myth continues with an obvious addition of south-western ideas: "There is another world under this, and it is like ours in everything — animals, plants, and people — save that the seasons are different. The streams that come down from the mountains are the trails by which we reach this underworld, and the springs at their heads are the doorways by which we enter it, but to do this one must fast and go to water and have one of the underground people for a guide. We know that the seasons in the underworld are different from ours, because the water in the springs is always warmer in winter and cooler in summer than the outer air."

Among other Cherokee myths having to do with the beginnings of things is a legend of the theft of fire — a tale widely distributed throughout America. The world was cold, says the myth, until the Thunders sent their lightnings to implant fire in the heart of a sycamore, which grew upon an island. The animals beheld the smoke and determined to obtain the fire to warm the world. First the birds attempted the feat, Raven and Screech Owl and Horned Owl and Hooting Owl, but came away only with scorched feathers or blinking eyes. Next the snakes, Black Racer and Blacksnake, in succession swam through the waters to the island, but succeeded only in blackening their own skins. Finally, Water-Spider spun a thread from her body and wove it into a *tusti* bowl which she fastened on her back and in which she succeeded in bringing home a live coal.[51] Game and Corn came into the world through the activities of two boys, one the son and one the foster-son of old man Lucky Hunter and his wife Corn. The boys followed their father into the woods, saw him open the rock entrance of the great cave in which the animals were confined, and afterward in mischief loosed all the animals, to people the world with game.[41] Their mother Corn they slew, and wherever her blood fell upon the ground there maize sprang up.[35] The parents went to the East and dwelt with the sunrise, but the boys themselves became the Thunderers and abode in the darkening West, and the songs which they taught to the hunters are still used in the chase of deer.

Like the Cherokee, the Yuchi held to the northern cosmogony — an upper world, containing the Elders of men and animals, and a waste of waters below. Animal after animal attempts to bring up earth from the deep, until, in this legend, the crayfish succeeds in lifting to the surface the embryonic ball whence Earth is to grow. The Yuchi add, however, an interesting element to the myth: The new-formed land was semi-fluid. Turkey-Buzzard was sent forth to inspect it, with the warning that he was not to flap his wings while soaring above earth's regions. But, becoming wearied, he did so, to avoid falling, and the effect upon the fluid land of the winds so created was the formation of hill and valley.

In contrast to these tales of a primeval descent or fall from an upper world are the cosmogonic myths of an ascent from a subterranean abode, which the Muskhogean tribes share with the Indians of the South-West. "At a certain time, the Earth opened in the West, where its mouth is. The earth opened and the Cussitaws came out of its mouth, and settled near by." This is the beginning of the famous migration-legend of the Creeks, as preserved by Gatschet.[31] The story recounts how the earth became angry and ate up a portion of her progeny; how the people started out on a journey

PLATE XIII

Human figure in stone, probably representing a deity; height 21½ inches. Found in Bartow County, Georgia. After *Report of the United States National Museum*, 1896, Plate XLIV.

toward the sunrise; how they crossed a River of Slime, then a River of Blood, and came to the King of Mountains, whence a great fire blazed upward with a singing sound. Here there was an assembly of the Nations, and a knowledge of herbs and of fire was given to men: from the East came a white fire, which they would not use; from the South a blue fire, neither would they have this; from the West came a black fire, and this, too, was refused; but the fire from the North, which was red and yellow, they took and mingled with the fire from the mountain, "and this is the fire they use today; and this, too, sometimes sings." On the mountain they found a pole which was restless and made a noise; they sacrificed a motherless child to it,[29] and then took it with them to be their war standard.[42] At this same place they received from singing plants knowledge of the herbs and purifications which they employ in the Busk.

The Choctaw, like the Creek, regard themselves as earth-born. In very ancient times, before man lived, Nane Chaha ("high hill") was formed, from the top of which a passage led down into the caverns of earth from which the Choctaw emerged, scattering to the four points of the compass. With them the grasshoppers also appeared, but their mother, who had stayed behind, was killed by men, so that no more of the insects came forth, and ever after those that remained on earth were known to the Choctaw as "mother dead." The grasshoppers, however, in revenge, persuaded Aba, the Great Spirit, to close the mouth of the cave; and the men who remained therein were transformed into ants.[46]

The Louisiana Choctaw continue their myth with the story of how men tried to build a mound reaching to the heavens, how the mound was thrown down and a confusion of tongues ensued, how a great flood came, and how the Choctaw and the animals they had taken with them into a boat were saved from the universal deluge[49]—all elements of an obviously Old-World origin; though the story of the smoking mountain, and of the cavern peopled by the ancestral animals and men, is to be found far in the North and West on the American continent, to which it is undoubtedly native.

V. ANIMAL STORIES[41]

To the most primitive stratum of myth belong those tales of the beginnings of things which have to do, not with the source of the world — for the idea that man's habitat is itself a single being, with beginning and end, is neither a simple nor a very primitive concept — but which recount the origins of animal traits. How Snake got his poison, why 'Possum has a large mouth, why Mole lives underground, why Cedar is red-grained — these are titles representative of a multitude of stories narrating the beginnings of the distinctive peculiarities of animals and plants as the Indian's fancy conjectures them. The Gulf-State region is particularly rich in tales of this type, and it has been urged very plausibly that the prevalence of similar and identical animal stories among the Indians and negroes points to a common and probably American source for most of them.

The snakes, the bees, and the wasps got their venom, according to the Choctaw story, when a certain water-vine, which had poisoned the Indians who came to the bayou to bathe, surrendered its poison to these creatures out of commiseration for men; the opossum got his big mouth, as stated by these same Indians, from laughter occasioned by a malevolent joke which he perpetrated upon the deer; the mole lives underground, say the Cherokee, for fear of rival magicians jealous of his powers as a love-charmer; and in Yuchi story the red grain of the cedar is due to the fact that to its top is fastened the bleeding head of the wizard who tried to kill the sun.

The motives inspiring the animal stories are various. Doubtless, the mere love of story-telling, for entertainment's sake, is a fundamental stimulus; the plot is suggested by nature, and the fancy enlarges upon it, frequently with a humorous or satirical vein. But from satire to moralizing is an easy turn; the story-teller who sees human foible in the traits of animals is well on the way to become a fabulist. Many of the Indian stories are intended to point a moral, just as many of them are designed to give an answer, more or less credible, to a natural difference that stimulates curiosity. Thus we find morals and science, mingling instruction with entertainment, in this most primitive of literary forms.

Vanity is one of the motives most constantly employed. The Choctaw story of the raccoon and the opossum tells how, long ago, both of these animals possessed bushy tails, but the opossum's tail was white, whereas the raccoon's was beautifully striped. At the raccoon's advice, the opossum undertook to brown the hairs of his tail at a fire, but his lack of caution caused the hair to burn, and his tail has been smooth ever since. A similar theme, with an obvious moral, is the Cherokee fable of the buzzard's topknot: "The buzzard used to have a fine topknot, of which he was so proud that he refused to eat carrion, and while the other birds were pecking at the body of a deer or other animal which they had found he would strut around and say: 'You may have it all, it is not good enough for me.' They resolved to punish him, and with the help of the buffalo carried out a plot by which the buzzard lost not his topknot alone, but nearly all the other feathers on his head. He lost his pride at the same time, so that he is willing enough now to eat carrion for a living."

Vengeance, theft, gratitude, skill, and trickery in contest are other motives which make of these tales not only explanations but lessons. The fable of the lion and the mouse has a Cherokee analogue in the story of the wolf whose eyes were plastered shut, while he slept, by a malicious raccoon; a bird, taking pity on the wolf, pecked the plaster from his eyes; and the wolf rewarded the bird by telling him where to find red paint with which he might colour the sombre feathers of his breast. This was the origin of the redbird. The story of the hare and the tortoise is recalled by the race of the crane and the humming-bird; the swift humming-bird outstripped the crane by day but slept at night; the lumbering crane, because of his powers of endurance, flying night and day, won the race. Even more suggestive of the same fable is the tale of how the terrapin beat the rabbit, who had challenged him to a race, by posting at each station on the course a member of his family, himself awaiting his antagonist at the finish.

Magic and transformation stories form still another class presenting many analogies to similar Old-World tales.[46] The Cherokee have a story, immediately reminiscent of German folk-tales, of a girl who found a bullfrog sitting beside the spring where she went for water; the bullfrog transformed himself into a young man, whom she married, but his face always had a froggish look. In other cases transformation is for the sake of revenge, as the eagle who assumed human form after his mate had been killed, and who took vengeance upon the tribe of the hunter. Probably the moral of the broken tabu lies at the basis of this story, for this is a frequent motive in tales where men are transformed into animals or animals assume human shape. Thus, a hungry hunter is turned into a snake for eating squirrel meat, which was tabu to him; another has his death foretold by a katydid whose song he ridicules; another is lured by a doe, which comes to life after he has slain her, to the cavern of the deer, and is there himself transformed into a deer, returning to his own people only to die. Stories of the Rip Van Winkle type develop from this theme of the hunter lured away by animals, as in the instance of the man who spent a night with the panthers, and found, upon his return, that he had been lost a whole season;[33] while European tales of merfolk find their parallels in stories of underwater towns to which fishermen are dragged or lured by wizard fishes.

VI. TRICKSTERS AND WONDER-FOLK[48]

The telling of animal stories leads naturally to the formation of groups of tales in which certain animals assume constant and characteristic *rôles*, and attain to the rank of mythic beings. The *Brer Rabbit* stories, made famous as negro tales by Joel Chandler Harris, appear as a veritable saga cycle among the Cherokee, from whom they are doubtless borrowed. There can be little question that "Brer Rabbit" — vain, tricky, malicious — is a southern and humorous debasement of the Great Hare, the Algonquian demiurge and trickster; while the Turtle, also important in northern cosmogony, is represented by the put-upon, but shifty, "Brer Terrapin" of the southern tales. The "tar baby" by which the thieving Rabbit was tricked and caught appears in Cherokee lore as a "tar wolf," set as a trap; the Rabbit, coming upon it by night, kicks it and is stuck fast; the wolf and the fox find him caught, and debate how he shall be put to death; the Rabbit pleads with them not to cast him into the thicket to perish, which accordingly they do, and thus he makes off. The escape of an animal from his captors through pretending fear of his natural element and thus inducing them to throw him into it is a frequent incident in animal tales, while the "tar baby" story has variants, as Mooney says, "not only among the Cherokee, but also in Mexico, Washington, and southern Alaska — wherever, in fact, the piñon or the pine supplies enough gum to be molded into a ball for Indian uses." Another legend found from coast to coast, and known to Cherokee and Creek, is the story of how the Rabbit dines the Bear (the "imitation of the host" theme, as it is called, which has endless variants throughout the continent): "The Bear invited the Rabbit to dine with him. They had beans in the pot, but there was no grease for them, so the Bear cut a slit in his side and let the oil run out until they had enough to cook the dinner. The Rabbit looked surprised, and thought to himself, 'That's a handy way. I think I'll try that.' When he started home he invited the Bear to come and take dinner with him. When the Bear came the Rabbit said, 'I have beans for dinner, too. Now I'll get grease for them.' So he took a knife and drove it into his side, but instead of oil, a stream of blood gushed out and he fell over nearly dead. The Bear picked him up and had hard work to tie up the wound and stop the bleeding. Then he scolded him, 'You little fool, I'm large and strong and lined all over with fat; the knife don't hurt me; but you're small and lean, and you can't do such things.'"

The world is peopled, however, with other wonder-folk besides the magic animals, and many of these mythic beings belong to ancient and wide-spread systems. Thus, the Cherokee Flint (Tawiskala) is obviously the evil twin of the northern Iroquois cosmogony; and although he has ceased to be remembered as a demiurgic Titan, his evil and unsociable nature remains the same.[45] In Choctaw tales, the Devil who is drowned by a maiden whom he has lured from her home, and whose body breaks into stony fragments, is apparently the same being.[38] The Ice Man, with his northerly winds and sleety rains, who quenched the fire that threatened to consume the world; the North who kept the South for Bride until the hot sun forced him to release her;[39] Untsaiyi, the Gambler, who games away his life, and flees to the world's end, where he is bound and pinned by the two brothers who have pursued him, there to writhe until the world's end[56] — all these are tales with familiar heroes, known in many tribes and lands.

Nor are the tribes of magic folk different in kind from those found elsewhere. There are the helpful spirit warriors, who dwell in rock and hill, the Nunnehi; there are the Little People, fairies good and evil;[36] there are the Tsundigewi, the Dwarfs who lived in nests scooped from the sand, and who fought with and were overcome by the cranes;[2] the Water-Cannibals, who live upon human flesh, especially that of children;[9] the Thunderers, whose steed is the great Uktena;

the horned snake with a diamond in his forehead,[50] and to whose cave a young man was lured by the Thunder's sister, only to find, when he returned to his folk to tell his story and die, that the night he had spent there comprised long years. Kanati, Lucky Hunter, the husband of Selu, Corn, and Tsulkalu, the slant-eyed giant, held dominion over the animals and were gods of the hunter; while the different animals, each in its kind, were under the supervision of the animal Elders,[40] such as the Little Deer, invisible to all except the greatest hunters, the White Bear, to whom wounded bears go to be cured of their hurts, Tlanuwa, the Hawk impervious to arrows, Dakwa, the great fish which swallowed the fisherman and from which he cut himself out, and the man-eating Leech, as large as a house.

Such is the general complexion of the Cherokee pantheon — hordes or kinds of nature-powers, with a few mightier personalities emerging above them, embryonic gods. Altogether similar are the conceptions of the Muskhogean tribes — giants and dwarfs, fairies and wizards, now human, now animal in shape, peopling hill and stream, forest and bayou.

VII. MYTHIC HISTORY[57]

Tribes, such as the Cherokee, Creek, and allied nations, with settled towns and elaborate institutions are certain to show some development of the historical sense. It is true that the Cherokee have no such wealth of historic tradition as have their northern cousins, the peoples of the Iroquois Confederacy; but at the same time they possess a considerable lore dealing with their past. Hero tales, narrating the deeds of redoubtable warriors of former days, and incidentally keeping alive the memory of the tribes with whom the Cherokee were at war in early days, naturally form the chief portion of such traditions; but there are also fabulous stories of abandoned towns, ancient mounds, and strange peoples formerly encountered.

In one particular the Cherokee are distinguished above all other tribes. In the first years of the nineteenth century Sequoya, having observed the utility of the white man's art of writing, invented the Cherokee alphabet, still employed for the native literature. He submitted his syllabary to the chief men of the nation; it was adopted, and in a few months thousands of the Cherokee had learned its use. Nevertheless, this innovation was not made without antagonism; and the opponents, to make strong their case, told a tale of how, when Indian and white man were created, the Indian, who was the elder, received a book, while the white was given bow and arrows. But since the Indian was neglectful of his book, the white man stole it, leaving the bow in its place, so that thenceforth the book belonged legitimately to the white man, while hunting with the bow was the Indian's rightful life. A similar tale makes the white man's first gift a stone, and the Indian's a piece of silver, these gifts becoming exchanged; while another story tells how the negro invented the locomotive, which the white man, after killing the negro, took from him.

To an entirely different stratum of historical myth belongs the story of the massacre of the Anikutani. These were a priestly clan having hereditary supervision of all religious ceremonies among the Cherokee. They abused their powers, taking advantage of the awe in which they were held, to override the most sacred rights of their fellow tribesmen, until finally, after one of the Anikutani had violated the wife of a young brave, the people rose in wrath and extirpated the clan. In later versions it is a natural calamity which is made responsible for the destruction of the wicked priests; so that here we seem to have a tale which records not only a radical change in the religious institutions of the tribe, but which is well on the way toward the formation of a story of divine retribution.[5]

The Creek "Migration Legend," edited by Gatschet, and recorded from a speech delivered in 1735 by Chekilli, head chief of the Creek, is a much more comprehensive historical myth than anything preserved for us by the kindred tribes. The legend begins with the account of how the Cussitaw (the Creek) came forth from the Earth in the far West; how they crossed a river of blood, and came to a singing mountain where they learned the use of fire and received their mysteries and laws. After this the related nations disputed as to which was the eldest, and the Cussitaw, having been the first to

Fig. 1. Birdlike Deity from Etowah Mound

Copper plate found in Etowah Mound, Georgia, representing a Birdlike Deity. Now in the United States National Museum, Washington

cover their scalp-pole with scalps, were given the place of honour. Since a huge blue bird was devouring the folk, the people gave it a clay woman to propitiate it and to induce it to cease its depredations. By this woman the bird became the father of a red rat, which gnawed its parent's bowstring. Thus the bird was unable to defend itself, and the people slew it, though they regarded it as a king among birds, like the eagle. They came to a white path, and thence to the town of

Coosaw, where they dwelt four years. A man-eating lion preyed upon the people of this town. "The Cussitaws said they would try to kill the beast. They digged a pit and stretched over it a net made of hickory bark. They then laid a number of branches crosswise, so that the lion could not follow them, and going to the place where he lay they threw a rattle into his den. The lion rushed forth in great anger and pursued them through the branches. Then they thought it better that one should die rather than all, so they took a motherless child[22] and threw it before the lion as he came near the pit. The lion rushed at it, and fell in the pit, over which they threw the net, and killed him with blazing pinewood. His bones, however, they keep to this day; on one side they are red, on the other blue. The lion used to come every seventh day to kill the people. Therefore, they remained there seven days after they had killed him. In remembrance of him, when they prepare for war they fast six days and start on the seventh. If they take his bones with them they have good fortune."[19] After this, the tribe continued its journey, seeking the people who had made the white path. They passed several rivers, and came to various towns; but when they shot white arrows into these towns, as a sign of peace, the inhabitants shot back red arrows. Sometimes the Cussitaw went on without fighting, sometimes they fought and destroyed the hostile people. Finally, "they came again to the white path, and saw the smoke of a town, and thought that this must be the people they had so long been seeking. This is the place where now the tribe of Palachucolas live. . . . The Palachucolas gave them black drink, as a sign of friendship, and said to them: Our hearts are white and yours must be white, and you must lay down the bloody tomahawk, and show your bodies, as a proof that they shall be white." The two tribes were united under a common chief. "Nevertheless, as the Cussitaws first saw the red smoke and the red fire and made bloody towns, they cannot yet leave their red hearts, which are, however, white on one side and red on the other. They now know that the white path was the best for them."

Such is the migration-legend of the Creek, altogether similar to other tales of tribal wandering both in the New World and the Old. Partly it is a mythical genesis; partly it is an exodus from a primitive land of tribulation and war into a land of peace; partly it is historical reminiscence, the tale of a conquering tribe journeying in search of richer fields. The sojourn by the mountain of marvels whence came the talismanic pole,[61] as well as knowledge of the law and the mysteries, recalls the story of Sinai, while the white path and the search for the land of peace suggest the promise of Canaan. The episodes of the man-devouring bird and the man-eating lion possess many mythic parallels, while both seem to hark back to a time when human sacrifice was a recognized rite.[29] Doubtless the whole tale is a complex of fact and ritual, partly veritable recollection of the historic past, partly a fanciful account of the beginnings of the rites and practices of the nation. Last of all, comes the bit of psychological analysis represented by the allegory of the parti-coloured heart of the Red Man who knows the better way, but, because of his divided nature, is not wholly capable of following it. This gives to the whole myth an aetiological rationality and a dramatically appropriate finish. The fall of man is narrated; his redemption remains to be accomplished.

Unquestionably many myths of the type of this Creek legend have been lost, for it is only by rare chance that such heroic tales survive the vicissitudes of time.

CHAPTER V

THE GREAT PLAINS

I. THE TRIBAL STOCKS

THE broad physiographical divisions of the North American continent are longitudinal. The region bounded on the east by the Atlantic seaboard extends westward to parallel mountain ranges which slope away on the north into the Labrador peninsula and Hudson's Bay, and to the south into the peninsula of Florida and the Gulf of Mexico. West of the eastward mountains, stretching as far as the vast ranges of the Rockies, is the great continental trough, whose southern half is drained by the Mississippi into the Gulf, while the Mackenzie and its tributaries carry the waters from the northern division into the Arctic Ocean. The eastern portion of this trough, to a line lying roughly between longitudes 90 and 95, is a part of what was originally the forest region; the western part, from far beyond the tree line in the north to the deserts of northern Mexico, comprises the Great Plains of North America, the prairies, or grass lands, which, previous to white settlement, supported innumerable herds of buffalo to the south and caribou to the north, as well as a varied and prolific life of lesser animals — antelope, deer, rabbits, hares, fur-bearing animals, and birds in multitude. Coupled with this plenitude of game was a paucity of creatures formidable to man, so that aboriginally the Great Plains afforded a hunting-ground with scarcely an equal on any continent. It was adapted to and did support a hale population of nomadic huntsmen.

As in similar portions of the earth having no natural barriers to passage and intercourse, the human aboriginals of the region fell into few and vast linguistic stocks. Territorially the greatest of these was the Athapascan, which occupied all central Alaska and, in Canada, extended from the neighbourhood of the Eskimo southward through the greater part of British Columbia and Athabasca into Alberta, and which, curiously enough, also bounded the Great Plains population to the south, Athapascan tribes, such as the Navaho and Apache, occupying the plains of southern Texas, New Mexico, and northern Mexico. Just south of the northern Athapascans a stratum of the Algonquian stock, including the important Cree and Blackfoot tribes, penetrated as far west as the mountains of Alberta and Montana, while north of the southern Athapascans, as it were reciprocally, a layer of the western Shoshonean stock extended eastward into central Texas, the Shoshonean Comanche forming one of the fiercest of the Plains tribes. Between these groups, occupying the greatest and richest portion of the prairie region in the United States, were the powerful and numerous Siouan and Caddoan peoples, the former, probably immigrants from the eastern forests, having their seat in the north, while the Caddo, whose provenance seems to have been southern, were divided into three segregated groups, Texan, Nebraskan, and Dakotan. The Pawnee, Wichita, Arikara, and Caddo proper are the principal tribes of the Caddoan stock; the Siouan stock is represented by many tribes and divisions, of whom the most famous are the Dakota or Sioux, the Omaha, Assinaboin, Ponca, Winnebago, Mandan, Crow, and Osage. It is of interest to note that five states, Missouri, Kansas, Nebraska, and the two Dakotas, either bear the designations of Siouan tribes or appellations of Siouan origin, while many towns, rivers, and counties are similarly named. Other important Plains tribes, occupying the region at the base of the Rocky Mountains, from Wyoming south to northern Texas, are the Arapaho and Cheyenne of the intrusive Algonquian stock and the Kiowa, linguistically unrelated to any other people.

The manner of life of the Plains tribes was everywhere much the same. They were in the main hunters, living in towns during the winter and in summer moving their portable camps from place to place within the tribal hunting range. The skin tipi, or Indian tent, was the usual type of dwelling, generally replacing the bark wigwam of the forests; but the Caddoan and some other tribes built substantial earth lodges — a form of dwelling which archaeological research shows to have been ancient and wide-spread along the banks of the great western rivers. Agriculture,[24] too, was more important and more highly developed among the earth-lodge dwellers, being partly a symbol and partly a consequence of their more settled life. It found its reflection, also, in ideas, the most significant and terrible instance being that underlying the Morning Star sacrifice of the Skidi Pawnee, which, like the similar rite of the Kandhs (or Khonds) of India, consisted in the sacrifice of a virgin, commonly a captive from a hostile tribe, whose body was torn to pieces and buried in the fields for the magical fructification of the grain.[29] One of the most romantic stories of the West is of the deed of Petalesharo, a Skidi warrior of renown.[58] A Comanche maiden was about to be sacrificed according to custom when Petalesharo stepped forward, cut the thongs which bound the captive, declaring that such sacrifices must be abolished, and bearing her through the crowd of his tribesmen, placed her upon a horse and conveyed her to the borders of her own tribal territories. This was in the early part of the nineteenth century, and it is said that his act put an end to the rite.

In warlike zeal and enterprise the Indians of the Plains [59] were no whit inferior to the braves of the East. The coming of the horse, presumably of Spanish introduction, added wonderfully to the mobility of the Indian camp, and opened to native daring a new field, — that of horse-stealing; so that the man who successfully stole his enemy's horses was little less distinguished than he who took hostile scalps. The Indian's

PLATE XIV

Pencil sketch by Charles Knifechief, representing the scaffold used by the Skidi Pawnee in the sacrifice to the Morning Star. See Note 58 (pp. 303-06). By courtesy of Dr. Melvin R. Gilmore.

West
North
South.
East

wars were really in the nature of elaborate feuds, giving opportunity for the display of prowess and the winning of fame, like the chivalry of the knight-errant; they were rarely intentional aggressions. Nor was Indian life wanting in complex rituals for the making of peace and the spread of a sense of brotherhood from tribe to tribe. Under the great tutelage of Nature noble and beautiful ceremonies were created, having at their heart truths universal to mankind; and nowhere in America were such mysteries loftier and more impressive than among the tribes of the Great Plains.

II. AN ATHAPASCAN PANTHEON[3]

Of all the great stocks of the Plains the Athapascan tribes (with the exception of the Navaho) show the least native advancement. The northern Athapascans, or Tinne tribes, in particular, while good hunters and traders, are far from warlike, even in self-defence, and their arts are inferior to the general level of the Plains peoples. The ideas of these tribes are correspondingly nebulous and confused. Father Jetté, who has made a study of the mind of the Yukon Indians, says of them that "whereas there is a certain uniformity in the practices" of these people, "there are very few points of belief common to several individuals, and these are of the vaguest kind." And he and other observers find a certain emptiness in the rites of the far north, as if the Indians themselves had forgotten their real significance.

Father Jetté gives a general analysis of the Yukon pantheon. The Tinne, he says, are incapable of conceiving really spiritual substances, but they think of a kind of aeriform fluid, capable of endless transformations, visible and invisible at will, penetrating all things and passing wherever they wish; and these are the embodiments of spiritual power. There is little that is personal and little that is friendly in these potencies; the religion of the Tinne is a religion of fear.

The four greater spirits among these powers are Man of Cold, Man of Heat, Man of Wind, and a Spirit of Plague (Tena-ranide), the evil that afflicts man's body, known by many names and appearing in many forms. Man of Cold "reigns during the winter months, causes the frost and the snow, kills people by freezing them to death, takes possession of the body at death, and faithfully covers the grave of the Tena with a shroud of snow." Man of Heat is the foe of Cold, whom he has conquered in the summer, as he succumbs in turn during the season of cold.[39] He is more friendly to man than is Cold, but still must be kept in check, for he, too, stifles and suffocates when the chance is offered him. Wind brings death and destruction in storm; while Tena-ranide is Death itself stalking the earth, and ever in wait for man — literally, says Father Jetté, the name means "the thing for man," that is, "the thing that kills man."

It is obvious enough that here we have the world-scheme of a people for whom the shifts of nature are the all-important events of life. Changes of season and weather are great and sudden in the continental interior of North America, becoming more perilous and striking as the Arctic zone is approached; and so we find, as we might expect, that the peoples of the northern inland make Heat and Cold and Windy Storm foremost of their gods, with the grisly form of ever-striking Death for their attendant. Below these greater spirits there is a multitude of confused and phantom powers. There are souls [20] of men and animals, the soul which is "next to" the body and makes it live; there are the similar souls of "those who are becoming again," or awaiting reincarnation; [18] finally, there is a strange shadow-world of doubles, not only for men and animals, but for some inanimate objects. The Yega ("picture," "shadow"), as the double is called, is "a protecting spirit, jealous and revengeful, whose mission is not to avert harm from the person or thing which it protects but to punish the ones who harm or misuse it." When a man is to die, his

Yega is first devoured by Tena-ranide or one of the malevolent Nekedzaltara, who are servants of the death-bringer. The familiars, or daemons, of the shamans, form another class of personal spirits, similar to the Tornait of the Eskimo Angakut, whose function is to give their masters knowledge of the hidden events and wisdom of the world, as well as power over disease and death.

The Nekedzaltara, "Things," form a class or classes of the hordes of nature-powers, visible and invisible, which people the world with terrors. Father Jetté gives a folk-tale description of one of these beings — one form out of a myriad. The story seems to be a version of the wide-spread North American tale of the hero who is swallowed by a water-dwelling monster, from whose body he cuts his way to freedom. The hero has just gotten into the Nekedzaltara's mouth:[2]

"Then he stopped and looked around him. He was in a kettle-shaped cave, the bottom of which was covered with boiling water; from this large bubbles were constantly coming forth. Looking up he saw stretching above his head a huge jaw; and looking down he saw another enormous jaw beneath him. Then he realized that he had put himself into the very mouth of a devil: he had gone into it unawares. He was deep in it, close to the throat, where the boiling water was bubbling up. The long twisting ropes were appendages to the devil's jaw, and now they began to encircle him and closed fast upon him. But he drew his sword and cut them. Then he ran out of the dreadful cave. Before going, as he saw the big teeth on the monster's jaw, he pulled out one of them and took it with him. . . . And he gave the devil's tooth to his master."

It is easy to see in this monster a whale, says the recorder; and certainly it is quite possible that this version of the story got its picturesque detail from the Arctic and the Eskimo, to whose beliefs those of the Tinne tribes show so many parallels. Of course, the story is known far to the South also,—in the episode of Hiawatha and the sturgeon, for example.

III. THE GREAT GODS OF THE PLAINS

On the plains there is a majestic completeness of almost every view of earth and sky. There are no valley walls to narrow the horizon; there are no forests to house men from the heavens. The circle of the horizon is complete and whole, and the dome of the sky, where the rainbow forms frequently in perfect arc, is vast and undiminished. To men accustomed to the broad spaces and simple lines of such vision, the brilliant blue of predominantly sunny skies, the green of the summer prairies, the sparkling white of the winter plains, the world seemed at once colossal and intelligible. Its plan was the plan of their own lodges: a flat and circular base over which was hung the tent of the skies, with door to the east, the direction of the rising sun. "If you go on a high hill," said a Pawnee priest, "and look around, you will see the sky touching the earth on every side, and within this circular enclosure the people dwell." The lodges of men were made on the same plan, to "represent the circle which Father Heaven has made for the dwelling-place of all the people"; and, in many tribes, the camp form was also circular, the tipis being ranged in a great ring, within which each clan had its assigned position.

The great gods of men in such a world form a natural, indeed an inevitable, hierarchy. Supreme over all is Father Heaven, whose abode is the highest circle of the visible universe.[6] Tirawa-atius is his Pawnee name. All the powers in heaven and on earth are derived from him; he is father of all things visible and invisible, and father of all the people, perpetuating the life of mankind through the gift of children. The Pawnee symbols of Tirawa are white featherdown, typifying the fleecy clouds of the upper heavens — and hence the cloud-bearing winds and the breath of life — and, in face-painting, a blue line drawn arch-like from cheek to cheek over the brow, with a straight line down the nose which symbolizes the path by which life descends from above. Yet the Pawnee

PLATE XV

Portrait of Tahirussawichi, a Pawnee priest, bearing in his hands an eagle-plume wand, symbol of Mother Earth, and a rattle marked with blue lines emblematic of the Sky. After *22 ARBE*, part 2, Plate LXXXV.

are not anthropomorphic in their ideas. "The white man speaks of a Heavenly Father; we say Tirawa-atius, the Father above, but we do not think of Tirawa as a person. We think of Tirawa as in everything, as the Power which has arranged and thrown down from above everything that man needs. What the power above, Tirawa-atius, is like, no one knows; no one has been there."

The priest who made this remark also said: "At the creation of the world it was arranged that there should be lesser powers. Tirawa-atius, the mighty power, could not come near to man, therefore lesser powers were permitted. They were to mediate between man and Tirawa." The Sun Father and Earth Mother were the two foremost of these lesser powers, whose union brings forth all the moving pageantry of life. The Morning Star, the herald of the Sun, is scarcely less important. The Winds from the four quarters of the world, the life-giving Vegetation, Water, the Hearth-Fire — all these are powers calling for veneration. In the intermediate heavens, below Sun and Moon, yet above man's reach, are the bird messengers, with the Eagle at their head, each with its special wisdom and guidance. Here, too, dwell the Visions which descend to the dreamer, giving him revelations direct from the higher powers; and here the dread Thunder wings his stormy course.

With little variation, these deities — Heaven, Earth, Sun, Moon, Morning Star, Wind, Fire, Thunder — form the common pantheon of the Plains tribes. The agricultural tribes, as the Pawnee and Mandan Indians, give the Corn Mother a prominent place. Animal-gods, the Elders of the animal kinds, are important according to the value of the animal as game or as a symbol of natural prowess. The Eagle is supreme among birds; the Bear, the Buffalo, the Elk, among quadrupeds; while the Coyote appears in place of the Rabbit as the arch-trickster. The animals, however, are not gods in any true sense, for they belong to that lesser realm of creation which, with man, shares in the universal life of the world.

IV. THE LIFE OF THE WORLD

It has recently been much the custom of writers dealing with Indian beliefs to assert that the conception of a Great Spirit or Great Mystery is imported by white teachers, that the untutored Indian knows no such being; the universality of the earlier tradition as to the native existence of this idea is regarded as of little consequence, almost as a studied misinterpretation. Nevertheless, when we find such definite conceptions as that of Kitshi Manito among the Algonquians or Tirawa-atius in Pawnee religion, or even such indefinite ones as that of the Carrier Indian's Yuttoere ("that which is on high"),[6] we begin to question the truth of the modern assertion. As a matter of fact, there is hardly a tribe that does not possess its belief in what may very properly be called a Great Spirit, or Great Mystery, or Master of Life. Such a being is, no doubt, seldom or never conceived anthropomorphically, seldom if ever as a formal personality; but if these preconceptions of the white man be avoided, and the Great Spirit be judged by what he does and the manner in which he is approached, his difference from the Supreme Deity of the white man is not so apparent.

Probably the Siouan conception of Wakanda, the Mystery that is in all life and all creation, has been as carefully studied as any Indian religious idea.[3] In general, Wakanda is the Siouan equivalent of the Algonquian Manito, not a being but an animating power, or one of a series of animating powers which are the invisible but potent causes of the whole world's life. "All the Indians," says De Smet, of the Assiniboin, "admit the existence of the Great Spirit, viz., of a Supreme Being who governs all the important affairs of life, and who manifests his action in the most ordinary events. . . . Every spring, at the first peal of thunder, which they call the *voice of the Great Spirit speaking from the clouds*, the Assiniboins offer it sacrifices. . . . Thunder, next to the sun, is their great

Wah-kon. . . . At the least misfortune, the father of a family presents the calumet to the Great Spirit, and, in prayer, implores him to take pity on him, his wives and children." "Prayer to Wakanda," another observer was told, "was not made for small matters, such as going fishing, but only for great and important undertakings, such as going to war or starting on a journey."

Doubtless the most illuminating analysis of this great Siouan divinity which is in all things is that made by Miss Fletcher in her study of the Omaha tribe. Wakanda, she says, "stands for the mysterious life power permeating all natural forms and forces and all phases of man's conscious life. . . . Visible nature seems to have mirrored to the Omaha mind the ever-present activities of the invisible and mysterious Wakonda and to have been an instructor in both religion and ethics. . . . Natural phenomena served to enforce ethics. Old men have said: 'Wakonda causes day to follow night without variation and summer to follow winter; we can depend on these regular changes and can order our lives by them. In this way Wakonda teaches us that our words and our acts must be truthful, so that we may live in peace and happiness with one another. Our fathers thought about these things and observed the acts of Wakonda and their words have come down to us.' . . . All experiences in life were believed to be directed by Wakonda, a belief that gave rise to a kind of fatalism. In the face of calamity, the thought, 'This is ordered by Wakonda,' put a stop to any form of rebellion against the trouble and often to any effort to overcome it. . . . An old man said: 'Tears were made by Wakonda as a relief to our human nature; Wakonda made joy and he also made tears!' An aged man, standing in the presence of death, said: 'From my earliest years I remember the sound of weeping; I have heard it all my life and shall hear it until I die. There will be parting as long as man lives on the earth. Wakonda has willed it to be so!' . . . Personal prayers were addressed directly to Wakonda.

A man would take his pipe and go alone to the hills; there he would silently offer smoke and utter the call, *Wakonda ho!* while the moving cause, the purport of his prayer, would remain unexpressed in words.[30] If his stress of feeling was great, he would leave his pipe on the ground where his appeal had been made. . . . Women did not use the pipe when praying; their appeals were made directly, without any intermediary. Few, if any, words were used; generally the sorrowful or burdened woman simply called on the mysterious power she believed to have control of all things, to know all desires, all needs, and to be able to send the required help."

The mere quotation of Indian utterances, the mere description of their simple rites, out-tell all commentary. Yet the testimony of one whose first and native education was in this belief may well be appended. "The worship of the 'great Mystery,'" says Dr. Eastman, "was silent, solitary, free from all self-seeking. It was silent, because all speech is of necessity feeble and imperfect; therefore the souls of my ancestors ascended to God in wordless adoration. It was solitary, because they believed that He is nearer to us in solitude, and there were no priests authorized to come between a man and his Maker. None might exhort or confess or in any way meddle with the religious experience of another. Among us all men were created sons of God and stood erect, as conscious of their divinity. Our faith might not be formulated in creeds, nor forced upon any who were unwilling to receive it; hence there was no preaching, proselyting, nor persecution, neither were there any scoffers or atheists. There were no temples or shrines among us save those of nature. Being a natural man, the Indian was intensely poetical. He would deem it sacrilege to build a house for Him who may be met face to face in the mysterious, shadowy aisles of the primeval forest, or on the sunlit bosom of virgin prairies, upon dizzy spires and pinnacles of naked rock, and yonder in the jeweled vault of the night sky! He who enrobes Himself in filmy veils of cloud, there on

PLATE XVI

Rawhide image of a Thunderbird for use as a head-band ornament in ceremonial dances. The image is beaded and painted, the zigzag lines representing the lightning issuing from the heart of the Thunderbird. See Note 32 (pp. 287–88), and compare Plates III, VI, XII, XXII, XXIV, XXVI, and Figure 1. After *14 ARBE*, part 2, p. 969.

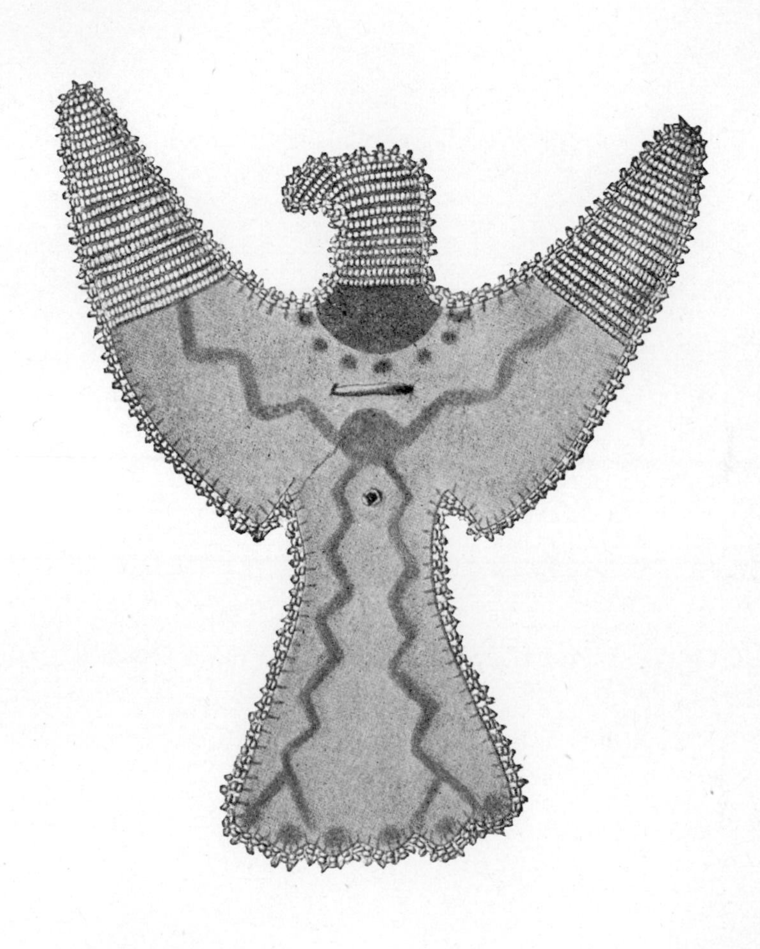

the rim of the visible world where our Great-Grandfather Sun kindles his evening camp-fire, He who rides upon the rigorous wind of the north, or breathes forth His spirit upon aromatic southern airs, whose war-canoe is launched upon majestic rivers and inland seas — He needs no lesser cathedral!"

V. "MEDICINE"[4]

To make the impersonal and pervasive life of nature more particularly his own, the Indian seeks his personal "medicine" — half talisman, half symbol. Usually the medicine is revealed in a fast-induced vision, or in a dream, or in a religious initiation. It then becomes a personal tutelary whose emblem is borne in its possessor's "medicine-bag" — to which miraculous powers are often attributed. "A skin of a weasel, heads and bodies of different birds stuffed, images made of wood and stone, of beads worked upon skin, rude drawings of bears, of buffalo bulls, wolves, serpents, of monsters that have no name, nor ever had an existence, in fact everything animate and inanimate is used, according to the superstition and belief of the individual. This object," continues Father De Smet, "is enveloped in several folds of skin, with a lock of some deceased relative's hair and a small piece of tobacco enclosed and the whole placed in a parfleche [buffalo skin stripped of hair and stretched over a frame] sack neatly ornamented and fringed, and this composes the arcanum of the medicine-sack. This sack is never opened in the presence of any one, unless the owner or some of his family fall dangerously ill, when it is taken out and placed at the head of his bed and the aid of the Great Spirit invoked through it. Ordinarily this sack is opened in secret; the medicine smoked and invoked and prayers and sacrifices made in its presence, and through it, as a tangible medium to the Great Spirit, who is unknown and invisible."

The Indian's "medicine" is, in fact, a symbol of superhuman power, just as his pipe is a portable altar of sacrifice; having these articles with him, he is equipped for all ordinary religious service. As the medicine was so often revealed in vision, so its potencies were partly to extend the knowledge of its owner by giving him guidance in the hour of need. Indeed, the fundamental demands underlying the Indian's use of his medicine were, first, for *clairvoyance*, the power to see behind the screen of appearances and to give man a longer time for adaptation to exigencies than his mere physical vision might allow, and, second, for *prowess*, the strength to cope with environing perils, be they human enemies, elemental dangers, or the insidious onslaughts of disease. The means for thus raising the tension of man's native abilities is the concentration of diffuse natural forces by means of the emblem, be it image or relic. With the more advanced Indians such "medicine" is regarded as no more than a symbol of the greater Medicine of nature — though still a symbol which is, in some vague sense, a key for the unlocking of nature's larger store.

Nor is "medicine" limited to private possession. Every Indian had his own "medicine-bag," but tribe and clan and religious society all owned and guarded sacred objects not differing in character from the individual's magic treasure, except for their greater powers and the higher veneration attached to them.

The "medicine" potency of objects is not limited to personal talismans and sacred things. The various tokens, such as eagle feathers, animal skins or teeth or claws, with which the Indian adorned his costume, were also supposed to have powers which entitled them to be treated with respect. Similarly, the painting of face and body, of robe and tipi, followed the strictest of rules, and was for the specific purpose of increasing the potencies of the owners of the decoration. The Indian's art was in a curious sense a private possession. If a man invented a song, it was his song, and no other had a right to sing it without his permission — usually, only after a formal ceremony of teaching. In similar fashion, societies had songs which could be sung only by their members; and there were chants that could be sung only at certain periods of the day or at fixed seasons of the year. So also in respect to pictorial design: certain patterns were revealed to the owner in dream or vision, and thereafter they were for his person or clothing or dwelling, and might not be copied or appropriated by any other, at least not without a proper transfer. All this was a part of the Indian's implicit belief that all nature, including human thought and action, represents one web of interknitted forces whose destined order may not be broken without peril. White men call this belief superstition, but in its essence it is not radically different from their own notion of a nature fabricated of necessity and law.

VI. FATHER SUN[13]

"Shakuru, the Sun, is the first of the visible powers," said the Pawnee priest, quoted above. "It is very potent; it gives man health, vitality, and strength. Because of its power to make things grow, Shakuru is sometimes spoken of as *atius*, 'father.' The Sun comes direct from the mighty power above; that gives it its great potency."

Here we have a compendium of the theology of sun-worship, perhaps the most conspicuous feature of the Plains Indian's religion. The sun was regarded as a mighty power, though not the mightiest; he was the first and greatest of the intermediaries who brought the power of Father Heaven down to earth, and he himself was addressed as "Father" or "Elder" because of his life-giving qualities. Especially potent were his first rays. "Whoever is touched by the first rays of the Sun in the morning receives new life and strength which have been brought straight from the power above. The first rays of the sun are like a young man: they have not yet spent their force or grown old." Inevitably this expression brings to mind the boy Harpocrates and the youth Horus, personations of the strength and splendour of the morning sun, as he leaped from the couch of night before the eyes of the priests of old Egypt.

Indeed, the Pawnee ritual in connexion with which this explanation was given seems to afford us a glimpse of just such a rite as must have been practised centuries before Heliopolis was founded or the temple of the Sphinx oriented to the morning sun. All night long, in a ceremonial lodge whose door is toward the east, priest and doctor chant their songs; as the hour of dawn approaches, a watcher is set for the Morning Star; and the curtain at the lodge door is flung back that the strength-giving rays may penetrate within. "As the Sun rises higher the ray, which is its messenger, alights upon the edge of the central opening in the roof of the lodge, right over the fireplace. We see the spot, the sign of its touch, and we know that the ray is there. The fire holds an important place in the lodge. . . . Father Sun is sending life by his messenger to this central place in the lodge. . . . The ray is now climbing down into the lodge. We watch the spot where it has alighted. It moves over the edge of the opening above the fireplace and descends into the lodge, and we sing that life from our Father the Sun will come to us by his messenger, the Ray." All day long the course of the life-giving beam is followed with songs of thankfulness. "Later, when the Sun is sinking in the west, the land is in shadow, only on the top of the hills toward the east can the spot, the sign of the ray's touch, be seen. . . . The ray of Father Sun, who breathes forth life, is standing on the edge of the hills. We remember that in the morning it stood on the edge of the opening in the roof of the lodge over the fireplace; now it stands on the edge of the hills that, like the walls of a lodge, inclose the land where the people dwell. . . . When the spot, the sign of the ray, the messenger of our Father the Sun, has left the tops of the hills and passed from our sight . . . we know that the ray which was sent to bring us strength has now gone back to the place whence it came. We are thankful to our Father the Sun for that which he has sent us by his ray."

Of Stonehenge and Memphis and Pekin and Cuzco, the most ancient temples of the world's oldest civilizations, this ritual is strangely and richly reminiscent. Far anterior to the olden temples must have been such shrines as the sacred if temporary lodges of the Indian's worship, within which the daily movements of the sun's ray were watched by faithful priests — Horus of the morning, Rê' of the midday, Atum of the sunset — and by which the first invention of the gnomon, and hence the beginnings of the measured calendar, were suggested. Who, remembering the sculptures of Amenophis IV, with rays reaching down from the Divine Disk to rest hands of benediction upon the king, but will feel the moving analogy of the Pawnee conception of the Ray, the Sun's messenger, touching his worshippers with life? Or, indeed, who will fail to find in the Indian's prayers to Father Sun the same beauty and aspiration that pervades the psalms of the heretic king?

The Sun-Dance of the Prairie tribes is their greatest and most important ritual.[39] This is an annual festival, occupying, usually, eight days, and it is undertaken in consequence of a vow, sometimes for an escape from imminent death, especially in battle; sometimes in hopes of success in war; sometimes as the result of a woman's promise to the Sun-God for the recovery of the sick. In the main, the ceremonies are dramatic, consisting of processions, symbolic dances, the recounting and enactment of deeds of valour, and the fulfilment of vows of various kinds undertaken during the year. The last and central feature is the building of a great lodge, symbolic of the home of man, in the centre of which is erected a pole, as an emblem of earth and heaven, sometimes cruciform, sometimes forked at the top, and adorned with symbols typifying the powers of the universe. Warriors under vow were formerly attached to this pole by ropes fastened to skewers inserted under the muscles of back and chest, and they danced about it until the lacerated body was freed;[21] but this and other forms of self-torture — a kind of atonement to the life-giving Sun for the life he had spared — were not essential to the ceremony, and in some tribes were never permitted; among the Kiowa the mere appearance of blood during the ceremony was regarded as an ill omen.

Not only were vows of atonement and propitiation fulfilled on the occasion of the Sun-Dance, but the dead of the year were mourned, babes had their ears pierced by the medicine-men, young men who had distinguished themselves were given formal recognition, and tribal and intertribal affairs and policies were discussed, for visiting tribes were often participants. The central feature, however, was a kind of cosmic thanksgiving, in which the people, through the Sun-Symbol, were brought directly into relation with Father Sun. The prayer of a chief directing this ceremony, in a recent performance of it, gives its meaning perhaps more fully than could any commentary:

"Great Sun Power! I am praying for my people that they may be happy in the summer and that they may live through the cold of winter. Many are sick and in want. Pity them and let them survive. Grant that they may live long and have abundance. May we go through these ceremonies correctly, as you taught our forefathers to do in the days that are past. If we make mistakes pity us. Help us, Mother Earth! for we depend upon your goodness. Let there be rain to water the prairies, that the grass may grow long and the berries be abundant. O Morning Star! when you look down upon us, give us peace and refreshing sleep. Great Spirit! bless our children, friends, and visitors through a happy life. May our trails lie straight and level before us. Let us live to be old. We are all your children and ask these things with good hearts" (McClintock, *The Old North Trail*, p. 297).

"We are all your children and ask these things with good hearts"! Is not this the essence of religious faith?

PLATE XVII

Sioux drawing, representing the Sun-Dance pole and tortures of devotees (see p. 89). After *11 ARBE*, Plate XLVIII. See Note 61 (p. 307).

VII. MOTHER EARTH AND DAUGHTER CORN[34]

"H'Uraru, the Earth," said the Pawnee priest, "is very near to man; we speak of her as Atira, Mother, because she brings forth. From the Earth we get our food; we lie down on her; we live and walk on her; we could not exist without her, as we could not breathe without Hoturu, the Winds, or grow without Shakuru, the Sun."

It is difficult to realize the deep veneration with which the Indian looks upon his Mother the Earth. She is omniscient; she knows all places and the acts of all men; hence, she is the universal guide in all the walks of life. But she is also, and before all, the universal mother — she who brings forth all life, and into whose body all life is returned after its appointed time, to abide the day of its rebirth and rejuvenation. The conception was not limited to one part of the continent, but was general. "The Sun is my father and the Earth is my mother; on her bosom I will rest," said Tecumseh to General Harrison; and from a chieftain of the far West, the prophet Smohalla, comes perhaps the most eloquent expression of the sense of Earth's motherhood in Occidental literature. Urged to settle his people in agriculture, he replied:

"You ask me to plow the ground! Shall I take a knife and tear my mother's bosom? Then when I die she will not take me to her bosom to rest.

"You ask me to dig for stone! Shall I dig under her skin for her bones? Then when I die I cannot enter her body to be born again.

"You ask me to cut grass and make hay and sell it, and be rich like white men! But how dare I cut off my mother's hair?

"It is a bad law, and my people cannot obey it. I want my people to stay with me here. All the dead men will come to life again. Their spirits will come to their bodies again. We must wait here in the homes of our fathers and be ready to meet them in the bosom of our mother."

On the Great Plains a remarkable ceremony, known to many tribes, represented the union of Heaven and Earth and the birth of Life. The fullest account of it is preserved from the Pawnee, though the Sioux and Omaha tribes have contributed many elements of the ritual. The Hako (*sacra*, or sacred objects, employed in the ceremony), as the Pawnee rite is called, is a dramatic prayer for life and children, for health and posterity. It is directed to the universal powers, to Father Heaven and the celestial powers, and to Mother Earth and the terrestrial powers, with the beautiful imagery of birds as the intermediaries between earth and heaven.[40] The central symbols of the mystery — for mystery it is, in the full classical sense — are the winged wands which represent the Eagle, the highest of the bird messengers; a plume of white featherdown, typifying the fleecy clouds of heaven, and hence the winds and the breath of life, "breathed down from above"; [60] and an ear of maize, symbol of "Mother Corn," daughter of Heaven and Earth.

"The ear of corn," said the priest, "represents the supernatural power that dwells in H'Uraru, the earth which brings forth the food that sustains life; so we speak of the ear as h'Atira, mother breathing forth life.[35] The power in the earth which enables it to bring forth comes from above; for that reason we paint the ear of corn with blue. . . . The life of man depends upon the Earth. Tirawa-atius works through it. The kernel is planted within Mother Earth and she brings forth the ear of corn, even as children are begotten and born of women. . . . We give the cry of reverence to Mother Corn, she who brings the promise of children, of strength, of life, of plenty, and of peace."

It is impossible to study the Hako ceremonial without being struck by the many analogies which it affords for what is known of the Eleusinian Mysteries. In the latter, as in the Hako, an ear of corn was the supreme symbol, while the central drama of both was the imaging of a sacred marriage of Heaven and

Earth and the birth of a Son, who symbolized the renewal of life, physical and spiritual, in the participants. The Hako did not, as the Eleusinian Mysteries did, convey a direct promise of life in a future world; but this is only a further step in symbolism easy to take, and it is by no means beyond reason to presume that the great religious mysteries of the ancients took their origin from ceremonies of the type for which the Indian rite furnishes us probably our purest and most primitive example.

VIII. THE MORNING STAR[14]

After the Sun the most important of the celestial divinities among the Plains tribes is the Morning Star (Venus). The Pawnee priest, Tahirussawichi, describes him thus:

"The Morning Star is one of the lesser powers. Life and strength and fruitfulness are with the Morning Star. We are reverent toward it. Our fathers performed sacred ceremonies in its honor. The Morning Star is like a man; he is painted red all over; that is the color of life. He is clad in leggings and a robe is wrapped about him. On his head is a soft downy eagle's feather, painted red. This feather represents the soft, light cloud that is high in the heavens, and the red is the touch of a ray of the coming sun. The soft, downy feather is the symbol of breath and life."

This is the star for which the Pawnee watch, as the herald of the sun, in the great ritual chant to the solar god. "The star comes from a great distance, too far away for us to see the place where it starts. At first we can hardly see it; we lose sight of it, it is so far off; then we see it again, for it is coming steadily toward us all the time. We watch it approach; it comes nearer and nearer; its light grows brighter and brighter." A hymn is sung to the star. "As we sing, the Morning Star comes still nearer and now we see him standing there in the heavens, a strong man shining brighter and brighter. The soft plume in his hair moves with the breath of the new day, and the ray of the sun touches it with color. As he stands there so bright, he is bringing us strength and new life. As we look upon him he grows less bright, he is receding, going back to his dwelling place whence he came. We watch him vanishing, passing out of our sight. He has left with us the gift of life which Tirawa-atius sent him to bestow."

Formerly the Skidi Pawnee were accustomed to sacrifice a captive virgin to the Morning Star, her body being used magically to fertilize the fields of maize. A similar association of ideas, though on the plane of mythic poetry rather than on that of barbarous rite, seems to underlie the Blackfoot legend of Poïa, "Scarface," the Star Boy.

Long ago, according to this story, a maiden, Feather Woman, was sleeping in the grass beside her tipi. The Morning Star loved her, and she became with child. Thenceforth she suffered the disdain and ridicule of her tribesfolk, until one day, as she went to the river for water, she met a young man who proclaimed himself her husband, the Morning Star. "She saw in his hair a yellow plume, and in his hand a juniper branch with a spider web hanging from one end. He was tall and straight and his hair was long and shining. His beautiful clothes were of soft-tanned skins, and from them came a fragrance of pine and sweet grass." Morning Star placed the feather in her hair and, giving her the juniper branch, directed her to shut her eyes; she held the upper strand of the spider's web in her hand and placed her foot on the lower, and in a moment she was transported to the sky. Morning Star led her to the lodge of his parents, the Sun and the Moon; and there she gave birth to a son, Star Boy (the planet Jupiter). The Moon, her mother-in-law, gave her a root digger, saying, "This should be used only by pure women. You can dig all kinds of roots with it, but I warn you not to dig up the large turnip growing near the home of Spider Man." Curiosity eventually got the better of caution; Feather Woman, with the aid of two cranes, uprooted the forbidden turnip, and found that it covered a window in the sky looking down to the earth she had left; at sight of the camp of her tribesfolk she became sad with home-sickness, and the Sun, her husband's father, decreed that she must be banished from the sky, and be returned to earth. Morning Star led her to the home of Spider Man, whose web had drawn her to the sky, and, with a "medicine-bonnet" upon her head, and her babe, Star Boy, in her arms, she was lowered in an elk's skin to earth. Here, pining for her husband and the lost sky-land, Feather Woman soon died, having first told her story to her tribesfolk. Her son, Star Boy, grew up in poverty, and, because of a scar upon his face, was named Poïa, "Scarface." When he became a young man, he loved a chieftain's daughter; but she refused him because of his scar. Since a medicine-woman told him that this could be removed only by the Sun-God himself, Poïa set out for the lodge of the solar deity, travelling westward to the Pacific. For three days and three nights he lay on the shore fasting and praying; on the fourth day he beheld a bright trail leading across the water, and following it he came to the lodge of the Sun. In the sky-world Poïa killed seven huge birds that had threatened the life of Morning Star, and, as a reward, the Sun not only removed the scar from Poïa's face, but also taught him the ritual of the Sun-Dance and gave him raven feathers to wear as a sign that he came from the Sun, besides a lover's flute and a song which would win the heart of the maid whom he loved. The Sun then sent him back to earth — by way of the short path, Wolf Trail (the Milky Way) — telling him to instruct the Blackfeet in the ritual of the dance. Afterward Poïa returned to the sky with the maiden of his choice.

"Morning Star," said the narrator of this myth, "was given to us as a sign to herald the coming of the Sun. . . . The 'Star that stands still' (North Star) is different from other stars, because it never moves. All the other stars walk round it. It is a hole in the sky, the same hole through which So-at-sa-ki

(Feather Woman) was first drawn up to the sky and then let down again to earth. It is the hole through which she gazed upon earth, after digging up the forbidden turnip. Its light is the radiance from the home of the Sun God shining through. The half circle of stars to the east (Northern Crown) is the lodge of the Spider Man, and the five bright stars just beyond (in the constellation of Hercules) are his five fingers, with which he spun the web, upon which Soatsaki was let down from the sky."

Corona Borealis is an important constellation in the mythic lore of nearly all the tribes of the Plains. According to the Pawnee, it is a circle of chiefs who are the guardians of the mystic sign of Tirawaatius, and the Pawnee society of Raritesharu (chiefs in charge of the rites given by Tirawa) paint their faces with the blue lines representing the arc of heaven and the path of descent, and wear upon their heads the featherdown symbol of celestial life. "The members of this society do not dance and sing; they talk quietly and try to be like the stars."

Ursa Major and the Pleiades are other constellations conspicuous in Indian myth. The Assiniboin regard the seven stars of Ursa Major as seven youths who were driven by poverty to transform themselves, and who rose to heaven by means of a spider's web. For the Blackfeet also these stars are seven brothers who have been pursued into the heavens by a huge bear (an interesting reversal of the Eskimo story). The Mandan believed this constellation to be an ermine; some of the Sioux held it to be a bier, followed by mourners. The Pleiades, in Blackfoot legend, are the "lost children," driven by poverty to take refuge in the sky.

Everywhere stars were associated with the dead. The Mandan considered them to be deceased men: when a child is born, a star descends to earth in human form; at death, it appears once more in the heavens as a star.[18] A meteor was frequently regarded as a forerunner of death; and the Milky Way, as with the eastern tribes, is the path by which souls ascend into heaven.

IX. THE GODS OF THE ELEMENTS[11]

The typical dwelling of the Plains folk, whether tipi or earth lodge, is circular in ground-plan, and, similarly, tribal encampments, especially for religious or ceremonial purposes, were round in form. On such occasions the entrance to the lodge faced the east, which was always the theoretic orientation of the camp. A cross, with arms directed toward the four cardinal points, and circumscribed by a circle, symbolizes the Plains Indian's conception of the physical world, and at the same time represents his analysis of the elemental powers of Nature, and hence of his analysis of the organization of human society, which is so directly dependent upon these potencies.

The circle of the horizon, the floor of the lodge of heaven; the circle of the tribal encampment; and the circular floor of the lodge, the home of the family — these might be said to typify so many concentrics, each a symbol of the universe, in the Indian's thought. In the Hako, the priest draws a circle with his toe, within which circle he places featherdown. "The circle represents a nest, and is drawn by the toe, because the eagle builds its nest with its claws. Although we are imitating the bird making its nest, there is another meaning to the action; we are thinking of Tirawa making the world for the people to live in. If you go on a high hill and look around, you will see the sky touching the earth on every side, and within this circular inclosure the people live. So the circles we have made are not only nests, but they also represent the circle Tirawa-atius has made for the dwelling place of all the people. The circles also stand for the kinship group, the clan, and the tribe."

The tribal circle of the Omaha was divided into two groups, the Sky-People occupying the northern, and the Earth-People the southern, semi-circle. The Sky represented the masculine, the Earth the feminine, element in nature; the human race was supposed to be born of the union of Earth-People and Sky-People;

and in the tribe marriage was not customary within either of these two groups, but only between members of Earth clans and members of Sky clans. Each group also had its own chieftain and ceremonial, so that the whole tribe possessed a dual organization, corresponding to the great dualism of nature.

J. O. Dorsey found a similar scheme prevalent throughout the Siouan stock, and this scheme he generalized by the figure of a quartered circle. The quarters of one half, which was the side of peace, were devoted respectively to Earth and Water; the quarters of the masculine, or Sky half, which was the side of war, were sacred to the spirits of Fire and Air. Powers of Earth, Water, Fire, and Air formed the great groups of the elemental gods. The Dakota name for the Earth-Power is Tunkan, "Boulder," [27] and it should be remembered that stones were not only the materials for the most important of aboriginal implements, but that they played an almost magical part in the venerated medicine rite of the sweat-bath lodge. The priests of the Pebble Society of the Omaha relate the following myth in this connexion: "At the beginning all things were in the mind of Wakonda. All creatures, including man, were spirits. They moved about in space between the earth and the stars. They were seeking a place where they could come into a bodily existence. They ascended to the sun, but the sun was not fitted for their abode. They moved on to the moon and found that it also was not fitted for their abode. Then they descended to the earth. They saw it was covered with water. They floated through the air to the north, the east, the south, and the west, and found no dry land. They were sorely grieved. Suddenly from the midst of the water uprose a great rock. It burst into flames and the waters floated into the air in clouds. Dry land appeared; the grasses and the trees grew. The hosts of spirits descended and became flesh and blood, fed on the seeds of the grasses and the fruits of the trees, and the land vibrated with their expressions of joy and gratitude to Wakonda, the maker of all things." [15]

The Water-Powers [9] were divided into two classes, those of the streams, which were masculine, and those of the subterranean waters, which were feminine. According to the Winnebago, the earth is upheld by the latter, which are sometimes represented as many-headed monsters — veritable leviathans. The Wind-Makers, occupying half the space devoted to the Sky-Powers, were especially associated with the four quarters whence the winds came, and with the animal gods or Elders, who came from the quarters. An Omaha cosmogony tells how, when the earth was covered with water and the souls were seeking their dwelling, an Elk came, and with a loud voice shouted to the four quarters, whereupon the four winds, in response, blew aside the waters, and exposed the rock which was the kernel of Earth. The tale of the diving of the different animals for mud, to expand the earth, is added to this legend.

Of the Fire-Powers, the Sun and the Thunderers or Thunderbirds were of first importance. The position of the Sun in the Prairie Indian's lore has been stated. The Thunders [32] were even more important among the aborigines of the central west than with their eastern cousins, perhaps because the electric storms of the Plains are so much more terrible and conspicuous. The Assiniboin regard the Thunder as "the voice of the Great Spirit speaking from the clouds," says De Smet; and the Dakota, he adds, "pretend that Thunder is an enormous bird, and that the muffled sound of the distant thunder is caused by countless numbers of young birds! The great bird, they say, gives the first sound, and the young ones repeat it: this is the cause of the reverberations. The Sioux declare that the young thunders do all the mischief, like giddy youth, who will not listen to good advice; but the old thunder, or big bird, is wise and excellent, he never kills or injures anyone."

The Thunder was pre-eminently the power of destruction, and, therefore, a tutelary of war.[59] When the boy was initiated into manhood, a lock of hair was cut from his crown by the priest, and dedicated to the Thunder. The hair, it must be borne in mind, was in many ways regarded by the Indian as a man's strength and life. Frequently a lock of the hair of a dead relative was preserved, and if carried by a pregnant woman it was thought to ensure the rebirth of the dead. When the hair on the boy's crown grew out once more, a special lock was parted in a circle from the rest, and braided by itself. Upon this lock war-honours were worn, and it was this that was taken when the dead enemy was scalped. It was more than a symbol; it was the magic vehicle of the vital strength of the slain man.[55]

In few Indian rites is the relation of the elemental powers to human society more impressively symbolized than in the Omaha ceremony of the sacred pole.[61] According to the legend, the tribe was threatened with disruption and was holding a council to determine by what means it could be kept intact. During this conference, a young hunter lost his way in the forest, and in the night he came upon a luminous tree. He made his way home and told his father, a chief of the tribe, of his discovery, whereupon the old man said to the Council: "My son has seen a wonderful tree. The Thunder birds come and go upon this tree, making a trail of fire that leaves four paths on the burnt grass that stretch toward the four Winds. When the Thunder birds alight upon the tree it bursts into flame and the fire mounts to the top. The tree stands burning, but no one can see the fire except at night." It was agreed that this marvel was sent from Wakanda. The warriors, stripped and painted, ran for the tree, and struck it as if it were an enemy; and after it had been felled and brought back to the camp, for four nights the chiefs sang the songs that had been composed for it. A sacred tent, decked with symbols of the sun, was made for the tree, which was trimmed and adorned. They called it a human being, and fastened a scalp-lock to it for hair. The tree, or pole, had keepers appointed for it, and it became the symbol of tribal unity and authority — a true palladium, which was carried on important excursions, and for which an annual rite was instituted, commemorating the manner of its discovery.

Perhaps the feeling of the Plains Indian for that great world of nature which surrounds him may best be summed up in the Blackfoot prayer to the Quarters, which is recorded by McClintock.[31] First, to the West: "Over there are the mountains. May you see them as long as you live, for from them you must receive your sweet pine as incense." To the North: "Strength will come from the North. May you look for many years upon 'the Star that never moves.'" To the East: "Old age will come from below where lies the light of the Sun." To the South: "May the warm winds of the South bring you success in securing food."

CHAPTER VI

THE GREAT PLAINS

(Continued)

I. ATHAPASCAN COSMOGONIES[15]

IN no portion of the American continent is intercourse of tribe with tribe easier than on the Great Plains. Of natural barriers there are none, and in the days of the aboriginal hunter, when all the prairie nations spent a part of each year in pursuit of the herds of game that crossed and recrossed their ill-defined hunting-grounds, it was inevitable that annually there should be encounters of people with people, and eventually of ideas with ideas. It was on the Plains that the sign language was developed and perfected, a mute *lingua franca*, serving almost the explicitness of vocal speech. The fundamental ceremonials of a ceremonial race varied little from tribe to tribe, and indeed were often conveyed from one people to another at the great intertribal gatherings, where feasting and trading and the recounting of the deeds of heroes were the order of the day. Loose confederacies were formed, and it was sometimes the custom for friendly nations to exchange children for a term that some might grow up in each nation acquainted with the language of the other. Not infrequently tribes or segments of tribes of quite distinct linguistic stocks lived together in a more or less coherent nationality, sharing the same territory and villages. Even in time of war there were well recognized rules, forming a kind of chivalric code, which obtained a general adherence; and one of the obvious outcomes of Indian warfare was the constant replenishment of tribal stocks with the blood of adopted captives.

With all these sources of intermingling it was natural that there should be interchange of stories, and indeed it is not unreasonable to suppose that the open country was the path by which many of the tales found in both the extreme north and the extreme south were transmitted from latitude to latitude, while similarly there was here a meeting-ground for the lore of the westward pressing tribes of the Forest Region and the eastward intrusions of the Mountain and Desert stocks. As a matter of fact, this meeting and commingling of myth is just what we find on the Plains, perhaps nowhere better illustrated than in the field of cosmogony.

Even among the remote Athapascans of the north cosmogonic myths are of diverse source. It is supposed that these Indians came originally from the north-west, and it is, therefore, no matter of wonder that they know and tell legends of the demiurgic Raven which form the characteristic cosmogony of the Pacific Coast tribes. They are also acquainted with the Forest Region tale of the deluge and of the animals that dived for the kernel of soil from which the earth grew; and they tell, likewise, the story known to the Eskimo, of the girl who bore children to a dog, from whom mankind are descended, or who, as in a Carrier version, became stars.[17] According to this recension, the girl was a virgin, who when her shame was discovered, was abandoned to die; but she contrived to find food for herself and her offspring, who were in the form of puppies. One night, coming back to her abode, she saw the footprints of children about the fireplace, and following this clue she returned surreptitiously to the lodge on the next occasion, and discovered her children in human form; she succeeded in destroying the dog-dress of her three boys, but the girl-child retransformed herself into a dog before her parent could interfere. After this, the mother (who seems very clearly to be the progenitress of all animal kinds, the Mother of Wild Life) taught her boys to hunt the different animals, their sister, the dog, aiding them in the chase; but one day brothers and sister pursued a herd of caribou up into the sky, where all became stars, the Pursuers (Orion) and the Herd (Pleiades).[14]

The tale of the two boys who were followed by their mother's head seems to be a Great Plains version of the cosmogonic stories of the Forest Region.[37] The mother of the boys was decapitated by her husband for illicit intercourse with a serpent;[50] but the head remained alive and gave chase to the children. With charms received from their father, the boys protected themselves, first, by a mountain, but the head turned itself into a wind and blew over it; second, by a heaven-reaching thorn-bush, which sprang from a drop of blood drawn from a wound in the head, but the head overleaped it; third, by a wall of fire, but the head passed through it.[62] Finally, driven into the midst of a lake, the elder brother struck the head with his knife, whereupon two water monsters emerged and swallowed it. It is easy to see in this pursuing head the body of the cosmic Titaness, the Earth Goddess, overcoming in turn earth, vegetation, and fire, and succumbing only to that primeval flood upon which the earth rests; and it is interesting to surmise in this legend the original of the gruesome tales of cannibal heads, known to tribes of the greater portion of North America.

A second part of the story tells of the adventures of the two brothers,[44] one of whom is captured and held by a magician, till he finally frees himself by proving his own greater magic; the other is slain by water monsters, but restored by his brother, although in the form of a wolf. The episode of the flood and the diving animals also appears.[49] All these themes are well known in Algonquian myth. The stories of the journey of the two young men to the village of souls, known as far as the Gulf Region; the universal legend of the theft of fire; the tradition of the creation of light; even the familiar South-Western tale of the ascent of the ancestral Elders from the under to the upper world, — each and every one is common among the northern tribes. And perhaps nowhere in America is there a more charming mythic conceit than that of the Chipewyans of the Arctic Barren Lands, relative to the Animal Age: "At the beginning there were no people, only animals; still they resembled human beings, and they could speak: when the animals could speak it was summer, and when they lost the power of speaking winter followed." [39] Here indeed we have a picture of the primeval world: the stillness of the dark Arctic winter, when even the animals were mute; the loveliness of summer, musical and living with the multitudinous voices of Nature.

II. SIOUAN COSMOGONIES [15]

The Assiniboin, the most northerly Siouan tribe, have a form of the story of the mother's head, but their own tales of the origins of things centre about the diving animals and the trickster hero, Inktonmi, a Siouan cousin of Manabozho. Further to the south the Mandan also possessed two cycles of cosmogonic myths. Apparently of southern provenance are the legends of the storeyed universe: [11] there were four storeys below and four above the earth. Before the flood, men lived in an underworld village, to which a grape-vine extended from the world above. Up this, first the animals, then men, climbed, until a very corpulent woman broke the vine. Next a flood destroyed most of the human race. A Kiowa version of this tale tells how the first people emerged from a hollow cottonwood log, until it came the turn of a pregnant woman, who was held fast — and this accounts for the small number of the Kiowa tribe.

The second Mandan cycle evidently belongs to the more properly Siouan version of the demiurgic pair. The Lord of Life created the First Man, who formed the earth out of mud brought up from the waters by a duck. Afterward the First Man and the Lord of Life quarrelled, and divided the earth between them. The Hidatsa believe that the Lord of Life, the Man-Who-Never-Dies, lives in the Rocky Mountains;[63] and they also say of the First Man, the Creator, that no one made him, and that he is immortal. To the Old-Woman-Who-Never-Dies,[34] the Grandmother, who is none other than the Earth, they ascribe a minor *rôle* in the creation; it was she who gave them the "two kettles," which are the tribal fetish, directing that they be preserved in memory of the great waters whence came all the animals dancing. When drought threatens they hold a feast, ceremonially using the two kettles and praying for rain. It seems altogether probable that these vessels are the "bowls of earth and sky," and so symbolize the universe.

The Dakota tell the story of the drowning of the younger brother of the First Man by the water monsters, and of his resuscitation after they had been slain.[49] He was brought to life, they say, by means of the sweat-bath, and it is not fanciful to connect the cosmic forces with the symbolism of the stones (earth) and steam (water) used in this rite.[27] Indeed, the Omaha make this symbolism definite. The idea of permanence, long life, and wisdom they typify by the stone; "man's restlessness, his questionings of fate, his destructiveness, are frequently symbolized by the wolf"; and in myth the wolf and the stone are the two demiurgic brothers — western duplicates of Flint and Sapling. One of the most interesting of Omaha rituals is that of the Pebble Society, sung to commemorate the great rock which Wakanda summoned from the waters, at the beginning of the world, to be a home for the animal souls that wandered about in primitive chaos (translated by Alice C. Fletcher, in 27 *ARBE*, p. 570): —

Toward the coming of the Sun
There the people of every kind gathered,
And great animals of every kind.
Verily all gathered together, as well as people.
Insects also of every description,
Verily all gathered there together,
By what means or manner we know not.

Verily, one alone of all these was greatest,
Inspiring to all minds,
The great white rock,
Standing and reaching as high as the heavens, enwrapped in mist,
Verily, as high as the heavens.
Thus my little ones shall speak of me,
As long as they shall travel in life's path, thus shall they speak of me.
Such were the words, it has been said.

Then next in rank
Thou, male of the crane, stoodst with thy long beak
And thy neck, none like to it in length,
There with thy beak didst thou strike the earth.

This shall be the legend
Of the people of yore, the red people,
Thus my little ones shall speak of me.

Then next in rank stood the male gray wolf, whose cry,
Though uttered without effort, verily made the earth to tremble,
Even the stable earth to tremble.
Such shall be the legend of the people.

Then next in rank stood Hega, the buzzard, with his red neck.
Calmly he stood, his great wings spread, letting the heat of the sun straighten his feathers.
Slowly he flapped his wings,
Then floated away, as though without effort,
Thus displaying a power often to be spoken of by the old men in their teachings.

III. CADDOAN COSMOGONIES[15]

Of the Caddoan stock the northerly Arikara were in close association with the Hidatsa and the Mandan. Among them it is natural to find again the story of the demiurgic pair — "Wolf and Lucky Man," as they name these heroes;[44] but the Arikara also have stories belonging to their own southerly origin, especially legends of Mother Corn, the great goddess of all the Caddoan tribes.[35] It was Mother Corn who, with the help of the animals, led the people from the under into the upper world, after which she apportioned territories, and taught the use of implements and ceremonial rites. Previous to their coming, the earth was inhabited by a race of people "so strong that they were not afraid of anybody, but they did not have good sense; they made fun of all the gods in heaven." This sounds curiously like the Greek myth of the race of Giants; nor is the sequel unlike the Greek. "Nesaru looked down upon them, and was angry. Nesaru said: 'I made them too strong. I will not keep them. They think that they are like myself. I shall destroy them, but I shall put away my people that I like and that are smaller.'" The giants were killed in a flood, while the animals and maize were preserved in a cave. Eventually, from an ear of maize which he had raised in heaven, Nesaru created a woman, Mother Corn, whom he sent into the underworld to deliver the people imprisoned there, and to lead them once more into the light of day — a Descent into Hell, like that of Ishtar or Persephone or many another Corn Goddess.

The Pawnee of Nebraska tell a more complicated tale of first things, with a suggestively astrological motive underlying the myth.[14] In the beginning were Tirawa, Chief of Tirawahut, the great circle of the heavens,[11] and Atira, his spouse, the Sky-Vault. Around them sat the gods in council, the place of each appointed by Tirawa. The latter spoke to the gods, saying: "Each of you gods I am to station in the heavens; and each of you shall receive certain powers from me, for I am about to create people who shall be like myself. They shall be under your care. I will give them your land to live upon, and with your assistance they shall be cared for." Then he appointed the station of Sakuru, the Sun, in the east, to give light and warmth; and that of Pah, the Moon, in the west, to illumine the night.[13] Also, he allotted the stations of the stars. To Bright Star, the evening star, he said, "You shall stand in the west. You shall be known as Mother of all things; for through you all beings shall be created." To Great Star, the morning star, he spake, "You shall stand in the east. You shall be a warrior. Each time you drive the people towards the west, see that none lag behind." To the Star-That-Does-Not-Move he appointed the north as station, and he made him the star-chief of the skies. And in the south he placed Spirit Star, "for you shall be seen only once in a while, at a certain time of the year." Four other stars he set over the quartered regions, north-east and north-west, and south-east and south-west, and commanding these four to move closer to him, he said to them: "You four shall be known as the ones who shall uphold the heavens. There you shall stand as long as the heavens last, and, although your place is to hold the heavens up, I also give you power to create people. You shall give them different bundles, which shall be holy bundles. Your powers will be known by the people, for you shall touch the heavens with your hands, and your feet shall touch the earth."

After this, Tirawa said to Bright Star, the west star: "I will send to you Clouds, Winds, Lightnings, and Thunders. When you have received these gods, place them between you and the Garden. When they stand by the Garden, they shall turn into human beings. They shall have the downy feather in their hair [symbol of the breath of life]. Each shall wear the buffalo robe for his covering. Each shall have about his waist a lariat of buffalo hair. Each shall also wear moccasins. Each of them shall have the rattle in his right hand [symbol of the garden of the Evening Star]. These four gods shall be the ones who shall create all things."

Then the Clouds gathered; the Winds blew; Lightnings and Thunders entered the Clouds. When space was canopied, Tirawa dropped a pebble into their midst, which was rolled about in the thick Clouds. The storm passed, and a waste of waters was revealed. Then to the Star-Gods of the World-Quarters Tirawa gave war-clubs, bidding them to strike the waters with them; and as they obeyed, the waters separated, and the earth was made.

When all this had come to pass, Tirawa commanded the Bright Star of the evening to tell the Star-Gods of the Quarters to sing of the formation of the earth. As they sang, the elemental gods, the Clouds and the Winds and the Lightnings and the Thunders, again assembled, and from the might of their storm earth was divided into hill and valley. Then again Tirawa bade, through Bright Star, that the Star-Gods of the Quarters should sing of timber and of vegetation, and again there was a storm, and earth was given a dress of living green. A third time they sang, and the waters of earth were cleansed and sweetened and coursed in flowing streams. A fourth time they sang, and all manner of seeds, which had been dropped to earth, sprouted into life.

Now, at the decree of Tirawa, the Sun and the Moon were united, and from their union was born a son; and the Morning and the Evening Stars were united, and from them a daughter was born. And these two, boy and girl, were placed upon the earth, but as yet they had no understanding. Then Tirawa again commanded: "Tell the four gods to sing about putting life into the children. . . . As the four gods rattled their gourds, the Winds arose, the Clouds came up, the Lightnings entered the Clouds. The Thunders also entered the Clouds. The Clouds moved down upon the earth, and it rained upon the two children. The Lightnings struck about them. The Thunders roared. It seemed to awaken them. They understood."

To this pair a son was born, and then "they seemed to understand all; that they must labor to feed the child and clothe him. Before this time they had not cared anything about clothing or food, nor for shelter." Tirawa saw their needs, and he sent the messenger gods to bear them gifts and to instruct them. To the woman they gave seeds and the moisture to fructify them; they bestowed upon her the lodge and the lodge altar, the holy place; they presented her with the fireplace, and they taught her the use of fire; the power of speech also was granted her; and the space about the lodge was to be hers; and the materials of the sacred pipes. To the man was given man's clothing and the insignia of the warrior: the war-club, "to remind him that with war-clubs earth was divided from the waters"; knowledge of paints, and the names of the animals; bow and arrows, and the pipes that should be sacred to the gods. "As each star came over the land, the young man went to the place where the Lightning had struck upon the mountains.[32] He found flint-stones with bows and arrows. When the gods had sung the songs about giving these things to these two people, the boy had seen the bow and arrows held up by his father, the Sun." [27]

After this, Bright Star came to the man in visions and revealed to him the rites of sacrifice and the making of the bundle of sacred objects which was to be hung up in the lodge. Meanwhile the gods had created other people, and to these also had been given bundles by the gods who had formed them; but as yet they did not know the rites that were appropriate to them. Then Bright Star said to the man: "Each of these bundles contains a different kind of corn, given by the gods. The Southwest people have the white corn; the Northwest people have the yellow corn; the Northeast people have the black corn; the Southeast people have the red corn." She promised that one would be sent to reveal the rites of the bundles. Thereupon Closed Man — for this was the chief's name — summoned the peoples from the four quarters, and a man who had learned the rituals in a vision taught them the songs and ceremonies. They made their camp in a circle, and ranged the people in imitation of the stations of the stars; and the priests performed a drama symbolizing the creation, making movements over a bowl of water "to show the people how the gods had struck the water when the land was divided from the waters."

Closed Man was the first chief. After he died, his skull was placed upon a bundle; "for before he had died he had told the people that Tirawa had told him, through Bright Star, that when he should die his skull should be placed upon the bundle, so that his spirit should have power, and be ever present with the Skidi people."

This extraordinary myth offers a multitude of analogies, not only with New-World, but also with Old-World cosmogonies. There is in it not a little that is suggestive of the Biblical Genesis, or of the time when the morning stars sang together and cloud and thick darkness were earth's swaddling-band. The Star-Gods of the Quarters, whose feet touch earth and whose hands uphold the heavens, are the very image of the cosmic Titans of old Mediterranean lore, and of the Homeric Strife, "who holdeth her head in the Heavens while her feet tread the Earth." In the earlier astronomical portion of the legend there is much that is reminiscent of Plato's account of creation, in the *Timaeus*, with its apportionments of the heavens among the stars and its delegation of the shaping of all save the souls of men to the Demiurge and the Star-Gods. Surely, there is sublimity in the Pawnee conception of Tirawa, in his abode above the circle of the heavens, passing his commands to the bright evening star, the Mother Star, mistress of the spirit garden of the West; of the Stars of the Quarters singing together their creative hymns; and of the Gods of the Elements, amid turmoil of cloud and wind and thunder and flame, shaping and fashioning the habitable globe, breathing the breath of life into stream and field, into physical seed and spiritual understanding, and striking the earth with the fires of purification.

IV. THE SON OF THE SUN[13]

The story of a woman of the primitive period ascending to the sky-world; of her marriage with a celestial god, son of the Sun Father; of her breaking a prohibition; and of her fall to earth, where a boy, or twin boys, is born to her; and tales of

PLATE XVIII

Kiowa drawing, representing (upper) the Woman who climbed to the Sky in pursuit of a Porcupine that turned out to be Son of the Sun, and (lower) who later fell to Earth, after digging the forbidden root (see p. 115). After *17 ARBE*, Plate LXVII.

M.W.H.

the future deeds of the son of the sky-god — all this is common, in part or in whole, to many tribes and to all regions of the American continent. Indeed, it has obvious affinities to world-wide myths of a similar type, of which Jack and the Beanstalk is the familiar example in English folk-lore.

The Iroquoian cosmogonic tale of the Titaness who is cast down from heaven to the waters of primeval chaos is a part of this mythic cycle, but it does not tell of the previous ascent of the woman into the sky-world. The beautiful and poetic Blackfoot tale of Poïa, the son of the girl who married the Morning Star, is a more complete version of the myth — or perhaps a transformation of the legend, for here it is no longer, as with the Iroquois, a cosmogony, but the tale of a culture hero. In different tribes it shifts from one character to the other — world origins and civilization origins — but in the main its central event seems to be the bringing of a golden treasure from the sky-world by a wonderful boy who becomes a teacher of mankind — a son of the Sun bringing to earth a knowledge of the Medicine of Heaven.

The Skidi Pawnee narrate the story almost exactly in its Blackfoot form, although they do not tell of the poetical translation to and from the heavens by means of a spider's web; but the Arikara, in their version of the "Girl Who Married a Star," give an account of this journey, which is by climbing an ever-growing tree that at last penetrates the sky-world — a means known not only to Jack of beanstalk fame, but to many another tale of the Old and the New Hemispheres.[42] It is in this form that the story is known to several tribes — Arapaho, Crow, Kiowa, Assiniboin.[14]

The events of the legend, as told in the very perfect Arapaho version, begin with the sky-world family: "their tipi was formed by the daylight, and the entrance-door was the sun." Here lived a Man and a Woman and their two boys — Sun and Moon. In search of wives the youths go along Eagle River, which runs east and west, the older brother, Sun, travelling down the stream; the younger, Moon, in the opposite direction. Sun takes for his wife a water animal, the Toad; but Moon decides to marry a mortal woman, and when he sees two girls in the field, he turns himself into a porcupine and climbs a tree. One of the girls starts to follow the animal up the tree, but it keeps ascending, and the tree continues growing. Finally the sky is pierced, and Moon, resuming the form of a young man, takes the girl to wife in the sky-world lodge. There a son is born to her. Meanwhile the father of Sun and Moon has presented his daughter-in-law with a digging stick, but her husband forbids her to dig a certain withered plant. Out of curiosity she disobeys and uncovers a hole through which she looks down upon the camp circle of her people. She undertakes to descend by means of a sinew rope, but just before she reaches earth with her son, Moon throws a stone, called Heated Stone, after her, saying, "I shall have to make her return to me" — a remark which, the Indians declare, shows that there is another place for dead people, the sky-world. The woman is killed by the stone, but the boy is uninjured. At first he is nourished from the breasts of his dead mother; but afterward he is found and cared for by Old Woman Night, who had come to the spot. "Well, well!" she says to him, "Are you Little Star? I am so happy to meet you. This is the central spot which everybody comes to. It is the terminus of all trails from all directions. I have a little tipi down on the north side of the river, and I want you to come with me. It is only a short distance from here. Come on, grandchild, Little Star." The old woman made bow and arrows for Little Star, and with these he slew a horned creature with blazing eyes which proved to have been the husband of Night.[50] She transformed the bow into a lance, and with this he began to kill the serpents which infested the world. While he was sleeping on the prairie, however, a snake entered his body and coiled itself in his skull. All the flesh fell from him, but his bones still held together, and "in this condition he gave his image to the people as a cross." Sense had not altogether deserted him; he prayed for two days of torrential rain and two of intense heat; and when these had passed the serpent thrust its panting head out of his mouth, whereupon he pulled it forth, and was restored to his living form. The reptile's skin he affixed to his lance, and thus equipped returned to the black lodge of Night, where he became the morning star.

In other versions — Crow, Kiowa — the Sun, not the Moon, is the celestial husband; and the porcupine, with his beautiful quills, would seem to be more appropriately an embodiment of the orb of day. The tabued plant, which the wife digs, appears as a constant feature in nearly every variant. That there is close association with the buffalo is indicated by the fact that a buffalo chip (dried dung of the buffalo) is substituted in the Crow story, and that in the Kiowa the tabu is a plant whose top had been bitten off by that animal. The Kiowa version gives the interesting variation that the boy, who is adopted in this instance by Spider Woman, the earth goddess, is split into twins by a gaming wheel (a sun-symbol) which he throws into the air. The story goes on with the drowning of one of the twins by water monsters, while the other transformed himself into "medicine," and in this shape gave himself to the Kiowa as the pledge and guardian of their national existence.

V. THE MYSTERY OF DEATH[16]

Why men die is a problem no less mysterious to the human mind than is the coming of life. One account of the origin of death, common to a number of Plains tribes, makes it the consequence of an unfavourable chance at the beginning of the world. As the Blackfeet tell it, Old Man and Old Woman debated whether people should die. "People will never die," said Old Man. "Oh," said Old Woman, "that will never do; because, if people live always, there will be too many people in the world." "Well," said Old Man, "we do not want to die forever. We shall die for four days and then come to life again." "Oh, no," said Old Woman, "it will be better to die forever, so that we shall be sorry for each other." Unable to agree, they leave the matter to a sign: Old Man throws a buffalo chip into the water; if it sinks, men are to die. "Now, Old Woman had great power, and she caused the chip to turn into a stone, so it sank. So when we die, we die forever." . . . We must have death in order that we may pity one another! — there is an elemental pathos in this simple motive, as in the not dissimilar Eskimo parable of the Old Woman who chose light and death rather than life amid darkness.

A tale of a different complexion, touched by the characteristic astrological genius of the tribe, is the Pawnee story of the origin of death.[14] Mankind had not yet been created when Tirawa sent the giant Lightning to explore the earth. In his sack — the tornado — given him by Bright Star, who has command of the elements, Lightning carried the constellations which Morning Star is accustomed to drive before him; and, after making the circuit of the earth, Lightning released the stars, to encamp there in their celestial order. Here they would have remained, but a certain star, called Fool-Coyote (because he deceives the coyotes, which howl at him, thinking him to be the morning star, whom he precedes), was jealous of the power of Bright Star, and he placed upon the earth a wolf, which stole the tornado-sack of Lightning. He released the beings that were in the sack, but these, when they saw that it was the wolf, and not their master Lightning, which had freed them, slew the animal; and ever since earth has been the abode of warfare and of death.

Another Pawnee myth, with the same astrological turn, tells of the termination that is to come to all earthly life. Various portents will precede: the moon will turn red and the sun will die in the skies. The North Star is the power which is to preside at the end of all things, as the Bright Star of evening was the ruler when life began. The Morning Star, the messenger of heaven, which revealed the mysteries of fate to the people, said that in the beginning, at the first great council which apportioned the star folk their stations, two of the people fell ill. One of these was old, and one was young. They were placed upon stretchers, carried by stars (Ursa Major and Ursa Minor), and the two stretchers were tied to the North Star. Now the South Star, the Spirit Star, or Star of Death, comes higher and higher in the heavens, and nearer and nearer the North Star, and when the time for the end of life draws nigh, the Death Star will approach so close to the North Star that it will capture the stars that bear the stretchers and cause the death of the persons who are lying ill upon these stellar couches. The North Star will then disappear and move away and the South Star will take possession of earth and of its people. "The command for the ending of all things will be given by the North Star, and the South Star will carry out the commands. Our people were made by the stars. When the time comes for all things to end our people will turn into small stars and will fly to the South Star, where they belong." Like other Indians, the Pawnee regard the Milky Way as the path taken by the souls after death. The soul goes first to the North Star, they say, which sets them upon the north end of the celestial road, by which they proceed to the Spirit Star of the south.

Yet not all the spirits of the dead go to the stars — at least, not directly. For the Indian the earth is filled with ghostly visitants, spirits of men and animals wandering through the places which life had made familiar. One of the most gruesome classes of these is formed by the Scalped Men. Men slain and scalped in battle are regarded as not truly dead; they become magic beings, dwelling in caves or haunting the wilds, for shame prevents them from returning to their own people. Their heads are bloody and their bodies mutilated, as left by their enemies, and one horribly vivid Pawnee tale tells how they address one another by names descriptive of the patches of hair still left upon their heads — "One-Hair, Forehead-Hair, Hair-Back-of-the-Head, all of you come!" [12]

The story in which this occurs is of a man who had lost wife and son, and in his bereavement was wandering over the prairies in quest of death. He was met by the Scalped Men of his tribe, and these, taking pity upon him, implored Tirawa to return the dead to the land of the living. The request was granted with certain restrictions — dead and living were to encamp for four days, side by side, without speaking to one another; the bereaved father might speak to his son, but might not touch him. The tribesfolk assembled in camp; they beheld a huge dust approaching; the spirits of their departed friends passed before them. But when the father saw his son among the dead, he seized hold of him and hugged him, and in his heart he said, "I will not let you go!" The people shrieked; the dead disappeared; and death has continued upon earth.[53]

Not less deeply pathetic is another Pawnee tale on the Orpheus and Eurydice theme. A young man joined a war-party in order to win ponies as a bridal fee for the girl of his desire. When her lover no longer appeared, the maiden, not knowing that he had gone to war, sickened and died. On the return of the war-party, it was noised through the village that the young brave had captured more ponies than any of the other men; and when he arrived at his father's lodge, his mother told him the tribal gossip, but failed to mention the girl's death. He went to the spring where the maidens go for water, the meeting-place of Indian lovers, but his sweetheart was not among them. The next day his mother remarked that a girl of the tribe had died during his absence, and then he knew that it was his love who was dead. When he learned this, he called for meat and a new pair of moccasins, and went forth in search of the girl's grave, for the people, following the buffalo, had moved from the place in which she had died. He came to the spot where the grave was and remained beside it for several days, weeping. Then he went on to the empty village, where the people had been when the girl died, for he saw smoke rising from one of the earth lodges. He peeped in, and there he saw his beloved, together with the buffalo robes and other objects which had been buried with her. As he stood gazing, the maiden said, "You have been standing there a long time. Come into the lodge, but do not come near me. Sit down near the entrance." Night after night he was allowed to return, each time coming a little nearer to the girl, but never being permitted to touch her. Finally, she told him that, if he would do in all things as she said, he might be allowed to keep her. After this, invisible dancers filled the lodge, each night becoming more visible, until at last he saw himself surrounded by a group of spirits of the girl's relatives. The leader said to him, "Young man, when you first started from the village where your people are you began to cry. We knew what you were crying about. You were poor in spirit because this girl had died. All of us agreed that we would send the girl back. You can see her now, but she is not real. You must be careful and not make her angry or you will lose her. You have been a brave man to stay with the girl when we came in, but this is the way we are. You can not see us, but some time we can turn into people and you can see us, though we are not real. We are spirits. There is one thing you must do before the girl can stay with you. We have smoked." The feat that remained to be accomplished was that, when her mortal relatives should return and approach her grave with meat-offerings, he must be able to seize and hold her in their presence. Four trials would be granted him; if he failed in each essay, she would vanish forever. Thrice he was thrown, and the girl escaped; the fourth time, with the aid of her uncles, he succeeded in holding her, and she became his wife. Only her mother seemed to be suspicious of her; the old woman took her hoe, went out to her daughter's grave, and dug till she found the bones; but when she returned, the girl said to her: "Mother, I know what you have done. You do not believe that I am your daughter; but, mother, I am your daughter. My body lies up there, but I am here with you. I am not real, and if you people do not always treat me properly, I will suddenly disappear."

The spirit bride gave birth to a son in due time, but the child was never allowed to touch the ground, and the mother never made moccasins for her husband. He had become a man of renown and he wished to take another wife. The spirit wife warned him not to do so, but he persisted. Eventually a quarrel came, due to the jealousy of the new wife, and the man struck his spirit wife. She said: "Do not strike me any more, for you know what I told you. For one thing I am glad, and that is I have a child. If I had remained in the Spirit Land I should never have been allowed to have a child. The child is mine. You do not love my child. . . . I love my child. When I am gone I shall take my child with me." The mother disappeared in a whirlwind, and the next morning the child was found dead. The man, too, died of grief and remorse, but the people buried him apart from the ghost wife's grave.

VI. PROPHETS AND WONDER-WORKERS

In the legendary lore of all Indian tribes the part played by wonder-workers in the affairs of men is the predominating theme. Sometimes these are demiurgic beings, exercising and evincing their might in the process of creation. Sometimes they are magical animals, endowed with shape-shifting powers. Sometimes they are human heroes who acquire wonderful potencies through some special initiation granted them by the Nature-Powers, and so become great prophets, or medicine-men. Frequently such human heroes are of obscure origin — in a very familiar type of story, a poor or an orphan boy who passes from a place despised into one of prominence and benefaction.

In these legends various motives are manifest — a feeling for history and the truth of nature, love of the marvellous, and moral allegory. G. A. Dorsey divides Pawnee myths into four great classes: (1) Tales of the heavenly beings, regarded as true, and having religious significance. (2) Tales of Ready-to-Give,[60] the culture hero,[69] especially pertaining to the guardian deity of the people in the matter of food-quests. (3) Stories of wonder-deeds on earth, the majority of them being concerned with the acquisition of "medicine"-powers by some individual. (4) Coyote tales, not regarded as true, but commonly pointing a moral. The coyote, among the Pawnee, usually appears as a low trickster, not as a magical transformer, as in his more truly mythic embodiments; and apparently he is with them a degraded mythological being, perhaps belonging to an older stratum of belief than their present astronomical theology, perhaps borrowed from other tribal mythologies. There is reason to believe, says Dorsey, that when the Pawnee were still residents of Nebraska the word coyote was rarely employed in these stories, and that the Wolf was the hero of the Trickster tales, this Wolf being the truly mythological being who was sent by the Wolf Star to steal the tornado-sack of Lightning, and so to introduce death upon earth. If the Wolf be indeed a kind of mythic embodiment of the tornado, which yearly deals death on some portion of the Great Plains, the Omaha description of "the male gray wolf, whose cry, uttered without effort, verily made the earth to tremble," will be at once full of significance; and it will inevitably call to mind the Icelandic dog, Garm, baying at world-destroying Ragnarok, and the wolf, Fenrir, loosed to war upon the gods of heaven.

Stories of the Trickster and Transformer are universal in North America.[48] In the eastern portion of the continent the Algonquian Great Hare (and his degenerate doublet, "Brer Rabbit") is the conspicuous personage, though he sometimes appears in human form, as in Glooscap and his kindred. On the Great Plains, and westward to the Pacific, the Coyote is the most common embodiment of this character. Sometimes he appears as a true demiurge, sometimes as the typical example for a well-shot moral or as the butt of satire and ridicule. Occasionally, the Trickster and the Coyote appear as doubles, as in some Arapaho stories of Nihançan, vying with Coyote in contests of trickery; the Assiniboin Tricksters, Inktonmi and Sitconski, have similar encounters with the Coyote or the Rabbit, and they are made heroes of tales which elsewhere have the animals themselves as central figures. Nihançan, Inktonmi, Sitconski, and the Athapascan trickster, Estas, all appear as heroes of cosmogonic events, though they are apparently in no sense deities, but only mythic personages of the Age of Giants and Titans, when animal-beings were earth's rulers. "Old Man" of the Blackfeet and "Old Man Coyote" of the Crow tribe play the same *rôle;* so that everywhere among the Plains tribes we seem to see a process of progressive anthropomorphization of a primitive Wolf god, who was the demiurgic hero. Whether such a being was ever worshipped, as are the heavenly gods in the cult of Sun and Stars, is a matter of doubt.

Among other animals the buffalo, and among birds the eagle, held places of first importance; [40] but all known creatures were regarded as having potencies worthy of veneration and desirable of acquisition. The Pawnee spoke of the animal-powers as Nahurak, whom they thought to be organized in lodges. Of these lodges, Pahuk on the Platte River was regarded as the most important. According to a story of which there are several variants, a chief slew his son — in one version as a sacrifice to Tirawa, in other forms of the legend because he was jealous of the son's medicine-powers — and cast the body into the Platte. The corpse was observed by the Kingfisher, who informed the animals at Pahuk. When the body floated down to their hill-side lodge, the animals took it, carried it in by the vine-hidden entrance, and sent to the animals of Nakiskat, the animal lodge to the west, to inquire whether life should be restored to the body of the slain youth. The animals of Nakiskat referred the matter to the animals of Tsuraspako, still westward on the Platte, and these sent him on to Kitsawitsak, southward in Kansas; there he was bidden to go to Pahua and thence again to Pahuk, all the lodges agreeing that the verdict should be left to the ruling Nahurak of Pahuk. The latter decided to restore life to the body and to send the youth back to his tribe instructed in the animal mysteries. There he became a great teacher and doctor, and taught the people to give offerings to the Nahurak of Pahuk, which was thenceforth a place of great sanctity.

A sojourn in the interior of a hill or a mountain which is the lodge of Nature-Powers who instruct the comer in medicinal mysteries is a frequent episode, especially in stories accounting for the origin of a certain cult or rite. The Cheyenne legend of the introduction of the Sun-Dance is a tale of this character.[5] In a time of famine a young medicine-man went into the wilderness with a woman, the wife of a chief, journeying until they came to a forest-clad mountain, beyond which lay a sea of waters. The mountain opened, and they entered; and Roaring Thunder, who talked to them from the top of the mountain-peak, instructed them in the ritual of the dance. "From henceforth, by following my teachings, you and your children shall be blessed abundantly," he said; "follow my instructions accurately, and then, when you go forth from this mountain, all of the heavenly bodies will move. The Roaring Thunder will awaken them, the sun, moon, stars, and the rain will bring forth fruits of all kinds, all the animals will come forth behind you from this mountain, and they will follow you home. Take this horned cap to wear when you perform the ceremony that I have given you, and you will control the buffalo and all other animals. Put the cap on as you go forth from here and the earth will bless you." Followed by herds of buffalo, which lay down as they camped and marched as they marched, they returned to their people, where the ritual was performed; while the horned head-dress was preserved as a sacred object and handed down in the tribe. In the Sun-Dance ceremonial the altar is made of a buffalo skull, and it is often by dragging buffalo skulls, attached by thongs to the muscles of the back, that vows are fulfilled and penance is performed. It is not difficult to see that the buffalo, as the great food animal of the Plains, is here the important personage, the gift of the heavenly powers; and it would be interesting to theorize on some similar origin for the bucrania which adorned the places of sacrifice of classical peoples.

VII. MIGRATION-LEGENDS AND YEAR-COUNTS[57]

The historical sense had reached a certain development among the Indians of the Plains as among those of the east. Not only are migration-legends to be found, such as that of the Creek, but pictographic records, like the *Walum Olum* of the Delaware, are possessed by more than one western tribe.

Among the most interesting of these migration-traditions — interesting because of their analogies with similar legends of the civilized Mexican peoples — are the Cheyenne myths reported by G. A. Dorsey. The tales begin with an origin story,[15] telling how, in the beginning, the Great Medicine created the earth and the heavenly bodies; and, in the far north, a beautiful country, an earthly Paradise where fruits and game were plentiful, and where winter was unknown. Here the first people lived on honey and fruits; they were naked, and wandered about like the animals with whom they were friends; they were never cold or hungry. There were three races of these men: a hairy race; a white race, with hair on their heads; and the Indians, with hair only on the top of the head. The hairy people went south, where the land was barren, and after a time the Indians followed them; the white, bearded men also departed, but none knew whither. Before the red men left this beautiful country, the Great Medicine blessed them and gave them that which seemed to awaken

PLATE XIX

Cheyenne drawing, representing the medicine-man and his wife who brought back the Sun-Dance from the Mountain of the Roaring Thunder (see p. 123). After *FCM* ix, Plate XIV.

their dormant minds, for hitherto they had been without intelligence. They were taught to clothe their bodies with skins and to make tools and weapons of flint.

The red men followed the hairy men to the south, where the latter had become cave-dwellers. These, however, were afraid of the Indians, were few in number, and eventually disappeared. Warned of a flood which was to cover the southland, the Indians returned to the north, to find that the bearded men and some of the animals were gone from there. Nor were they able, as before, to talk with the animals, but they tamed the panther and bear and other beasts, teaching them to catch game for the people. Afterward they went once more to the south, where the flood had subsided, and where the land was become beautiful and green. Another inundation came, however, and scattered them here and there in small bands, so that they never again were united as one people. This deluge laid the country waste, and to escape starvation they journeyed north once more, only to find the lands there also barren. After hundreds of years, the earth shook, and the high hills sent forth fire and smoke; with the winter came floods, so that all the red men had to dress in furs and live in caves, for the winter was long and cold, and it destroyed all the trees. The people were nearly starved when spring came; but the Great Medicine gave them maize to plant and buffalo for meat, and after that there were no more famines.

A second myth of the same people, which is in some degree a doublet of the preceding, tells how the ancestors of the Cheyenne dwelt in the far north, beyond a great body of water. They were overpowered by an enemy and in danger of becoming slaves, when a medicine-man among them, who possessed a marvellous hoop and carried a long staff, led them from the country. On the fourth night of their journey, they saw before them a bright light, a little above the ground, and this went in front of them as they advanced. When they came to the water, the medicine-man told them that he was going to lead them to a land where they should live forever. He sang magic songs; the waters divided; and the people crossed on dry land. The fire now disappeared, and when day came they found themselves in a beautiful country.

In these events the missionary influence is obvious: the Exodus of Israel is adapted to Cheyenne history. The story goes on, however, with elements that seem truly aboriginal. In the new country the Cheyenne were physically strong, but mentally weak. They could carry off large animals on their backs; they tamed the bear and the panther. Animals, too, were huge. One variety was in the form of the cow, though four times as large; it was tame by nature, and men used its milk; twenty men and boys could get upon the back of one of these creatures at a time. Another species resembled the horse, but had horns and long, sharp teeth; this was a man-eater, and could trail human beings through the rivers and tall grass by scent; fortunately, beasts of this kind were few in number. Most of the animals were destroyed in a great flood, after which the Cheyenne who survived were strong in mind, but weak in body.

It is tempting to see in these stories vague memories of great physiographical changes, reaching back perhaps to the glacial age, and to the period when the elephant kind was abundant in North America, and the great sabre-tooth not yet extinct. On the other hand, the northerly and southerly wanderings of the tribe may well be historical, for it is altogether in keeping with what is known of the drift of the tribal stocks; naturally, such migrations in search of food would be accompanied by changes in the conditions of life, in fauna and in flora. The legend of the bearded white men in the far north is interesting, both as recalling the Nahuatlan myths of Quetzalcoatl, and for its suggested reminiscence of the Northmen: for may it not be possible that the hairy men of the first races in the extreme north were the fur-clad Eskimo, and that the bearded men, who came and disappeared, none knew whither, were descendants of the Scandinavian colonizers of Greenland?

Myths having to do with the gift of maize and of the buffalo to mankind are of frequent occurrence. A Cheyenne tale recounts the adventures of two young men who entered a hill by diving into a spring which gushed from it.[44] Inside they found an old woman cooking buffalo meat and maize in two separate pots; and they saw great herds of buffalo and ponies and all manner of animals, as well as fields of growing maize. The ancient crone[7] gave them the two bowls with maize and meat, commanding them to feed all the tribe, last of all an orphan boy and an orphan girl, the contents of the vessels being undiminished until it came the turn of the orphans, who emptied the dishes.[62] Buffalo arose from the spring, while from the seed that the young men brought maize was grown, this cereal being thereafter planted every year by the Cheyenne. It is easy to see in the episode of the orphans the symbol of plenty, for with wild tribes the lot of the orphan is not secure: it is the orphan child that is sacrificed in the hour of danger, the orphan who is left to starve in time of famine, the orphan, too, who is sometimes led to a wonderful career by the pitying powers of nature.[22]

The Dakota divide their national history by the epochal descent of the Woman-from-Heaven,[7] which, in the chronology of Battiste Good (Wapoctanxi), a Brulé, occurred in the year 901 A. D. All the tribes of the Dakota nation were assembled in a great camp, when a beautiful woman appeared to two of the young men, saying, "I came from Heaven to teach the Dakotas how to live and what their future shall be. . . . I give you this pipe;[30] keep it always." Besides the pipe, she bestowed upon them a package containing four grains of maize — one white, one black, one yellow, one variegated — with the words, "I am a buffalo, the White Buffalo Cow. I will spill my milk [the maize] all over the earth, that the people may live."[35] She pointed to the North: "When you see a yellowish cloud toward the north, that is my breath; rejoice at the sight of it, for you shall soon see buffalo. Red is the blood of the buffalo, and by that you shall live." Pointing to the east, symbolized by blue: "This pipe is related to the heavens, and you shall live with it" — that is, the blue smoke of the pipe is akin to the heavenly blue to which it ascends. Southward: "Clouds of many colors may come up from the south, but look at the pipe and the blue sky and know that the clouds will soon pass away and all will become blue and clear again." Westward: "When it shall be blue in the west, know that it is closely related to you through the pipe and the blue heavens, and by that you shall grow rich. . . . I am the White Buffalo Cow; my milk is of four kinds; I spill it on the earth that you may live by it.[31] You shall call me Grandmother. If you young men will follow me over the hills you shall see my relatives." And with this revelation she disappeared.[40]

Battiste Good's chronology, or "Cycles," is one of the most interesting pictographic records made by an Indian north of Mexico. It recalls the Nahuatlan historical documents by its cyclic character, although the numerical period, seventy years, is different. Each cycle is represented by a circle, surrounded by tipis, and containing emblems recalling noteworthy events. Occurrences from 901, the year of the mythic revelation, to 1700 are legendary, but from 1700 onward each year is marked by an image emblematic of some event of an historical character. The veracity of the record is proved in part by the existence of other Dakotan "Winter-Counts" (so called because the Dakota chiefly choose winter events to mark their chronology) with corroborative statements. Similar pictographic chronologies have been discovered elsewhere, those of the Kiowa showing a division of the year into summer and winter and even into moons, or months; but in no other part of the American continent, north of Mexico, do we find an antiquity of reference equal to that claimed for the Siouan records.

PLATE XX

Kiowa calendar, painted on buckskin. The bars, twenty-nine in number, represent the years from 1864 onward. The crescents, thirty-seven in number, represent a lunar record, separate from the year-count. The figures attached to these signs are symbols of the events which mark the periods indicated. Compare, for other forms of pictographic and mnemonic record, Plates V, X, XXX, and Figure 2. After *17 ARBE*, Plate LXXX.

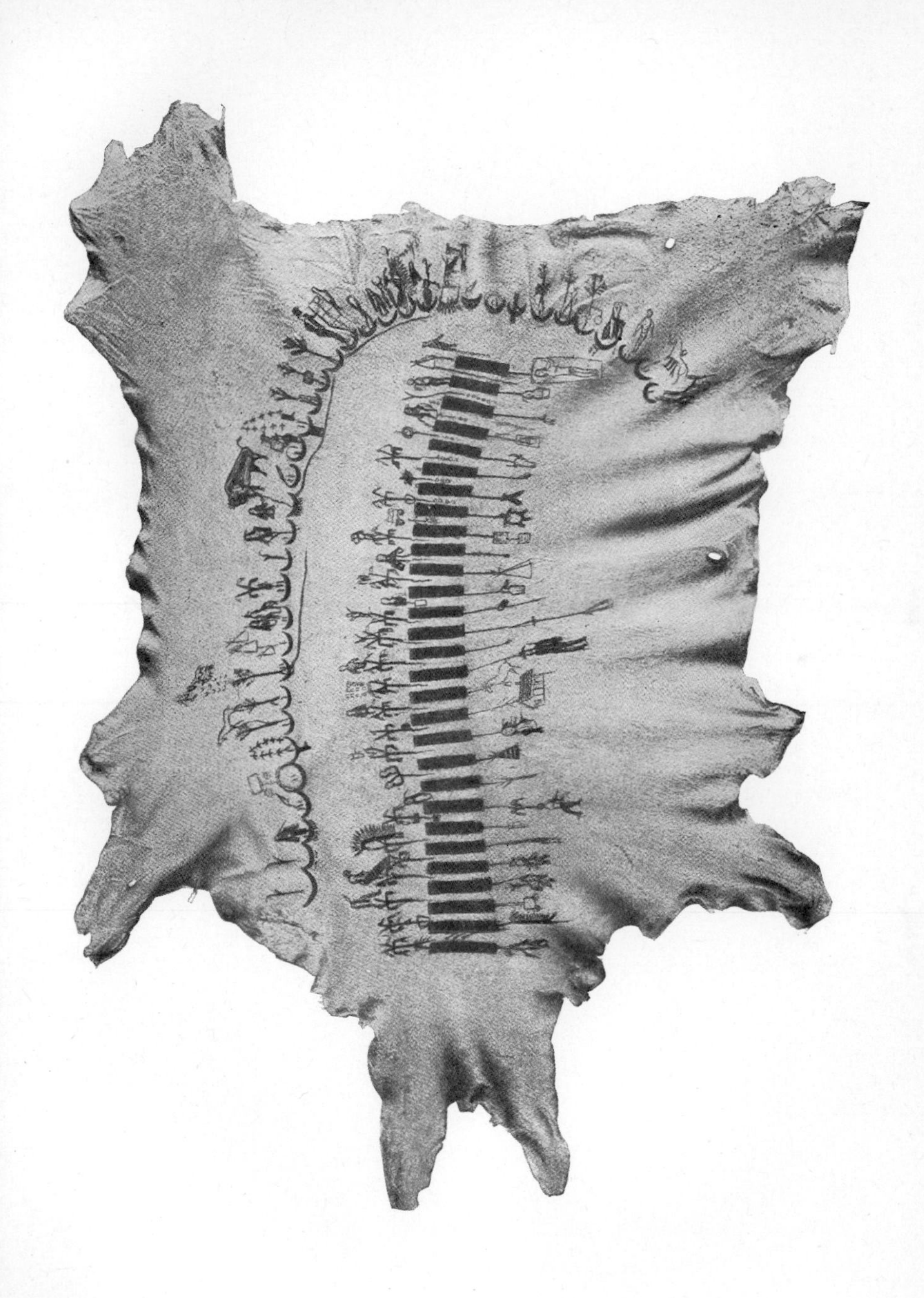

CHAPTER VII

MOUNTAIN AND DESERT

I. THE GREAT DIVIDE

WEST of the Great Plains, and extending almost the full length of the continent, rises the long wall of the Rocky Mountains — the Great Divide of North America. To the east of this chain lie the open prairies, grassy and watered, and beyond these the ancient forest lands, rich in vegetation. To the west, extending to the coastal ranges which abruptly overlook the Pacific, is a vast plateau, at its widest occupying a full third of the continental breadth, the surface of which is a continuous variegation of mountain and valley, desert and oasis. To the north this plateau contracts in width, becoming more continuously and densely mountainous as it narrows in the high ranges and picturesque glaciers of the Canadian Rockies. In the central region it opens out into broad intermontane valleys, like that of the Columbia, and eventually expands into the semi-arid deserts of the south-west, the land of mesa and canyon, wonderfully fertile where water is obtainable, but mainly a waste given over to cactus and sagebrush. Still farther south the elevated area contracts again into the central plateau of Mexico, which becomes more fruitful and fair as the Tropic of Cancer is passed, until it falls away at the Isthmus of Tehuantepec.

This plateau region of North America is well-nigh as distinct ethnically as it is physiographically. In the mountains of British Columbia and up into central Alaska its aboriginals are Athapascan tribes, whose congeners hold the Barren

Lands of the north and the Plains as far as Hudson's Bay; and in the south, in eastern New Mexico, in Arizona and southern Texas, and on into Mexico itself, Athapascans are again found in the Navaho and Apache peoples. Between these limits, however — penetrating now westward to the Pacific, now eastward into the Plains — is a succession of linguistic stocks who are the characteristic autochthones of the mountain and desert region, colouring with their beliefs and civilization other intrusive tribes who have taken a habitation beside them.

The northerly of these stocks is the Salishan, comprising more than sixty tribes, of whom the Flathead and Pend d'Oreille are perhaps best known. Southern British Columbia, western Montana, and most of Washington, where they surrounded Puget Sound and held the Pacific coast, is territory which was once almost wholly Salishan; although, around the headwaters of the Columbia, the Kutenai formed a distinct stock consisting of a single tribe. Adjoining the Salish to the south, and extending from the Columbia valley in Washington and Oregon eastward to central Idaho, were the tribes of the Shahaptian stock, made famous by the Nez Percé and their great Chief Joseph. From central Oregon and Idaho, through the deserts of Nevada, Utah, and southern California, eastward into the mountains of Wyoming and Colorado, and finally out through the lower hills of New Mexico into the Texas plains, were the tribes of the great Shoshonean family — Bannock and Shoshoni in the north, Paiute and Ute in the central belt, Hopi in Tusayan, and Comanche on the Great Plains. To the south dwell the most characteristically desert peoples of all — the Yuman Mohave and Cocopo of Arizona and Lower California, the Pima and Papago of southern Arizona, whose kindred extend far south into western Mexico. Another group, culturally the most interesting of all, although territorially the most limited, is formed by the Pueblo Indians — tribes of various stocks forming little islets of race amid the engulfing

Athapascans of Arizona and New Mexico — but to these a separate chapter must be devoted.

The cultural characteristics of these peoples vary from zone to zone, both in form and in originality. In the north, where the headwaters of the Columbia and the Missouri approach each other, and where the valleys of these rivers form easy paths that lead down to the sea or out into the plains, it is to be expected that we should find, as we do find, the civilization of the Salish and the Shahaptian approximating in form and idea to that of the neighbouring peoples of coast and prairie. In the central region, where the mountain barriers on each side are huge and the distances are immense, it is equally natural to discover among the sparse and scattered Shoshonean peoples a comparatively isolated culture — inept and crude, with that reliance upon roots and herbs to eke out their meagre supply of animal food which has won for many of them the epithet "Digger Indians." In the more open south, agriculture was practised in some degree by every people — Yuman, Piman, Athapascan, and Pueblo — and civilization was accordingly higher, the arts of pottery, basketry, and weaving being developed into skilled industries, especially among the more gifted tribes. Here, however, there is a sharp line between the dwellers in well-built pueblos and the campers, content with grass hut or brush wikiup in summer and earth-covered hogan in winter — a difference reflected in social organization and in ideas.

The subsistence of the tribes of the mountain and desert area had its own character. The range of the buffalo, nowhere found in such numbers as on the Plains, was restricted to the eastern portion of the region; and the deer kind and other large animals, such as the bear and mountain goat, were not sufficiently numerous to form an economic equivalent. Of smaller animals the hare was perhaps most important, and his dignity is reflected in his mythic *rôles*. Horses were early used, and in recent times the Navaho have become accomplished herdsmen. The dog was, of course, ubiquitous. Vegetable subsistence is abundant in places where water is sufficient, but these are few, and hence it comes that a great part of the religion, especially of the agricultural tribes of the South-West, revolves about rain-making and the rain-bringing powers.

II. THE GODS OF THE MOUNTAINS

The prairie tribes, and even tribes of the forest region, held the western mountains in veneration, for to them the Rockies were the limits of the known world. They regarded them as the pillars of heaven, whose summits were the abode of mighty beings, who spoke in the thunders and revealed themselves in the lightning's flash. There, too, on the Mountains of the Setting Sun, many a tribe placed the Village of Souls, to reach which the adventurous spirit must run a gauntlet of terrors — snow-storm and torrent, shaking rock and perilous bridge; only the valiant soul could pass these obstacles and arrive at last in the land of plenty and verdure which lay beyond. Again, the mountains were the seats of revelation; thither went mighty medicine-men, the prophets of the nations, to keep their solitary vigils, or to receive, in the bosom of these lodges of the gods, instruction in the mysteries which were to be the salvation of their people.

It is not extraordinary that the mountains exercised a like fascination over the mythopoetic imaginations of the tribes who inhabited their valleys or dwelt on the intermontane plateau. There are many myths accounting for the formation of natural wonders, and the wilds are peopled with monstrous beings, oft-times reminiscent of European folk-lore.[2] Giants, dwelling in stone houses or armoured with stone shirts, are familiar figures, as are also eaters of human flesh, fang-mouthed and huge-bellied. The cannibal's wife, who warns and protects her husband's visitors, even to the point where they destroy him, is a frequent theme; and the Ute tell stories of mortal men capturing bird-women by stealing their bird-clothes while they are bathing — exactly as the swan-maidens are taken in Teutonic and Oriental folk-lore.[46] The home of these bird-women is far away in the mountains, whither the human hero makes his adventurous flight with magic feathers and a mantle of invisibility.[62] In a Shoshonean tale, published by Powell, Stone Shirt,[38] the giant, slays Sikor, the crane, and carries away the wife of the bird, but her babe is left behind and is reared by his grandmother. One day a ghost appears and tells the boy of the fate of his parents. He returns to his grandmother: "Grandmother, why have you lied to me about my father and mother?" — but she answers nothing, for she knows that a ghost has told him all; and the boy sobs himself to sleep. There a vision came to him, promising him vengeance, and he resolved to enlist all nations in his enterprise; but first he compelled his grandmother to cut him in twain with a magic axe, which, when she had done, lo, there were two boys, whole and beautiful, where before there had been only one.[44] With Wolf and Rattlesnake as their counsellors, the brothers set out across the desert. From a never-failing cup they gave water to their followers, when threatened with death from thirst; and when hunger beset them, all were fed from the flesh of the thousand-eyed antelope which was the watchman of Stone Shirt, but which Rattlesnake, who had the power of making himself invisible, approached and slew. In the form of doves the brothers spied out the home of Stone Shirt, to which they were taken by the giant's daughters, to whom the two birds came while the maidens bathed. In the form of mice, they gnawed the bowstrings of the magic bows which the young girls owned; and when Stone Shirt appeared, glorying in his strength and fancied immunity, the Rattlesnake struck and hurt him to the death. The two maidens, finding their weapons useless, sang their death-song and danced their death-dance, and passed away beside their father. The girls were buried on the shore of the lake where their home had been, but the bones of Stone Shirt were left to bleach as he had left the bones of Sikor, the crane.

This myth surely recounts the conquests of the mountains by the animal-powers, with the birds at their head. The northern Shoshoni say that formerly there were numerous Stone Giants (Dzoavits) dwelling in the hills; many of these were killed by the Weasels, but most of them were destroyed by birds who built fires which exterminated the race. In a familiar western form of the Theft of Fire, it is a mountain genius who is the fire's jealous guardian, and from whom, by craft and fleetness, the animals steal the precious element for the succour of a cold and cheerless world.

It is not always the animals, however, who war against the mountains. On the Columbia River, the canyon by which it passes through the Cascade Range was at one time, the Indians say, bridged by rock, a veritable Bridge of the Gods; but the snow-capped hills of the region engaged in war, hurling enormous boulders at one another, and one of these, thrown by Mt. Hood at Mt. Adams, fell short of its mark, struck and broke the bridge, and dammed the river where is now the great cascade. A Salishan legend tells that this bridge was made by Sahale, the creator, to unite the tribes of men who dwelt on either side of the mountains. He stationed Loowit, the witch, on guard at this bridge, where was the only fire in the world,[51] but she, pitying the Indians, besought Sahale to permit her to bestow upon them the gift of fire. This was done, to the end that men's lot was vastly bettered, and Sahale, pleased with the result, transformed Loowit into a beautiful maiden. But the wars brought on by the rivalry of two chiefs, Klickitat and Wiyeast, for the hand of Loowit were so disastrous to men that Sahale repented his act, broke down the bridge, and, putting to death the lovers and their beloved, reared over them, as memorials, the three great mountains — over Loowit the height that is now St. Helens, over Wiyeast Mt. Hood, and over Klickitat Mt. Adams.

Another great elevation of the vicinity, Mt. Tacoma, has its own legends. Of its beautiful Paradise Valley, near the snow-line, the Indians made a sanctuary, a place of refuge for the pursued, upon attaining which none dared harm him, a place of penance for the repentant, a place of vigil for the seeker after visions. But beyond this valley, toward the mountain-top, no Indian ventured. Long ago, they said, a man was told in a dream that on the mountain's top was great wealth of shell money. He made his way thither, and under a great rock, elk-shaped like the spirit that had directed him, he found stores of treasure; but in his greed he took all, leaving naught as an offering to the mountain. Then it, in its anger, shook and smoked and belched forth fire; and the man, throwing down his riches, fell insensible. When he awoke, he was at his old camp in Saghalie Illahie, "the Land of Peace," now called Paradise Valley; but the time he had passed, instead of a single day, had been years, and he was now an old man, whose remaining life was passed as a counsellor of his tribe, venerated because of his ascent of the divine mountain.[33]

III. THE WORLD AND ITS DENIZENS

Men's ideas of the form of the world, in the pre-scientific stage of thinking, are determined by the aspect of their natural environment: dwellers by the sea look upon the land as an island floating like a raft on cosmic waters; plains-folk believe the earth to be a circle overcanopied by the tent of heaven; mountaineers naturally regard the mountains as the pillars of the firmament supporting the sky-roof over the habitable valleys. The Thompson River Indians, of Salishan stock, dwelling amid the dense mountains that stand between the Fraser and Columbia rivers, consider the earth to be square, says Teit,[11] the corners directed to the points of the compass. It is comparatively level toward the centre, but rises in mountain chains at the outer borders, where, too, clouds and mists ascend from the encircling lakes. The earth rises toward the north; hence it grows colder as one travels in this direction.

Long ago, these Indians say, earth was destitute of trees and of many kinds of vegetation; there were no salmon nor berries. The people of the time, though they had human form, were really animals, gifted with magical powers.[40] Into the world then came certain transformers,[48] the greatest of whom were the Coyote and the Old Man,[63] and these were the beings who put the earth in order, giving the mountains and valleys their present aspects and transforming the wicked among the ancient world denizens into the animal shapes which are still theirs; the descendants of the good among these pristine beings are the Indians of today. Many of these creatures, too, were transformed into rocks and boulders: on a certain mountain three stone men may be seen sitting in a stone canoe; they are three human beings who escaped thither when the deluge [49] overtook the world; Coyote alone survived this flood, for he transformed himself into a piece of wood, and floated until the waters subsided.

It was Coyote's son, created by his father from quartz, who climbed to the sky-world on a tree which he made to grow by lifting his eyelids.[42] In that realm he found all sorts of utensils useful to man, but when he chose one, the others attacked him, so that he cursed them all thenceforth to be servants of the human race. He returned to the world of man by means of a basket which Spider lowered for him; and on earth, in a series of miracles, he distributed the food animals for the people to live upon. The place where Coyote's son came back from the sky is the centre of the earth.

There is a world below the world of men as well as a world above. In the world below the people are Ants, very active and gay and fond of the game of lacrosse. On a certain day one of two brothers disappeared; the remaining brother searched far and wide, but could find no trace of him. Now the

Ants had stolen him, and had carried him away to the underworld, where he played with them at lacrosse. But one day, as he was in the midst of a game, he began to weep, and the Ants said that some one must have struck him with a lacrosse stick. "No! Nobody struck me," he answered. "I am sorrowful because while I was playing a tear fell on my hand. It was my brother's tear from the upper world, and I know by it that he is searching for me and weeping." Then the Ants in pity sent a messenger to the upper world to tell the bereaved one that his brother was well and happy in the underworld. "How can I see my brother?" he asked. "I must not tell you," replied the Ant. "Go to the Spider, and he may tell you." But the Spider said, "I cannot let you down, as my thread is too weak. Go to the Crow." The Crow answered, "I will not tell you with my mouth, but I will tell you in a dream"; and in the vision he was told to lift the stone over the fireplace in his lodge, and there would be the entrance to the lower world. He was to close his eyes, leap downward, and, when he alighted, jump again. Four times he was to leap with closed eyes. The bereaved brother did so, and the fourth jump brought him to the lowest of the worlds, where he was happy with his brother. This myth presents analogies not only with the Navaho conception of an ant-infested series of underworlds, but far to the south, in Central America, with the Cakchiquel legend of the two brothers who played at ball with the powers of the underworld;[44] and again, on a world canvas, with the myriad tales of the bereaved one, god or mortal, seeking the ghost of his beloved in gloomy Hades.[53]

These same Indians tell a story that seems almost an echo of the Greek tale of Halcyone or of Tereus lamenting the lost Itys.[46] A certain hunter, they say, commanded his sister never to eat venison while he was on the hunt, but she disobeyed, and he struck her. In chagrin she transformed herself into a golden plover and flew away, while he, since he really loved his sister, began to weep and bemoan his fate, until he, too, became a bird, crying disconsolately, "Na xlentcetca," — "Oh, my younger sister!"

Like the southern tribes, the Salish tell of a time when the Sun was a man-slayer, nearer to earth than now.[13] Across a bridge of fog an unlucky gambler [56] made his way to the Sun's house, where the Sun's son concealed him from his cannibal father.[19] "Mum, mum, mum! There must be a man here," said the Sun; but his son persuaded him that there was none, and sent the gambler back to earth, burdened with riches.

The Thunderbird is not so huge as the bird of the Plains tribes; he is in fact a small, red-plumaged creature which shoots arrows from his wing as from a bow, the rebound of the wing making the thunder, while the twinkling of his eyes is the lightning; [32] the large black stones found in the country are the Thunder's arrows.[27] The winds are people, dwelling north and south; some describe the wind as a man with a large head and a body thin and light, fluttering above the ground. Long ago the South-Wind People gave a daughter in marriage to the North, but their babe was thrown into the water by the bride's brother, whose southern warmth was unable to endure the little one's colder nature; and the child became ice floating down the river. Where the powerful Chinook wind blows, capable of transforming the temperature from winter to summer in a few hours, the Indians tell of a great struggle, a wrestling-match of long ago, in which five brothers of the Warm-Wind People were defeated and decapitated by the Cold-Wind Brothers; but the son of one of the Warm-Wind Brothers grew up to avenge his uncles, and defeated the Cold-Wind Brothers, allowing only one to live, and that with restricted powers. Both the stories — of the north marrying the south and of the wrestling winds, or seasons — are found far east among the Algonquians and Iroquois; but the allegory is too natural to necessitate any theory of borrowing — any more than we might suppose the bodiless cherubs of the old Italian painters to be akin to the Salish wind-people.[39]

IV. SHAHAPTIAN AND SHOSHONEAN WORLD-SHAPERS

The Nez Percé are the most important tribe of the Shahaptian stock. In the primeval age, they say,[41] there was a monster in what is now central Idaho whose breath was so powerful that it inhaled the winds, the grass, the trees, and different animals, drawing them to destruction. The Coyote, who was the most powerful being of the time, counselled by the Fox, decided to force an entrance into this horrible creature, and there he found the emaciated people, their life being slowly drawn out of them, chill and insensible. He kindled a fire from the fat in the monster's vitals, revived the victims, and then, with the knives with which he had provided himself, cut their way out into the sunlight. From the different parts of the body of the hideous being he created the tribes of men, last of all making the Nez Percé from its blood, mingled with water. Here is another world-wide myth, the tale of the hero, swallowed by the monster, making his way again to light; though in this Nez Percé version it seems to be a true cosmogony, the monster being the world-giant from whose body all life emerges.

The Shoshoni, or Snake, who border upon the Nez Percé, regard the firmament as a dome of ice, against which a great serpent, who is none other than the rainbow, rubs his back.[50] From the friction thus produced particles of ice are ground off, which in winter fall to earth as snow, while in summer they melt into rain. Thunder they do not ascribe to birds, but to the howling of Coyote, or, some say, to a celestial mouse running through the clouds.[32] A great bird they know, Nunyenunc, which carries off men, like the roc of Arabian tales, but he is not connected with the thunder. Like neighbouring tribes, they tell of a time when the sun was close to the earth, killing men with its heat. The Hare was sent to slay it, and he shattered the sun into myriad fragments; but these set the world ablaze, and it was not until the Hare's eyes burst, and a flood of tears issued forth, that the conflagration was quenched. Thereafter the sun was conquered, and its course regulated.[13]

The tale of the theft of fire recurs in many forms.[51] The familiar type is that in which the flame is guarded by its first owners in some mountain lodge, until the tribes of animals who dwell in cold and gloom decide to steal it. Entrance is gained to the home of the guardians by craft, and a bit of the fire is smuggled out under the coat or blanket of the thief. He is discovered and pursued by the owners of the flame, but succeeds in passing it on to another animal, which in turn gives it to another, and this one to yet another, until it is distributed in all nature, or, perhaps, hidden in trees or stones. A Shoshoni version makes the great animal hero of this region, the Coyote, the thief. With the aid of the Eagle he steals the fire from its guardian, the Crane. Blackbird and Rock-Squirrel are the animals who carry the flame farther, while Jack-Rabbit revives the fallen fire-carriers. The Thompson River Indians make the Beaver the assistant of the Eagle in the theft; and they also tell a story of the Pandora type, of a man who guarded fire and water in two boxes till an Elk, out of curiosity, opened the receptacles and set the elements free. A Nez Percé variant also makes the Beaver the thief; the Pines were the fire's first guardians, but the Beaver stole a live coal, hid it in his breast, and distributed it to willows and birches and other trees which as yet did not possess it; and it is from these woods that the Indians now kindle fire by rubbing.

Perhaps the most dramatic fire-myth of all is the elaborate Ute version, in which Coyote is again the hero. It was in the age when Coyote was chief, but when the animals had no fire, though the rocks sometimes got hot. Once a small piece of burnt rush, borne by the winds, was discovered by Coyote, and then he knew that there was fire. He made for himself a head-dress of bark fibre, summoned the animals in council, and dispatched the birds as scouts to discover the flame country. The Humming-Bird descried it; and headed by Coyote, they made a visit to the fire-people, who entertained them with dance and feast. As they danced, Coyote came nearer and nearer to the flame, took off his bark wig, and with it seized the fire. Then all fled, pursued by the enraged guardians. Coyote passed the fire to Eagle, Eagle to Humming-Bird, thence to Hawk-Moth, to Chicken-Hawk, to Humming-Bird again, and once more to Coyote, who, nearly caught, concealed himself in a cavern where he nourished the one little spark that remained alive. The disappointed fire-people caused rain and snow, which filled the valleys with water; but directed by the Rabbit, Coyote discovered a cave containing dry sage-brush. Here he took a piece of the dry sage-brush, bored a hole in it, and filled it with coals. With this under his belt he returned home and summoned the people who were left; then he took the stick, made a hole in it with an arrow-point, and whittled a piece of hard greasewood. After this he bored the sage-brush with the greasewood, gathered the borings, and put them in dry grass; blowing upon this he soon had a fire. "This dry pine-nut will be burned hereafter," he said. "Dry cedar will also be burned. Take fire into all the tents. I shall throw away the rocks. There will be fire in every house."

V. COYOTE[48]

The animal-powers bulk large in the myths of the tribes of the Mountain and Desert region. Doubtless in their religion, apart from myth, the animal-powers are secondary; the Shoshoni, says De Smet, swear by the Sun, by Fire, and by the Earth, and what men swear by we may be reasonably sure marks their intensest convictions. The ritual of the calumet, directed to the four quarters, to heaven, and to earth, is familiar here as elsewhere among the Red Men; and there is not wanting evidence of the same veneration of a "Great Spirit" which is so nearly universal in America.[6] Even in myth there is a considerable degree of anthropomorphism.

The Transformer is not always an animal, but is often the "Old One" or "Old Man," the Ancient who is the true creator.[63] Other manlike beings, good and evil, hold or have held the rulership of certain provinces of nature; and in the Age of Animals, before men were, the beasts themselves are said to have had human form: their present shapes were imposed upon them by the Transformers. Nevertheless, they were truly animals, in nature and disposition, and the heroic age of Indian myth is the period of their deeds.

Among all these creatures Coyote is chief. It is difficult to obtain a clear conception of the part which Coyote plays in the Indian's imagination. The animal itself, the prairie wolf, is small and cowardly, the least imposing of the wolf kind. In multitudes of stories he is represented as contemptible — deceitful, greedy, bestial, with an erotic mania that leads him even to incest, often outwitted by the animals whom he endeavours to trick, without gratitude to those that help him; and yet, with all this, he is shown as a mighty magician, reducing the world to order and helping man with innumerable benefactions, perhaps less the result of his intention than the indirect outcome of his own efforts to satisfy his selfish appetite. It is impossible to regard such a being as a divinity, even among those tribes who make him the great demiurge; it is equally out of the question to regard him as a hero, for his character abuses even savage morals. In general he resembles the Devil of mediaeval lore more than perhaps any other being — the same combination of craft and selfishness, often defeating its own ends, of magic powers and supernatural alliances. The light in which the Indians themselves regard him may best be indicated by the statement made to Teit by an old Shuswap: "When I was a boy, very many stories were told about the Old One or Chief, who travelled over the country teaching people, and putting things to rights. Many wonderful tales were related of him; but the men who told these stories are now all dead, and most of the 'Old One' tales have been forgotten. The majority of the Coyote tales have survived, however, and are often told yet; for they are funny, and children like to hear them. Formerly Coyote stories were probably commonest of all. Long before the arrival of the first white miners, a Hudson Bay half-breed told the Shuswap that after a time strange men would come among them, wearing black robes (the priests). He advised them not to listen to these men, for although they were possessed of much magic and did some good, still they did more evil. They were descendants of the Coyote, and like him, although very powerful, they were also very foolish and told many lies. They were simply the Coyote returning to earth in another form."

Coyote stories have a wide distribution. They are told by Athapascans in the north and in the south, and by men of the stocks that lie between, from the prairies to the western coast. Their eastern counterparts are the tales of the Great Hare; but the two beings, Hare and Coyote, appear together in many stories, often as contestants, and the Hare, or Rabbit, is an important mythic being among the Shoshonean Ute as well as among the Algonquian Chippewa. Nevertheless, in the west it is Coyote who holds the first and important place among the animal-powers; and it may reasonably be assumed that his heroship is a creation of the plateau region.

Like the Hare, Coyote is frequently represented as having a close associate, or helper. Sometimes this is a relative, as Coyote's son; sometimes another animal, especially the Fox; sometimes it is the Wolf, whose character is, on the whole, more dignified and respectable. A most interesting Shoshonean myth, published by Powell, tells how Wolf and his brother debated the lot of mortals. The younger of the pair said: "Brother, how shall these people obtain their food? Let us devise some good plan for them. I was thinking about it all night, but could not see what would be best, and when the dawn came into the sky I went to a mountain and sat on its summit, and thought a long time; and now I can tell you a good plan by which they can live. Listen to your younger brother. Look at these pine trees; their nuts are sweet; and there on the plain you see the sunflower, bearing many seeds—they will be good for the nation. Let them have all these things for their food, and when they have gathered a store they shall put them in the ground, or hide them in the rocks, and when they return they shall find abundance, and having taken of them as they need, shall go on, and yet when they return a second time there shall still be plenty; and though they return many times, as long as they live the store shall never fail; and thus they shall be supplied with abundance of food without toil." "Not so," said the elder brother, "for then will the people, idle and worthless, and having no labor to perform, engage in quarrels, and fighting will ensue, and they will destroy each other, and the people will be lost to the earth; they must work for all they receive." Then the younger brother went away grieving, but the next day he came with the proposition that, though the people must work for their food, their thirst should be daily quenched with honey-dew from heaven. This, too, the elder brother denied; and again the younger departed in sorrow. But he came to the Wolf, his brother, a third time: "My brother, your words are wise; let the women gather the honey-dew with much toil, by beating the reeds with flails. Brother, when a man or a woman or a boy or a girl, or a little one dies, where shall he go? I have thought all night about this, and when the dawn came into the sky I sat on the top of the mountain and did think. Let me tell you what to do: When a man dies, send him back when the morning returns, and then will all his friends rejoice." "Not so," said the elder; "the dead shall return no more." Then the younger went away sorrowing. But one day he beheld his brother's son at play, and with an arrow slew him; and when Wolf, the father, sought his boy in anguish, his younger brother, the Coyote, said to him: "You made the law that the dead shall never return. I am glad that you are the first to suffer."[16] In such a tale as this, it is self-evident that we are hearing, not of heroes of romance, but of fate-giving divinities; and it is not far to go back in imagination to a time when the Wolf was a great tribal god.

VI. SPIRITS, GHOSTS, AND BOGIES

Giants, dwarfs, talking animals, ogre-like cannibals, many-headed water monsters, man-stealing rocs, sky-serpents, and desert witches are all forms which, in the jargon of the north-west, are regarded as *tamanos*, or powerful, though they are neither gods nor spirits, and, indeed, may be destroyed by an adroit and bold warrior. These beings must be put in the general class of bogies, and, though one is tempted to see, especially in the prevalence and ferocity of cannibal tales, some reminiscence of former practices or experiences, there is probably nothing more definite behind them than the universal fancy of mankind.

To a somewhat different category belong the tutelaries, or daemons attached as guardians to individuals, and the residua of once-living beings which correspond to the European's conceptions of ghosts and souls. Both of these classes of beings are related to visionary experience. The Indian's tutelary [4] is commonly revealed to him in a fast-induced vision, especially in the period of pubescence; from the nature of the revelation comes his own conception of himself — vision of a weapon or a scalp will mean that he is to be a warrior, of a game-animal that he will succeed in the chase, of a ghostly being that he will be a medicine-man of renown; and from it he fashions an image or fabricates a bundle which is to be his personal and potent medicine; sometimes, he even derives his name — the secret name, which he may reveal only after some exploit has justified it — from the same source. Similarly, ghosts and their kind are likeliest seen in the course of spirit-journeys, in trance or dream; or, if beheld by the eyes of flesh, they may be dispelled by the taunt, "Thou art only a ghost! Get thee gone."

On the other hand, a ghost that is feared may be a fatal antagonist.

Ghosts and souls are distinct. In several tribes ghosts are regarded as the shadows of souls; they dress and appear like the man himself. Souls may make journeys from the living body and return again; in the case of shamans they may reach the land of souls itself, and still come back. Souls of the dead may be reincarnated in human bodies; usually this is in their own families; some tribes say that only children are so reborn. Again, souls are frequently regarded as manikins, a few inches high — a conception found all over the earth; and the noises of the spirit-world, especially the voices of the shades, are thin and shrill or like the crying of a child.[20]

Ghosts, as distinguished from souls or spirits, are of a more substantial character.[12] They are wraiths of the dead, but they assume material forms, and at times enter into human relations with living people, even marriage and parentage. Often the ghost is detected as such only when his body is seen transparent, with the skeleton revealed — and we are reminded of the Eskimo ghosts, men when beheld face to face, but skeletons when perceived from behind. Reminiscent of another Eskimo idea, the Cannibal Babe, is the Montana legend of the Weeping Child.[19] A traveller passing a certain place would hear an infant crying; going thither, he would find the babe and take it in his arms and give it his finger to quiet it; but the child would suck all the flesh from his bones, so that a great pile of skeletons marked its monstrous lair. The Klickitat, a Shahaptian tribe of the lower Columbia, have a story of the union of a mortal and a ghost curiously like the Pawnee tale of "The Man who Married a Spirit." The Klickitat buried their dead on islands of the river, and it was here that the body of a young chief was carried. But neither his soul, on the isle of the dead, nor the mind of his beloved, who was with her people, could forget one another, and so he came to her in a vision and called her to him. At night her father took her in a canoe to the isle and left her with the dead. There she was conducted to the dance-house of the spirits, and found her lover more beautiful and strong than ever he was upon earth. When the sun rose, however, she awoke with horror to find herself surrounded by the hideous remains of the dead, while her body was clasped by the skeleton arm of her lover. Screaming she ran to the water's edge and paddled across the river to her home. But she was not allowed to remain, for the fear of the departed was now upon the tribe; and again she was sent back, and once more passed a night of happiness with the dead. In the course of time a child was born to her, more beautiful than any mortal. The grandmother was summoned, but was told that she must not look upon the child till after the tenth day; unable to restrain her curiosity, she stole a look at the sleeping babe, whereupon it died. Thenceforth, the spirit-people decreed, the dead should nevermore return, nor hold intercourse with the living.[53]

The path from the land of the living to the land of the dead is variously described by the different tribes. Generally it lies westward, toward the setting sun, or downward, beneath the earth. Often it is a journey perilous, with storms and trials to be faced, narrow bridges and yawning chasms to be crossed — a hard way for the ill-prepared soul. Teit has given us a full account — of which the following is a paraphrase — of the road to the soul's world, as conceived by the Thompson River tribes[8] — a description interesting for its analogies to the classical Elysium, lying beyond Styx, and the three judges of the dead:

The country of the souls is underneath us, toward the sunset; the trail leads through a dim twilight. Tracks of the people who last went over it, and of their dogs, are visible. The path winds along until it meets another road which is a short cut used by the shamans when trying to intercept a departed soul. The trail now becomes much straighter and smoother, and is painted red with ochre. After a while it winds to the westward, descends a long gentle slope, and terminates at a wide shallow stream of very clear water. This is spanned by a long slender log, on which the tracks of the souls may be seen. After crossing, the traveller finds himself again on the trail, which now ascends to a height heaped with an immense pile of clothes — the belongings which the souls have brought from the land of the living and which they must leave here. From this point the trail is level, and gradually grows lighter. Three guardians are stationed along this road, one on either side of the river and the third at the end of the path; it is their duty to send back those souls whose time is not yet come to enter the land of the dead. Some souls pass the first two of these, only to be turned back by the third, who is their chief and is an orator who sometimes sends messages to the living by the returning souls. All of these men are very old, grey-headed, wise, and venerable. At the end of the trail is a great lodge, mound-like in form, with doors at the eastern and the western sides, and with a double row of fires extending through it. When the deceased friends of a person expect his soul to arrive, they assemble here and talk about his death. As the deceased reaches the entrance, he hears people on the other side talking, laughing, singing, and beating drums. Some stand at the door to welcome him and call his name. On entering, a wide country of diversified aspect spreads out

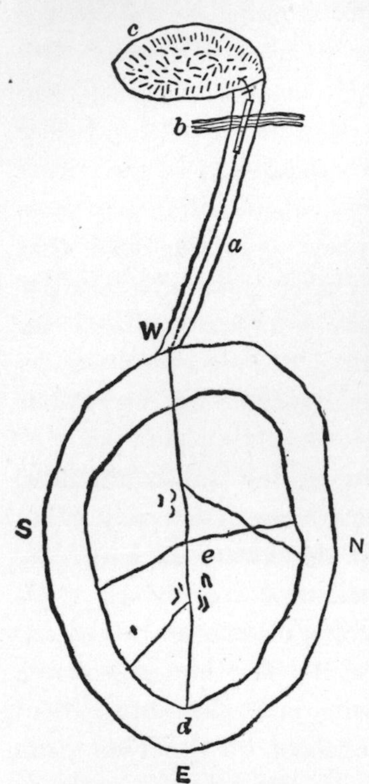

Fig. 2. Sketch of the World

Map of the world as drawn by a Thompson River Indian. (a) Westward trail to the Underworld. (b) River. (c) Land of the Dead. (d) Sunrise point. (e) Middle place. After *MAM* ii, 343.

before him. There is a sweet smell of flowers and an abundance of grass, and all around are berry-bushes laden with ripe fruit. The air is pleasant and still, and it is always light and warm. More than half the people are dancing and singing to the accompaniment of drums. All are naked, but do not seem to notice it. The people are delighted to see the new comer, take him up on their shoulders, run around with him, and make a great noise.

VII. PROPHETS AND THE GHOST-DANCE[5]

A spirit-journey and a revelation is the sanction which creates an Indian prophet. Shaman and medicine-man alike claim this power of spiritual vision, and the records of investigators sufficiently show that the Indian possesses in full degree this form of mystic experience. Behind nearly every important movement of the Indian peoples lies some trance of seer or prophet, to whom the tribes look for guidance. Underneath the "conspiracy of Pontiac" were the visions and teachings of a Delaware prophet, who had visited the Master of Life and received from him a message demanding the redemption of the Indian's lands and life from white pollution; the trances of Tenskwatawa were the inspiration of his brother, the great chief Tecumseh, in the most formidable opposition ever organized by Indians against the whites; Kanakuk, the prophet of the Kickapoo, talked with the Great Spirit, and brought back to his tribe a message of sobriety and industry, peace and piety.

Of the later prophets the most notable have been men of the far West. Smohalla, chief of a small Shahaptian tribe of Washington, who was called by his people "The Shouting Mountain" because they believed that his revelation came from a living hill which spoke to him as he lay entranced, founded a sect of Dreamers, whose main tenet was hostility to the ways of the white man and insistence that the land of the Indian should be Indians' land: "My young men shall never work," he said; "men who work cannot dream, and wisdom comes to us in dreams." This was the doctrine which inspired Chief Joseph and his Nez Percé in the wonderful exploit which marked the exodus of his tribe in 1877 — "the Earth is our Mother; she shall not be torn by plow nor hoe; neither shall she be sold, nor given from the hand of her children."

Very similar is the teaching of the Paiute prophet, Wovoka, the Indian "messiah," whose promises of a regeneration of the life of the Red Man, with the foreigner destroyed or driven from his ancient holdings, spread throughout all the tribes of the Plains and Mountains, and eventuated in the Sioux uprising of 1890 and the tragedy of Wounded Knee. Wovoka is the son of a prophet; his home a strip of valley prairie surrounded by the dark walls of volcanic sierras. Here, when he was about thirty-three, in the year "when the sun died" (probably the eclipse of January 1, 1889), he declared that he went up to heaven, and saw God, and received a message to all Indians that they must love one another, that they must not fight, nor steal, nor lie, and he received also a dance which he was to bring to them as pledge and promise of their early redemption from the rule of the whites. The dead are all alive again, the prophet taught; already they have reached the boundaries of earth, led by the spirit captain in the form of a cloud. When they arrive, the earth will shake, the sick be healed, the old made young, and the free life of the Indian again restored. Among many of the tribes the dance which they were to continue until the day of the advent assumed the form of ecstasy and trance, in which visionary souls would perceive the advancing hosts of the spirit Indians, the buffalo once more filling the prairies, and the Powers of the Indian's universe returning to their ancient rule. Better than aught else the Ghost-Dance songs, collected by Mooney from the various tribes among whom the religion spread, give the true spirit of the creed, and at the same time afford an insight into the religious feeling which goes far deeper in the Indian's experience than story-made

PLATE XXI

Ghost-Dance, painted on buckskin by a Ute captive among the Cheyenne in 1891. Cheyenne and Arapaho are the dancers; the prostrate forms in the centre represent persons entranced; the round object is a blanket; before it stands a medicine-man hypnotizing a subject. Now in United States National Museum. After *14 ARBE*, part 2, Plate CIX.

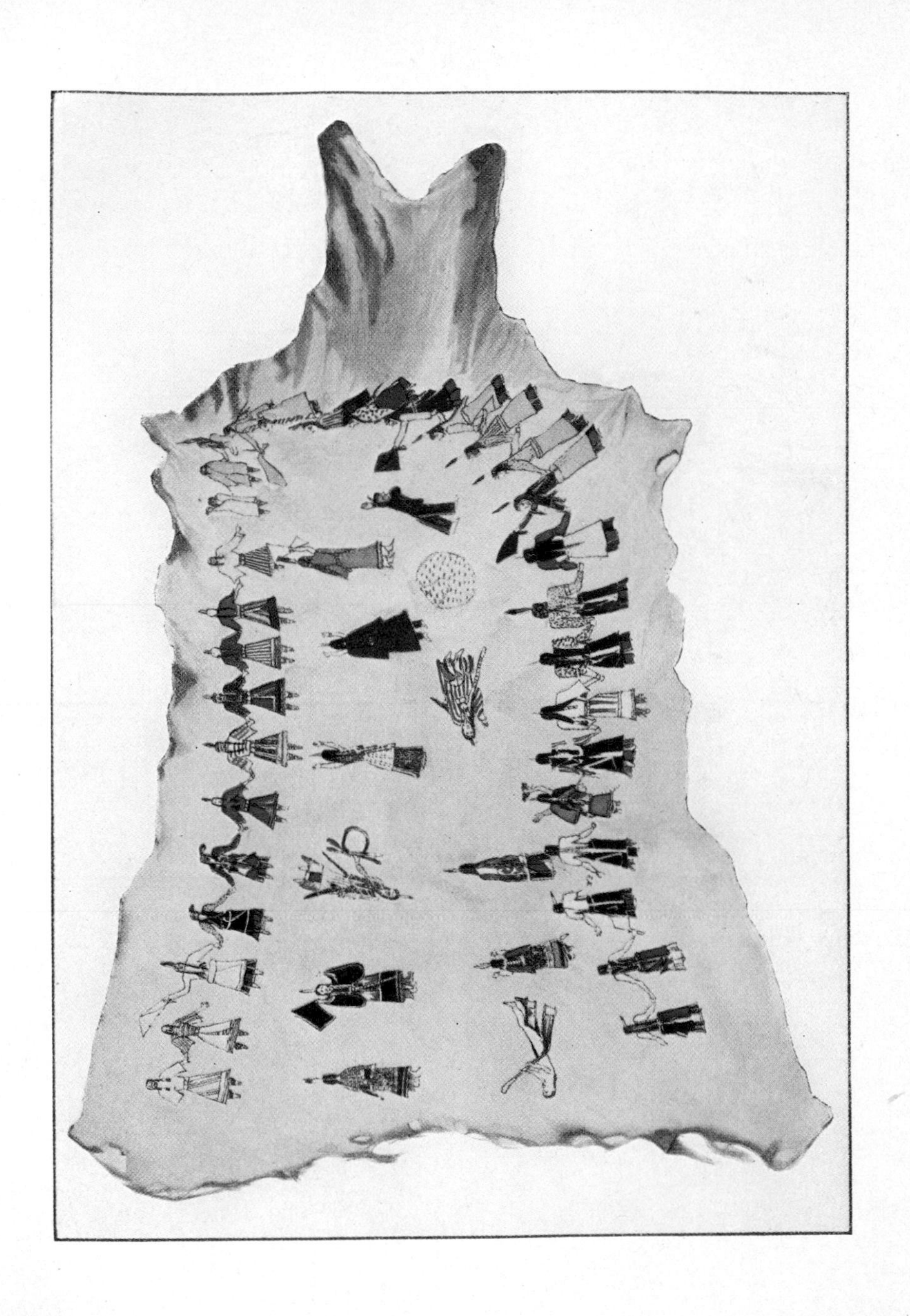

myth (See James Mooney, "The Ghost-Dance Religion," in *14 ARBE*, Part 2, pp. 953–1103).

A curious and lovely feature of these Indian hymns of the Ghost-Dance is their intense visualization of Nature. The words are elemental and realistic, but no song is without its inner significance, either as symbolic of indwelling Powers or as vocables of individual experiences too full for complete expression. Among the Paiute songs one seems to be a promise of the advancing spirits, approaching by the Path of Souls to an earth clothed in a kindred purity —

> The snow lies here — *ro'rani!*
> The snow lies here — *ro'rani!*
> The snow lies here — *ro'rani!*
> The Milky Way lies there!

Others tell of rejuvenated animal and vegetable life —

> A slender antelope, a slender antelope,
> He is wallowing upon the ground.

And —

> The cottonwoods are growing tall,
> They are growing tall and verdant.

Again it is the elements, astir with expectancy of the great regeneration —

> The rocks are ringing,
> The rocks are ringing,
> They are ringing in the mountains!

And especially there is the whirlwind, advancing, like the Spirit Captain, as a cloud that foretokens the new life of earth —

> There is dust from the whirlwind,
> There is dust from the whirlwind,
> The whirlwind on the mountain!
>
> The Whirlwind! The Whirlwind!
> The snowy Earth comes gliding, the snowy Earth comes gliding!

The more beautiful and intellectual Ghost-Dance songs come, however, not from the Paiute, who originated the ceremony, but from the Plains tribes who developed it to its intensest form. Especially fine are the Arapaho songs. The Whirlwind is still the mighty power — the Psychopompos, leading the ghostly visitants —

Our father, the Whirlwind —
By its aid I am running swiftly,
By which means I saw our father.

The Whirlwind is personified thus —

I circle around,
I circle around
The boundaries of the Earth,
Wearing the long wing feathers as I fly.

Many songs are devoted to the bird messengers of the Ghost-Dance, to the mythical Thunderbirds and to the Crow which is the sacred bird of the dance; and in these there is almost always a note of exaltation —

I fly around yellow,
I fly around yellow,
I fly with the wild rose on my head,
On high — *He'e'e'!*
On high — *He'e'e'!*

Uplifted, too, and exultant is the note of another Arapaho song, to the Father —

Father, now I am singing it — *Hi'ni'ni!*
Father, now I am singing it — *Hi'ni'ni!*
That loudest song of all,
That resounding song — *Hi'ni'ni!*

Again, the note struck is cosmogonic, with a reference back to the old beliefs of the Indians — in this case to the Algonquian conception of the Turtle whose carapace supports the Earth —

At the beginning of human existence — *I'yehe'eye'!*
It was the Turtle who gave this grateful gift to me,
The Earth — *I'yahe'eye'!*
Thus my father told me — *Ahe'eye'–he'eye'!*

But the commonest note of all, and the one that best summarizes the whole spirit, not only of the Ghost-Dance, but of the prophecy of the Indians through all the later period when they have felt themselves inevitably succumbing before the hard encroachments of the white race, is the note of sorrowful supplication, a pleading for help. The most pathetic of these songs, "sung," says Mooney, "to a plaintive tune, sometimes with tears rolling down the cheeks of the dancers," is that which he calls the Indian's Lord's Prayer —

> Father, have pity on me,
> Father, have pity on me;
> I am crying for thirst,
> I am crying for thirst;
> All is gone — I have nothing to eat.

The hunger and thirst here meant are of the spirit, and the sustenance that the Indian supplicates is the spiritual food and drink which will support him through the harsh trials of a changing life.

CHAPTER VIII

MOUNTAIN AND DESERT

(Continued)

I. THE NAVAHO AND THEIR GODS

THE Navaho speak an Athapascan tongue, but in blood they are one of the most mixed of Indian peoples, with numerous infusions from neighbouring tribes, additions having come to them from the more civilized Pueblo dwellers as well as from the wandering tribes of the desert. But various as is their origin, the Navaho have a cultural unity and distinction setting them in high relief among Indian peoples. They practise a varied agriculture, are herdsmen even more than huntsmen, and have developed arts, such as blanket weaving and silversmithing, which have made them pre-eminent among Indian craftsmen. It is chiefly in the matter of habitation that they are inferior to the tribes of the pueblos, for until recently they have persistently adhered to temporary dwellings (partly, it is supposed, because of the superstition which calls for the abandonment of a house in which a death has occurred) — the hogan, or earth hut, for winter, the brush shelter for summer residence.

In particular the Navaho have developed an artistic power which has won for them the admiration of the white race, with whom their work finds a ready market; though it is perhaps in the unmerchantable wares of the mind, in myth and poetry, and their curiously ephemeral sand-painting that their powers are revealed at their best. Their religious rituals are characterized by elaborate masques, far more in the nature of drama than of dance; by cycles of unusually poetic song (though their melodic gift is not comparable with that of some other tribes); and by an elaboration and concatenation of myth which truly deserves the name of a mythology, for it is no mere aggregation of unconnected legends, but an organized body of teaching. Among all peoples on the way toward civilization there is a tendency to organize the confused and contradictory stories of uncritical savagery into consistently connected systems; and the Navaho are well advanced in this direction. Very many of the tales found elsewhere in North America as disjointed episodes have been incorporated by them into dramatic series; and in no small sense is their artistic skill manifested by the cleverness with which these stories are assimilated to not wholly congruous contexts — for it is obvious that in their mythology, as in their arts, the Navaho have been wide borrowers, though in both art and mythology they have bettered these borrowings in relation and design.

Another evidence of advancement in Navaho culture is the degree of personification—anthropomorphic personification—attained in their pantheon. Animal-beings are consistently of less importance than manlike divinities, and in the conception of nature-powers the phenomenon is more likely to be the instrument than the embodiment of the potency — lightning is the arrow or missile of the war-god or storm-god, the rainbow is a bridge, light and clouds are robes or bundles, the sun itself is dependent upon the Sun-Carrier, Tshohanoai, who hangs the blazing disk in his lodge at the end of the day's journey. All this represents that consistent intellectualization of nature-myth, which finds one of its earliest expressions in the replacing of immanent nature-powers by manlike gods who make of nature their tool. In their curiously geometrical representations of the gods, it is not animals, nor part animals, that the Navaho draw, but conventionalized men and women, and in their ceremonial masques the divine beings still have recognizably human form and feature.

Of course there are abundant traces of the more primitive

type of thinking. The background of the mythic world of the Navaho is filled in with classes of beings, sometimes emerging into distinct individuals, sometimes sinking back into vague kinds, such as are found in the protean strata of every mythology — beings like the Satyrs, Panes, Keres, and Daimones of the Greeks, or the local and household godlings of the Romans. The Yei of the Navaho, for the most part *genii locorum*, number among them many such kinds:[3] fire-godlings and godlings of the chase, corn spirits and harvest deities, such as the Ganaskidi, or "Humpbacks," who bear cloud-humps upon their backs and ram's horns on their heads, and sometimes appear in the guise of the Rocky Mountain sheep. Other Yei approach the dignity and importance of great gods, though their homes are the wild places—mountains and caverns—of earth: among these Thonenli, the Water Sprinkler, and especially Hastsheyalti, the Talking God (also known as Yebitshai, "Maternal Grandfather of the Gods"), and Hastshehogan, the House-God, hold high positions in the Navaho pantheon and figure importantly in myth and ritual. Hastsheyalti is god of the dawn and the east, Hastshehogan of evening and the west; white maize is Hastsheyalti's and yellow Hastshehogan's; and it is from white and yellow maize that man and woman are created by the gods under the supervision of these two Yei chieftains.[35]

The Yei are in the main beneficent and kindly to man. Another class, the Anaye, or Alien Gods, are man-destroyers — monsters, giants, beasts, or bogies.[2] The worst of them were slain by the Sons of the Sun long ago, but the race is not yet utterly destroyed. Still another evil kind is made up of the Tshindi, or Devils, ugly and venomous, — among whom is numbered the Corpse Spirit, which remains with the body when the soul departs to the lower world.[12] Other classes comprise the Animal Elders, such as are universal in Indian lore; the Digini, half wizard, half sprite, dwelling in the strange and fantastic formations with which volcanic fire and eroding waters

PLATE XXII

Navaho gods, from a dry- or sand-painting. The figure with the rectangular head is a female divinity, with arms covered with yellow pollen. The round-headed figures are male deities, the one carrying a lightning bow and a rattle, the other having a cloud-sack on his back and a basket before him. The colours and ornaments are symbolic of maize and other vegetation, of rain, lightning, fertility, etc. After *MAM* vi, Plate VIII.

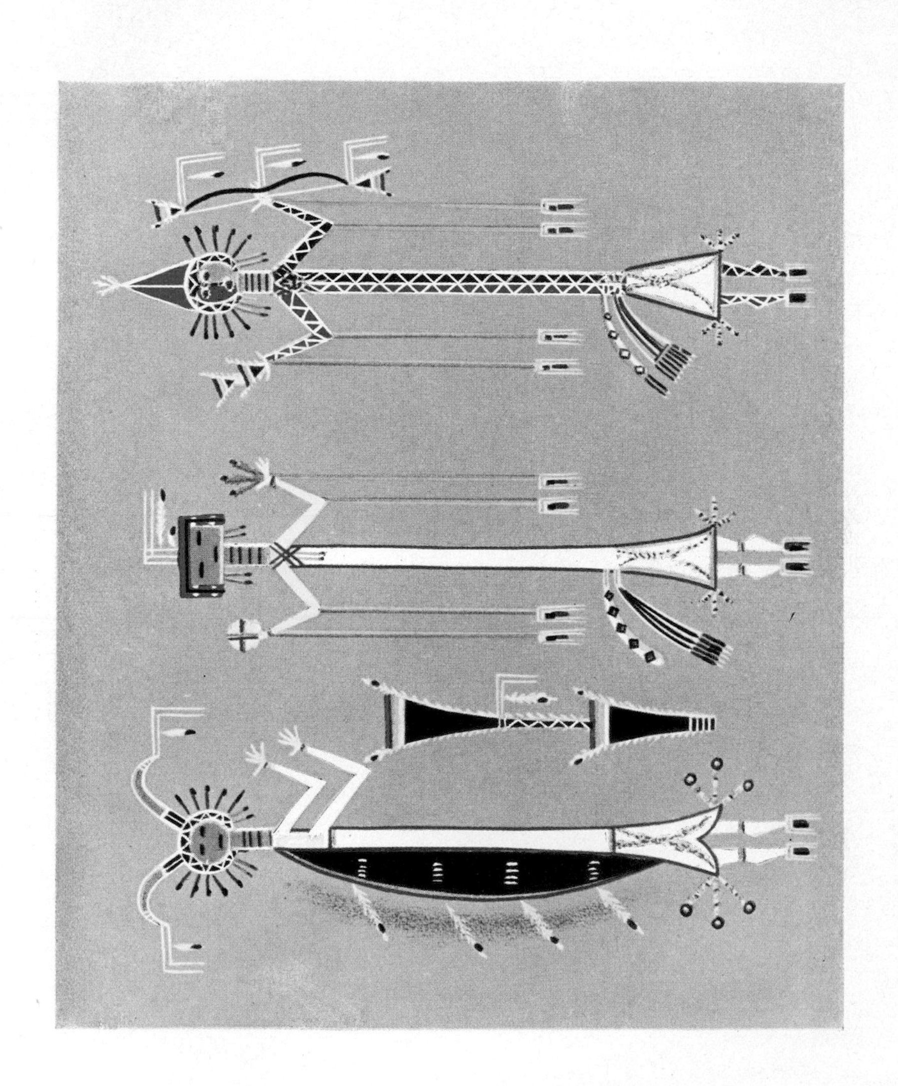

have made the Navaho country picturesque; and the Water-Powers, among whom Tieholtsodi, of the waters beneath the earth, is the most powerful.[9]

The highest place in the Navaho pantheon is held by Estsanatlehi,[7] the "Woman Who Changes" — for, like the Phoenix, when she becomes old, she transforms herself again into a young girl and lives a renewed life.[46] Though she originated on earth, her home is now in the west, on an island created for her by the Sun-Carrier, who made her his wife. From that direction come the rains that water the Navaho country and the winds that foretell the spring; and it is therefore appropriate that the goddess of nature's fruitfulness should dwell there. The younger sister of Estsanatlehi is Yolkai Estsan, the White Shell Woman, wife of the Moon-Carrier, Klehanoai. The white shell is her symbol, and she is related to the waters, as her sister, whose token is the turquoise, is akin to the earth; white is the colour of the dawn and the east, blue of midday and the south, and it is with the magic of these colours that the two sisters kindle the sun's disk and the moon's — although, according to Navaho myth, which is by no means always consistent, the Sun-God and the Moon-God were in existence before the sisters were created.

Of the male deities worshipped by the Navaho, the most important are the brothers, Nayanezgani, Slayer of the Alien Gods, and Thobadzistshini, Child of the Waters.[44] In some stories these are represented as twins of the Sun-Carrier and Estsanatlehi; in others, Thobadzistshini is the child of Water and Yolkai Estsan. These two brothers are the new generation of gods which overthrow the monsters and bring to an end the Age of Giants. Their home is on a mountain in the centre of the Navaho country, to which warriors betake themselves to pray for prowess and success in war. Klehanoai, the Moon-Carrier, is sometimes identified with a deity by the name of Bekotshidi, represented as an old man, and regarded as the creator of many of the beasts, especially the larger game and the domestic animals; his home is in the east, and many of the Navaho think that he is the god worshipped by the white men.

Another mythic pair of importance are the First Man, Atse Hastin, and the First Woman, Atse Estsan, who were created in the lower world from ears of maize; it is they who led the First People into the world in which we live. Coyote,[48] who is a conspicuous figure in adventures serious and ludicrous, though he never plays the *rôle* of demiurge, such as he sustains among many Indian tribes, is sometimes represented as accompanying these two Elders from the lower world. Spider Woman is an underground witch (the large spiders of the South-West make their nests in the ground), friendly with her magic; and Niltshi, the Wind, saves many a hero by whispering timely counsels in his ear. Other beings are little more than lay figures: such are Mirage Boy, Ground-Heat Girl, White-Corn Boy, Yellow-Corn Girl, Rock-Crystal Boy, Pollen Boy, Grasshopper Girl, etc. — a few out of the multitude which seem to be, in many cases, merely personifications of objects important in ritual practices.

The most important cult-symbols employed by the Navaho are arranged in groups according to their system of colour-symbolism [31] — white, the mantle of dawn, for the east; blue, the robe of the azure sky, for the south; yellow, the raiment of the sunset, for the west; black, the blanket of night, for the north. Thus, the "jewels" of the respective quarters are: east, white shell beads and rock-crystal; south, turquoise; west, haliotis shell (regarded by the Navaho as yellow); north, black stones or cannel-coal.[27] Birds are similarly denoted by the hues of their feathers; animals by their hides; maize by the colour of its kernels — white, blue, yellow, and, for the north, variegated (the north is sometimes all-colours, instead of black). The colours are used also in the sand-paintings, or drawings, which form an important and distinctive feature of Navaho rites; and in the painting of the prayer-sticks, frequently adorned with feathers,[60] which, with pollen and tobacco, in the form of cigarettes, are the principal articles offered in sacrifice.[30] Navaho rituals comprise many elaborate ceremonies, a conspicuous feature of which are masques, or dramatic representations of myths, in which the actors personate the gods. A convention of these masques is the representation of male deities with rounded, and of female with rectangular faces, a distinction which is maintained in the sand-paintings.

II. THE NAVAHO GENESIS[15]

The Navaho believe that the world is built in a sequence of storeys, the fifth of these being the earth on which men now dwell.[11] The genesis-legend of this tribe divides into four episodic tales, the first of which, the Age of Beginnings, narrates the ascent of the progenitors of Earth's inhabitants from storey to storey of the Underworld, and their final emergence upon Earth. The second, the Age of Animal Heroes, tells of the setting in order of Earth, its illumination by the heavenly bodies, and the adventures of its early inhabitants. The third, the Age of the Gods, recounts the slaying of the giants and other monsters by the War-Gods and the final departure of the great goddess to the West. The fourth, the Patriarchal Age, chronicles the growth of the Navaho nation in the days of its early wanderings; to this age, too, belong most of the revelations which prophets and visionaries bring back in the form of rites, acquired in their visits to the abodes of the gods.

The lowest of the world-storeys, where the Navaho myth begins, was red in colour, and in its centre was a spring from which four streams flowed, one to each of the cardinal points, while oceans bordered the land on all sides. Tieholtsodi, the water monster, the Blue Heron, Frog, and Thunder were chiefs in this world; while the people who "started in life there" were ants, beetles, dragon-flies, locusts, and bats (though some say First Man, First Woman, and Coyote were in existence even here). For the sin of adultery these people were driven out by a flood raised by the Underworld gods,[49] and as they flew upward, seeking a place of escape, a blue head was thrust from the sky and directed them to a hole leading into the next storey. This second world was blue, and was inhabited by the Swallow People. Here they lived till, on the twenty-fourth night, one of the strangers made free with the wife of the Swallow chief; and they were commanded to leave. Again they flew upward, and again a voice — that of Niltshi, the Wind — directed them to an opening by which they escaped into the third storey. Here they were in a yellow world, inhabited by Grasshoppers; but exactly what happened in the world below was repeated here, and once more directed by a Wind they flew up into the fourth storey, which was all-coloured.[31]

The fourth world was larger than the others and had a snow-covered mountain at each of the cardinal points. Its inhabitants were Kisani (Pueblo Indians), who possessed cultivated fields and gave the wanderers maize and pumpkins. The four gods of this world were White Body, Blue Body, Yellow Body, and Black Body, and these created Atse Hastin (First Man) and Atse Estsan (First Woman), from ears of white and yellow maize respectively.[35] To this pair came five births of twins, of whom the first were hermaphrodites,[64] who invented pottery and the wicker water-bottle. The other twins intermarried with the Mirage People, who dwelt in this world, and with the Kisani, and soon there was a multitude of people under the chieftainship of First Man.

"One day they saw the Sky stooping down and the Earth rising to meet it." At the point of contact Coyote and Badger sprang down from the world above; Badger descended into the world below, but Coyote remained with the people. It was at this time that the men and women quarrelled and tried the experiment of living apart; at first the women had plenty of food, but eventually they were starving and rejoined the men. Two girls, however, who were the last to cross the stream that had separated the sexes, were seized by Tieholtsodi, and dragged beneath the waters.[29] Guided by the gods, a man and a woman descended to recover them, but Coyote surreptitiously accompanied them and, unperceived, stole two of the offspring of the Water Monster. Shortly afterward, a flood was sent by the Monster, "high as mountains encircling the whole horizon." The people fled to a hill and various animals attempted to provide a means of escape by causing trees to outgrow the rising waters, but it was not until two men appeared, bearing earth from the seven sacred mountains of what is now the Navaho's land, that a soil was made from which grew a huge hollow reed, reaching to the sky.[42] The last of the people were scarcely in this stalk, and the opening closed, before they heard the loud noise of the surging waters outside. But there was still no opening in the sky above. They sent up the Great Hawk, who clawed the heaven till he could see light shining through; the Locust followed, and made a tiny passage to the world above, where he was met by four Grebes from the four quarters, and in a magic contest won half of their world; finally, the Badger enlarged the hole so that people could go through, and all climbed into the fifth world, whose surface is our earth.

The place of emergence was an islet in the middle of a lake, but the gods opened a passage, and they crossed to the shores. It was here that they sought to divine their fate, and a hide-scraper was thrown into the water: "If it sinks we perish, if it floats we live." It floated, but Coyote cast in a stone, saying, "Let me divine: if it sinks we perish, if it floats we live." It sank, and in answer to the execrations of the people, he said: "If we all live and continue to increase, the earth will soon be too small to hold us. It is better that each of us should live but a time on this earth and make room for our children."[16]

But the peril of the flood was not yet escaped, for waters were observed welling up from the hole of emergence. Then it was discovered that Coyote had with him the stolen offspring of Tieholtsodi. At once the people threw them into the hole, and with a deafening roar the waters subsided. Shortly after this, the first death occurred, and two hunters, looking down into the lower world, beheld the deceased combing her hair, as she sat beside a river. The two men died very soon; so that the people knew that a ghost is a thing ill seen.

First Man and First Woman, Black Body and Blue Body, built the seven mountains of the Navaho land, one at each cardinal point, and three in the centre. "Through Tsisnadzini [Pelado Peak, New Mexico], in the east, they ran a bolt of lightning to fasten it to earth. They decorated it with white shells, white lightning, white corn, dark clouds, and he-rain. They set a big bowl of shell on its summit, and in it they put two eggs of the Pigeon to make feathers for the mountain. The eggs they covered with a sacred buckskin to make them hatch [there are many wild pigeons in this mountain now]. All these things they covered with a sheet of daylight, and they put the Rock-Crystal Boy and the Rock-Crystal Girl into the mountain to dwell."[27] Mount Taylor, of the San Mateo range, is the southern mountain, and this was pinned to earth with a great stone knife, adorned with turquoise, mist, and she-rain, nested with bluebird's eggs, guarded by Turquoise Boy and Corn Girl, and covered with a blanket of blue sky. San Francisco, in Arizona, the mountain of the west, was bound with a sunbeam, decked with haliotis shell, clouds, he-rain, yellow maize and animals, nested with eggs of the Yellow Warbler, spread with yellow cloud, and made the home of White-Corn Boy and Yellow-Corn Girl. San Juan, in the north, was fastened with a rainbow, adorned with black beads, nested with eggs of the Blackbird, sheeted with darkness, and made the abode of Pollen Boy and Grasshopper Girl.[31] In a similar fashion the three central mountains were built.

The Sun-Disk, the Moon-Disk, and the Stars were then made by First Man and First Woman, and two men from among the people were appointed to be the Sun-Carrier and the Moon-Carrier,[13] these being the same two men who had caused the reed to grow, by means of which the folk had ascended from the world below.

The earth was now formed, but its inhabitants were not yet in order. The myth goes on to tell of the birth of the giants and other man-devouring monsters — the dread Anaye.[19] They were the offspring of women who had resorted to evil practices during the separation of the sexes in the world below. The first-born was the headless and hairy being, Theelgeth; the second the harpylike Tsanahale, with feathered back; the third was the giant whose hair grew into the rock, so that he could not fall, and who kicked people from the cliff as they passed; the fourth birth produced the limbless twins, the Binaye Ahani, who slew with their eyes; and there were many other monsters besides these, born of sinful women to become destroyers of men.[2]

The next event in this age was the descent of a gambler from the heavens, He-Who-Wins-Men, who enslaved the greater part of mankind by inducing them to bet their freedom.[56] Now we first hear of the beneficent Yei, Hastsheyalti and Hastshehogan, with their assistants, Wind, Darkness, the animal-gods, and others. By their aid a young Navaho defeated the Gambler, and with a magic bow shot him into the sky whence he came, and whence he was sent back into the world to become the ruler of the Mexicans.

Coyote [48] now appears upon the scene in a series of adventures such as are told of him by neighbouring tribes; the unsuccessful imitation of his host, in which Coyote comes ingloriously to grief in endeavouring to entertain, first Porcupine, then Wolf, as they had entertained him; a tradition of Coyote's hunt, in which he rounds up game by driving them with fire from a faggot of shredded cedar-bark — a story with many resemblances to the Ute version of the theft of fire; the tale of the blinding of Coyote, who attempts to imitate birds whom he sees toss up their eyes and catch them again in the sockets, and of the substitution of gum eyes, which melt as fire is approached, for the eyes he has lost; the story of how Coyote killed a giant by pretending to break and heal his own leg, and inducing the giant to follow his example; and the legend, which is apparently a version of the fire-theft tale, of how Coyote marries a witch who is unable to kill him, is concealed by her from her man-devouring brothers, steals fire from their lodge, is persecuted by animals at the instigation of the brothers, and is avenged by his wife, who is transformed into a bear. The youngest brother, however, with the aid of the winds, escapes the Bear Woman and eventually kills her, causing her to live again in the form of the several animals, which spring from the parts of her body as he cuts it up.

Here end the adventures of the Age of Animals. The ensuing is the Age of the New Gods. The Yei, under the leadership of Hastsheyalti, create Estsanatlehi — the great goddess who rejuvenates herself whenever she grows old — from an image of turquoise, and her sister, Yolkai Estsan, from white shell. Each sister gives birth to a son; Estsanatlehi becomes the mother of Nayanezgani, whose father is the Sun; Yolkai Estsan of Thobadzistshini, Son of the Waters.[44] Counselled by Niltshi, the Wind, and aided by Spider Woman, who gives them life-preserving feathers, the boys journey to the home of the Sun-Carrier — passing, with magic aids, clashing rocks which, like the Symplegades, close upon those who go between them; a plain of knifelike reeds and another of cane cactuses, which rush together and destroy travellers, and finally a desert of boiling sands.[8] Bear guardians, serpent guardians, and lightning guardians still bar their way to the Sun's house, but these, too, they overcome by means of the Spider's spells. In the lodge of the Sun, which is of turquoise and stands on the shore of a great water, the children of the Sun-Carrier conceal them in a bundle; but the Sun-Carrier knew of their coming, and when he had arrived at the end of the day's journey, and had taken the Sun from his back and hung it on a peg on the west wall of his lodge, he took down the parcel. "He first unrolled the robe of dawn with which they were covered, then the robe of blue sky, next the robe of yellow evening light, and lastly the robe of darkness." In a series of tests he tried to slay the boys, but, finding at last that he could not do so, he acceded to their request for weapons with which to fight the beings that were devouring mankind — armour from every joint of which lightning shot, a great stone knife, and arrows of lightning, of sunbeams, and of the rainbow. The brothers returned to earth on a lightning flash, and in a series of adventures, like the labours of Hercules, cleansed the world of the greater part of the man-devouring monsters which infested it. On a second visit to the Sun, they received four hoops by means of which their mother, Estsanatlehi, raised a great storm which brought to an end the Age of Monsters and formed the earth anew, shaping the canyons and hewing pillars of rock from the ancient bluffs. "Surely all the Anaye are now killed," said Estsanatlehi; but Old Age, Cold, Poverty, and Hunger still survived, and were allowed to live on; for should they be slain, they said, men would prize neither life nor warmth nor goods nor food.[16]

When this had been accomplished, the brothers returned to the mountain which is their home, and whither warriors go to pray for success in war.[59] Then the Sun-God, after creating the animals which inhabit the earth, departed for the far West where he had made a lodge, beyond the waters, for Estsanatlehi, who became his wife and the great goddess of the west, the source of the life-bringing rains. Every day, as he journeys toward the west, the Sun-Carrier sings:

"In my thoughts I approach,
The Sun-God approaches,
Earth's end he approaches,
Estsanatlehi's hearth approaches,
In old age walking the beautiful trail.

"In my thoughts I approach,
The Moon-God approaches,
Earth's end he approaches,
Yolkai Estsan's hearth approaches,
In old age walking the beautiful trail."

For Yolkai Estsan, too, became the bride of a god. But before she departed for the divine lodge, she remained for some time solitary. It was then, in the days of her loneliness, that Hastsheyalti came to her, and it was decided that a new race of men should be created. With the assistance of all the gods a man was formed from a white, and a woman from a yellow, ear of maize. Niltshi gave them the breath of life; the Rock-Crystal Boy gave them mind; the Grasshopper Girl gave them voices. Yolkai Estsan gave them fire and maize, and married the man to Ground-Heat Girl and the woman to Mirage Boy, and from these two couples is descended the first gens of the Navaho tribe — the House of the Dark Cliffs, "so named because the gods who created the first pair came from the cliff houses."

III. THE CREATION OF THE SUN[13]

In the Navaho Genesis, just recounted, there is a brief description of the creation of the Sun-Disk. A somewhat different and fuller version, recorded by James Stevenson, is as follows:

"The first three worlds were neither good nor healthful. They moved all the time and made the people dizzy. Upon ascending into this world the Navaho found only darkness and they said, 'We must have light.'" Two women were summoned — Ahsonnutli (Estsanatlehi) and Yolaikaiason (Yolkai Estsan) — and to them the Indians told their desire. "The Navaho had already partially separated light into its several colors. Next to the floor was white, indicating dawn; upon the white blue was spread for morning; and on the blue yellow for sunset; and next was black representing night.[31] They had prayed long and continuously over these, but their prayers had availed nothing. The two women on arriving told the people to have patience and their prayers would eventually be answered.

"Night had a familiar, who was always at his ear. This person said, 'Send for the youth at the great falls.' Night sent as his messenger a shooting star. The youth soon appeared and said, 'Ahsonnutli has white beads in her right breast and turquoise in her left. We will tell her to lay them on darkness and see what she can do with her prayers.' This she did. The youth from the great falls said to Ahsonnutli, 'You have carried the white-shell beads and the turquoise a long time; you should know what to say.' Then with a crystal [27] dipped in pollen she marked eyes and mouth on the turquoise and on the white-shell beads, and forming a circle round these with the crystal she produced a slight light from the white-shell beads and a greater light from the turquoise, but the light was insufficient.

"Twelve men lived at each of the cardinal points. The forty-eight men were sent for. After their arrival Ahsonnutli sang a song, the men sitting opposite to her; yet even with their presence the song failed to secure the needed light. Two eagle feathers were placed upon each cheek of the turquoise and two on the cheeks of the white-shell beads and one at each of the cardinal points.[60] The twelve men of the east placed twelve turquoises at the east of the faces. The twelve men of the south placed twelve white-shell beads at the south. The men of the west placed twelve turquoises on that side, and the men of the north twelve white-shell beads at the north, and with a pollen-dipped crystal a circle was drawn around the whole. But the wish remained unrealized. Then Ahsonnutli held the crystal over the turquoise face, whereupon it lighted into a blaze. The people retreated far back on account of the great heat, which continued increasing. The men from the four points found the heat so intense that they arose, but they could hardly stand, as the heavens were so close to them. They looked up and saw two rainbows, one across the other from east to west and from north to south. The heads and feet of the rainbows almost touched the men's heads. The men tried to raise the great light, but each time they failed.

"Finally, a man and a woman appeared, whence they knew not. The man's name was Atseatsine [Atse Hastin] and the woman's name was Atseatsan [Atse Estsan]. They were asked, 'How can this sun be got up?' They replied, 'We know; we heard the people down here trying to raise it, and this is why we came.' 'Sunbeams,' exclaimed the man, 'I have the sunbeams; I have a crystal from which I can light the sunbeams, and I have the rainbow; with these three I can raise the sun.' The people said, 'Go ahead and raise it.' When he had elevated the sun a short distance it tipped a little and burned vegetation and scorched the people, for it was still too near. Then the people said to Atseatsine and Atseatsan, 'Raise the sun higher,' and they continued to elevate it, and yet it continued to burn everything. They were then called to lift it higher still, but after a certain height was reached their power failed; it would go no farther.

"The couple then made four poles, two of turquoise and two of white-shell beads, and each was put under the sun, and with these poles the twelve men at each of the cardinal points raised it. They could not get it high enough to prevent the people and grass from burning. The people then said, 'Let us stretch the world'; so the twelve men at each point expanded the world.[62] The sun continued to rise as the world expanded, and began to shine with less heat, but when it reached the meridian the heat became great and the people suffered much. They crawled everywhere to find shade. Then the voice of Darkness went four times around the world telling the men at the cardinal points to go on expanding the world. 'I want all this trouble stopped,' said Darkness; 'the people are suffering and all is burning; you must continue stretching.' And the men blew and stretched, and after a time they saw the sun rise beautifully, and when the sun again reached the meridian it was only tropical. It was then just right, and as far as the eye could reach the earth was encircled first with the white dawn of day, then with the blue of early morning, and all things were perfect. And Ahsonnutli commanded the twelve men to go to the east, south, west, and north, to hold up the heavens [Yiyanitsinni, the holders up of the heavens], which office they are supposed to perform to this day."

IV. NAVAHO RITUAL MYTHS[5]

The myth of the creation of the sun, just quoted, gives a vivid picture of a primitive ritual, with its reliance upon mimetic magic and the power of suggestion; the magic depicted is that of the gods, but all Navaho ceremonials, and indeed Indian rituals generally, are regarded as derived from the great powers. The usual form of transmission is through some prophet or seer who has visited the abodes of the powers, and there has been permitted to observe the rites by means of which the divine ones attain their ends. On returning to his people, the prophet brings the ceremony (or "dance," as such rites are frequently called, although dancing is commonly a minor feature) to his people, where it is transmitted from generation to generation of priests or shamans. It is interesting to note that among the Navaho it is usually the younger brother of the prophet, not the prophet himself, who conducts the rite, when once it is learned;[44] and it is their custom to choose younger brothers to be educated as shamans (though the elder brothers are not deterred from such a career, if they so choose) the Navaho reason being that the younger brother is likely to be the more intelligent.

Indian rites may be broadly divided into three classes: (1) rites pertaining to the life-history of the individual — birth, pubescence, death; and to social life — clan and fraternity rites, rites for the making of war and the cementing of peace; (2) rites connected with the elements and seasons, maize festivals, rain dances, the magic fructification of fields and the magic invocation of game; and (3) mysteries or medicine rites, designed to bring health, both physical and spiritual, and to ensure life and prosperity to individual and tribe, — a therapeutic which recognizes that all men are at all times ailing and in need of some form of divine aid. The various elements of the different types interlace, but in general, those of the first class fall into a biographical or an historical series, those of the second class tend to assume a ferial character, and those of the third class depend upon the chance of necessity or of desire for their performance — upon the fulfilment of a vow, the need of the sick for cure, or the like.

Navaho ceremonials are mainly of the latter kind and are in sharp contrast to the calendric rites of their Pueblo neighbours. They are medicine ceremonies, undertaken in the interest of the sick, who individually defray the expenses, although the rite is supposed to benefit the whole tribe; and they are performed at no stated times, but only in response to need. There is, however, some restriction: the Night Chant, the most popular of all Navaho ceremonies, may be held only in the winter, when the snakes are hibernating — perhaps because serpents are regarded as underworld-powers, and related to the maleficent deities of the region of the dead; a similar motive produces a reverse effect on the Great Plains, where the Hako Ceremony and the Sun-Dance are observed only when the world is green and life is stirring.[39]

The Night Chant, like some other Navaho ceremonies, has a nine-day period. On the first day holy articles and the sacred lodge are prepared; on the second, the sweat-house and the first sand-painting are made, and the song of the approach of the gods is sung: prayers and a second sweat-house are features of the third day, while the fourth is devoted to preparations for the vigil which occupies the fourth night, at which the

PLATE XXIII

Navaho dry- or sand-painting connected with the Night Chant ceremony. The encircling figure is the Rainbow goddess. The swastika-like central figure represents the whirling logs with Yei riding upon them (see p. 173). At the East is Hastsheyalti (white); at the West, Hastshehogan (black). Rain spirits, with cloud-sacks and baskets, are North and South. Symbols of vegetation are between the arms of the cross. After *MAM* vi, Plate VI.

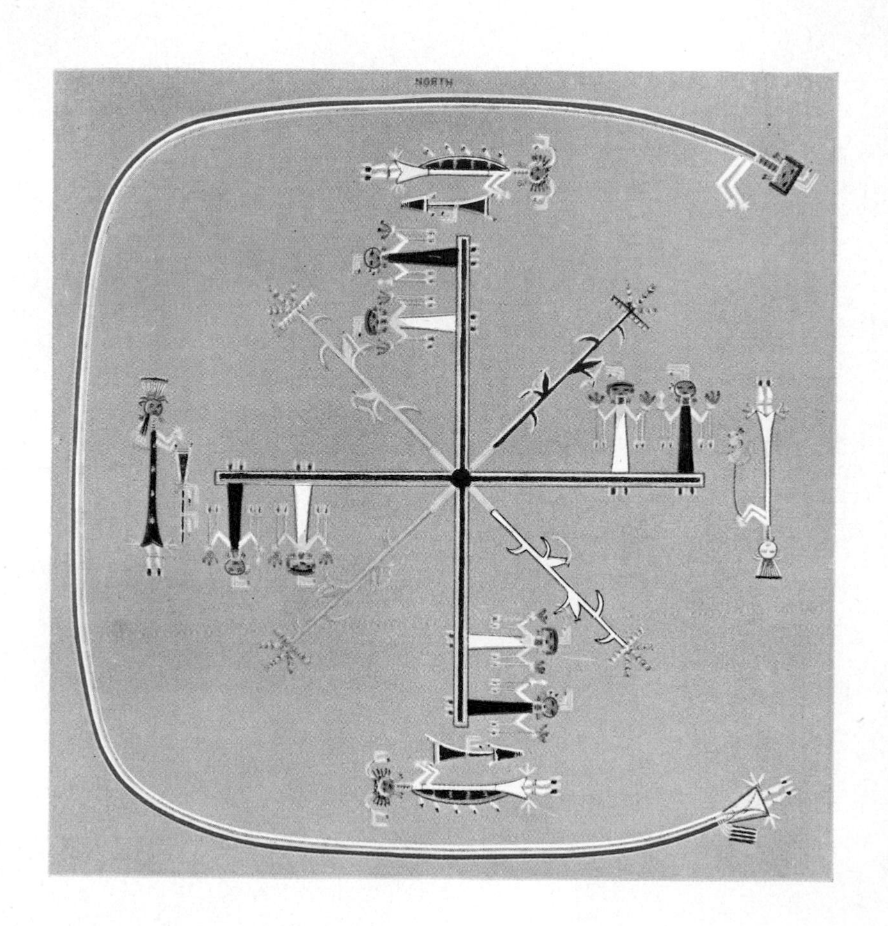
NORTH

sacred masks [65] of the gods are sprinkled with pollen and water and a communal supper is followed by a banquet; the principal feature of each of the next four days is the preparation of an elaborate sand-painting of the gods, each picture symbolizing a mythic revelation, and the touching of the affected parts of the bodies of the sick with the coloured sands from the analogous parts of the divine images; the ninth day is devoted to preparations for the great ceremony which marks the ninth night, at which the masque of the gods is presented. It is from this masque of the ninth night that the Night Chant gets its name, and this is the night, too, of that prayer to the dark bird who is the chief of pollen which is perhaps the most poetic description of the genius of thunder-cloud and rain in Indian literature, and which runs thus, abridged from Matthews's translation [32]: —

In Tsegihi,
In the house made of dawn,
In the house made of evening twilight,
In the house made of dark cloud,
In the house made of rain and mist, of pollen, of grasshoppers,
Where the dark mist curtains the doorway,
The path to which is on the rainbow,
Where the zigzag lightning stands high on top,
Where the he-rain stands high on top,
Oh, male divinity!
With your moccasins of dark cloud, come to us,
With your leggings and shirt and head-dress of dark cloud, come to us,
With your mind enveloped in dark cloud, come to us,
With the dark thunder above you, come to us soaring,
With the shapen cloud at your feet, come to us soaring.
With the far darkness made of the dark cloud over your head, come to us soaring,
With the far darkness made of the rain and the mist over your head, come to us soaring.
With the zigzag lightning flung out on high over your head,
With the rainbow hanging high over your head, come to us soaring.
With the far darkness made of the dark cloud on the ends of your wings,

With the far darkness made of the rain and the mist on the ends of your wings, come to us soaring,
With the zigzag lightning, with the rainbow hanging high on the ends of your wings, come to us soaring.
With the near darkness made of the dark cloud of the rain and the mist, come to us,
With the darkness on the earth, come to us.
With these I wish the foam floating on the flowing water over the roots of the great corn.
I have made your sacrifice,
I have prepared a smoke for you,
My feet restore for me.
My limbs restore, my body restore, my mind restore, my voice restore for me.
Today, take out your spell for me,
Today, take away your spell for me.
Away from me you have taken it,
Far off from me it is taken,
Far off you have done it.
Happily I recover,
Happily I become cool,
My eyes regain their power, my head cools, my limbs regain their strength, I hear again.
Happily for me the spell is taken off,
Happily I walk; impervious to pain, I walk; light within, I walk; joyous, I walk.
Abundant dark clouds I desire,
An abundance of vegetation I desire,
An abundance of pollen, abundant dew, I desire.
Happily may fair white corn, to the ends of the earth, come with you,
Happily may fair yellow corn, fair blue corn, fair corn of all kinds, plants of all kinds, goods of all kinds, jewels of all kinds, to the ends of the earth, come with you.
With these before you, happily may they come with you,
With these behind, below, above, around you, happily may they come with you,
Thus you accomplish your tasks.
Happily the old men will regard you,
Happily the old women will regard you,
The young men and the young women will regard you,
The children will regard you,
The chiefs will regard you,
Happily, as they scatter in different directions, they will regard you,
Happily, as they approach their homes, they will regard you.

May their roads home be on the trail of peace,
Happily may they all return.
In beauty I walk,
With beauty before me, I walk,
With beauty behind me, I walk,
With beauty above and about me, I walk.
It is finished in beauty,
It is finished in beauty.

The Tsegihi of the first verse of this impressive prayer is one of the sacred places with which the Navaho country abounds. The myths which explain most of their rites frequently recount the visits of prophets to such places, and it was from such a trip that the Night Chant was brought back: a hunter found his arm paralysed when he attempted to draw the bow upon four mountain sheep; after the fourth endeavour the sheep appeared to him in their true form, as Yei, and conducted him to their rocky abode, where he was taught the mystery and sent home to his people. This same man became a great prophet: he made a strange voyage in a hollow log, with windows of crystal, guided by the gods; finally, at a place sacred to the Navaho, a whirling lake with no outlet and no bottom, he beheld the "whirling logs" — a cross upon which rode eight Yei, two on each arm; and by these he was instructed in a mystery of healing, in which maize and rain and life-giving magic play the chief *rôles*. There are other myths representing similar journeys in god-steered logs, from which the hero returns with a magic gift: on one such trip, the prophet is said to have gone as far as the sea — "the waters that had a shore on one side only" — and there to have learned the art of mixing colours and the use of maize, a food till then unknown to the Navaho.

Upon another myth is based the ceremony of the Mountain Chant. Like the Night Chant, this rite is characterized by a nocturnal masque of the gods, depicting the mythic adventure, and in it the hero ascends to the world above the sky, where the people were Eagles. Here, with the aid of Spider

Woman's magic, he defeated the Bumble-Bees and Tumble-Weeds who were the Eagles' foemen, and in return was given the sacred rite. He, however, used his powers to trick the Pueblo people into surrendering their wealth to him; and in a great shell which he obtained from them he was lifted by ropes of lightning up into the heavens, surrounded by his treasure.[56] The story recalls similar ascents in the legends of northern Indians.

Of all the ritual myths of the Navaho the most pathetic is the story of the Stricken Twins.[44] They were children of a mortal girl by a god; and in childhood one was blinded, the other lamed. Driven forth by relatives too poor to keep them, they wandered from one abode of the gods to another in search of a cure, the blind boy carrying the lame. At each sacred place the Yei demanded the fee of jewels which was the price of cure, and when they found that the children had nothing sent them on with ridicule. Their father, Hastsheyalti, secretly placed food for them, for he wished to keep his paternity concealed, and finally gave them a cup containing a never-failing supply of meal.[62] After twice making the rounds of the sacred places, rejected at all, the children's paternity was discovered, and the gods, taking them to the sweat-house, undertook to heal them, warning them that they must not speak while there; but when the blind one became faintly conscious of light, in joy he cried, "Oh, younger brother, I see!"; and when the lame one felt returning strength, he exclaimed, "Oh, elder brother, I move my limbs!" And the magic of the gods was undone. Again blind and halt, they were sent forth to secure the fee by which alone they could hope for healing. The gods aided them with magic, and they tricked the wealthy Pueblo dwellers into giving them the needed treasure. Provided with this, they returned once more to the abode of the Yei, and in an elaborate ceremony — a nine days' rite — they were at last made perfect. The ritual they took back to their people, after which they returned to the gods, one to become a rain genius, the other a guardian of animals.[22] In this myth the abodes of the Yei are usually represented as crystal-studded caverns, which are entered through rainbow doorways. An interesting feature, as touching the primitive philosophy of sacrifice, is the reason given by the Yei for refusing a cure: you mortals, they say, have certain objects, tobacco, pollen, feathers, jewels, which we lack and desire; in return for our healing, you should give them to us: *do ut des*. The gods of the Navaho are not represented as omnipotent, nor as much more powerful than men: to save the passenger in the floating log from capture by mortals, they must resort to the magic device of raising a storm and concealing their hero — as Aeneas is driven forth by the angry waves, or as Hector is hidden from peril in a cloud.

V. APACHE AND PIMAN MYTHOLOGY

The mythology of the Apache, who like the Navaho are of Athapascan stock, is of the same general character as that of their kindred tribe, except that it lacks the organization and poetry of Navaho myth, and in general reflects the inferiority of Apache to Navaho culture. The same gods reappear, frequently with the same names; similar stories are told of them, though in a fragmentary fashion; rites and ceremonies show many common elements. Occasionally, an Apache version reveals a dramatic superiority to the Navaho, as in the Jicarilla story of the emergence, where a feeble old man and old woman were left behind when the First People ascended into this world. "Take us out," they called, but the people heeded them not, and the deserted ones cried after them, "You will come back here to me"; and now they are rulers of the dead in the lower world.[16] Such improvements, however, are incidental; the bulk of Apache lore is on an inferior level, with an emphasis on the coarser elements and on the unedifying adventures and misadventures of Coyote.

Similar in grade is the mythology of the other two wide-spread stocks of the South-West, the Piman and Yuman, who occupy the territories to the west and south-west of the Navaho country, far into Mexico and Lower California, and who form, in all probability, the true autochthones of the arid region. In material culture these peoples are perhaps superior to the Apache, their hereditary foe, for they are successful agriculturists on the scale which their lands permit; yet they are in no sense the equals of the Navaho. Their mythology and religion have been slightly reported, but enough is known to make clear the general relations of their ideas.

Among tribes of the Piman stock Sun, Moon, and Morning Star are the great deities governing the world, while Earth Doctor and Elder Brother are the important heroes of demiurgic myth.[13] The Moon is the wife of Father Sun, the pair being identified by some of the half-Christianized Mexican peoples with the Virgin and the Christian God. Coyote is the son of Sun and Moon according to the Pima, and all the tribes of this stock have their full quota of tales of Coyote and his kindred. The Devil is a mighty power in the eyes of the Tarahumare, a Mexican tribe of Piman stock, and no mean antagonist for Tata Dios ("Father God"), whom he slays twice before he is finally cast down. Death, it may be noted, is no annihilation in Piman view, for, as one shaman remarked, "the dead are very much alive." It is among the Cora of Mexico, that Chulavete, the Morning Star,[14] is most important, though the other tribes recognize him (or her, for with the Pima "Visible Star" is a girl). Star-myths are found in various tribes, an interesting instance being the legend, which occurs in analogous forms in Tarahumare and Tepehuane lore, of the women who commit the sin of cannibalism and flee from their husbands into the heavens: there they are transformed into stars, the Pleiades or Orion's Belt, while the husband who has vainly pursued them is changed into a coyote. The use of the cross,[61] apparently an ancient and indigenous symbol of the Sun Father, and the cult of the peyote (a species of plant, especially the cactus *Lophophora Williamsii*, used to exalt and intensify the imaginative faculties) are features of the ritual of tribes of this stock; the peyote, deified as Hikuli, the four-faced god who sees all things, being one of the important deities of the pagan Tarahumare.

Piman cosmogony [15] contains the typically south-western ascent of the First People from the Underworld and the universal story of the deluge, but the form and embellishment of these incidents are original. As told by a shaman of the Pima tribe: "In the beginning there was nothing where now are earth, sun, moon, stars, and all that we see. Ages long the darkness was gathering, until it formed a great mass in which developed the spirit of Earth Doctor, who, like the fluffy wisp of cotton that floats upon the wind, drifted to and fro without support or place to fix himself. Conscious of his power, he determined to try to build an abiding place, so he took from his breast a little dust and flattened it into a cake. Then he thought within himself, 'Come forth, some kind of plant,' and there appeared the creosote bush." Three times the earth-disk upset, but the fourth time it remained where he had replaced it. "When the flat dust cake was still he danced upon it singing:

'Earth Magician shapes this world.
  Behold what he can do!
Round and smooth he molds it.
  Behold what he can do!

'Earth Magician makes the mountains.
  Heed what he has to say!
He it is that makes the mesas.
  Heed what he has to say!

'Earth Magician shapes this world;
  Earth Magician makes its mountains;
Makes all larger, larger, larger.
  Into the earth the magician glances;
  Into its mountains he may see.'"

Assuredly this is an extraordinary genesis, with its conception of a primeval void and fiat creation, to come from the untaught natives, and it is possible that mission teachings may have influenced its form, though the matter seems to be aboriginal. The story goes on with the creation of insects; then of a sky-dome which the Earth Doctor commanded Spider to sew to the earth around the edges; then of sun, moon, and stars, the two first from blocks of ice flung into the heavens, —

"I have made the sun!
I have made the sun!
Hurling it high
In the four directions.
To the east I threw it
To run its appointed course," —

the stars from water which he sprayed from his mouth. Next Earth Doctor created living beings, but they developed cannibalism and he destroyed them. Then he said: "I shall unite earth and sky; the earth shall be as a female and the sky as a male, and from their union shall be born one who shall be a helper to me.[34] Let the sun be joined with the moon, also even as man is wedded to woman, and their offspring shall be a helper to me." [13] Earth gave birth to Elder Brother, who in true Olympian style later became more powerful than his creator; and Coyote was born from the Moon. Elder Brother created a handsome youth who seduced the daughter of South Doctor, and the unrestrainable tears of the child of this union threatened to destroy all life in a mighty flood.[49] Elder Brother, however, escaped by enclosing himself in a pot which rolled about beneath the waters; Coyote made a raft of a log; while Earth Doctor led some of the people through a hole which he made to the other side of the earth-disk. After the flood Elder Brother was the first of the gods to appear, and he therefore became the ruler. He sent his subordinates in search of earth's navel, and when the central mountain had been discovered, they set about repeopling the world.

PLATE XXIV

Apache medicine-shirt, painted with figures of gods, centipedes, clouds, lightning, the sun, etc. After *9 ARBE*, Plate VI.

The myth continues with incidents having to do with the origin of fire and the cremation of the dead; the freeing of the animals, by the wile of Coyote,[48] from the cave in which they were imprisoned; the coming of the wicked gambler, who is finally defeated and is changed into a vicious, man-devouring Eagle; the birth and destruction of a cannibal monster, Ha-ak, and the origin of tobacco from the grave of an old woman who had stolen Ha-ak's blood; [30] and finally the destruction of Elder Brother by the Vulture, his journey to the underworld, and his return to conquer the land with the aid of some of the antediluvians who had escaped to the other side of the world.

VI. YUMAN MYTHOLOGY[15]

The tribes of the Yuman stock — of which the Mohave, Maricopa, Havasupai, Walapai, Diegueño, and Yuma proper are the most important in the United States — occupy territory extending from the southern Californian coast and the peninsula of Lower California eastward into the arid highlands. Geographically they are thus a connecting link between the tribes of the South-West and the Californian stocks, and their customs and beliefs show relation to both groups; but their traditions assign their origin to the inland, and because of this and of their great territorial extension, which is in contrast with the limited areas held by the stocks of the coastal region, they may best be classed with the tribes of the desert region.

The little that is recorded of their mythology tells of a time when Earth was a woman and Sky was a man.[34] Earth conceived (some say from a drop of rain that fell upon her while she slept), and twin sons were born of her (some say from a volcano), Kukumatz and Tochipa (Mohave), or Hokomata and Tochopa (Walapai, etc.). Earth at this time was close in the embrace of Sky, and the first task of the twins was to raise the heavens, after which they set the cardinal points, defined the land, and created its inhabitants — though the Mohave say that the First People were created by Mustamho, who was himself the son of a second generation born of Earth and Sky; and the Walapai tell how the first man, Kathatakanave, Taught-by-Coyote, issued with his friend Coyote from the Grand Canyon.

The Walapai myth goes on to recount how Kathatakanave prayed to Those Above (the *di superi*) to create companions for him; how Coyote broke the spell by speaking before all men had been created and so slunk away, ashamed; how Tochopa instructed the human race in the arts and was beloved accordingly, and how Hokomata out of jealousy taught them war and thus brought about the division of mankind. The Havasupai tell also of the feud between the brothers, and that Hokomata in his rage brought about a deluge which destroyed the world.[49] Before the waters came, however, Tochopa sealed his beloved daughter, Pukeheh, in a hollow log, from which she emerged when the flood had subsided; she gave birth to a boy, whose father was the sun, and to a girl, whose father was a waterfall (whence Havasupai women have ever been called "Daughters of the Water"); and from these two the world was repeopled. In the Mohave version, Mustamho took the people in his arms and carried them until the waters abated.

The origin of death is told by the Diegueño. "Tuchaipai thought to himself, 'If all my sons do not have enough food and drink, what will become of them?'" He gave men the choice of living forever, dying temporarily, and final death; but while they were debating the question, the Fly said, "'Oh, you men, what are you talking so much about? Tell him you want to die forever.' . . . This is the reason why the fly rubs his hands together. He is begging forgiveness of the people for these words."[16]

Another myth, which the Yuman tribes share with the Piman, tells of Coyote's theft of the heart from a burning corpse. As the Diegueño tell it, it is Tuchaipai, slain through the malevolence of the Frog, whose body is placed upon the pyre; the Mohave recount the same event of the remains of Matyavela, the father of Mustamho, who may be a doublet of Tuchaipai, or Tochipa. When the pyre is ready, Coyote is sent away on an invented errand, for his presence is feared; but seeing the smoke of the cremation, he hurries back in time to snatch the heart from the burning body, and this he carries off to the mountains. "For this reason men hate the Coyote."[48] It is tempting to see in this myth, coming to peoples whose kindred extend far into Mexico, some relation to the Nahuatlan human sacrifice, in which the heart was torn from the victim's body, which was not infrequently thereafter burned.[29]

CHAPTER IX

THE PUEBLO DWELLERS

I. THE PUEBLOS

ONE of the most interesting and curious groups of people, not only of North America but of the world, is composed of the Pueblo dwellers of New Mexico and Arizona. The Pueblo Indians get their name (given them by the Spaniards) from the fact that they live in compact villages, or pueblos, of stone or adobe houses, which in some instances rise to a height of five storeys. These villages suggest huge communal dwellings, or labyrinthine structures like the "house of Minos," but in fact each family possesses its own abode, the form of building being partly an economy of construction, but mainly for ready defence; for the pueblos are islets of sedentary culture in the midst of what was long a sea of marauding savagery. For this same protective reason sites were chosen on the level tops of the mesas, or villages were built in cliff walls, hollowed out and walled in (the "cliff dwellings" of the desert region have been identified as former, and probably the earliest, seats of Pueblo culture); but under the influence of their modern freedom from attack many of the villages are gradually disaggregating into local houses. Anciently the Pueblo territory extended from central Colorado and Utah far south into Mexico; now about three hundred miles separate Taos in the east from Oraibi in the west, while the north and south distance, from Taos to Acoma, is half of this. Within the modern area the pueblos fall into two main groups: those of northern and central New Mexico, clustered along the Rio Grande, and those of the Moqui or Hopi reservation in Arizona; between these, and to the south, are the large pueblos of Laguna, Acoma, and Zuñi, all in New Mexico.

The Pueblo tribes are of four linguistic stocks; three of them, the Tanoan, Keresan, and Zuñian, are unknown elsewhere; the fourth constitutes a special group of Shoshonean dialects, the language of the Hopi of Arizona, related to the Ute and Shoshoni in the north and perhaps to the Aztec far to the south. But if there is divergence in language, there is little difference in the degree of aboriginal evolution (though power to preserve it under the pressure of white civilization varies greatly). The most astonishing feature of this development is that it is based primarily upon agriculture.[24] The Pueblo culture is located, and apparently has evolved, in what is agriculturally the least promising part of North America south of the Arctic barren lands. The South-West is an arid plateau, watered by scant rains and traversed by few streams. Its one favourable feature is that where water is obtainable for irrigation the returns in vegetation are luxuriant; but irrigation, even where feasible, requires both toil and intelligence, and it seems truly extraordinary that the most varied agriculture of the continent, north of Mexico, should have developed in so unpromising a region. It is not, however, surprising that the religion of the Pueblo agriculturists should be found to centre about the one recurrent theme of prayer for rain; to few other peoples is a dry year so terrible.

But it is not alone in agriculture and housing that the Pueblo dwellers show advancement. In the industrial arts of basketry, pottery, weaving, and stone-working they were and are in the forefront of the tribes, and it is altogether probable that it is to the Pueblos that the neighbouring Navaho owe their skill in these industries. In decorative art they display an equal pre-eminence, both geometric and naturalistic design being pleasingly adapted to their elaborate symbolism. Socially the Pueblo dwellers form a distinctive group. Each village is a tribal unit, with a republican system of government, formed of a group of clans, originally exogamous and frequently, though not invariably, with matrilinear descent. There is no inferiority of the women to the men, though there is a division of privilege: the family home is the property of the wife, but in each pueblo there is a type of building — varying in number from one, in the smaller, to a dozen or more in the larger villages — called the "kiva," which is characteristically the men's house. The kiva is partly temple, partly clubhouse or lounging room; the more primitive type is circular, the later rectangular, like the houses; sometimes it is subterranean. In the kiva men gather for work or amusement, and in the kiva occur the secret rites of the various fraternities and priesthoods. Women are rarely admitted, except in those pueblos where they have a kiva of their own, or rites demanding one. It is regarded as probable that the kiva is the original nucleus of the pueblo — the primitive "men's house," converted into a temple, around which first grew the fortified refuge, and later the settled and permanent town.

Where the pagan religion of the Pueblo dwellers persists — and in matters of belief they have shown themselves to be among the most conservative of Indians — their elaborate and spectacular rites are in charge of fraternities or priesthoods, each with its own cult practices and its proper *fêtes* in the calendar. These festivals are devoted to the three great objects of securing rain, and hence abundant crops, healing the sick, and obtaining success in war. Practically all Pueblo men are initiates into one or more fraternities, to some of which women are occasionally admitted. In certain pueblos, as the Hopi, the fraternities appear to have originated from the warrior and medicine societies of the various clans, such societies being found in almost every Indian tribe; in others, clan origin cannot be traced if it ever existed, admission being gained either by the exhibition of prowess (as formerly in the warrior societies), by the fact of being healed by the rites of the fraternity, or by some such portent as that to which is ascribed the Zuñi Struck-by-Lightning fraternity, which was founded by a number of Indians, including, besides Zuñi men, one Navaho and a woman, who were severely shocked by a thunderbolt.[32] In many of the fraternities there are orders or steps of rank, and the head men or priests of the societies hold a power over the pueblo which sometimes amounts, as at Zuñi, to theocratic rule. In spite of differences of language and origin, the general resemblances of the Pueblos to one another, in the matter of ritual and myth as in outward culture, is such as to make of them an essential group. At least this is indicated from the results which have been recorded for Sia, Zuñi, and the Hopi towns — of Keresan, Zuñian, and Shoshonean stock respectively — which are the only groups as yet deeply studied.

II. PUEBLO COSMOLOGY[11]

The symbolism of the World-Quarters, of the Above, and of the Below is nowhere more elaborately developed among American Indians than with the Pueblos.[31] Analogies are drawn not merely with the colours, with plants and animals, and with cult objects and religious ideas, but with human society in all the ramifications of its organization, making of mankind not only the theatric centre of the cosmos, but a kind of elaborate image of its form.

According to their Genesis, the ancestors of the Pueblo dwellers issued from the fourfold Underworld through a Sipapu, which some regard as a lake, and thence journeyed in search of the Middle Place of the World, Earth's navel, which the various tribes locate differently; in Zuñi, for example, it is in the town itself. The world is oriented from this point and the sunrise — east is "the before," as in the ancient lore of the Old World — the four cardinals, the zenith, and the nadir defining the cosmic frame of all things. It may be of interest to note that if these points be regarded as everywhere equidistant from the centre, and that if they then be circumscribed by circles in every plane about the centre, the resulting figure will be a sphere; and it is not improbable that from such a procedure arose the first conception of the spherical form of the universe; the swastika and the swastika inscribed in a circle are cosmic symbols in the South-West as in many other parts of the world, and while no Indians had attained to the concept of a world-sphere, the Pueblos at least were upon the very threshold of the idea.[66] Each of the six regions — the Quarters, the Above, and the Below — possesses its symbolic colour: in the Zuñi and Hopi systems, the white of dawn is the colour of the East; the blue of the daylit sky is the tint of the West, toward which the sun takes his daily journey; red, the symbol of fire and heat, is the hue of the South; and yellow, for sunrise and sunset, perhaps for the aurora as well, is the Northern colour; all colours typify the Zenith; black is the symbol of the Nadir. As the colours, so the elements are related to the Quarters: to the North belongs the air, element of wind and breath, for from it come the strong winter winds; the West is characterized by water, for in the Pueblo land rains sweep in from the Pacific; fire is of the South; while the earth and the seeds of life which fructify the earth are of the East. In their rituals the Zuñi address the points in this order: prayer is made first to the Middle Place, then to the North with whom is the breath which is the prime essential of life, to the West whose rain-laden clouds first break the hold of winter, to the South, the East, the Zenith, the Nadir which holds in its bosom the caverns of the dead, and once again the Middle Place. The tribal clans are grouped and organized with respect to these same points, while human activities, as represented by the fraternities having them symbolically in charge, are similarly oriented — war is of the North, peace and the chase of the West, husbandry of the South, rite and medicine of the East; to the Zenith belong the life-preservers, and to the Nadir the life-generators, for not only do the dead depart thither to be born again, but it is from Below that the ancestors of all men first came; to the Middle Place, the heart or navel of the world, belong the "Mythic Dance Drama People," representing all the clans, and having in charge the presentation of the masques of the ancestral and allied divinities. This sevenfold division is reflected in the six kivas and shrine of the Middle Place of the town itself; and may be associated with the original seven towns of the ancestral community, for it is taken as established that the Seven Cities of Cibola, whose fame brought Coronado and his expedition from the south, were the ancestral pueblos of the present Zuñi.[67]

III. GODS AND KATCINAS

In such a frame are set the world-powers venerated by the Pueblo dwellers. These cosmic potencies may be classed in two great categories: the gods, which represent the powers and divisions of nature; and the Katcinas, primarily the spirits of ancestors, but in a secondary usage the spirit-powers of other beings, even of the gods.

Father Sun[13] and Mother Earth are the greater deities of the pantheon; but each is known by many names, and may indeed be said to separate into numerous personalities — among the Hopi, for example, the Sun is called Heart of the Sky, while Mother of Germs or Seed, Old Woman, Spider Woman, Corn Maid, and Goddess of Growth are all appellations of the Earth.[34] Superior even to this primeval pair, the Zuñi recognize Awonawilona, the supreme life-giving power, the initiator and embodiment of the life of the world, referred to as He-She, whose earliest avatar was the person of the Sun Father, but whose pervasive life is confined to no one being.[6] No similar Hopi being is reported.

Along with the Sun are other celestial gods, the Moon Mother and the Morning and Evening Stars, the Galaxy, Pleiades, Orion, Ursa Major and Ursa Minor, the Polar Star,[14] and the knife-feathered monster whom the Zuñi name Achiyalatopa.[38] Sun and Moon are masked by shields as they traverse the skies, but, little by little, Awonawilona draws aside the veil from Moon Mother's shield and as gradually replaces it, thus imaging the course of man's life from infancy to the fulness of maturity and thence to the decline of age. These, with the meteorological beings, the cloud-masked rain-bringers, are the *di superi*, "Those Above." The *di inferi*, "Those Below," dwellers in the bosom of Mother Earth, include the twin Gods of War,[59] who in the years of the beginnings delivered mankind from the monsters; the Corn Father and Corn Mother, the latter being Earth or Earth's Daughters;[35] and the mineral "Men" and "Women" representing Salt, Red Shell, White Shell, and Turquoise;[27] as well as the animal-gods, or Ancients, which are the intermediaries between men and the higher gods, and which also act as the tutelaries or patrons of the several fraternities.[40] Another deity, associated with both the subterranean and the celestial powers, is the Plumed Serpent, called Koloowisi by the Zuñi, Palulukoñ by the Hopi.[50] This god is connected both with the lightning and with fertility: a moving serpent is a natural symbol for the zigzag flash of lightning, and it is probably this analogy which has given rise in the South-West to the myth of sky-travelling snakes; on the other hand, lightning is associated with rainfall, and rain, according to the South-Western view, is carried aloft from the subterranean reservoirs of water; the connexion of rain with fertility is obvious; in the Zuñi initiation of boys into the Kotikili (of which all who may enter the Dance-House of the Gods, after death, must be members), Koloowisi is represented by a large image from whose mouth water and maize issue, and in the highly dramatic Palulukoñti of the Hopi Indians there are several acts which seem to represent the fructification of the maize by the Plumed Snake. Possibly this deity is of Mexican origin, for far to the south, among the Mayan and Nahuatlan peoples, the Plumed Serpent is a potent divinity.

PLATE XXV

Zuñi masks for ceremonial dances. Upper mask of a Warrior God; lower, mask of the Rain Priest of the North. After *23 ARBE*, Plates XVI, LIV. See Note 65 (pp. 309–10), and compare Frontispiece and Plates III, IV, VII, XXXI.

PLATE XXV

Zuñi masks for ceremonial dances. Upper mask of a Warrior God; lower, mask of the Rain Priest of the North. After *23 ARBE*, Plates XVI, LIV. See Note 65 (pp. 309–10), and compare Frontispiece and Plates III, IV, VII, XXXI.

1

2

The second great group of higher powers is composed of the ancestral and totemic Katcinas which play an important part in the Pueblo scheme of things.[65] "While the term Katcina," says Fewkes, "was originally limited to the spirits, or personified medicine power, of ancients, personifications of a similar power in other objects have likewise come to be called Katcinas. Thus the magic power or medicine of the sun may be called Katcina, or that of the earth may be known by the same general name, this use of the term being common among the Hopis. The term may also be applied to personations of these spirits or magic potencies by men or their representation by pictures or graven objects, or by other means." The number of Katcinas is very great, for every clan has its own, not to be personated by members of any other clan; while others are introduced by being adopted as a result of initiation into the rites of neighbouring pueblos. In general, the Katcinas are anthropomorphic. In ritual and in picture they appear as masked, and to their representation is due the long series of masques which characterize Pueblo ceremonial life.

The mask is certainly more than a symbolic disguise. The mythology of the South-West, despite the extensive appearance of animal-powers and the use of animal fetishes, is predominantly anthropomorphic in cast: the Sun and the Moon are manlike beings, hidden by shields; clouds are shields or screens concealing the manlike Rain-Bringers. The Hopi place cotton masks upon the faces of their dead, and the Zuñi blacken the countenances of their deceased chieftains. Now the dead depart to the Underworld [10] (though the Zuñi believe that members of the warrior society, the Bow Priesthood, ascend to the Sky, thence to shoot their lightning shafts, while the Rain-makers roll their thunderous gaming stones),[32] there to become themselves rain-bringers, or at least more potent intercessors for rain than are their mortal brethren. "The earth," Mrs. Stevenson writes, "is watered by the deceased Zuñi, of both sexes, who are controlled and directed by a council composed of ancestral gods. These shadow people collect water in vases and gourd jugs from the six great waters of the world, and pass to and fro over the middle plane, protected from the view of the people below by cloud masks." These six great waters are the waters of the six springs in the hearts of the six mountains of the cosmic points. The Uwannami, as the Zuñi name these shadowy rain-makers, are carried by the vapour which arises from these springs, each Uwannami holding fast a bunch of breath-plumes[60] to facilitate ascension. Clouds of different forms have varying significance: cirrus clouds tell that the Uwannami are passing about for pleasure; cumulus and nimbus that the earth is to be watered. Yet it is not from, but through, the clouds that the rain really comes: each cloud is a sieve into which the water is poured directly or sprinkled by means of the plumed sticks, such as the Zuñi use in their prayers for rain. Of this same tribe Mrs. Stevenson says again: "These people rarely cast their eyes upward without invoking the rain-makers, for in their arid land rain is the prime object of prayer. Their water vases are covered with cloud and rain emblems, and the water in the vase symbolizes the life, or soul, of the vase." This picturesque conception of the office of the ancestral gods is not shared by the Hopi, who regard the rain as coming directly from a special group of gods, the Omowuhs; but the Hopi do believe that the dead are potent intercessors with these deities, and they call the mask which is placed over the face of the deceased a "prayer to the dead to bring rain."

Pueblo maskers personate divine and mythological beings of many descriptions, as well as the ancestral dead, and to the masks themselves attaches a kind of veneration, due to their sacred employment. Besides the masks, however, many other objects are used as ritualistic *sacra*. Sticks painted with symbolic colours, and adorned with plumes which convey the breath of prayer upward to the gods, are offered by the thousand, the placing of such prayer-plumes at notable shrines being a feature of the ceremonial life of each individual.[60] The fraternities, or cult societies, erect elaborate altars, sand-paintings, images, and symbolic objects, indicating the powers to which they are devoted. Meal and pollen, seeds, cords of native cotton, maize of various colours, tobacco in the form of cigarettes, and stone implements, nodules, and figures are all important adjuncts of worship. What are called fetishes are employed in numbers, and vary in character from true fetishes to true idols. Many of the stone fetishes are private property, of the nature of the "medicine" universal in North America.[4] Others are properties of the fraternities, and are in the keeping of certain priests or initiates who bring them forth on the occasion of the appropriate festivals. Still others are of the nature of tribal palladia, in charge of the higher priesthoods. Thus, at Zuñi, the images of the Gods of War (wooden stocks with crudely drawn faces, such as must have been the most ancient xoana) are under the guardianship of the Bow Priesthood, who are servants of the Lightning-Makers.[61]

In Zuñi the supreme sacerdotal group consists of the Ashiwanni, the rain priesthood, which comprises fourteen rain priests, two priests of the bow, and the priestess of fecundity.[5] Six of the rain priests are known as Directors of the House, this house being the chamber which marks the Middle Place of the world, in which is kept the fetish of the rain priests of the North, who are supposed to be exactly over the very heart of the world. The priest of the sun and the director and deputy of the Kotikili, added to the Ashiwanni, form the whole body of Zuñi priests duplicating in the flesh the Council of the Gods, which assembles in Kothluwalawa, the Dance-House of the Gods. The Kokko constitute the entire group of anthropic gods worshipped by the Zuñi. The Kotikili is the society of those who may personate them in masques (including in its membership all of the men and a few of the women of Zuñi); and it is only the members of the Kotikili who are admitted into Kothluwalawa after death. The other fraternities of Zuñi have in charge the service of animal, not anthropic, deities — beings regarded rather as powerful intermediaries between men and gods, and as magical assistants of hunters and doctors, than as rulers of creation. In the Hopi towns priests and fraternities likewise form the sacerdotal organization, though with a clearer dependence upon what is evidently a more ancient and primitive system of clan worship.[5]

IV. THE CALENDAR[39]

Agriculture makes a people not only non-migratory, but close observers of the seasons, and hence of the yearly stations of the sun. The count of time by moons is sufficient for nomadic peoples, or for tribes whose subsistence is mainly by the chase, but in a settled agricultural community the primitive lunar year is sooner or later replaced by a solar year, determined by the passage of the sun through the solstitial and equinoctial points. The lunar measure of time will not be abandoned, but it will be corrected by the solar, and gradually give way to the latter. Such, indeed, is the outline of all calendric development.

The Zuñi year is divided into two seasons, inaugurated by the solstices, each of which is composed of six months — lunations, subdivided into three ten-day periods. The significations of the month names are interesting: the month of the winter solstice, which is the beginning of the year, is called Turning-Back, in reference to the Sun Father's return from the south; it is followed by Limbs-of-the-Trees-Broken-by-Snow, No-Snow-in-the-Road, Little-Wind, Big-Wind, and No-Name. For the remaining half of the year, these appellations, though now inappropriate, are used again, the months of the second half-year being, strictly speaking, nameless. A similar duplication occurs in the Hopi calendar, where the names of five moons are repeated, but in summer and winter rather

PLATE XXVI

Wall decoration in the room of a Rain Priest, Zuñi. Beneath the cloud-symbols are Plumed Serpents, while a sacred Frog, wearing a cloud cap and shooting forth lightnings, stands on their protruding tongues. After *23 ARBE*, Plate XXXVI.

than in the solstitial division, which, however, plays an important *rôle* in the ferial calendar. Fewkes records an interesting remark that may give the true reason for the arrangement: "When we of the upper world are celebrating the winter Pa moon," said the priest, "the people of the under world are engaged in the observance of the Snake or Flute [summer festivals], and vice versa." The priest added that the prayer-sticks which were to be used by the Hopi in their summer festivals were prepared in winter during the time when the underworld folk were performing these rites. "From their many stories of the under world," writes Fewkes, "I am led to believe that the Hopi consider it a counterpart of the earth's surface, and a region inhabited by sentient beings. In this under world the seasons alternate with those in the upper world, and when it is summer in the above it is winter in the world below." Ceremonies are said to be performed there, as here.

Both Zuñi and Hopi have priests whose special duty it is to observe the annual course of the sun, and hence to determine the dates for the great festivals of the winter and summer solstices.[13] The Zuñi sun priest uses as his gnomon a petrified stump which stands at the outskirts of the village, and at which he sprinkles meal and makes his morning prayers to the sun, until, on the day when that luminary rises at a certain point of Corn Mountain, the priesthood is informed of the approaching change. Every fourth morning, for twenty days, the sun priest offers prayer-plumes to the Sun Father, the Moon Mother, and to departed sun priests; on the twentieth morning he announces that in ten days the rising sun will strike the Middle Place, in the heart of Zuñi, and the ceremony will begin. This rite occupies another twenty-day period, beginning with prayers to the gods and ending in days of carnival and giving; during this time the gods are supposed to visit the town, images and fetishes are brought forth and adorned, prayer-plumes are deposited by each family in honour of its ancestral rain-bringers, boys are initiated by ceremonial flogging,[21] the sacred fire is kindled by the fire-maker, and there is a great house cleaning, moral as well as physical, for personators of the gods make it a part of their duty to settle family quarrels and to reprimand the delinquents, young and old. At each solstice the sun is believed to rest in his yearly journey (the Hopi speak of the solstitial points as "houses"); when the sun strikes a certain point on Great Mountain five days in succession, the second change of the year takes place. The ceremonies of the summer solstice include pilgrimages to shrines and elaborate dances, and this is also the season when it is especially lucky to fire pottery, so that all the kilns are smoking. An instructive feature is the igniting of dried grass and trees and bonfires generally; for the Zuñi believe clouds to be akin to smoke, and by means of the smoke of their fires they seek to encourage the Uwannami to bring rain.[62] The ceremony of the summer solstice, in fact, is the inauguration of the series of masques in which they, in common with the other Pueblos, implore moisture from heaven for the crops that are now springing up.

The Hopi sun priests make use of thirteen points on the horizon for the determination of ceremonial dates. Their ritual year begins in November with a New Fire ceremony, which is given in an elaborate and extended form every fourth year, for it then includes the initiation of novices into the fraternities. Other cer monies are similarly elaborated at these same times; while still other rites, as the Snake- and Flute-Dances, occur in alternate years. The Hopi year is divided into two unequal seasons, the greater festivals occurring in the longer season, which includes the cold months. Five and nine days are the usual active periods for the greater festivals, though the total duration from the announcement to the final purification is in some instances twenty days. Of the greater festivals, the New Fire ceremony of November is followed at the winter solstice by the Soyaluña, in which the germ god is supplicated and the return of the sun, in the form of a bird, is dramatized; the Powamu, or Bean-Planting, comes in February, its main object being the renovation of the earth for the coming sowing and the celebration of the return of the Katcinas, to be with the people until their departure at Niman, following the summer solstice; the famous Snake-Dance of the Hopi alternates with the Flute-Dance in the month of August. These are only a few of the annual festivals, a striking feature of which is the arrival and departure of the Katcinas. The period during which these beings remain among the Hopi is approximately from the winter to the summer solstice, and it may be supposed that their absence is due in some way to their function as intercessors for rain during the remaining half-year. A secondary trait, found only in Katcina ceremonies, is the presence of clowns or "Mudheads" — a curious type of funmaker whose presence in Zuñi Cushing ascribes to the ancient union of a Yuman tribe with the original Zuñian stock.

Neither Zuñi nor Hopi succeed in entirely co-ordinating the primitive lunar and solar years. The lunations and sunstations are observed, rather than counted in days; apparently no effort is made to keep a precise record of time nor to correct the calendar, unless indeed the uncertainty which Fewkes found among the Hopi priests as to the true number of lunations in the year, twelve according to some, thirteen and even fourteen according to others, may represent such an attempt. On a sun shrine near Zuñi there are marks said to represent year-counts; certain it is that few North American Indians have a more ancient and verifiable tradition than is possessed by the Pueblo dwellers.[57]

Analogies between the Pueblo periods and festivals and those of the more civilized peoples of ancient Mexico seem to point to a remote identity — the five-, nine-, and twenty-day periods,[68] the general character of many of the rites and mythological beings, the significance of the heart as the seat of life.[29] But one in search of parallels need not confine himself to the New World. The great summer solstice festival of the Celts, with its balefires, is of a kind with that of the Zuñi, while the purification ceremonies of the winter solstice have points of identity with the Roman Lupercalia, the Anthesteria of the Greeks, and similar festivals, which close analysis would multiply. The quadrennial and biennial character of many Pueblo ceremonies, as well as the division into greater and lesser rites, are still other noteworthy analogues of Greek usage.

V. THE GREAT RITES AND THEIR MYTHS

Perhaps no feature of Pueblo culture is more distinctive than the calendric arrangement of their religious rites. Other tribes in North America have ceremonies as elaborate as any in the pueblos, and probably in most cases these rituals are regarded as appropriate only to certain seasons of the year, but it is not generally the season that brings the performance: sickness and the need for cure, the fulfilment of a vow, the munificence or ambition of a rich man, are the commoner occasions. In the pueblos, on the other hand, not a moon passes without its necessary and distinctive festivals, which are fruit of the season rather than of individual need or impulse, thus marking a great step in the direction of social solidarity and cultural advancement.

The origin of these ceremonies harks back to the genesis of the tribes. Most of these are formed of an amalgam of clans which from time to time have joined themselves to the initial tribal nucleus, and have eventually become welded into a single body. Each of these clans has brought to the tribe its own rites, the mythic source of which is zealously recounted; and thus the general corpus of the tribal ritual has been enriched. But the joining of clan to tribe has entailed a modification: by adoption and initiation new members have been added, from without the clan, to the ceremonial body, and eventually (a process which seems to have gone farthest in Zuñi) a cult society, or fraternity, has replaced the clan as the vehicle of the rite; again, clans with analogous or synchronous rites have united their observances into a new and complicated ceremony, partly public, partly secret — for the esoteric aspect is never quite lost, each organization having its own rites, such as the preparation of ceremonial objects, the erecting of altars, etc., shared only by its initiates and usually taking place in its proper kiva.

A famous ceremony of the type just named is the Snake-Dance of the Hopi Indians, the most examined of all Pueblo rites.[50] This ritual occurs biennially in five of the Hopi villages; remnants of a similar observance have been recorded from Zuñi and the eastern group of pueblos; and it is probable that a form of it was celebrated in pre-Columbian Mexico. The participants in the Hopi Snake-Dance are the members of two fraternities — the Snake and the Antelope — each of which conducts both secret and public rites during the nine days of the festival. In the early part of the ceremony serpents are captured in the fields and brought to the kiva of the Snake priests, where the reptiles undergo a ritual bathing and tending; the building of the Snake altar, with personifications of the Snake Youth and Snake Maid, the initiation of novices, the singing of songs, and the recitation of prayers are other rites of the secret ceremonial. The Antelope priests meantime erect their own altar, on which are symbols of rain-clouds and lightning, as well as of maize and other fruits of the earth; and lead in a public dance in which symbols of vegetation and water are displayed. The Antelope priests, moreover, are the first to appear in the public dance on the final day, when the snakes are brought forth from the Snake kiva. These are carried in the mouths of the dancing Snake priests, who are sprinkled with meal by the women; and finally the serpents are taken far into the fields and loosed, that they may bear to the Powers Below the prayers for rain and fertility which is the object of the whole ceremony.

The symbolism of the Snake-Dance is in part explained by the myth which, in varying versions, the Hopi tell of the Snake Youth and Maid. It is a story very similar to the Navaho tale of the Floating Log. A youth, a chief's son, spent his days beside the Grand Canyon, wondering where all the water of the river flowed to and thinking, "That must make it very full somewhere." Finally, he embarks in a hollow log and is borne to the sea, where he is hailed by Spider Woman, who becomes his wizardly assistant. Together they visit the kiva of the mythic Snake People, at the moment human in shape, who subject the young man to tests, which, with the aid of Spider Woman, he successfully meets. The Snake People then assume serpentine form; at the instigation of Spider Woman he seizes the fiercest of these, whereupon the reptile becomes a beautiful girl who, before the transformation, had caught the youth's fancy. This is the Snake Maid, whom he now marries and leads back to his own country. The first offspring of this union is a brood of serpents; but later human children are born, to become the ancestors of the Snake Clan. In some versions, the Snake Maid departs after the birth of her children, never to return; or her offspring are driven forth, from them springing a strange goddess of wild creatures, a sorceress who gambles for life with young hunters, and who carries a child that is never born.

In this mythic medley it is easy to see that the forces of generation are the primary powers. The Snake Maid, from the waters of the west, is the personification of underworld life, the life that appears in the cultivated maize of the fields and the reproduction of animals in the wilds (there are many indications that other animals besides snakes were formerly important in the rite). Fewkes regards her as the Corn Goddess herself and in one Hopi myth a Corn Maid is transformed into a snake.[35] The Snake Youth is probably a sky-power, for in at least one version the Sun-Man bears the youth on his back in his course about the earth. The significance of the antelope in the ceremony is not so clear, though the altar of the Antelope priests is obviously associated also with the powers of fertility; but it may not be amiss to assume that the horn of the antelope, like the horn of the ram in Old-World symbolism, is also a sign of fertility; certainly the conception of descent from an ancestral horn is not foreign to South-Western myth.[40]

The Flute Ceremony, which alternates with the Snake-Dance, has a similar purpose, though here the emblem of the Sun, an adorned disk encircled by eagle feathers and streamers, is significant of the pre-eminence of the Powers Above; and in the Lalakoñti, which follows, in September, the Flute or Snake Ceremony of August, the women, who have charge of the festival, erect an altar on which images of the Growth Goddess and the Corn Goddess are conspicuous.[7] In this ritual the women dance, carrying baskets, while the two Lakone maids, adorned with horn and squash-blossom symbols of fertility, throw baskets and gifts to the spectators — all a dramatic plea for a bountiful harvest.

The Corn Maidens[35] are omnipresent in Pueblo rites, one of the most sacred and guarded of the Zuñi ceremonials being the quadrennial drama representing their visit to their ancestors, an observance occurring, like the Snake-Dance, in August. When their fathers issued from the lower world, the Zuñi say, the ten Corn Maidens came with them and for four years accompanied them, unseen and unknown, but at Shipololo, the Place of Fog, witches discovered them and gave them seeds of the different kinds of maize and the squash. Here the Maidens remained while the Ashiwi, the fathers of the Zuñi, continued on their journey; they whiled away their hours bathing in the dew and dancing in a bower walled with cedar, fringed with spruce, and roofed with cumulus cloud; each maiden held in her hand stalks of a beautiful plant, with white, plumelike leaves, brought from the lower world. Once the Divine Ones, twins of the Sun and Foaming Waters, while on a deer hunt, found the Maidens in their abode, and when their discovery was related they were sent, at the command of the Sun priest, to lead them to the people. The Maidens came and danced before them all in a court decorated with a meal-painting of cloud-symbols. But as they danced the people fell asleep, for it was night, and during their slumber Payatamu, the diminutive flower-crowned god who plays his flute in the fields, causing the flowers to bloom and the butterflies to crowd after him (Pied Piper and god Pan in one), came near and saw the Maidens dancing. He thought them all beautiful, but deemed the Yellow Corn Maiden the loveliest of all. They read his thoughts, and in fear kept on dancing until he, too, fell asleep, when they fled away, by the first light of the morning star, to the Mist and Cloud Spring, where the gods, in the form of ducks, spread their wings and concealed the Maidens hiding in the waters. But famine came to the people, and in their distress they called upon the Gods of War to find the Corn Maidens for them. These two besought Bitsitsi, the musician and jester of the Sun Father, to aid them, and he from a height beheld the Maidens beneath the spreading feathers of a duck's wings. In their kiva the Ashiwanni were sitting without fire, food, drink, or smoke: "all their thoughts were given to the Corn Maidens and to rain." Bitsitsi, borne by the Galaxy, who bowed to earth to receive him, went to the Maidens with the message of the Ashiwanni, which he communicated without words; "all spoke with their hearts; hearts spoke to hearts, and lips did not move." He promised them safety and brought them once more to the Ashiwi, before whom they enacted the ceremonial dance which was to be handed down in the rites of their descendants. Even Payatamu assisted. His home is a cave of fog and cloud with a rainbow door, and thence he came bringing flutes to make music for the dancers. "The Corn Maidens danced from daylight until night. Those on the north side, passing around by the west, joined their sisters on the south side, and, leaving the hampone [waving corn], danced in the plaza to the music of the choir. After they had all returned

PLATE XXVII

Altar of the Antelope Priests of the Hopi. The central dry-painting represents rain-clouds and lightning. About this are arranged symbols of vegetation, prayer sticks, offerings of meal, etc. After *19 ARBE*, Plate XLVI.

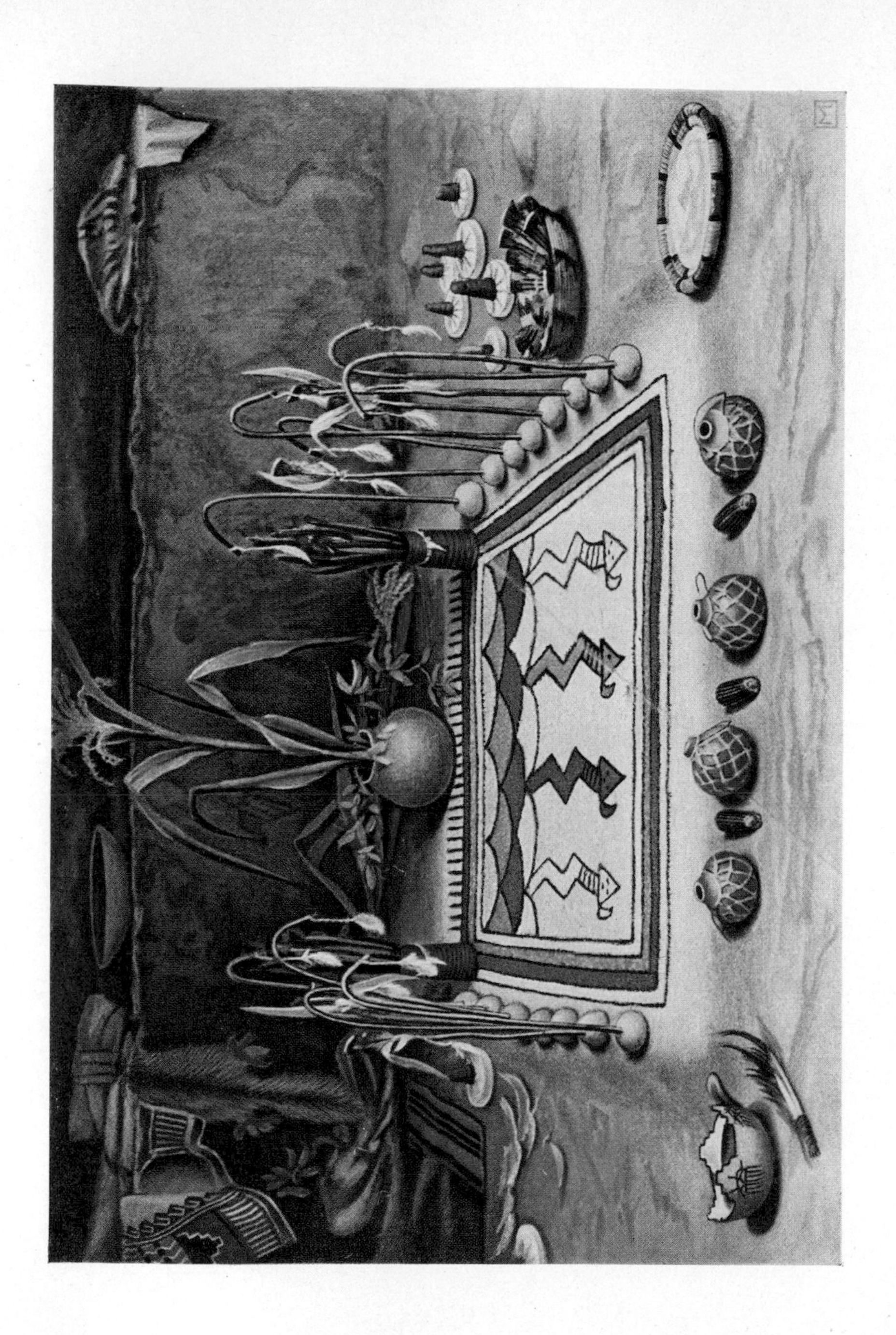

to their places the Maidens on the south side, passing by the west, joined their sisters on the north, and danced to the music, not only of the choir, but also of the group of trumpeters led by Payatamu. The Maidens were led each time to the plaza by either their elder sister Yellow Corn Maiden, or the Blue Corn Maiden, and they held their beautiful *thlawe* (underworld plant plumes) in either hand. The Corn Maidens never again appeared to the Ashiwi."

Not all myths connected with the maize are as innocent or poetic as this. The witches that gave the seed to the Corn Maidens were the two last comers from the Underworld at the time of the emergence. At first the Ashiwi were in favour of sending them back, but the witches told them that they had in their possession the seeds of all things, in exchange for which they demanded the sacrifice of a youth and a maid, declaring, "We wish to kill the children that the rains may come." So a boy and a girl, children of one of the Divine Ones, were devoted, and the rain came, and the earth bore fruit — bitter fruit it was, at first, till the owl and the raven and the coyote had softened and sweetened it. Here we have one of the many legends of the South-West telling of the sacrifice of children to the Lords of the Waters which seem to point to a time when the Pueblo dwellers and their neighbours, like the Aztecs of the south, cast their own flesh and blood to the hard-bargaining Tlaloque.[29]

The one theme of Pueblo ritual is prayer for rain. When asked for an explanation of his rites, says Fewkes (*Annual Report of the Smithsonian Institution*, 1896, pp. 698–99), there are two fundamentals always on the lips of the Hopi priest. "We cling to the rites of our ancestors because they have been pronounced good by those who know; we erect our altars, sing our traditional songs, and celebrate our sacred dances for rain that our corn may germinate and yield abundant harvest." And he gives the call with which the town crier at dawn announces the feast:

All people awake, open your eyes, arise,
Become children of light, vigorous, active, sprightly.
Hasten clouds from the four world quarters;
Come snow in plenty, that water may be abundant when summer
comes;
Come ice, cover the fields, that the planting may yield abundance.
Let all hearts be glad!
The knowing ones will assemble in four days;
They will encircle the village dancing and singing their lays . . .
That moisture may come in abundance.

VI. SIA AND HOPI COSMOGONIES[15]

No Indians are more inveterate and accomplished tellers of tales than are the Pueblo dwellers. Their repertoire includes its full quota of coyote traditions and stories of ghosts, bugaboos, cannibals, ogres,[2] and fairies, as well as legends of migration and clan accession, of cultural innovations and the founding of rites, the historical character of which is more or less clear. But for insight into fundamental beliefs the cosmogonic myths of these, as of other peoples, are the most valuable of all. To be sure, not all the beings who play leading *rôles* in cosmogony are equally important in cult: many of them belong to that "elder generation" of traditionary powers which appear in every highly developed mythic system; and often the potencies for which there is a real religious veneration are symbolized in myth by more or less strange personifications — as Spider Woman, in the South-West, appears to be only an image of the Earth Goddess, suggested by the uncannily huge earth-nesting spiders of that region. Nevertheless, it is to cosmogonies that we must look for the clearest definition of mythic powers.

In their general outlines the cosmogonies of the Pueblo dwellers are in accord with the Navaho Genesis, with which they clearly share a common origin. They differ from this, and among themselves, in the arrangement and emphasis of incidents, as well as in dramatic and conceptual imagination.

The cosmogony of the Sia is very near in form to that of the Navaho. The first being was Sussistinnako, Spider, who drew a cross in the lower world where he dwelt,[66] placed magic parcels at the eastern and western points, and sang until two women came forth from these, Utset, the mother of Indians, and Nowutset, the parent of other men. Spider also created rain, thunder, lightning, and the rainbow, while the two women made sun and moon and stars. After this there was a contest of riddles between the sisters, and Nowutset, who, though stronger, was the duller of the two, losing the contest, was slain by Utset and her heart cut from her breast.[29] This was the beginning of war in the world. For eight years the people dwelt happily in the lower world, but in the ninth a flood came and they were driven to the earth above, to which they ascended through a reed.[42] Utset led the way, carrying the stars in a sack; the turkey was last of all, and the foaming waters touched his tail, which to this day bears their mark.[41] The locust and the badger bored the passage by which the sky of the lower world was pierced, and all the creatures passed through. Utset put the beetle in charge of her star-sack, but he, out of curiosity, made a hole in it, and the stars escaped to form the chaotic field of heaven, although a few remained, which she managed to rescue and to establish as constellations.[14] The First People, the Sia, gathered into camps beside the Shipapo, through which they had emerged, but they had no food. Utset, however, "had always known the name of corn," though the grain itself was not in existence; accordingly, she now planted bits of heart, and, as the cereal grew, she said, "This corn is my heart, and it shall be to my people as milk from my breasts." [35] The people desired to find the Middle Place of the world, but the earth was too soft, and so Utset requested the four beasts of the quarters — cougar, bear, wolf, and badger — to harden it; but they could not, and it was a Spider Woman and a Snake Man who finally made a path upon which the people set forth on their journey. The quarrel of the men and women, their separation, and the birth of cannibal beings from the women — events which the Navaho place in the Underworld — now occur; a little while later the sexes reunite, and a virgin, embraced by the Sun, gives birth to Maasewe and Uyuuyewe, the diminutive twin Warriors, who visit their Sun Father, and are armed to slay the monsters, as in Navaho myth.[44] After the departure of the Warrior Twins, the waters of the Underworld began to rise, and the people fled to the top of a mesa, the flood[49] being placated only by the sacrifice of a youth and a maiden. When the earth was again hardened, the people resumed their search for the Middle Place, which they reached in four days and where they built their permanent home. Shortly afterward a virgin gave birth to a son, Poshaiyanne,[56] who grew up, outcast and neglected, to become a great magician; gambling with the chief, he won all the towns and possessions of the tribe, and the people themselves, but he used his power beneficently and became a potent bringer of wealth and game. Finally, he departed, promising to return; but on the way he was attacked and slain by jealous enemies. A white, fluffy eagle feather fell and touched his body, and as it came in contact with him, it rose again, and he with it, once more alive. Somewhere he still lives, the Sia say, and sometime he will come back to his people. Here we meet a northern version of the famous legend of Quetzalcoatl.[69]

Hopi myths of the beginnings contain the same general incidents. In the Underworld there was nothing but water; two women,[7] Huruing Wuhti of the East and Huruing Wuhti of the West, lived in their east and west houses, and the Sun made his journey from one to the other, descending through an opening in the kiva of the West at night and emerging from a similar aperture in the kiva of the East at dawn. These deities decided to create land, and they divided the waters that the earth might appear. Then from clay they formed, first, birds, which belonged to the Sun, then animals, which were the property of the two Women, and finally men, whom the Women rubbed with their palms and so endowed with understanding.[70] At first the people lived in the Underworld in Paradisic bliss, but the sin of licentiousness appeared, and they were driven forth by the rising waters, escaping only under the leadership of Spider Woman, by means of a giant reed, sunflower, and two kinds of pine-tree.[42] Mocking-Bird assigned them their tribes and languages as they came up, but his songs were exhausted before all emerged and the rest fell back into nether gloom. At this time death entered into the world, for a sorcerer caused the son of a chief to die. The father was at first determined to cast the guilty one back into the Sipapu, the hole of emergence, but relented when he was shown his dead son living in the realm below: "That is the way it will be," said the sorcerer, "if anyone dies he will go down there." [16]

The earth upon which the First People had emerged was dark and sunless,[13] and only one being dwelt there, Skeleton, who was very poor, although he had a little fire and some maize. The people determined to create Moon and Sun, such as they had had in the Underworld, and these they cast, with their carriers, up into the sky. They then set out to search for the sunrise, separating into three divisions — the White People to the south, the Indians to the north, and the Pueblos in the centre. It was agreed that whenever one of the parties arrived at the sunrise, the others should stop where they stood. The whites, who created horses to aid them, were the first to attain their destination, and when they did so a great shower of stars informed the others that one of the parties had reached the goal, so both Indians and Pueblo dwellers settled where they now live. The legends of the flood and of the sacrifice of children are also known to the Hopi, while the Warrior Brothers — Pookonghoya and Balongahoya — perform the usual feats of monster-slaying.[44] Additional incidents of a more wide-spread type are found in Hopi and other Pueblo mythologies: the killing of the man-devouring monster by being swallowed and cutting a way to light, thus liberating the imprisoned victims; the creation of life from the flesh of a slain animal; the freeing of the beasts from a cave, to people the world with game;[41] the adventures of young hunters with Circe-like women of the wilderness — all of them myths which represent the detritus of varied cosmogonies.

VII. ZUÑI COSMOGONY[15]

Of all the Pueblo tales of the origin of the universe the Zuñi account is the most interesting, for it alone displays some power of metaphysical conceptualization. "In the beginning Awonawilona with the Sun Father and the Moon Mother existed above, and Shiwanni and Shiwanokia, his wife, below. . . . (Shiwanni and Shiwanokia labored not with hands but with hearts and minds; the Rain Priests of the Zuñi are called Ashiwanni and the Priestess of Fecundity Shiwanokia.) . . . All was shipololo (fog), rising like steam. With breath from his heart Awonawilona created clouds and the great waters of the world. . . . (He-She[64] is the blue vault of the firmament. The breath-clouds of the gods are tinted with the yellow of the north, the blue-green of the west, the red of the south, and the silver of the east of Awonawilona. The smoke clouds of white and black become a part of Awonawilona; they are himself, as he is the air itself; and when the air takes on the form of a bird it is but a part of himself — is himself. Through the light, clouds, and air he becomes the essence and creator of vegetation.) . . . After Awonawilona created the clouds and the great waters of the world, Shiwanni said to Shiwanokia, 'I, too, will make something beautiful, which will give light at night when the Moon Mother sleeps.' Spitting in the palm of his left hand, he patted the spittle with the palm of his right hand, and the spittle foamed like yucca suds and then formed into bubbles of many colors, which he blew upward; and thus he created the fixed stars and constellations. Then Shiwanokia said, 'See what I can do,' and she spat into the palm of her left hand and slapped the saliva with the fingers of her right, and the spittle foamed like yucca suds, running over her hand and flowing everywhere; and thus she created Awitelin Tsita, the Earth Mother." [34]

Light and heat and moisture and the seed of generation — these are the forces personified in this thinly mythic veil. In the version rendered by Cushing there is a still more single beginning: "Awonawilona conceived within himself and thought outward in space, whereby mists of increase, steams potent of growth, were evolved and uplifted. Thus, by means of his innate knowledge, the All-container made himself in person and form of the Sun whom we hold to be our father and who thus came to exist and appear.[13] With his appearance came the brightening of the spaces with light, and with the brightening of the spaces the great mist-clouds were thickened together and fell, whereby was evolved water in water; yea, and the world-holding sea. With his substance of flesh outdrawn from the surface of his person, the Sun-father formed the seed-stuff of twin worlds, impregnating therewith the great waters, and lo! in the heat of his light these waters of the sea grew green and scums rose upon them, waxing wide and weighty until, behold! they became Awitelin Tsita, the 'Four-fold Containing Mother-earth,' and Apoyan Tachu, the 'All-covering Father-sky.' From the lying together of these twain upon the great world-waters, so vitalizing, terrestrial life was conceived; whence began all beings of earth, men and the creatures, in the Four-fold womb of the World. Thereupon the Earth-mother repulsed the Sky-father, growing big and sinking deep into the embrace of the waters below, thus separating from the Sky-father in the embrace of the waters above.

"As a woman forebodes evil for her first-born ere born, even so did the Earth-mother forebode, long withholding from birth her myriad progeny and meantime seeking counsel with the Sky-father. 'How,' said they to one another, 'shall our children, when brought forth, know one place from another, even by the white light of the Sun-father?' . . . Now like all the surpassing beings the Earth-mother and the Sky-father were changeable, even as smoke in the wind; transmutable at thought, manifesting themselves in any form at will, like as dancers may by mask-making. . . . Thus, as a man and woman, spake they, one to another.

"'Behold!' said the Earth-mother as a great terraced bowl appeared at hand and within it water, 'this is as upon me the homes of my tiny children shall be. On the rim of each world-country they wander in, terraced mountains shall stand, making in one region many, whereby country shall be known from country, and within each, place from place. Behold, again!' said she as she spat on the water and rapidly smote and stirred it with her fingers. Foam formed, gathering about the terraced rim, mounting higher and higher. 'Yea,' said she, 'and from my bosom they shall draw nourishment, for in such as this shall they find the substance of life whence we were ourselves sustained, for see!' Then with her warm breath she blew across the terraces; white flecks of the foam broke away, and, floating over above the water, were shattered by the cold breath of the Sky-father attending, and forthwith shed downward abundantly fine mist and spray! 'Even so, shall white clouds float up from the great waters at the borders of the world, and clustering about the mountain terraces of the horizons be borne aloft and abroad by the breaths of the surpassing soul-beings, and of the children, and shall hardened and broken be by thy cold, shedding downward, in rain spray, the water of life, even into the hollow places of my lap! For therein chiefly shall nestle our children, mankind and creature-kind, for warmth in thy coldness.' . . . Lo! even the trees on high mountains near the clouds and the Sky-father crouch low toward the Earth-mother for warmth and protection! Warm is the Earth-mother, cold the Sky-father, even as woman is the warm, man the cold being! . . .

"'Even so,' said the Sky-father; 'Yet not alone shalt thou helpful be unto our children, for behold!' and he spread his hand abroad with the palm downward and into all the wrinkles and crevices thereof he set the semblance of shining yellow corn-grains; in the dark of the early world-dawn they gleamed like sparks of fire, and moved as his hand was moved over the bowl, shining up from and also moving in the depths of the water therein. 'See!' said he, pointing to the seven grains clasped by his thumb and four fingers, 'by such shall our children be guided; for behold, when the Sun-father is not nigh, and thy terraces are as the dark itself (being all hidden therein), then shall our children be guided by lights — like to these lights of all the six regions turning round the midmost one — as in and around midmost place, where these our children shall abide, lie all the other regions of space! Yea! and even as these grains gleam up from the water, so shall seed-grains like to them, yet numberless, spring up from thy bosom when touched by my waters, to nourish our children.' Thus and in other ways many devised they for their offspring."

The Zuñi legend continues with events made familiar in other narratives. As in the Navaho Genesis, the First People pass through four underworlds before they finally emerge on earth: "the Ashiwi were queer beings when they came to this world; they had short depilous tails, long ears, and webbed feet and hands, and their bodies and heads were covered with moss, a lengthy tuft being on the fore part of the head, projecting like a horn"; they also gave forth a foul odour, like burning sulphur, but all these defects were removed by the Divine Ones, under whose guidance the emergence and early journeying of the First People took place. These gods, Kowwituma and Watsusi, are twins of the Sun and Foam, and are obviously doublets of the Twin Gods of War (whose Zuñi names are variants of those known to the Sia), by whom they are later replaced.[44] Other incidents of the Zuñi story tell of the origins of institutions and cults near the place of emergence, of the hardening of the world, of the search for the Middle Place, and of the cities built and shrines discovered on the way. Incidents of the journey include the incest of a brother and sister, sent forward as scouts,[17] to whom a sterile progeny was born, and who created Kothluwalawa, the mountain home of the ancestral gods; the accession and feats of the diminutive twins, the Gods of War; the coming of the Corn Maidens, already recounted; the flood[49] and the sacrifice of a youth and a maid, which caused the waters to recede;[29] the assignment of languages and the dispersal of tribes; stories of Poshaiyanki,[69] the culture hero, and of the wanderings of Kiaklo, who visited Pautiwa, the lord of the dead, and returned to notify the Ashiwi of the coming of the gods to endow them with the breath of life "so that after death they might enter the dance house at Kothluwalawa before proceeding to the undermost world whence they came."[10]

In the cosmogonies of the Pueblo dwellers, thus sketched, the events fall into two groups: gestation of life in the underworld and birth therefrom, and the journey to the Middle Place — Emergence and Migration, Genesis and Exodus. The historical character of many of the allusions in the migration-stories has been made plausible by archaeological investigations, which trace the sources of Pueblo culture to the old cliff-dwellings in the north. Characteristically these abodes are in the faces of canyon walls, bordering the deep-lying streams whose strips of arable shore formed the ancient fields. May it not be that the tales of emergence refer to the abandonment of these ancient canyon-set homes, never capable of supporting a large population? Some of the tribes identify the Sipapu with the Grand Canyon — surely a noble birthplace! — and when in fancy we see the First People looking down from the sunny heights of the plateau into the depths whence they had emerged and beholding, as often happens in the canyons of the South-West, the trough of earth filled with iridescent mist, with rainbows forming bridgelike spans and the arched entrances to cloudy caverns, we can grasp with refreshened imagination many of the allusions of South-Western myth. Possibly a hint as to the reason which induced the First People to come forth from so fairylike an abode is contained in the Zuñi name for the place of emergence, which signifies "an opening in the earth filled with water which mysteriously disappeared, leaving a clear passage for the Ashiwi to ascend to the outer world."

One other point in South-Western myth is of suggestive interest. This is the moral implication which clearly appears and marks the advancement of the thought of these Indians over more primitive types. In the world below the First People dwelt long in Paradisic happiness; but sin (usually the sin of licentiousness) appeared among them, and the angry waters drove them forth, the wicked being imprisoned in the nether darkness. The events narrated might be ascribed to missionary influence, were it not that these same events have close analogues far and wide in North American myth, and for the further fact of the pagan conservatism of the Pueblos. That the people are capable of the moral understanding implied is indicated by the reiterated assertion of priest and story that "the prayer is not effective except the heart be good."

CHAPTER X

THE PACIFIC COAST, WEST

I. THE CALIFORNIA-OREGON TRIBES

A GLANCE at the linguistic map of aboriginal North America will reveal the fact that more than half of the radical languages of the continent north of Mexico — nearly sixty in all — are spoken in the narrow strip of territory extending from the Sierras, Cascades, and western Rockies to the sea, and longitudinally from the arid regions of southern California to the Alaskan angle. In this region, nowhere extending inland more than five degrees of longitude, are, or were, spoken some thirty languages bearing no relation to one another, and the great majority of them having no kindred tongue. The exceptional cases, where representatives of the great continental stocks have penetrated to the coast, comprise the Yuman and Shoshonean tribes occupying southern California, where the plateau region declines openly to the sea; small groups of Athapascans on the coasts of California and Oregon; and the numerous Salishan units on the Oregon-Washington coast and about Puget Sound.

It is this latter intrusion, the Salishan, which divides the Coast Region into two parts, physiographically and ethnically distinct. From Alaska to Mexico the Pacific Coast is walled off from the continental interior by high and difficult mountain ranges. There are, in the whole extent, only two regions in which the natural access is easy. In the south, where the Sierra Nevada range subsides into the Mohave Desert, the great Southern Trail enters California; and here we find the aborigines of the desert interior pressing to the sea. The Northern, or Oregon, Trail follows the general course of the Missouri to its headwaters, crosses the divide, and proceeds down the Columbia to its mouth; and this marks the general line of Salishan occupancy, which extends northward to the more difficult access opened by the Fraser River. The Salishan tribes form a division, at once separating and transitionally uniting a northern and a southern coastal culture of markedly distinct type. Indeed, the Salish form a kind of key to the continent, touching the Plains civilization to the east and that of the Plateau to the south, as well as the two coastal types; so that there is perhaps no group of Indians more difficult to classify with respect to cultural relationships.

The linguistic diversity of the southern of the two Coast groups bounded by the Salish is far greater than that of the northern. In California alone over twenty distinct linguistic stocks have been noted, and Oregon adds several to this score. Such a medley of tongues is found nowhere else in the world save in the Caucasus or the Himalaya mountains — regions where sharply divided valleys and mountain fastnesses have afforded secure retreat for the weaker tribes of men, at the same time holding them in sedentary isolation. Similar conditions prevail in California, the chequer of mountain and valley fostering diversity. Furthermore, the nature of the littoral contributed to a like end. The North-Western coast, from Puget Sound to Alaska, is fringed by an uninterrupted archipelago; the tribes of this region are the most expert in maritime arts of all American aborigines; and the linguistic stocks, owing to this ready communication, are relatively few. From the mouth of the Columbia to the Santa Barbara Islands, on the contrary, the coast is broken by only one spacious harbour — the bay of San Francisco — and little encouragement is offered to seafarers. Among the tribes of this coast the art of navigation was little known: the Chinook, on the Columbia, and the Chumashan Indians, who occupied the Santa Barbara Islands, built excellent canoes, and used them with skill; but among the intervening peoples rafts and balsas, crudest of water transports, took the place of boats, and even sea-food was little sought, seeds and fruits, and especially acorn meal, being the chief subsistence of the Californian tribes.

In the general character of their culture the tribes of this region form a unity as marked as is their diversity of speech. Socially their organization was primitive, without centralized tribal authority or true gentile division. They lived in village communities, whose chiefs maintained their ascendancy by the virtue of liberal giving; and a distinctive feature of many of the Californian villages was the large communal houses occupied by many families. Grass, tule, brush, and bark were the common housing materials, for skill in woodworking was only slightly advanced; northward, however, plank houses were built, such as occur the length of the North-West Coast. Of the aboriginal arts only basket-making, in which the Californian Indians, and especially the Athapascan Hupa, excel all other tribes, was the only one highly developed; pottery-making was almost unknown. In other respects these peoples are distinctive: they were unwarlike to the point of timidity; they did not torture prisoners; and in common with the Yuman and Piman stocks, but in contrast to most other peoples of North America, they very generally preferred cremation to burial. Intellectually they are lethargic, and their myths contain no element of conscious history; they regard themselves as autochthones, and such they doubtless are, in the sense that their ancestors have continuously occupied California for many centuries. Physical and mental traits point to a racial unity which is in part borne out by their language itself; for although their speech is now divided into many stocks between which no relationship can be traced — a clear indication of long and conservative segregation, — yet there is a similarity in phonetic material, the Californian tongues being notable, among Indian languages, for vocalic wealth and harmony.

II. RELIGION AND CEREMONIES

The religious life and conceptions of the Californian tribes reflect the simplicity of their social organization. In northern California and Oregon the religious life gains in complexity as the influence of the North-West becomes stronger, and a similar increase in the importance of ceremonial is observed in the south; but in the characteristic area of the region, central California, the development of rites is meagre. The shaman is a more important personage than the priest and ritual is of far less consequence than magical therapy; in fact, the Californian Indians belong to that primitive stratum of mankind for which shamanism is the engrossing form of religious interest, the western shamans, like the majority of Indian "medicine-men," acquiring their powers through fast and vision in which the possessing tutelary is revealed.[5]

Of ceremonies proper, the most distinctive on this portion of the Coast is the annual rite in commemoration of the dead, known as the "burning" or the "cry" or the "dance of the dead." This is an autumnal and chiefly nocturnal ceremony in which, to the dancing and wailing of the participants, various kinds of property are burned to supply the ghosts; the period of mourning is then succeeded by a feast of jollity. In few parts of America are the tabus connected with the dead so stringent: typical customs include the burning of the house in which death occurs; the ban against speaking the name of the deceased, or using, for the space of a year, a word of which this name is a component; and the marking of a widow by smearing her with pitch, shearing her hair, or the like, until the annual mourning releases her from the tabu. Such usages, along with cremation, disappear as the North-West is approached.

A second group of rites have to do with puberty. Her first menstruation is marked by severe tabus for the girl concerned; and a dance is given when the period is passed. Boys undergo an initiation into the tribal mysteries, the ceremony including the recounting of myths. Rites of this character are not always compulsory, nor are they limited to boys, since men who have passed the age period without the ceremony sometimes participate later. The body of initiates forms a kind of Medicine Society, having in charge the religious supervision of the village. Still a third ceremonial group includes magic dances intended to foster the creative life of nature, the number of such rites varying from tribe to tribe.

Ceremonial symbolism, so elaborate in many portions of America, is little developed in the West-Coast region. Pictographs are unknown and fetishes little employed; nor is there anything approaching in character the complicated use of mask personations which reaches its highest forms in the neighbouring South-West and North-West. Mythic tales and ritual songs have a similar inferiority of development, the extremes of the region, north and south, showing the greatest advancement in this as in other respects. In one particular the Californians stand well in advance: throughout the central region, their idea of the creation is clearly conceptualized; and it is their cosmogonic myths, with the idea of a definite and single creator, which form their most unique contribution to American Indian lore. The creator is sometimes animal, sometimes manlike, in form, but he is usually represented as dignified and beneficent, and there is an obvious tendency to humanize his character.

Northern California and Oregon, however, know less of such a single creator. In this section stories of the beginnings start with the Age of Animals — or rather, of anthropic beings who on the coming of man were transformed into animals — whose doings set the primeval model after which human deeds and institutions are copied. Here is a cycle assimilated to the myth of the North-West, just as the lore of the south Californian tribes approaches the type of the plateau and desert region.

PLATE XXVIII

Maidu image for a woman, used at the Burning Ceremony in honour of the dead (see p. 215). After *BAM* xvii, Plate XLIX.

III. THE CREATOR[15]

In the congeries of West-Coast peoples it is inevitable that there should be diversity in the conception of creation and creator, even in the presence of a general and family likeness. But the differences in the main follow geographical lines. To the south, while creation is definitely conceived as a primal act, the creative beings are of animal or of bird form, for the winged demiurge is characteristic of the Pacific Coast throughout its length.[48] In the central region of California and Oregon the creator is imaged in anthropomorphic aspect, the animals being assistants or clumsy obstructionists in his work. To the north, and along the coast, the legend of creation fades into a delineation of the First People, whose deeds set a pattern for mankind.

Tribes of the southerly stocks very generally believed in primordial waters, the waters of the chaos before Earth or of the flood enveloping it. Above this certain beings dwell — the Coyote and the birds. In some versions they occupy a mountain peak that pierces the waves, and on this height they abide until the flood subsides; in others, they float on a raft or rest upon a pole or a tree that rises above the waters. In the latter case, the birds dive for soil from which to build the earth; it is the Duck that succeeds, floating to the surface dead, but with a bit of soil in its bill[49] — like the Muskrat in the eastern American deluge-tales. The Eagle, the Hawk, the Crow, and the Humming-Bird are the winged folk who figure chiefly in these stories, with the Eagle in the more kingly *rôle;* but it is Coyote — though he is sometimes absent, his place being taken by birds — who is the creator and shaper and magic plotter of the way of life.

In the region northward from the latitude of San Francisco — among the Maidu, Pomo, Wintun, Yana, and neighbouring tribes — the Coyote-Man, while still an important demiurgic being, sinks to a secondary place; his deeds thwart rather than help the beneficent intentions of the creator, toil, pain, and death being due to his interference. "I was the oldest in the olden time, and if a person die he must be dead," says Coyote to Earth-Maker in a Maidu myth, reported by Dixon.[16] The first act of this Maidu creation already implies the covert antagonism:

"When this world was filled with water, Earth-Maker floated upon it, kept floating about. Nowhere in the world could he see even a tiny bit of earth. No person of any kind flew about. He went about in this world, the world itself being invisible, transparent like the sky. He was troubled. 'I wonder how, I wonder where, I wonder in what place, in what country we shall find a world!' he said. 'You are a very strong man, to be thinking of this world,' said Coyote. 'I am guessing in what direction the world is, then to that distant land let us float!' said Earth-Maker." The two float about seeking the earth and singing songs: "Where, O world, art thou?" "Where are you, my great mountains, my world mountains?" "As they floated along, they saw something like a bird's nest. 'Well that is very small,' said Earth-Maker. 'It is small. If it were larger I could fix it. But it is too small,' he said. 'I wonder how I can stretch it a little!' . . . He extended a rope to the east, to the south he extended a rope, to the west, to the northwest, and to the north he extended ropes. When all were stretched, he said, 'Well, sing, you who were the finder of this earth, this mud! "In the long, long ago, Robin-Man made the world, stuck earth together, making this world." Thus mortal men shall say of you, in myth-telling.' Then Robin sang, and his world-making song sounded sweet. After the ropes were all stretched, he kept singing; then, after a time, he ceased. Then Earth-Maker spoke to Coyote also. 'Do you sing, too,' he said. So he sang, singing, 'My world where one travels by the valley-edge; my world of many foggy mountains; my world where one goes zigzagging hither and thither; range after range,' he said, 'I sing of the country I shall travel in. In such a world I shall wander,' he said. Then Earth-Maker sang — sang of the world he had made, kept singing, until by and by he ceased. 'Now,' he said, 'it would be well if the world were a little larger. Let us stretch it!' 'Stop!' said Coyote. 'I speak wisely. The world ought to be painted with something so that it may look pretty. What do ye two think?' Then Robin-Man said, 'I am one who knows nothing. Ye two are clever men, making this world, talking it over; if ye find anything evil, ye will make it good.' 'Very well,' said Coyote, 'I will paint it with blood. There shall be blood in the world; and people shall be born there, having blood. There shall be birds born who shall have blood. Everything — deer, all kinds of game, all sorts of men without any exception — all things shall have blood that are to be created in this world. And in another place, making it red, there shall be red rocks. It will be as if blood were mixed up with the world, and thus the world will be beautiful!'" After this Earth-Maker stretched the world, and he inspected his work, journeying through all its parts, and he created man-beings in pairs to people earth's regions, each with a folk speaking differently. Then he addressed the last-created pair, saying: "'Now, wherever I have passed along, there shall never be a lack of anything,' he said, and made motions in all directions. 'The country where I have been shall be one where nothing is ever lacking. I have finished talking to you, and I say to you that ye shall remain where ye are to be born. Ye are the last people; and while ye are to remain where ye are created, I shall return, and stay there. When this world becomes bad, I will make it over again; and after I make it, ye shall be born,' he said. (Long ago Coyote suspected this, they say.) 'This world will shake,' he said. 'This world is spread out flat, the world is not stable. After this world is all made, by and by, after a long time, I will pull this rope a little, then the world shall be firm. I, pulling on my rope, shall make it shake. And now,' he said, 'there shall be songs, they shall not be lacking, ye shall have them.' And he sang, and kept on singing until he ceased singing. 'Ye mortal men shall have this song,' he said, and then he sang another; and singing many different songs, he walked along, kept walking until he reached the middle of the world; and there, sitting down over across from it, he remained."

In another myth of the Maidu, Earth-Maker descends from heaven by a feather rope to a raft upon which Turtle and a sorcerer are afloat. Earth-Maker creates the world from mud brought up by the Turtle, who dives for it, and Coyote issues from the Underworld to introduce toil and death among men. The Maidu Earth-Maker has close parallels among neighbouring tribes,[6] perhaps the most exalted being Olelbis, of the Wintun: "The first that we know of Olelbis is that he was in Olelpanti. Whether he lived in another place is not known, but in the beginning he was in Olelpanti (on the upper side), the highest place." Thus begins Curtin's rendering of the myth of creation. The companions of Olelbis in this heaven-world — completing the triad which so often recurs in Californian cosmogonies — are two old women, with whose aid he builds a wonderful sweat-house in the sky: its pillars are six great oaks; its roof is their intertwining branches, from which fall endless acorns; it is bound above with beautiful flowers, and its four walls are screens of flowers woven by the two women; "all kinds of flowers that are in the world now were gathered around the foot of that sweat-house, an enormous bank of them; every beautiful color and every sweet odor in the world was there."[42] The sweat-house grew until it became wonderful in size and splendour, the largest and most beautiful thing in the world, placed there to last forever — perhaps the most charmingly pictured Paradise in Indian myth.

Other creators, in the myths of this region, are Taikomol, He-Who-Goes-Alone, of the Yuki; Yimantuwinyai, Old-One-Across-the-Ocean, of the Hupa; K'mukamtch, Old Man, of the Klamath, tricky rather than edifying in character; and the

Wishosk Maker Gudatrigakwitl, Old-Man-Above, who performs his creative work by "joining his hands and spreading them out." Among these the Hupa creator seems not to have existed forever: "It was at Tcoxoltcwedin he came into being. From the earth behind the inner house wall he sprang into existence. There was a ringing noise like the striking together of metals at his birth. Before his coming smoke had settled on the mountain side. Rotten pieces of wood thrown up by someone fell into his hands. Where they fell there was fire." This surely implies a volcanic birth of the universe, natural enough in a land where earthquakes are common and volcanoes not extinct. Something of the same suggestion is conveyed by a myth of the neighbouring Coos Indians, in which the world is created by two brothers on a foundation of pieces of soot cast upon the waters.[44] In this Kusan myth the third person of the recurrent Californian triad is a medicine-man with a red-painted face, whom the brothers slay, spilling his blood in all directions — an episode reminiscent of the *rôle* of Coyote in the Maidu genesis. When the world is completed, the brothers shoot arrows upward toward the heavens, each successive bolt striking into the shaft of the one above, and thus they build a ladder by means of which they ascend into the sky.

IV. CATACLYSMS[49]

The notion of cataclysmic destructions of the world by flood or fire, often with a concomitant falling of the sky, is frequent in West-Coast myth. Indeed, many of the creation-stories seem to be, in fact, traditions of the re-forming of the earth after the great annihilation, although in some myths both the creation and the re-creation are described. One of the most interesting is the genesis-legend of the Kato, an Athapascan tribe closely associated with the Pomo, who are of Kulanapan stock.

The story begins with the making of a new sky, to replace

the old one, which is soon to fall. "The sandstone rock which formed the sky was old, they say. It thundered in the east; it thundered in the south; it thundered in the west; it thundered in the north. 'The rock is old, we will fix it,' he said. There were two, Nagaitcho and Thunder. 'We will stretch it above far to the east,' one of them said. They stretched it.[62] They walked on the sky." So the tale begins. Nagaitcho, the Great Traveller, and Thunder then proceed to construct an outer cosmos of the usual Californian type: a heaven supported by pillars, with openings at each of the cardinal points for winds and clouds and mist, and with winter and summer trails for the sun's course. They created a man and a woman, presumably to become the progenitors of the next world-generation. Then upon the earth that was they caused rain to fall: "Every day it rained, every night it rained. All the people slept. The sky fell. The land was not. For a very great distance there was no land. The waters of the oceans came together. Animals of all kinds drowned. Where the water went there were no trees. There was no land. . . . Water came, they say. The waters completely joined everywhere. There was no land or mountains or rocks, but only water. Trees and grass were not. There were no fish, or land animals, or birds. Human beings and animals alike had been washed away. The wind did not then blow through the portals of the world, nor was there snow, nor frost, nor rain. It did not thunder nor did it lighten. Since there were no trees to be struck, it did not thunder. There were neither clouds nor fog, nor was there a sun. It was very dark. . . . Then it was that this earth with its great, long horns got up and walked down this way from the north. As it walked along through the deep places the water rose to its shoulders. When it came up into shallower places, it looked up. There is a ridge in the north upon which the waves break. When it came to the middle of the world, in the east under the rising of the sun, it looked up again. There where it looked up will be a large land near to the coast. Far away to the south it continued looking up. It walked under the ground. Having come from the north it traveled far south and lay down. Nagaitcho, standing on earth's head, had been carried to the south. Where earth lay down Nagaitcho placed its head as it should be and spread gray clay between its eyes and on each horn. Upon the clay he placed a layer of reeds and then another layer of clay. In this he placed upright blue grass, brush, and trees. 'I have finished,' he said. 'Let there be mountain peaks here on its head. Let the waves of the sea break against them.'"

The Wintun creation-myth, narrated by Curtin, possesses a plot of the same type. Just as he perceives that the end of the First World and of the First People is approaching, Olelbis, He-Who-Sits-Above, builds his paradisic sweat-house in the sky-world to become a refuge for such as may attain to it. The cataclysm is caused by the theft of Flint from the Swift, who, for revenge, induces Shooting Star, Fire Drill, and the latter's wife, Buckeye Bush, to set the world afire.[51] "Olelbis looked down into the burning world. He could see nothing but waves of flame; rocks were burning, the ground was burning, everything was burning. Great rolls and piles of smoke were rising; fire flew up toward the sky in flames, in great sparks and brands. Those sparks are sky eyes, and all the stars that we now see in the sky came from that time when the first world was burned. The sparks stuck fast in the sky, and have remained there ever since. Quartz rocks and fire in the rocks are from that time; there was no fire in the rocks before the world fire. . . . During the fire they could see nothing of the world below but flames and smoke." Olelbis did not like this; and on the advice of two old women, his Grandmothers, as he called them, he sent the Eagle and the Humming-Bird to prop up the sky in the north, and to summon thence Kahit, the Wind, and Mem Loimis, the Waters, who lived beyond the first sky.[9] "The great fire was blazing, roaring all over the earth, burning rocks, earth, trees, people, burning everything. Mem Loimis started, and with her Kahit. Water rushed in through the open place made by Lutchi when he raised the sky. It rushed in like a crowd of rivers, covered the earth, and put out the fire as it rolled on toward the south. There was so much water outside that could not come through that it rose to the top of the sky and rushed on toward Olelpanti. . . . Mem Loimis went forward, and water rose mountains high. Following closely after Mem Loimis came Kahit. He had a whistle in his mouth; as he moved forward he blew it with all his might, and made a terrible noise. The whistle was his own; he had had it always. He came flying and blowing; he looked like an enormous bat with wings spread. As he flew south toward the other side of the sky, his two cheek feathers grew straight out, became immensely long, waved up and down, grew till they could touch the sky on both sides." Finally the fire was quenched, and at the request of Olelbis, Kahit drove Mem Loimis, the Waters, back to her underworld home, while beneath Olelpanti there was now nothing but naked rocks, with a single pool left by the receding waters. The myth goes on to tell of the refashioning and refurnishing of the world by Olelbis, assisted by such of the survivors of the cataclysm of fire and flood as had managed to escape to Olelpanti. A net is spread over the sky, and through it soil, brought from beyond the confines of the sky-capped world, is sifted down to cover the boulders. Olelbis marks out the rivers, and water is drawn to fill them from the single lakelet that remains. Fire, now sadly needed in the world, is stolen from the lodge of Fire Drill and Buckeye Bush — the parents of flame — without their discovering the loss (an unusual turn in the tale of the theft of fire). The earth is fertilized by Old Man Acorn and by seed dropping down from the flower lodge of Olelbis in the skies. Many animals spring into being from the feathers and bits of the body of Wokwuk, a large and beautiful bird, with very red eyes; while numerous others are the result of the transformations wrought by Olelbis, who now metamorphoses the survivors of the first world into the animals and objects whose nature they had in reality always possessed.[41] A particularly charming episode tells of the snaring of the clouds. These had sprung into being when the waters of the flood struck the fires of the conflagration, and they were seeking ever to escape back to the north, whence Kahit and Mem Loimis had come. Three of them, a black, a white, and a red one, are captured; the skin of the red cloud is kept by the hunters, who often hang it up in the west, though sometimes in the east; the black and the white skins are given to the Grandmothers of Olelbis. "Now," said the two old women, "we have this white skin and this black one. When we hang the white skin outside this house, white clouds will go from it, — will go away down south, where its people began to live, and then they will come from the south and travel north to bring rain. When they come back, we will hang out the black skin, and from it a great many black rain clouds will go out, and from these clouds heavy rain will fall on all the world below." The Pacific Coast is a land of two seasons, the wet and the dry, and these twin periods could scarcely be more beautifully symbolized.[39]

V. THE FIRST PEOPLE[40]

A little reflection upon the operations of animistic imagination will go far to explain the conception of a First People, manlike in form, but animal or plant or stone or element in nature, which is nowhere in America more clearly defined than on the West Coast.[3] The languages of primitive folk are built up of concrete terms; abstract and general names are nearly unknown; and hence their thought is metaphorical in cast and procedure. Now the nearest and most intelligible of metaphors are those which are based upon the forms and traits of men's own bodies and minds: whatever can be made familiar in terms of human instinct and habit and desire is truly familiar, — "Man is the measure of all things," and primitive mythic metaphor is the elementary form of applying this standard. At first it is the activities rather than the forms of things that are rendered in terms of human nature; for it is always the activities, the powers of things, that are important in practical life; the outward, the aesthetic, cast of experience becomes significant only as people advance from a life of need to a life of thought and reflection. Hence, at first, mythopoetic fancy is content to ascribe human action and intention, human speech and desires, to environing creation; the physical form is of small consequence in explaining the conduct of the world, for physical form is of all things the most inconstant to the animistic mind, and it is invariably held suspect, as if it were a guise or ruse for the deluding of the human race. But there comes a period of thought when anthropomorphism — an aesthetic humanizing of the world — is as essential to mental comfort and to the sense of the intelligibility of nature as is the earlier and more naïve psychomorphism: when the phantasms, as well as the instincts and powers, of the world call for explanation.

Such a demand, in its incipiency, is met by the conception of the First People. This is a primeval race, not only regarded as human in conduct, but imagined as manlike in form. They belong to that uncertain past when all life and all nature were not yet aware of their final goal — a period of formation and transformation, of conflict, duel, strife, of psychical and physical monstrosities, before the good and the bad had been clearly separated. "As the heart is, so shall ye be," is the formula ever in the myth-maker's half unconscious thought, and the whole process of setting the earth in order seems to consist of the struggle after appropriate form on the part of the world's primitive forces.[46]

West-Coast lore is in great part composed of tales of the First People, and it is instructive that the stories and events in this mythology are far more constant than are the personalities of the participants. This harks back to the prime importance of the action: it is as if the motives and deeds of the natural world were being tried out, fitted, like vestments, now upon this type of being, now upon that, with a view to the discovery of the most suitable character. It indicates, too, that the tales are probably far older than the environment, which they have been gradually transformed to satisfy. To be sure, certain elements are constant, for they represent unchangeable factors in human experience — as the relation of Earth and Sky, Light and Darkness, Rain, Fire, Cloud, and Thunder; but the animal personalities, and to a less extent the monstrous beings, vary for the same plot in different tribes and different tellings — vary, yet with certain constancies that deserve note. Coyote, over the whole western half of North America, is the most important figure of myth: usually, he is not an edifying hero, being mainly trickster and dupe by turns; yet he very generally plays a significant *rôle* in aiding, willy-nilly, the First People to the discovery of their final and appropriate shapes. He is, in other words, a great transformer; he is frequently the prime mover in the theft of fire, which nearly all tribes mark as the beginning of human advancement; and in parts, at least, of California, his deeds are represented as almost invariably beneficent in their outcomes; he is a true, if often unintentional, culture hero. Other animals — the Elk, the Bear, the Lion — are frequent mythic figures, as are certain reptiles — the Rattlesnake, the exultant Frog Woman, who floats on the crest of the world-flood, and the Lizard who, because he has five fingers and knows their usefulness, similarly endows man when the human race comes to be created. But it is especially the winged kind — the birds — that play, after Coyote, the leading *rôles* in West-Coast myth. The Eagle, the Falcon, the Crow, the Raven, and to a less degree the Vulture and the Buzzard, are most conspicuous, for it is noticeable that among birds, as among animals, it is the stronger, and especially the carnivorous, kinds that are the chiefs of legend. Nevertheless, this is no invariable rule, and the Woodpecker, whose red head-feathers were used as money among the Californian tribes, the Humming-Bird, and indeed most other birds known to them, figure in the myths of the region. Nor are smaller creatures — the Louse, the Fly, and the Worm — too insignificant for the maker of traditions.

All of these beings, in the age of the First People, were human in form; the present order of existence began with their transformation into the birds and animals we now know. In West-Coast myth, this metamorphosis often follows directly upon the cataclysm of fire or flood by which the First World was destroyed, thus giving the two periods a distinctness of separation not common in Indian thought. In many versions the transformation is the work of the world-shaper — Coyote or another — as in the myth of Olelbis, who apportions to each creature its proper shape and home after the earth has been restored. Even more frequently there is a contest of some sort, the outcome of which is that victor and vanquished are alike transformed. This may be a battle of wits, as in the Coos story of the Crow whose voice was thunder and whose eyes flashed lightning:[32] a certain man-being persuaded the Crow first to trade voices with him, and then to sell the lightnings of his eyes for the food left by the ebb-tide, whereupon the Crow degenerated into what he now is, a glutton with a raucous voice, while the man became the Thunderer. Again, the struggle may be of the gaming type: in a Miwok legend Wek-wek, the Falcon, participated with a certain winged giant, Kelok, in a contest at which each in turn allowed himself to be used as a target for red-hot stones hurled by his opponent; through over-confidence Wek-wek is slain, but he is restored to life again by Coyote, who is shrewd enough to beat the giant at his own game; while from the body of the slain monster is started the conflagration that destroys the world.[33] In a third case, the contest is one of sorcery: the story of the Loon Woman tells how she fell in love with the youngest of her ten brothers as they danced in the sweat-lodge; by her magic she compelled him to accompany her, but he escaped, and the brothers, with the aid of their elder sister, Spider Woman, ascended to heaven in a basket; Loon Woman perceived them, set fire to the sweat-house, and all save the Eagle fell back into the flames; their bodies were burned and Loon Woman made herself a necklace of their hearts. Nevertheless, her triumph was brief, for the Eagle succeeded in slaying her, and placing her heart along with those of his brothers in a sweat-house, brought them all back to life, but with the forms and dispositions which they now possess.[17]

The creation of the human race [70] marks the close of the age of the First People. Usually the World-Maker is also the shaper of men, and it is the West-Coast mode to conceive the process quite mechanically: men are fashioned from earth and grass, or appear as the transformations of sticks and feathers; the Kato story is altogether detailed, telling how Nagaitcho made a trachea of reed and pounded ochre to mix with water and make blood. A more dignified creation was that of Gudatrigakwitl, the Wishosk Maker, who used no tools, but formed things by spreading out his hands. "When Gudatrigakwitl wanted to make people, he said, 'I want fog.' Then it began to be foggy. Gudatrigakwitl thought: 'No one will see it when the people are born.' Then he thought: 'Now I wish people to be all over, broadcast. I want it to be full of people and full of game.' Then the fog went away. No one had seen them before, but now they were there." Most imaginative of all is the Modoc myth, recorded by Curtin. Kumush, the man of the beautiful blue, whose life was the sun's golden disk, had a daughter. He made for her ten dresses: the first for a young girl, the second the maturity raiment in which a maiden clothes herself when she celebrates the coming of womanhood, the third to the ninth festal and work garments such as women wear, the tenth, and most beautiful of all, a burial shroud. When the girl was within a few days of maturity, she entered the sweat-house to dance; there she fell asleep and dreamed that some one was to die, and when she came out she demanded of Kumush her burial dress. He offered her each of the others in turn, but she would have only this; when she had donned it, she died, and her spirit set out for the west, the home of them that had passed away. Kumush, however, would not let her go alone, and saying, "I know all things above, below, and in the world of ghosts; whatever is, I know," he accompanied her down into the caverns of the dead. There father and daughter dwelt, by night dancing with the spirits, which became skeletons by day. But Kumush wearied of this, and determined to return to earth and restore life upon it. He took a basketful of the bones and set out, but they resisted and dug sharply into his body. Twice he slipped and fell back, but the third time he landed in the world above, and sowing there the bones of the ghosts, a new race sprang up from them — the race of men who have since inhabited the earth.

VI. FIRE AND LIGHT [51]

In the beginning the First World was without light or heat; blackness and cold were everywhere, or if there were light and warmth, they were distant and inaccessible: "the world was dark and there was no fire; the only light was the Morning, and it was so far away in the high mountains of the east that the people could not see it; they lived in total darkness" — with this suggestive image of valley life begins a Miwok tale of the theft of Morning. Sometimes it is Morning or Daylight that is stolen, sometimes it is the Sun, oftenest it is Fire; but the essential plot of the story seldom varies: on the confines of the world there is a lodge in which the Light or the Fire is guarded by jealous watchmen, from whom their treasure must be taken by craft; generally, the theft is discovered and a pursuit is started, but relays of animals succeed in bearing off a fragment of the treasure.

Coyote is the usual plotter and hero of myths of fire and light.

In a dramatic Kato story he dreams of the sun in the east.[13] With three mice for companions he sets out, coming at last to the lodge where two old women have the sun bound to the floor. When they sleep, the mice gnaw the bands that hold the sun, and Coyote seizes it, pursued by the awakened women, whom he changes into stone. From the stolen sun he fashions all the heavenly bodies: "Moon, sun, fly into the sky. Stars become many in it. In the morning you shall come up. You shall go around the world. In the east you shall rise again in the morning. You shall furnish light." Not always, however, is the venture so successful; in the Miwok tale the stealing of the sun results in the transformation of the First People into animals, and the like metamorphosis follows on the theft of fire as narrated by the Modoc. Sometimes the fire-origin story is literal and simple, as in the Wishosk legend of the dog who kindled the first flame by rubbing two sticks; sometimes it is dramatic and grim, as in the duel of magicians, which the Coos tradition narrates, in which one is eaten by maggots till he is nothing but bones, before he finally succeeds in so terrifying his opponent that the latter flees, and his wealth of fire and water — a unique combination — is taken.[21] Again, there are poetic versions — the Shasta story which makes Pain and his children the guardians of fire; or the Miwok tale of the Robin who got his red breast from nestling his stolen flame, to keep it alive; or that of the Mouse who charmed the fireowners with music and hid a coal in his flute.

The Maidu, naturally enough, make Thunder and his Daughters (who must be the lightnings) the guardians of fire.[32] They tell, in a hero story, how the elder of two brothers is lured away by, and pursues, a daughter of Thunder. He shoots an arrow ahead of her, and secures it from her pack-basket (the storm-cloud) without harm. He makes his way through a briar field by the aid of a flint which cuts a path for him. Protected by moccasins of red-hot stone, he follows her through a field of rattlesnakes, and when he finds her he cuts off the serpent teeth which surround her vagina (a variant of one of the most wide-spread of North American myth-incidents). On his moccasins he crosses a frozen lake, and with the assistance of a feather — the universal symbol of life — he fords a deep river and passes the Valley-of-Death-by-Old-Age.[8] Arrived at the house of Thunder, he avoids poisoned food, breaks a pitch-log for firewood, escapes a water monster that nearly drowns him, and slays a grizzly bear which pursues him, when on a deer-hunt, by shooting it in the left hind foot, its only vulnerable spot. These labours performed, the North American Hercules takes the daughter of Thunder to wife, and returns to his home.

This is one of the many hero tales in which the West-Coast mythology is rich. The red-hot moccasins suggest the personification of volcanic forces, so that the whole myth may well be the story of a volcano, wedded to its lightnings, cleaving lake and river and valley, and overcoming the mighty of earth. A similar origin may be that of the Miwok giant Kelok, hurling his red-hot rocks and setting the world ablaze — surely a volcanic Titan.

Another type of hero is the child of the Sun.[48] The Maidu story of the exploits of the Conquerors, born at one birth to Cloud Man and a virgin, is strikingly like the South-Western tales of the divine twins, sons of the Sun; and a somewhat similar legend is narrated by the Yuki.[44] The kind of hero more distinctive of the West Coast, however, is "Dug-from-the-Ground." In the Hupa recension a virgin, forbidden by her grandmother to uproot two stocks (the mandrake superstition), disobeys, and digs up a child. He grows to manhood, visits the sky-world, and finally journeys to the house of the sun in the east, where he passes laborious tests, and in the game of hockey overcomes the immortals, including Earthquake and Thunder. Tulchuherris is the Wintun name for this hero; he is dug up by an old woman, and when he emerges a noise like thunder is heard in the distant east, the home of the sun.

Curtin regards Tulchuherris as the lightning, born of the fog which issues from the earth after sunrise.

In another story, one of the most popular of Californian tales,[52] the Grizzly Bear and the Doe were kindred and friends, living together and feeding in the same pasture. One day while afield the Bear killed the Doe, but her two Fawns discovered the deed, and beguiling the murderess into letting them have her cub for a playmate, they suffocated it in a sweat-house. Pursued by the Bear, they were conveyed to heaven by a huge rock growing upward beneath them; and there they found their mother. The story has many forms, but the Fawns are always associated with fire. Sometimes they trap the mother bear, but usually they kill her by hurling down red-hot rocks. They themselves become thunders, and it is instructive that the Doe, after drinking the waters of the sky-world, dies and descends to earth — clearly she is the rain-cloud and her Fawns are the thunders. The legend of the heaven-growing rock, lifting twins to the skies, occurs more than once in California, most appropriate surely when applied to the great El Capitan of the Yosemite.[42]

It is perhaps too easy to read naturalistic interpretations into primitive myth. In many instances the meaning is unmistakably expressed and seems never to be lost, as in the Promethean theft of fire; but in others — and the hero of Herculean labours is a fair example — it is by no means certain that long and varied borrowing has not obscured the original intention. Volcanic fire, lightning, and sunlight itself seem to be the figures suggesting the adventures; but it may well be that for the aboriginal narrators these meanings have long since vanished.

VII. DEATH AND THE GHOST-WORLD

The source of death, no less than the origin of life, is a riddle which the mind of man early endeavours to solve; and in the

New World, as sometimes in the Old, the event is made to turn upon a primal choice. In the New-World tales, however, it is not the creature's disobedience, but deliberate selection by one of the primal beings that establishes the law. The typical story is of a conflict of design:[16] the Author of Life intends to create men undying, but another being, who is Coyote far more often than any other, jealous of the new race, wishes mortality into the world, and his wish prevails. In very many versions, neither rational nor ethical principle is concerned in the choice; it is a result of chance; but on the West Coast not a few examples of the legend involve both reason and morals. As it is told, one of the First People loses a child; its resurrection is contemplated; but Coyote interferes, saying, "Let it remain dead; the world will be over-peopled; there will be no food; nor will men prize life, rejoicing at the coming of children and mourning the dead." "So be it," they respond, for Coyote's argument seems good. But human desires are not satisfied by reason alone, as is shown in the grimly ironical conclusion: Coyote's real motive is not the good of the living; selfishness and jealousy prompt his specious plea; now his own son dies, and he begs that the child be restored to life; but "Nay, nay," is the response, "the law is established."

The most beautiful myth of this type that has been recorded is Curtin's "Sedit and the Two Brothers Hus," of the Wintun. Sedit is Coyote; the brothers Hus are buzzards. Olelbis, about to create men, sends the brothers to earth to build a ladder of stone from it to heaven; half way up are to be set a pool for drink and a place for rest; at the summit shall be two springs, one for drinking and the other for bathing — internal and external purification — for these are to be that very Fountain of Youth whose rumour brought Ponce de Léon from Spain to Florida. When a man or a woman grows old, says Olelbis, let him or her climb to Olelpanti, bathe and drink, and youth will be restored. But as the brothers build, Coyote, the tempter, comes, saying, "I am wise; let us reason"; and he pictures contemptuously the destiny which Olelbis would bestow: "Suppose an old woman and an old man go up, go alone, one after the other, and come back alone, young. They will be alone as before, and will grow old a second time, and go up again and come back young, but they will be alone, just the same as at first. They will have nothing on earth whereat to rejoice. They will never have any friends, any children; they will never have any pleasure in the world; they will never have anything to do but to go up this road old and come back down young again." "Joy at birth and grief for the dead is better," says Coyote, "for these mean love." The brothers Hus are convinced, and destroy their work, though not until the younger one says to Coyote: "You, too, shall die; you, too, shall lie in the ground never to rise, never to go about with an otter-skin band on your head and a beautiful quiver at your back!" And when Coyote sees that it is so, he stands muttering: "What am I to do now? I am sorry. Why did I talk so much? Hus asked me if I wanted to die. He said that all on earth here will have to die now. That is what Hus said. I don't know what to do. What can I do?" Desperate, he makes himself wings of sunflowers — the blossoms that are said always to follow the sun — and tries to fly upward; but the leaves wither, and he falls back to earth, and is dashed to death. "It is his own deed," says Olelbis; "he is killed by his own words; hereafter all his people will fall and die."

Such is the origin of death; but death is, after all, not the end of a man; it only marks his departure to another world than this earth. The body of a man may be burned or buried, but his life is a thing indestructible; it has journeyed on to another land. The West-Coast peoples find the abode of the dead in various places.[10] Sometimes it is in the world above, and many are the myths detailing ascents to, and descents from, the sky; sometimes it is in the underworld; oftenest, it is in the west, beyond the waters where the sun is followed by night. Not always, however, are mortals content to let their loved ones depart, and over and again occurs the story of the quest for the dead, at times almost in the form of Orpheus and Eurydice.[53] Thus the Yokut tell of a husband grieving beside his wife's grave, until, one night, her spirit rises and stands beside him. He follows her to the bridge that arches the river separating the land of the living from the realm of them that have passed away, and there wins consent from the guardians of the dead for her return to earth, but he is forbidden to sleep on the return journey; nevertheless, slumber overtakes him on the third night, and he wakes in the morning to find that he lies beside a log. The Modoc story of Kumush and his daughter and of the creation of men from the bones of the dead is surely akin to this, uniting life and death in one unbroken chain. This conception is brought out even more clearly in a second version of the Yokut tale, wherein the man who has visited the isle of the dead tells how, as it fills, the souls are crowded forth to become birds and fish.

That the home of those who have gone hence should lie beyond the setting sun is a part of that elemental poetry by which man sees his life imaged and painted on the whole field of heaven and earth: the disk of morning is the symbol of birth, noon is the fullness of existence, and evening's decline is the sign of death. But dawn follows after the darkness with a new birth, for which the dead that be departed do but wait — where better than in those Fortunate Isles which all men whose homes have bordered on the western sea have dreamed to lie beyond its gleaming horizons?

CHAPTER XI

THE PACIFIC COAST, NORTH

I. PEOPLES OF THE NORTH-WEST COAST

FROM Puget Sound northward to the neighbourhood of Mt. St. Elias and the Copper River the coast is cut by innumerable fiords and bays, abutted by glaciated mountains, and bordered by an almost continuous archipelago. The rainy season is long and the precipitation heavy on this coast, which, on the lower levels, is densely forested, conifers forming the greater part of the upper growth, while the shrubbery of bushes furnishes a wealth of berries. The red cedar (*Thuja plicata*) is of especial importance to the natives of the coast, its wood serving for building and for the carvings for which these people are remarkable, while its bark is used for clothing, ropes, and the like. Deer, elk, bear, the wolf, the mountain goat, the beaver, the mink, and the otter inhabit the forest, the hills, and the streams, and are hunted by the Indians; though it is chiefly from the sea that the tribes of this region draw their food. Besides molluscs, which the women gather, the waters abound in edible fish: salmon and halibut, for which the coast is famous, herring, candlefish, from which the natives draw the oil which is an important article of their diet, and marine mammals, such as the seal, sea-lion, and whale. The region is adapted to support a considerable population, even under aboriginal conditions of life, while at the same time its easy internal communication by water, and its relative inaccessibility on the continental side, encourage a unique and special culture.

Such, indeed, we find. While no less than six linguistic divisions are found on the North-West Coast, accompanied by a corresponding diversity of physical types, the general culture of the region is one, and of a cast unlike anything else on the continent. Its foundation is maritime, the Indians of this region building large and shapely canoes, and some tribes, such as the Nootka and Quileute, even attacking the whale in the open sea. Villages are built facing the beach, and the timber houses, occupied by several families, represent the highest architectural skill of any Indian structures north of the pueblos. The wood-working craft is nowhere in America more developed, not only in the matter of weapons and utensils, but especially in carvings, of which the most famous examples are the totem-poles [61] of the northern tribes. Work in shell, horn, and stone is second in quality only to that in wood, while copper has been extensively used, even from aboriginal times. Basketry and the weaving of mats and bark-cloth are also native crafts. In art the natives of the North-West attained a unique excellence, their carvings and drawings showing a type of decorative conventionalizing of human and animal figures unsurpassed in America, as is also the skill with which these elements are combined. The impulse of this art is almost wholly mythical, and it finds its chief expression in heraldic poles, grave-posts, and house-walls, in ceremonial masks and rattles, and in the representation of ancestral animals on clothing and utensils.

The social structure of the peoples of the North-West reflects their advancement in the crafts. The majority of the tribes are organized into septs and clans determining descent and marriage relations. In the northern area descent is counted matrilinearly, in the southern by the patrilinear rule. The Kwakiutl have an institution which seems to mark a transition between the two systems: descent follows the paternal line, but each individual inherits the crest of his maternal grandfather. In some village-groups parents are at liberty to place their children in either the maternal or the paternal clan. Clan exogamy is the rule. Within the tribe the various clans are not of equal status; consequently, there is a similar gradation in the rank of the nobles who are the clan heads or chiefs. These nobles are the real rulers of the North-West peoples, whose government is thus of an oligarchic type. Clan membership carries with it the right to use the ancestral crest, certain totems involving the privileges of rank, while others mark plebeian caste. Slavery is another institution prominent in the North-West, slaves being either prisoners of war or hopeless debtors.

Perhaps the most distinctive feature of these tribes is the Potlatch. Primarily this word designates a festival at which a chieftain or a man of means distributes a large amount of property, often the accumulation of years. These riches are not, however, a free presentation, since the recipients are bound to return, with interest, the gifts received, so that a wealthy man thus ensures to himself competence and revenue, as well as importance in the tribal councils. Rivalry of the intensest sort is generated between the great men of the several clans, each striving to outdo the others in the munificence of his feasts, which thus become a matter of family distinction, entitled to record on the family crest. The recognized medium of exchange is the blanket, but a curious and interesting device is the "Copper" — the bank-note of the North-West — a hammered and decorated sheet of copper of a special form, having the value of many hundred or of several thousand blankets, according to the amount offered for it at a festal sale. These Coppers are, in fact, insignia of wealth; and since the destruction of property is regarded as the highest evidence of social importance, they are sometimes broken, or even entirely destroyed, as a sign of contempt for the riches of a less able rival.

Of the stocks of the North-West the most northerly is the Koluschan, comprising the Tlingit Indians, whose region extends from the Copper River, where they border upon the Eskimoan Aleut, south to Portland Canal. The Skittagetan stock, of the Queen Charlotte Islands and the southern part of Prince of Wales Island, is formed of the Haida tribes; while on the opposite mainland, following the Nass and Skeena rivers far inland, is the district of the Tsimshian and other Chimmesyan peoples. South of these begin the territories of the Wakashan stock, which extend on the mainland to Johnston Strait and, beyond, over the whole western part of the island of Vancouver. Powell divided this stock into the Aht and Haeltzuk (Bellabella) tribes, but later authorities prefer Kwakiutl and Nootka, the latter holding the seaward side of Vancouver. The fifth group comprises the Coast Salish: a northern division, about Dean Inlet and the Salmon and Bella Coola rivers, adjoining the Wakashan territories; a central division extending from the head of the Strait of Georgia southward to Chinook lands about the Columbia; and a southern group holding the Oregon coast south of the Chinook peoples. A single tribe, the Quileute, about Cape Flattery in Washington, represents the almost extinct Chimakuan stock. In general, the culture of the Tlingit and Haida tribes show an identity of form which distinguishes them as a group from the like community manifested by the Tsimshian, Kwakiutl, Nootka, and North-Coast Salish.

II. TOTEMISM AND TOTEMIC SPIRITS[3]

The ceremonies of the tribes of the North-West fall into two classes, following their social and ceremonial organization. The social division into clans, which are matrilinear and exogamic in the north, while patrilinear or mixed systems prevail in the south, finds outward expression in totemic insignia and in ceremonial representations of the myths narrating the beginnings of the septs. These origins are ascribed to an ancestor who has been initiated by animal-beings into their mysteries, or dances, thus conferring upon him the powers of the initiating creatures; the animals themselves are not regarded as ancestral,

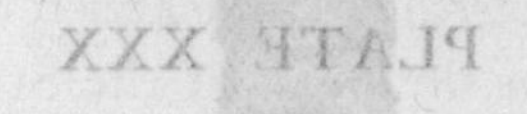

PLATE XXX

Frame of Haida house with totem-pole. After *MAM* viii, Plate XI.

nor are the members of the clan akin to the totemic being, except in so far as they possess the powers and practise the rites obtained through the ancestral revelation. The manner of revelation is precisely that in which the Indian everywhere in North America acquires his guardian or tutelary, his personal totem: in fast or trance the man is borne away by the animal-being, taken perhaps to the lodge of its kind, and there given an initiation which he carries back to his people. The distinctive feature of the North-Western custom, however, is that a totem so acquired may be transmitted by inheritance, so that a man's lineage may be denoted by such a series of crests as appears upon the totem-pole.[61] Correspondingly, the number and variety of totemic spirits become reduced, animals or mythic beings of a limited and conventionalized group forming a class fixed by heredity. Yet the individual character of the totem never quite disappears; what is transmitted by birth is the right to initiation into the ancestral mysteries; without this ceremony the individual possesses neither the use of the crest nor knowledge of its myths and songs.

The animal totems of the Tlingit, as given by Boas, are the Raven and the Wolf; of the Haida, the Raven and the Eagle; of the Tsimshian, Raven, Eagle, Wolf, and Bear; of the Heiltsuk Kwakiutl, Raven, Eagle, and Killer Whale; while the Haisla (like the Heiltsuk Kwakiutl of Wakashan stock) have six totems, Beaver, Eagle, Wolf, Salmon, Raven, and Killer Whale. Among the remaining tribes of the region — Nootka, Kwakiutl, and Salishan — family crests, rather than clan totems, are the marks of social distinction; but even in the north, where the totemic clan prevails, crests vary among the clan families: thus, the families of the Raven clan of the Stikine tribe of the Tlingit have not only the Raven, but also the Frog and the Beaver, as hereditary crests.

In addition to acquisition by marriage and inheritance, rights to a crest may pass from one family or tribe to another through war; for a warrior who slays a foe is deemed to have acquired the privileges of the slain man's totem; if this be one foreign to the conqueror's tribe, slaves may be called upon to give the proper initiation, which is still essential. Thus the rights to certain crests pass from clan to clan and from tribe to tribe, forming the foundation for a kind of intertribal relationship of persons owning like totems. Wars were formerly waged for the acquisition of desired totemic rights, and more than once, the legends tell, bitter conflicts have resulted from the appropriation of a crest by a man who had no demonstrable right to it, for no prerogatives are more jealously guarded in the North-West. Only persons of wealth could acquire the use of crests, for the initiation must be accompanied by feasting and gift-giving at the expense of the initiate and his kindred. On the other hand, the possession of crests is a mark of social importance; hence, they are eagerly sought.

The origin of crests was referred to mythic ancestors. The Haida are divided into Eagles and Ravens. The ancestress of the Raven clan is Foam Woman, who rose from the sea and is said to have had the power of driving back all other supernatural beings with the lightnings of her eyes; Foam Woman, like Diana of the Ephesians, had many breasts, at each of which she nourished a grandmother of a Raven family of the Haida. The oldest crest of this clan is the Killer Whale, whose dorsal fin, according to tradition, adorned the blanket of one of the daughters of Foam Woman; but they also have for crests the Grizzly Bear, Blue Hawk, Sea-Lion, Rainbow, Moon, and other spirits and animals. Curiously enough, the Raven crest among the Haida does not belong to families of the Raven clan, but to Eagles, whose ancestor is said to have obtained it from the Tsimshian. All the Eagles trace their descent from an ancestress called Greatest Mountain, probably denoting a mainland origin of this clan, but the Eagle is regarded as the oldest of their crests. The animals themselves are not held to be ancestors, but only to have been connected in some significant fashion with the family or clan progenitor; thus, an Eagle chief appeared at a feast with a necklace of live frogs, and his family forthwith adopted the frog as a crest.

Many creatures besides animals appear as totemic or family crests, and the double-headed snake (represented with a head at each end and a human head in the middle), known to the Kwakiutl as Sisiutl, is one of the most important of these beings.[50] A Squawmish myth tells of a young man who pursued the serpent Senotlke for four years, finally slaying it; as he did so, he himself fell dead, but he regained life and, on his return to his own people, became a great shaman, having the power to slay all who beheld him and to make them live again — a myth which seems clearly reminiscent of initiation rites. The Sisiutl is able to change itself into a fish, whose flesh is fatal to those who eat it, but for those who obtain its supernatural help it is a potent assistant. Pieces of its body, owned by shamans, are powerful medicine and command high prices. The Bella Coola believe that its home is a salt-water lake behind the house of the supreme goddess in the highest heaven, and that the goddess uses this mere as a bath. The skin of the Sisiutl is so hard that it cannot be pierced by a knife, but it can be cut by a leaf of holly. In one Bella Coola myth the mountain is said to have split where it crawled, making a passage for the waters of a river. It would appear from these and other legends that the Sisiutl, like the horned Plumed Snake of the Pueblos, is a genius of the waters, perhaps a personification of rain-clouds. A Comox tradition, in many ways analogous to the South-Western story of the visit of the Twin Warriors to the Sun, tells of the conquest of Tlaik, chief of the sky, by the two sons of Fair Weather, and of the final destruction of the sky-chief, who is devoured by the double-headed snake — a tale which suggests clearly enough the effacement of the sun by the clouds.

Another being important in clan ritual is the Cannibal woman (Tsonoqoa, Sneneik),[19] whose offspring are represented as wolves, and in whose home is a slave rooted to the ground from eating the food which the demoness gave her. This anthropophagous monster dwells in the woods and carries a basket in which she puts the children whom she steals to eat, and she also robs graves; but at last she is slain by a sky-boy to whose image, reflected in the water, she makes love. Komokoa, the Rich One,[7] is the protector of seals, and lives at the bottom of the sea; the drowned go to him, and stories are narrated of persons who have penetrated to his abode and afterward returned to give his crest to their descendants. A frequent form of legend recounts how hunters harpoon a seal and are dragged down with incredible velocity until the home of Komokoa is reached; there they are initiated, and receive crests and riches with which they go back to their kindred, who have believed them long since dead. The Thunderbird,[32] described as a huge creature carrying a lake on its back and flashing lightnings from its eyes, is also a crest, traditions telling of clan ancestors being carried away to its haunts and there initiated. Whales are said to be its food, and the bones of cetaceans devoured by it may be seen upon the mountains. Monstrous birds are of frequent occurrence in the myths of the North-West, as in California, many of them seeming to derive their characteristics from the Thunderbird, while the latter is sometimes asserted to resemble types of the *Falconidae*, as the hawk or the eagle.

The wooden masks, carved and painted, employed in the initiation ceremonies connected with the clan totems are the ritual representations of the clan myth.[65] Many of these masks are double, the inner and outer faces representing two moods or incidents in the mythic adventure. Frequently the outer is an animal, the inner a human, face — a curious expression of the aboriginal belief in a man-soul underlying the animal exterior. Masks are not regarded as idols; but that a kind of fetishistic reverence attaches to wood-carvings of supernatural beings in the North-West is shown by the number of myths telling of such figures manifesting life. "The carvings on the house posts wink their eyes," is a Haida saying denoting excellence in art, and more than one myth is adorned with tales of houses in which the sculptured pillars or the painted pictures are evidently alive, while stories of living persons rooted to the floor apparently have a similar origin. The carving of a wife out of wood is a frequent theme, and occasionally she, like Galatea, is vivified; when the husband's name is Sitting-on-Earth, we may suspect that here, too, we have a myth connected with the house-post. In creation stories the first human pair are sometimes represented as carved from wood by the demiurge and then endowed with life, although this may be a version of the Californian legend of the creation of men from sticks, modified by a people with a native genius for wood carving.[70]

III. SECRET SOCIETIES AND THEIR TUTELARIES

Of even greater ceremonial significance than the possession of crests is membership in the secret societies of the North-West. Everywhere in North America, as the clan system loosens in rigidity, the Medicine Lodge or the Esoteric Fraternity grows in importance. In its inception the medicine society is seldom unrelated to the clan organization, but it breaks free from this either in the form of a ceremonial priesthood, as among the Pueblo, or in that of a tribal or inter-tribal religious order, as in the mystery societies of the Great Plains. Among the peoples of the North-West the fraternities have had a development of their own. Apparently they originated with the Kwakiutl tribes, among whom the social organization is either a compromise or a transitional stage between the matrilinear clans of the northward stocks and the patriarchal family or village-groups of the southerly Coast-Dwellers. Membership in the secret societies is in a sense dependent upon heredity, for certain of the tutelary spirits of the societies are supposed to appear only to members of particular clans or families; but with this restriction the influence of the clan upon society membership ends. Perhaps no sharper indication of the difference could be given than the very general custom of changing the names of the society members, during the season of their ceremonials, from their clan names to the spirit names given them at the time of their initiation; [20] the family system temporarily yields place to a mystic division into groups defined by patron spirits, the genii or guardians of the societies.

These spirits are distinguished from the totems that mark descent in that the latter are not regarded as giving continued revelations of themselves: the totem appeared to the ancestor and revealed his mystery, which then became traditionary; the spirits of the societies manifest themselves to, and indeed must take possession of, every initiate; they still move among men, and the ceremonials in their honour take place in the winter season, when these supernatural beings are supposed to be living in association with their neophytes.[39] The most famed and dreaded of the secret society tutelaries is the Cannibal, whose votaries practise ceremonial anthropophagy, biting the arms of non-initiates (in former times slaves were killed and partly eaten).[19] Cannibals are common characters in the myths of the North-West, as elsewhere; but the Cannibal of the society is a particular personage who is supposed to dwell in the mountains with his servants, the man-eating Grizzly Bear and the Raven who feeds upon the eyes of the persons whom his master has devoured, and who is a long-beaked bird which breaks men's skulls and finds their brains a dainty morsel. The cult of the Cannibal probably originated among the Heiltsuk Kwakiutl, whence it passed to neighbouring tribes in comparatively recent times. The Warrior of the North is a second spirit, his gifts being prowess in war, and resistance to wounds and disease. Still others are the Bird-Spirit which makes one able to fly, and the ghosts who bestow the power of returning to life after being slain. The Dog-Eating Spirit, whose votaries kill and eat a dog as they dance, is the inspirer of yet another society with a wide-spread following. The more potent spirits

PLATE XXXI

Kwakiutl ceremonial masks. Upper, an ancestral or totemic double mask, the bird mask, representing the totem being opened out to show the inner man-faced mask. Lower, mask representing the Sisiutl, or double-headed and horned serpent. After *MAM* viii, Plates XLIX, LX.

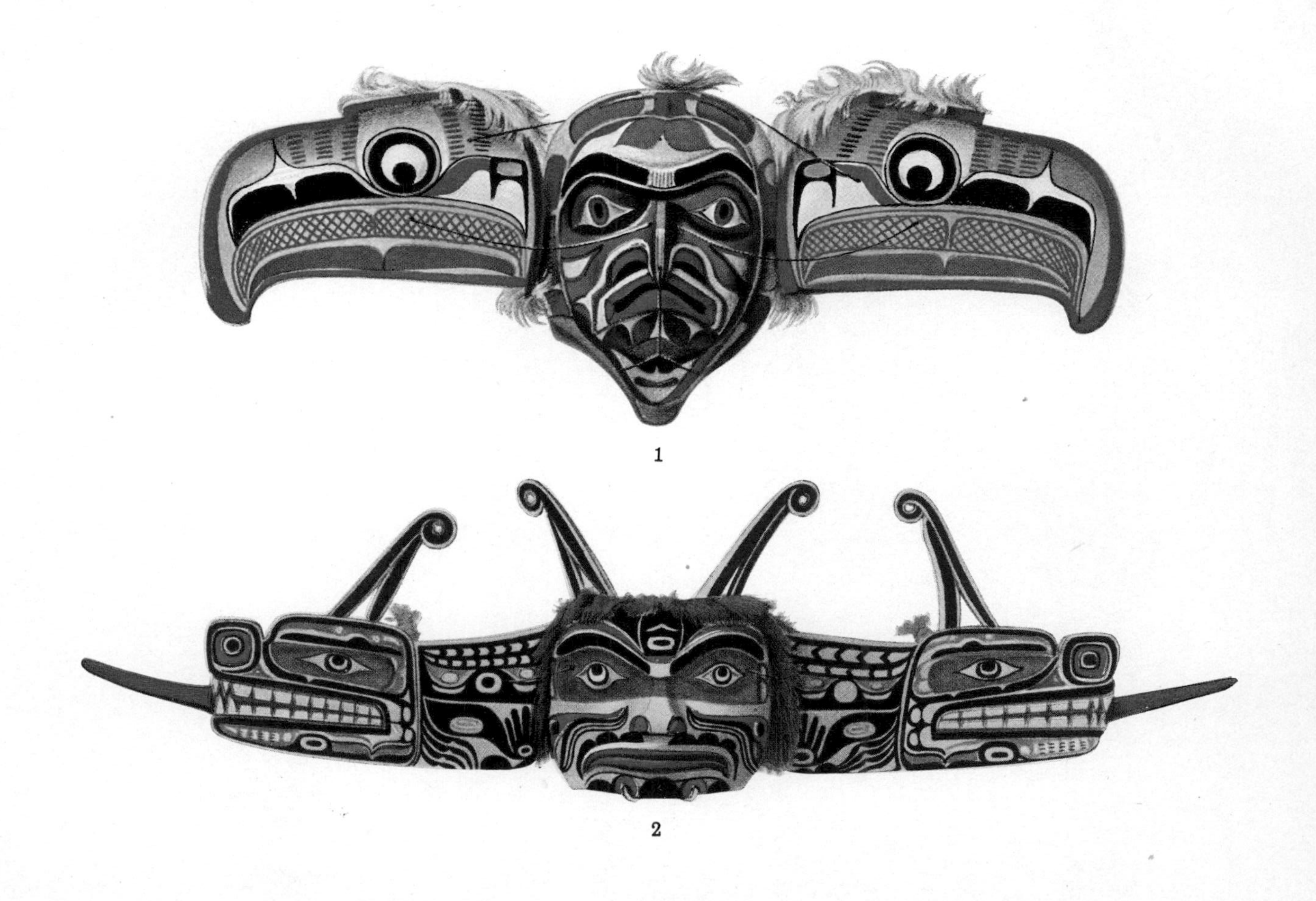
1
2

are regarded as malignant in character, but there are milder beings and gentler forms of inspiration derived from the greater powers, some of these latter types belonging to societies exclusively for women.

The winter ceremonials, accompanying initiations into the secret societies, are the great festivals of the North-West. They are made the occasion for feasts, mask dances of the clan initiates in honour of their totems, potlatches, with their rivalries, and varied forms of social activity and ceremonial purification. The central event, however, is the endowment of the neophyte with the powers which the genius of the society is believed to give. The underlying idea is shamanistic;[5] the initiate must be possessed by the spirit, which is supposed to speak and act through him: he must become as glass for the spirit to enter him, as one myth expressively states. The preparation of the novice is various: sometimes he is sent into the wilderness to seek his revelation; sometimes he is ceremonially killed or entranced; but in every instance seizure by the controlling spirit is the end sought. The Haida call this "the spirit speaking through" the novice; and an account of such possession by the Cannibal Spirit, Ulala, is given by Swanton: "The one who was going to be initiated sat waiting in a definite place. He always belonged to the clan of the host's wife. When the chief had danced around the fire awhile, he threw feathers upon the novice, and a noise was heard in the chief's body. Then the novice fell flat on the ground, and something made a noise inside of him. When that happened, all the 'inspired' said, 'So and so fell on the ground.' A while after he went out of the house. Walala (the same as Ulala) acted through him. The novice was naked; but the spirit-companions wore dancing skirts and cedar-bark rings, and held oval rattles (like those used by shamans) in their hands. Wherever the novice went in, the town people acted as if afraid of him, exclaiming, 'Hoy-hoy-hoy-hoy hiya-ha-ha hoyi!' Wherever he started to go in, the spirit-companions went in first in a crowd. All the uninitiated hid themselves; not so the others. When he passed in through the doorway, he made his sound, 'Ap ap ap!' At the same time the Walala spirit made a noise outside. As he went around the fire he held his face turned upward. In his mouth, too, something (a whistle) sounded. His eyes were turned over and showed the whites." The cannibal initiate among the Kwakiutl is called "hamatsa"; and Boas has recorded (*Report of the United States National Museum*, 1895, pp. 458–62) a number of hamatsa songs which reveal the spirit of the society and its rites better than mere description. The poetry of the North-West tribes, like their mythology, seems pervaded with a spirit of rank gluttony, which naturally finds its most unveiled expression in the cannibal songs:—

Food will be given to me, food will be given to me, because I obtained this magic treasure.
I am swallowing food alive: I eat living men.
I swallow wealth; I swallow the wealth that my father is giving away [in the accompanying Potlatch].

This is an old song, and typical. A touch of sensibility and a grimly imaginative repression of detail is in the following:—

Now I am going to eat.
My face is ghastly pale.
I shall eat what is given to me by Baxbakualanuchsiwae.

Baxbakualanuchsiwae is the Kwakiutl name for the Cannibal Spirit, and the appellation signifies "the first to eat man at the mouth of the river," i. e., in the north, the ocean being conceived as a river running toward the arctic regions. In some of the songs the cosmic significance of the spirit is clearly set forth: —

You will be known all over the world; you will be known all over the world, as far as the edge of the world, you great one who safely returned from the spirits.
You will be known all over the world; you will be known all over the world, as far as the edge of the world. You went to Baxbakualanuchsiwae, and there you first ate dried human flesh.

You were led to his cannibal pole, in the place of honor in his house, and his house is our world.
You were led to his cannibal pole, which is the milky way of our world.
You were led to his cannibal pole at the right-hand side of our world.

From the abode of the Cannibal, the Kwakiutl say, red smoke arises. Sometimes the "cannibal pole" is the rainbow, rather than the Milky Way; but the Cannibal himself is regarded as living at the north end of the world (as is the case with the Titanic beings of many Pacific-Coast myths), and it is quite possible that he is originally a war-god typified by the Aurora Borealis. A Tlingit belief holds that the souls of all who meet a violent death dwell in the heaven-world of the north, ruled by Tahit, who determines those that shall fall in battle, of what sex children shall be born, and whether the mother shall die in child-birth.[10] The Aurora is blood-red when these fighting souls prepare for battle, and the Milky Way is a huge tree-trunk (pole) over which they spring back and forth. Boas is of opinion that the secret societies originated as warrior fraternities among the Kwakiutl, whose two most famed tutelaries are the Cannibal and Winalagilis, the Warrior of the North. Ecstasy is supposed to follow the slaying of a foe; the killing of a slave by the Cannibal Society members is in a sense a celebration of victory, since the slave is war booty; and it is significant that in certain tribes the Cannibals merely hold in their teeth the heads of enemies taken in war.

IV. THE WORLD AND ITS RULERS[11]

The usual primitive conception of the world's form prevails in the North-West. It is flat and round below and surmounted above by a solid firmament in the shape of an inverted bowl. As the people of this region are Coast-Dwellers, Earth is regarded as an island or group of islands floating in the cosmic waters. The Haida have a curious belief that the sky-vault rises and falls at regular intervals, so that the clouds at times strike against the mountains, making a noise which the Indians say they can hear. The world above the firmament is inhabited, and one Haida myth (which closely resembles the Pueblo cosmogony) tells of Raven, escaping from the rising flood in the earth below, boring his way through the firmament and discovering five successive storeys in the world above; a five-row town is the more characteristically North-West conception, given in another version. The Bella Coola believe that there are five worlds, one above the other, two being heaven-worlds, two underworlds, and our Earth the mid-world — an arrangement which is of significance in their theology. Belief in an underworld, and especially in undersea towns and countries, is universal in this region; while the northern tribes all regard the Earth itself as anchored in its mobile foundation by a kind of Atlas, an earth-sustaining Titan. According to the Haida, Sacred-One-Standing-and-Moving, as he is called, is the Earth-Supporter; he himself rests upon a copper box, which, presumably, is conceived as a boat; from his breast rises the Pillar of the Heavens, extending to the sky; his movements are the cause of earthquakes. The Bella Coola, following a myth which is clearly of a South-Coast type, also believe in the Earth-Titan, who is not, however, beneath the world, but sits in the distant east holding a stone bar to which the earth island is fastened by stone ropes; when he shifts his hold, earthquakes occur. The Tsimshian and Tlingit deem the Earth-Sustainer to be a woman. The earth, they say, rests upon a pillar in charge of this Titaness, Old-Woman-Underneath;[7] and when the Raven tries to drive her from the pillar, earthquake follows.

The sun, moon, stars, and clouds are regarded as material things,—sometimes as mechanically connected with the firmament; sometimes as the dwellings of celestial creatures; sometimes, as in the South-West, as masks of these beings.[13] The winds are personified according to their prevailing directions, but there is little trace in the North-West of the four-square conception of the world, amounting to a cult of the Quarters.[31] As might be expected among seafarers, tide-myths are common. Among the southern tribes animal heroes control the movement of the sea, as in the Kwakiutl story of the Mink who stole the tail of the Wolf that owned the tides, and caused them to ebb or flow by raising or lowering it. In the north a different conception prevails: the Haida regard the command of the tide as the possession of an Old Man of the Sea, from whom the ebb and flow were won by the craft of the Raven, who wished to satisfy his gluttony on the life of the tide-flats; the same story is found among the Tlingit, who, however, also believe the tide to issue from and recede into a hole at the north end of the world, an idea which is similar to the Bella Coola notion of an undersea man who twice a day swallows and gives forth the waters.

The universe so conceived is peopled by an uncountable number of spirits or powers, whom the Tlingit call Yek.[3] According to one of Swanton's informants, everything has one principal and several subordinate spirits, "and this idea seems to be reflected in shamans' masks, each of which represents one main spirit and usually contains effigies of several subsidiary spirits as well." There is a spirit on every trail, a spirit in every fire, the world is full of listening ears and gazing eyes — the eyes so conspicuous in the decorative emblems of the North-West. Earth is full and the sea is full of the Keres loosed by Pandora, says Hesiod, and an anonymous Greek poet tells how the air is so dense with them that there is no chink or crevice between them; for the idea is universal to mankind.

Among these spirits appear, up and down the Coast, almost every type of being known to mythology.[2] There are the one-eyed Cyclops, the acephalous giant with eyes in his breast; the bodiless but living heads and talking skulls, sea-serpents, mermen, Circes, the siren-like singers of Haida lore, anthropophagi of many types, Harpy-like birds, giants, dwarfs, treasure-wardens, witches, transformers, werefolk, ghosts, and a multitude of *genii locorum*, to say nothing of magically endowed animals, birds, and fishes. The Haida even have a double nomenclature for the animal kinds; as "Gina teiga" they are creatures of their several sorts, and the proper prey of the hunter; as "Sgana quedas" they are werefolk or man-beings, capable of assisting the human race with their magic might.[40] The Haida make another interesting distinction between the world-powers, classifying them, as their own tribes are divided, into Ravens and Eagles; and they also arrange the ruling potencies in a sort of hierarchy, sky, sea, and land having each its superior and subordinate powers.

The greatest of these potencies is a true divinity, who is named Power-of-the-Shining-Heavens,[6] and who, in a prayer recorded by Swanton, is thus addressed: "Power-of-the-Shining-Heavens, let there be peace upon me; let not my heart be sorry." He is not, however, a deity of popular story, although a legend is told of his incarnation. Born of a cockle-shell which a maiden dug from the beach, he became a mighty getter of food; a picturesque passage tells how he sat "blue, broad and high over the sea"; and at his final departure for heaven, he said, "When the sky looks like my face as my father painted it there will be no wind; in me (i. e., in my days) people will get their food." It is Power-of-the-Shining-Heavens who determines those that are to die, although Wigit, another celestial deity, who is the same as the Raven, is the one who apportions the length of life of the new-born child, according as he draws a long or a short stick from the faggot which he keeps for this purpose. The Tsimshian have a conception of the sky-god similar to that of the Haida, their name for him being Laxha.

The idea of a Fate in the sky-world, deciding the life of men, is common to the northern tribes. Tahit, the Tlingit divinity of this type, has already been mentioned; and the same god (Taxet, "the House Above") is recognized by the Haida, though here he is the one who receives the souls of those slain by violence, rather than the determiner of death. The Bella Coola have an elaborate system of Fates. When Senx creates the new-born child, an assistant deity gives it its individual features, while a birth goddess rocks it in a pre-natal cradle; and this is true also of animals whose skins and flesh are foreordained for the food and clothing of man. Death, according to the Bella Coola, is predestined by the deities who rule over the winter solstice (the season of the great ceremonies): two divinities stand at the ends of a plank, balanced like a seesaw, while the souls of men and animals are collected about them; and as the plank rises or falls, the time of the passing of the souls is decided.

It is among the Bella Coola that the hierarchic arrangement of the world-powers has reached, apparently, the most systematic and conscious form on the North Pacific. As stated above, this tribe separates the universe into five worlds or storeys, two above and two below the earth. In the upper heaven resides Qamaits,[7] who is also called "Our Woman" and "Afraid-of-Nothing." The house of this goddess is in the east of the treeless and wind-swept prairie which forms her domain, and behind her home is the salt-water pond in which she bathes and which forms the abode of the Sisiutl. In the beginning of the world she is said to have waged war against the mountains, who made the world uninhabitable, and to have conquered them and reduced them in height. Qamaits is regarded as a great warrior, but she is not addressed in prayer, and her rare visits to earth cause sickness and death. In the centre of the lower heaven stands the mansion of the gods, called the House of Myths. Senx, the Sun,[13] is master of this house, "the Sacred One" and "Our Father" are his epithets; and it is to him that the Bella Coola pray and make offerings. Almost equal in rank to Senx is Alkuntam, who, with the sun, presided over the creation of man.[70] Alkuntam's mother is described as a Cannibal, who inserts her long snout into the ears of men and sucks out their brains. She seems to be a personification of the mosquito, for in a myth frequent throughout the North-West these insects spring from the ashes to which the Cannibal is reduced in the effort to destroy her.[37] Various inferior gods, including the Fates and the ten deities presiding over the great ceremonies, dwell in the House of Myths; at the rear of it are two rooms, in the first of which lives the Cannibal, organizer of the Cannibal Society, and in the second another ecstasy-giving god: these two are the sons of Senx and Alkuntam. Intercessors and Messengers, Sun Guardians and Sky Guardians (whose business it is to feed the sky continually with firewood), the Flower Goddess, and the Cedar-Bark Goddess are other personages of the Bella Coola pantheon. Four brothers, dwellers in the House of Myths, gave man the arts, teaching him carving and painting, the making of canoes, boxes, and houses, fishing, and hunting.[69] They are continually engaged in carving and painting, and seem to be analogous to the Master Carpenter, who often appears in Haida myths. Earth, in Bella Coola lore, is the home of a multitude of spirits — chiefly Animal Elders — and in the ocean are similar beings, though there seems to be no power corresponding to the Haida Neptune, The-Greatest-One-in-the-Sea. The two underworlds have their own *raison d'être*, the upper one belonging to *revenant* spirits, who are at liberty to return to heaven, whence they may be reborn on earth; and the lower being the abode of those who die a second death, from which there is no release.[18]

V. THE SUN AND THE MOON [13]

The place of sunrise, according to the Bella Coola, is guarded by the Bear of Heaven,[52] a fierce warrior, inspirer of martial zeal in man; and the place of sunset is marked by an enormous pillar which supports the sky. The trail of the Sun is a bridge as wide as the distance between the winter and summer solstices; in summer he walks on the right-hand side of the bridge, in winter on the left; the solstices are "where the sun sits down." Three guardians accompany the Sun on his course, dancing about him; but sometimes he drops his torch, and then an eclipse occurs.

Not many Pacific-Coast tribes have as definite a conception of the Sun as this, and generally speaking the orb of day is of less importance in the myths of the northern than in those of the southern stocks of the North-West. It is conceived both as a living being, which can even be slain, and as a material object — a torch or a mask — carried by a Sun-Bearer. One of the most wide-spread of North-Western legends is a Phaethon-like story of the Mink, son of the Sun, and his adventures with his father's burden, the sun-disk. A woman becomes pregnant from sitting in the Sun's rays; she gives birth to a boy, who grows with marvellous rapidity, and who, even before he can talk, indicates to his mother that he wants a bow and arrows; other children taunt him with having no father, but when his mother tells him that the Sun is his parent, he shoots his arrows into the sky until they form a ladder whereby he climbs to the Sun's house; the father requests the boy to relieve him of the sun-burden, and the boy, carelessly impatient, sweeps away the clouds and approaches the earth, which becomes too hot — the ocean boils, the stones split, and all life is threatened; whereupon the Sun Father casts his offspring back to earth condemning him to take the form of the Mink. In some versions the heating of the world results in such a conflagration that those animal-beings who escape it, by betaking themselves to the sea, are transformed into the men who thereafter people the earth. It is obvious that in these myths we have a special North-Western form of the legend of the Son of the Sun who climbs to the sky, associated with the cataclysm which so frequently separates the Age of Animals from that of Man.

A curious Kwakiutl tradition tells of a Copper given up by the sea and accidentally turned so that the side bearing a pictured countenance lay downward; for ten days the sun failed to rise or shine: then the Copper was laid face upward, and the light again appeared. It would seem from this that copper is associated with the sun. Other myths tell of a hero who marries a copper woman, whose home — an underworld or undersea mansion — is also made of copper. The connexion of the bones of the dead with an abundance of food and mineral wealth would imply that the hero of this tale, Chief Wealthy, is a kind of Pluto. One of the most widely disseminated of North-Western legends, in which the Raven is usually the principal figure, tells of a time when darkness reigned throughout the world. The sun, or daylight, was kept imprisoned in a chest, under the jealous protection of a chieftain. The hero of the story realizes that daylight cannot be obtained by force, so he enters the womb of the chieftain's daughter when she comes to the spring for water; thence he is born, an infant insatiate until he gets possession of the precious box, from which the light is freed. A Salish version makes the Gull the guardian of the chest; the Raven wishes a thorn into the Gull's foot; then he demands light to draw the thorn; and thus day and light are created. Still another tale (which seems to be derived from the South-West) narrates how the Raven bored his way through the sky or persuaded the beings above to break it open, thus permitting sunlight to enter the world below.

The origin of fire[51] is sometimes associated with the sun, as in a Salish account which tells how men lived "as in a dream" without fire until the Sun took pity upon them and gave it to them; but in very many North-Western myths the element is secured, curiously enough, from the ocean — perhaps a reminiscence of submarine volcanoes. Thus another Salish story recounts how the Beaver and the Woodpecker stole fire from the Salmon and gave it to the ghosts; the Mink captured the head of the ghost-chief and received fire as its ransom. Possibly the salmon's red flesh may account for its connexion with the igneous element, but the most plausible explanation of the fire as the gift of the sea is in the popular tale which ascribes its theft to the stag. An old man had a daughter who owned a

wonderful bow and arrow; in the navel of the ocean, a gigantic whirlpool, pieces of wood suitable for kindling were carried about, and when the daughter shot her arrows into this maelstrom the wood was cast ashore, and her father lit a huge fire and became its keeper; but the stag, concealing bark in his hair, entered by craft, lay down by the flame as if to dry himself, caught the spark, and made off with the treasure.

The Sun and the Moon are sometimes described as husband and wife, and the Tlingit say that eclipses are caused by the wife visiting her husband. Again, they are the "eyes of heaven," and it is quite possible that the prominence of eyes and eyelashes in North-Western myth is associated primarily with these heavenly bodies. The Sun's rays are termed his eyelashes; one of the sky-beings recognized by the Haida is called Great Shining Heaven, and a row of little people is said to be suspended, head down, from his eyelashes. The Haida, Kwakiutl, and Tlingit believe that they see in the moon figure a girl with a bucket, carried thither by the Moon; and the Kwakiutl have also a legend of his descent to earth, where he made a rattle and a medicine lodge from an eagle's beak and jaw, and with the power so won created men, who built him a wonderful four-storeyed house, to be his servants. An interesting Tsimshian belief makes the Moon a kind of half-way house to the heavens, so that whoever would enter the sky-world must pass through the Home of the Moon. The Keeper of this abode is Pestilence, and with him are four hermaphrodite dwarfs.[64] When the quester appears, he must cry out to the Keeper, "I wish to be made fair and sound"; then the dwarfs will call, "Come hither, come hither!" If he obeys them, they will kill him; but if he passes on, he is safe.[8] A certain hero found his way to the Moon's House by the frequent mode of the arrow ladder, and was there made pure and white as snow. Finally the Keeper sent him back to the world, with the command: "Harken what you shall teach men when you return to Earth. I rejoice to see men upon the Earth, for otherwise there would be no one to pray to me or to honor me. I need and enjoy your worship. But when you undertake to do evil I will thwart you. Man and wife shall be true to one another; ye shall pray to me; and ye shall not look upon the Moon when attending to nature's needs. I rejoice in your smoke. Ye shall not spend the evening in riotous play. When you undertake to do what I forbid I will deny you." This revelation of the law is a truly primitive mixture of morality and tabu, based upon the *do ut des* relationship of god and man so succinctly expressed in a Haida prayer recorded by Swanton: "I give this to you for a whale; give one to me, Chief."

VI. THE RAVEN CYCLE[48]

The most characteristic feature of the mythology of the North-West is the cycle of legends of which the hero is the Raven — the Yetl of the Northern tribes. Like Coyote in the tales of the interior, Raven is a transformer and a trickster — half demiurge, half clown; and very many of the stories that are told of Coyote reappear almost unchanged with Raven as their hero; he is in fact a littoral and insular substitute for Coyote.

Nevertheless, he is given a character of his own. Like Coyote, he is greedy, selfish, and treacherous, but gluttony rather than licentiousness is his prevailing vice. He is engaged in an insatiable food-quest: "Raven never got full," says a Tlingit teller, "because he had eaten the black spots off of his own toes. He learned about this after having inquired everywhere for some way of bringing such a state about. Then he wandered through all the world in search of things to eat." The journeys of Raven form the chief subject of most of the myths; he travels from place to place, meets animals of every description, and in contests of wit usually succeeds in destroying and eating them or in driving them off and securing their stores of food. As is the case with Coyote, he himself is occasionally overcome, but always manages to make good his escape, even (again like Coyote) returning to life after having been slain. A touch of characteristic humour is added to his portrait by the derisive "Ka, ka," with which he calls back to his opponents as he flies away — frequently through the smoke-hole, to which he owes his blackness, having once been uncomfortably detained in this aperture.

Despite all their ugliness and clownishness, the acts of Raven have a kind of fatefulness attached to them, for their consequence is the establishment of the laws that govern life, alike of men and animals. A Haida epithet for Raven is He-Whose-Voice-is-Obeyed, because whatever he told to happen came to pass, one of his marked traits being that his bare word or even his unexpressed wish is a creative act. In one Haida version there is a suggestion of Genesis in the Raven's creative laconism: "Not long ago no land was to be seen. Then there was a little thing on the ocean. This was all open sea. And Raven sat upon this. He said, 'Become dust.' And it became Earth." The Haida, Swanton says, make a distinction between the events in the first portion of the Raven story — the truly creative acts — and the mad adventures of the later anecdotes: the first division is called "the old man's story," and the chiefs will not allow the young men to laugh while it is being told, hilarity being permissible only during the latter part.

Raven is not, apparently, an object of worship, although it is said that in former times people sometimes left food on the beach for him. Rather he is numbered among those heroes of the past about whom indecorous tales may be narrated without sullying the spirit of reverence which attaches to the regnant gods. One of the most comprehensive of Raven stories — a Tlingit version — states that at the beginning of things there was no daylight; the world was in darkness.[15] In this period lived Raven-at-the-Head-of-Nass, who had in his house the sun, moon, stars, and daylight. With him were two aged men, Old-Man-Who-Foresees-All-Trouble-in-the-World and He-

Who-Knows-Everything-that-Happens, while Old-Woman-Underneath was under the world. Raven-at-the-Head-of-Nass had a sister, who was the mother of many children, but they all died young, the reason, according to the legend, being the jealousy of her brother, who did not wish her to have any male offspring. Advised by Heron, who had already been created, she circumvented his malicious intent by swallowing a red-hot stone, as a consequence of which she gave birth to Yetl, the Raven, who was as hard as rock and so tough that he could not easily be killed. Nascakiyetl (Raven-at-the-Head-of-Nass) thereupon made Raven the head man over the world. Nascakiyetl appears as the true creator in this myth, however, for it is he who brought mankind into existence. He undertook to make people out of a rock and a leaf at the same time, but the rock was slow and the leaf quick; therefore human beings came from the latter. Then the creator showed a leaf to the new race and said, "You see this leaf. You are to be like it. When it falls off the branch and rots there is nothing left of it." And so death came into the world.[16]

A striking Tsimshian myth tells how a woman died in the throes of child-birth; how her child lived in her grave, nourished by her body; how he later ascended to heaven, by means of Woodpecker's wings, and married the Sun's daughter; and how her child by him was cast down to earth and adopted by a chieftain there, but abandoned because the gluttonous infant ate the tribe out of provisions; this child was the Raven. Usually, however, the myth begins abruptly with the wandering Raven. The world is covered with water and Raven is seeking a resting-place. From a bit of flotsam or a rocky islet upon which he alights he creates the earth. His adventures, creative in their consequences rather than in intention, follow. He steals the daylight and the sun, moon, and stars from an old man who keeps them in chests or sacks and who seems to be a kind of personification of primeval night, Raven's mode of theft being to allow himself to be swallowed by the

PLATE XXXIII

Chilkat blanket. The design is interpreted as a Killer Whale motive. Above the lower fringe are two kites in profile. Above these the mouth and teeth of the whale, whose nostrils are central in the mouth. The whale's eyes are just above, the figure between them representing water from the blowhole, which is indicated by the central human face. The body of the whale is denoted by the upper face, the figures on either side of the two faces representing fins. The upper eyes represent the lobes of the whale's tail; the figure between them, the dorsal fin. After *MAM* iii, Plate XXVII.

old man's daughter, from whom he is born again. He steals water from its guardian, the Petrel, and creates the rivers and streams, and he forces the tide-keeper to release the tides. He captures fire from the sea and puts it in wood and stone for the use of man. He seizes and opens the chest containing the fish that are to inhabit the sea, also creating fish by carving their images in wood and vivifying them; or he carries off the Salmon's daughter and throws her into the water, where she becomes the parent of the salmon kind.[41] In addition he enters the belly of a great fish, where he kindles a fire, but his ever-present greed causes him to attack the monster's heart, thereby killing it; he wishes the carcass ashore, and is released by the people who cut up its body. In some versions the walrus is Raven's victim, the story being a special North-West form of the myth of the hero swallowed by the monster, which is found from ocean to ocean in North America. Finally, in various ways he is responsible for the flood which puts an end to the Age of Animal Beings and inaugurates that of Men.[49] A Haida legend repeats the Tlingit tale of the jealous uncle, who is here identified with the personified Raven, Nankilstlas (He-Whose-Voice-is-Obeyed). The sister gives birth to a boy, as a result of swallowing hot stones, but the uncle plots to destroy the child, and puts on his huge hat (the rain-cloud?), from which a flood of water pours forth to cover the earth. The infant transforms himself into Yetl, the Raven, and flies heavenward, while the hat of Nankilstlas rises with the inundation; but when Yetl reaches the sky, he pushes his beak into it and, with his foot upon the hat, presses Nankilstlas back and drowns him. This tale appears in many forms in the North-West, the flood-bringing hat often belonging to the Beaver. After the deluge, the surviving beings of the first age are transformed into animals, human beings are created, with their several languages, and the present order of the world is established — all as in Californian myths. One curious inversion of events, in a Kwakiutl story, tells how the antediluvian wolves, after the subsidence of the flood, took off their wolf-masks and became human beings.[46]

VII. SOULS AND THEIR POWERS

In no section of America is the belief in possession by spirits and spiritistic powers more deeply seated than in the North-West; shamanism is the key to the whole conception of life which animates myth and rite. Scarcely any idea connected with spiritualism is absent: stories of soul-journeys are frequent, while telepathic communication, prophetic forewarnings of death and disaster, and magic cures through spirit aid are a part of the scheme of nature; there are accounts of crystal-gazing, in which all lands and events are revealed in the translucent stone, which recurs again and again as a magic object; and there are tales of houses haunted by shadows and feathers, of talking skulls and bones that are living beings by night, and of children born of the dead, which are only abortively human. There is also a kind of psychology which is well developed among some tribes.[20] The disembodied soul is not a whole or hale being: "Why are you making an uproar, ghosts? You who take away men's reason!" is a fragment of Kwakiutl song; and a certain story tells how a sick girl, whose heart was painted, went insane because the colouring was applied too strongly. The Haida have three words for "soul"; two of these apply to the incarnate soul, and are regarded as synonyms; the third designates the disembodied soul, although the latter is not the same as the ghost, which is marked by a distinct name. A curious feature of Haida psychology is that the word for mind is the same as that for throat — less strange, perhaps, when we reflect upon the importance of speech in any description of the mind's most distinctive power, that of reason.

The origin of death is explained in many ways.[16] A Tlingit story has been given, and a Nootka tale tells of a chieftain who kept eternal life in a chest; men tried to steal it from him and almost succeeded, but their final failure doomed them to mortality. A significant Wikeno (Kwakiutl) myth recounts the descent from heaven of two ancestral beings who wished to endow men with everlasting life, but a little bird wished death into the world: "Where will I dwell," he asked, "if ye always live? I would build my nest in your graves and warm me." The two offered to die for four days, and then arise from the tomb; but the bird was not satisfied, so finally they concluded to pass away and be born again as children. After their death they ascended to heaven, whence they beheld men mourning them; whereupon they transformed themselves into drops of blood, carried downward by the wind. Sleeping women inbreathe these drops and thence bear children.

The abodes of the dead are variously placed.[10] Beneath the sea is one of the most frequent, and there is an interesting story telling of the waters parting and the ghost, in the form of a butterfly, rising before a young man who sat fasting beside the waters. The Haida believe that the drowned go to live with the killer whales; those who perish by violence pass to Taxet's house in the sky, whence rebirth is difficult, though not impossible for an adventurous soul; while those who die in the sickbed pass to the Land of Souls — a shore land, beyond the waters, with innumerable inlets, each with its town, just as in their own country. Although the dying could decide for themselves to what town in the Land of Souls they wished their own spirits to go, there is occasionally, nevertheless, an apportionment of the future abode on a moral basis; thus, in Tlingit myth, after Nascakiyetl has created men, he decrees that when the souls of the dead come before him, he will ask: "What were you killed for? What was your life in the world?" Destiny is determined by the answer; the good go to a Paradise above; the wicked and witches are reborn as dogs and other animals. The Bella Coola assign the dead to the two lower worlds, from the upper of which alone is return possible through reincarnation. An old woman who, in trance, had seen the spirit world, described it as stretching along the banks of a sandy river. When it is summer in the world above, it is winter in the earth below (an idea which appears in Hopi conceptions of the world order); and the ghosts, too, are said to walk with their heads downward. They speak a different language from that in the world above, and each soul receives a new name on entering the lower realms.

The ever-recurring and ever-pathetic story of the dead wife and of her grieving lord's quest for her — the tale of Orpheus and Eurydice — appears in various forms in the North-West.[53] Sometimes it is the story of a vain journey, without even a sight of the beloved, though the Land of the Dead be discovered; sometimes the searcher is sent back with gifts, but not with the one sought; sometimes the legend is made a part of the incident of the carved wife — the bereaved husband making a statue of the lost spouse, which may show a dim and troubled life, as if her soul were seeking to break through to him; and again it is the true Orphean tale with the partial success, the tabu broken through anxiety or love, and the spirit wife receding once more to the lower world. It is not necessary to invoke the theory of borrowings for such a tale as this; the elemental fact of human grief and yearning for the departed will explain it. Doubtless a similar universality in human nature and a similar likeness in human experiences will account for the multitude of other conceptions which make the mythic universe of the men of the Old World and the men of the New fundamentally and essentially one.

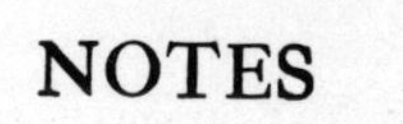

NOTES

NOTES

1. SPELLING. — *Kabluna* (*kavdlunâk*, *qadluna* are variants) is the Eskimo's word for "white man"; *kablunait* is the plural. Similarly, *tornit* (*tunnit*) is the plural of *tunek* (*tuniq*, *tunnek*); *tornait* of *tornak* (*tornaq*, *tornat*); *angakut* of *angakok*, other forms of which are *angekkok*, *angatkuk*, *angaqok*, etc. These differences in spelling are due in part to dialectic variations in Eskimo speech, in part to the phonetic symbols adopted by investigators. Their number in a language comparatively so stable as is Eskimo illustrates the difficulties which beset the writer on American Indian subjects in choosing proper representation for the sounds of aboriginal words. These difficulties arise from a number of causes. In the first place, aboriginal tongues, having no written forms, are extremely plastic in their phonetics. Dialects of the same language vary from tribe to tribe; within a single tribe different clans or families show dialectic peculiarities; while individual pronunciation varies not only from man to man but from time to time. In the second place, the printed records vary in every conceivable fashion. Divergent systems of transliteration are employed by different investigators, publications, and ethnological bureaux; translations from French and Spanish have introduced foreign forms into English; usage changes for old words from early to later times; and finally few men whose writings are extensive adhere consistently to chosen forms; indeed, not infrequently the form for the same word varies in an identical writing. In formulating rules of spelling for a general work, a number of considerations call for regard. First, it is undesirable even to seek to follow the phonetic niceties represented by the more elaborate transliterative systems, which represent sound-material unknown in English or other European tongues. Aboriginal phonetics is important to the student of linguistics; it is unessential to the student of mythology; and it is detrimental to that literary interest which seeks to make the mythological conceptions available to the general reader; for the mythologist or the literary artist a symbol conforming to the genius of his own tongue is the prime desideratum. In the light of these considerations the following rules of spelling for aboriginal terms have been adopted for the present work:

(1) In the spelling of the names of tribes and linguistic stocks the usage of the *Handbook of American Indians North of Mexico* (30

BBE) has been chosen as the standard. The same form (as a rule) is used for the singular and for the collective plural; also, frequently, for the adjective.

(2) Where a term has attained, through considerable usage, a frequent English form, especially if this has literary (as distinct from scientific) sanction, such form is preferred. This rule is necessarily loose and difficult to apply. Thus the term *manito*, which has many variants, is almost equally well known under the French form *manitou*, for which there is the warrant of geographical usage. Again, *Manabozho* is preferred to *Nanabozho* (used for the title of the article in *30 BBE*) for the reason that *Manabozho* is more widely employed in non-technical works.

(3) In adaptations of transliterations all special characters are rendered by an approximation in the Anglo-Roman alphabet and all except the most familiar diacritical marks are omitted. This is an arbitrary rule, but in a literary sense it seems to be the only one possible.

(4) Vowels have the Italian values. Thus *tipi* replaces the older form *teepee*. Changes of this type are not altogether fortunate, but the trend of usage is clearly in this direction. In a few cases (notably from Longfellow's *Hiawatha*) older literary forms are kept.

2. Monsters. — Monstrous beings and races occur in the mythology of every American tribe, and with little variation in type. There are: (a) manlike monsters, including giants, dwarfs, cannibals, and hermaphrodites; (b) animal monsters, bird monsters, water monsters, etc.; (c) composite and malformed creatures, such as one-eyed giants, headless bodies and bodiless heads, skeletons, persons half stone, one-legged, double-headed, and flint-armoured beings, harpies, witches, ogres, etc. As a rule, these creatures are in the nature of folk-lore beings or bogies. In some cases they have a clear-cut cosmologic or cosmogonic significance; thus, myths of Titans and Stone Giants are usually cosmogonic in meaning; legends of serpents and giant birds occur especially in descriptions of atmospheric and meteorological phenomena; the story of the hero swallowed by a monster is usually in connexion with the origin of animals. See Notes 9, 12, 19, 32, 36, 37, 38, 40, 41, 49, 50, 64. *The principal text references are:* Ch. I. i (cf. Rink, Nos. 54, 55). — Ch. II. vii. — Ch. IV. vi (Mooney [b], pp. 325–49). — Ch. V. ii (Jetté [a]). — Ch. VII. ii (Lowie [b], Nos. 10–15, 31; Teit [a], Nos. 29–30; Powell, pp. 45–49). — Ch. VIII. i, ii. — Ch. IX. vi (Cushing [c], Lummis, Voth). — Ch. XI. iv.

3. Animism. — The Eskimo's Inue belong to that universal group of elementary powers commonly called "animistic," though some writers object to this term on the ground that it implies a clear-cut

spiritism in aboriginal conceptions (cf. Clodd, Hartland, et al., in *Transactions of the Third International Congress for the History of Religions*, Oxford, 1908; Marett, *Threshold of Religion*, London, 1909; Lang, "Preanimistic Religion," in *Contemporary Review*, 1909; see also, Powell, *1 ARBE*, pp. 29–33). Taking *anima* in its primitive sense of "breath," "wind," no other word seems really preferable as a description of the ancient notion of indwelling lives or powers in all things, — "panzoism," if that term be preferred. The American forms under which this idea appears are many, *manito*, *orenda*, and *wakanda* being the terms most widely known. The application of the words varies somewhat. (a) *Manito*, the Algonquian name, designates not only impersonal powers, but frequently personified beings. (b) *Orenda*, an Iroquoian term, is applied to powers, considered as attributes. (c) *Wakanda*, the Siouan designation, connotes, in the main, impersonal powers, though it is sometimes used of individuals, and apparently also for the collective or pantheistic power of the world as a whole. Usually in Indian religion there is some sense of the difference between a personality as a cause and its power as an attribute, but in myths the tendency is naturally toward lively personification. Cf. Note 4. *Text references:* Ch. I. iii (*inua*, plural *inue*, is cognate with *inuk*, "man," and means "its man" or "owner"). — Ch. II. iii (BRINTON [a], p. 62; HEWITT [a], pp. 134, 197, note *a; JR* v. 157, 175; lxvi. 233 ff.). — Ch. V. ii (JETTÉ [a], [b]); iv (FLETCHER and LA FLESCHE, pp. 597–99). — Ch. VIII. i (MATTHEWS [a]). — Ch. X. v. — Ch. XI. ii (BOAS [f]; SWANTON [a], chh. viii, ix); iv (SWANTON [e], p. 452).

4. MEDICINE. — The term "medicine" has come to be applied in a technical sense to objects and practices controlling the animistic powers of nature, as the Indian conceives them. "Medicine" is, therefore, in the nature of private magical property. It may exist in the form of a song or spell known to the owner, in the shape of a symbol with which he adorns his body or his possessions, or in the guise of a material object which is kept in the "medicine-bag," in the "sacred bundle," or it may be present in some other fetishistic form. It may appear in a "medicine dance" or ceremony, or in a system of rites and practices known to a "medicine lodge" or society. The essential idea varies from fetishism to symbolism. On the fetishistic level is the regard for objects themselves as sacred and powerful, having the nature of charms or talismans. Such fetishes may be personal belongings — the contents of the "medicine-bag," etc. (sometimes even subject to barter) — or they may be tribal or cult possessions, such as the sacred poles and sacred bundles of the Plains tribes, or the fetish images, masks, and *sacra* of the Pueblo and North-West stocks; a not infrequent form is the sacred

drum or rattle. Symbolism is rarely absent even from the fetishistic object, and usually the fetish is lost in the symbol, which is the token of the union of interests between its owner and his "helper," or tutelary. It is in this latter sense, as designating the relation between the owner and his guardian or tutelary, that the Algonquian term "totem" is most used. The totem is not a thing materially owned, as is the fetish; it is a spirit or power, frequently an animal-being, which has been revealed to the individual in vision as his tutelary, or which has come to him by descent, his whole clan participating in the right. The Tornait of the Eskimo belong to this latter class; the word "totem," however, is not used in connexion with such guardians, and indeed is now mainly restricted to the tutelaries of clans, right to which passes by inheritance. *Text references:* Ch. I. iii. — Ch. V. v (De Smet, pp. 1068–69). — Ch. VII. vi. — Ch. IX. iii (Cushing [a]; M. C. Stevenson [c]; Fewkes, *passim*).

5. Shamanism. — The terms applied to Indian priests and wonder-workers are many, but they do not always bear a clear distinction of meaning. The word "shaman" is especially common in works on the Eskimo and the North-West tribes; "medicine-man" is used very largely with reference to the eastern and central tribes; "priest" is particularly frequent in descriptions of Pueblo institutions. In general, the following definitions represent the distinctions implied:

(a) *Shaman.* A wonder-worker and healer directly inspired by a "medicine"-power, or group of such powers, "shamanism" signifying the recognition of possession by powers or spirits as the primary *modus operandi* in all the essential relations between man and the world-powers.

(b) *Medicine-Man, Doctor.* Not radically different from shaman, though the employment of naturalistic methods of healing, such as the use of herbal medicines, the sweat-bath, crude surgery, etc., is often implied, especially where the term "doctor" is employed.

(c) *Priest.* One authorized to preside over the celebration of traditional ceremonies. Such persons must be initiates in the society or body owning the rites, which are sometimes shamanistic in character, though more frequently the shaman is supposed to get his powers as the result of an individual experience.

Every degree of relationship is found for these offices. In tribes of low social organization (e. g. the Eskimo and the Californians) the shaman is the man of religious importance; in tribes with well developed traditional rites the priestly character is frequently combined with the shamanistic (as in the North-West); still other peoples (as the Pueblo) elevate the priest far above the medicine-man, who may be simply a doctor, or medical practitioner, or who, on the shamanistic level, may be regarded as a witch or wizard, with an evil reputation. The tendency toward formal and hereditary priesthoods is naturally confined to the socially advanced peoples (of whom the Creek and Pueblo are examples), while "mystery" societies and ceremonies, the aim of which is spiritual and physical well-being, and often material prosperity in addition, occur in all but the lowest tribal stocks. *The principal text references are:* Ch. I. iii. — Ch. IV. vii (MOONEY [b], p. 392). — Ch. VI. vi (G. A. DORSEY [b], pp. 46–49). — Ch. VII. vii (MOONEY [d], for translated songs, pp. 958–1012, 1052–55). — Ch. VIII. iv (MATTHEWS [a], "Natinesthani," "The Great Shell of Kintyel"; [c], "The Visionary," "So," "The Stricken Twins," "The Whirling Logs"; JAMES STEVENSON, "The Floating Logs," "The Brothers"; cf. GODDARD [a], Nos. 18, 22, 23). — Ch. IX. iii (M. C. STEVENSON [c], pp. 32–33, 62–67, 289–90; FEWKES [a], pp. 310–11). — Ch. X. ii. — Ch. XI. iii (SWANTON [a], pp. 163–64; BOAS [f]).

6. GREAT SPIRIT. — The Greenlander's Tornarsuk is another example of the *fainéant* supreme being for which Lang so astutely argued (*Myth, Ritual and Religion*, 3d ed., London, 1901, Introd.), citing Atahocan and Kiehtan as early instances. Writers on American Indian religion frequently assert that the idea of a "Great Spirit" is not aboriginal (cf. Brinton [a], p. 69; Fewkes [f], p. 688). Thus Morgan (Appendix B, sect. 62): "The beautiful and elevating conception of the Great Spirit watching over his red children from the heavens and pleased with their good deeds, their prayers, and their sacrifices, has been known to the Indians only since the Gospel of Christ was preached to them." Yet in the section just preceding, on Indian councils, he says: "The master of ceremonies, again rising to his feet, filled and lighted the pipe of peace from his own fire. Drawing three whiffs, one after the other, he blew the first toward the zenith, the second toward the ground, and the third toward the Sun. By the first act he returned thanks to the Great Spirit for the preservation of his life during the past year, and for being permitted to be present at this council. By the second, he returned thanks to his Mother, the Earth, for her various productions which had ministered to his sustenance. And by the third, he returned thanks to the Sun for his never-failing light, ever shining upon all." No one questions the aboriginal character of this pipe ritual, its pre-Columbian antiquity, or its universality (cf., e. g., De Smet, *Index*, "Calumet"); and equally there is abundant evidence that Morgan's interpretation of its meaning is correct: the first whiff is directed to the Great Spirit, the Master of Life, whose abode is the upper heaven. Very commonly this being is referred to as "Father Heaven," and invariably he is regarded as beneficent and all-seeing, and as "pleased with the good deeds of his red children." The only truth in the as-

sertion that the Indian's idea of a Great Spirit is derived from white missionaries is that the Indian conception is less anthropomorphic than that commonly entertained by an unphilosophic white (though it is one that would have been readily comprehended by the Stoics of antiquity, and would not have seemed remote to the thought of Plato or Aristotle). If a separation of ideas be made, and the Biblical epithet "Heavenly Father" be understood for what it doubtless originally was, a name for a being who was (1) the sky-throned ruler of the world, and (2) its creator, a better comprehension of Indian ideas will follow; for it is rare in America to find Father Heaven in the creative *rôle* (the Zuñi and Californian cosmogonies are exceptions). It is partly for this reason that he plays so small a part in myth; he belongs to religion rather than to mythology proper. Lang is probably wrong in regarding the Supreme Being as *fainéant*, a do-nothing; occasionally the Indian expresses himself to this effect, but no one can follow the detail of Indian ritual without being impressed by his intense reverence for the Master of Life and his firm conviction in his goodness. That the Indian more often addresses prayer to the intermediaries between himself and the ruler of the high heaven, or makes offerings to them, is as natural as that a Latin should approach his familiar saints. A particularly good bit of evidence, if more were needed, for the aboriginal character of the heaven-god is given by Swanton ([a], p. 14). "The-Chief-Above" is the Haida name for God, as taught them by the missionaries; "Power-of-the-Shining-Heavens" is their aboriginal Zeus: "Some Masset people once fell to comparing The-Chief-Above with Power-of-the-Shining-Heavens in my presence. They said they were not the same. The idea that I formed of their attitude toward this being was, that, just as human beings could 'receive power' or 'be possessed' by supernatural beings, and supernatural beings could receive power from other supernatural beings, so the whole of the latter got theirs in the last analysis from the Power-of-the-Shining-Heavens." The same idea of a hierarchy in space with the heaven-god at its summit appears in the ritual of the Midewiwin, in the Hako Ceremony, and in the Olelbis myth. These are only a few instances from different parts of the continent; there are numerous other examples, for wherever the breath of Heaven is identified with the descent of life from on high, and the light of day is regarded as the symbol of blessings bestowed upon man, the conception of Father Heaven, the Great Spirit, is found. See Notes 13, 15, 25, 26, 30, 34, 63. *Text references:* Ch. I. iii (cf. Boas [a], p. 583: "The Central Eskimo . . . believe in the Tornait of the old Greenlanders, while the Tornarsuk (i. e. the great Tornaq of the latter) is unknown to them"). — Ch. II. ii (*JR* xxxiii. 225); iv (see Note

28). — Ch. V. iii (FLETCHER, pp. 27, 216, 243); iv (MORICE [b]; DE SMET, p. 936; EASTMAN [b], pp. 4–6). — Ch. VII. v. — Ch. IX. iii (M. C. STEVENSON [c], pp. 22–24). — Ch. X. iii (KROEBER [c], pp. 184, 348; [e], p. 94; GODDARD [b], No. 1; GATSCHET [c], p. 140; CURTIN [a]; [b], pp. 39–45). — Ch. XI. iv (SWANTON [a], pp. 13–15, 190; [b], p. 284; [c], pp. 26–30).

7. GODDESSES. — There are several occurrences in North American mythology of a goddess as the supremely important deity of a pantheon. Nerrivik, "Food Dish," is the epithet given by Rasmussen to the divinity called Arnarksuagsak, "Old Woman," by Rink, Arnakuagsak by Thalbitzer, and Sedna and Nuliajoq by Boas. Her character as the ruler of sea-food sufficiently accounts for her importance in the far North. A somewhat similar goddess appears among the North-West Coast tribes; she is the owner of the food animals of the sea which come forth from a chest that is always full (Boas [g], xx. 7). Foam Woman, the Haida ancestral divinity, is perhaps the same personage. The Bella Coola deity, Qamaits, who dwells in the highest heaven, belongs to a different class; apparently she is the one example of a truly supreme being in feminine form in North America, for she is a cosmic creator and ruler rather than a food-giver; on the other hand, the fact that she has a lake of salt water as her bath may indicate a marine origin. In the South-West goddesses are important both in cosmogony and in cult. There is no higher personage in the Navaho pantheon than Estsanatlehi, and her doublets in Pueblo myth enjoy nearly equal rank. Again it is her association with food-giving from which this goddess derives her status, for in the South-West the Great Goddess of the West presides over the region whence come the fructifying rains. Cosmogonic Titanesses occur in many myths, in almost every instance as personifications of the Earth, which in turn is almost universally recognized as the great giver of life and food. See Notes 34, 35, 43. *Text references:* Ch. I. iii (cf. RASMUSSEN, pp. 142, 151; RINK, p. 40; BOAS [a], pp. 583–87). — Ch. VI. vii. — Ch. VIII. i (MATTHEWS [a]). — Ch. IX. v (see Note 35 for references), vi. — Ch. XI. ii: The marine god of the North-West Coast is a masculine equivalent of Sedna (BOAS [f], p. 374; [g], *passim*); iv (BOAS [j], pp. 27–28).

8. THE PERILOUS WAY. — Descriptions of the dangers besetting the journey to the Land of Spirits, whether for the dead souls that are to return no more, the adventurous spirits of shamans, or the still more daring heroes of myth who seek to traverse the way in the flesh, are found in practically all Indian mythologies. The analogues with Old-World myth will occur to every reader. The special perils associated with the moon in journeys to the sky-world are interestingly similar in Greenland and on the North-West Coast. Cf. Notes

10, 42, 53. *Text references:* Ch. I. iii, iv. — Ch. III. vii (*JR* vi. 181; Converse, pp. 51–52; De Smet, p. 382). — Ch. VII. vi. — Ch. VIII. ii. — Ch. X. vi. — Ch. XI. v.

9. Water Monsters. — There is a striking similarity in the personnel of the mythic sea-powers among the Eskimo and on the North-West Coast, nearly every type of being in the one group having its equivalent in the other — mermen, phantom boatmen, mouth-prowed and living boats, and, most curious of all, the Fire-People. Nowhere else in North America, except for the Nova Scotian Micmac, has any considerable body of marine myths been preserved. Everywhere, however, there are well defined groups of under-water beings, sometimes reptilian or piscine, sometimes human in form. Among the important myths in which under-water monsters are conspicuous are: (a) the common legend of a hero swallowed by a huge fish or other creature (not always a water-being; cf. Note 41), from whose body he cuts his way to freedom, or is otherwise released; (b) the flood story, in which the hero's brother, or companion, is dragged down to death by water monsters which cause the deluge when the hero takes revenge upon them (see Note 49); (c) the South-Western myth of the subterranean water monster who threatens to inundate the world in revenge for the theft of his two children, and who is appeased only by the sacrifice of other two children or of a youth and a maid (cf. Note 29). *Text references:* Ch. I. iv (Rink, p. 46; Rasmussen, pp. 307–08). — Ch. II. vii. — Ch. III. iv. — Ch. IV. vi (Mooney [b], pp. 320, 349). — Ch. V. ix (J. O. Dorsey [d], p. 538; Fletcher and La Flesche, p. 63). — Ch. VIII. i. — Ch. X. iv.

10. Abode of the Dead. — Cavernous underworlds, houses in heaven, the remotely terrene village beyond the river, or the earthly town on the other side of the western sea are all included in the American's mythic homes of the dead. In the Forest and Plains regions a western village, situated beyond a river which the living cannot cross even if they win to its banks, is perhaps the most common idea, though throughout this portion of the continent the Milky Way is the "Pathway of Souls." In the South-West the subterranean land of souls is usual, and on the Pacific the spirits of the dead are supposed to fare to oversea isles; but nowhere is there great consistency of belief. The idea of divergent destinies for different classes of people finds what is doubtless its most primitive form in the notion that those who die by violence, especially in war, and women in child-birth have a separate abode in the after-life. The Eskimo, Tlingit, and Haida place the dwelling-place of persons so dying in the skies, and it is interesting to note that the same distinction was observed by the Aztecs, who believed that men dying

in battle, persons sacrificed to the gods (except underworld gods), and women dead in child-birth all went to the house of the Sun, others to a subterranean Hades. The Norse Valhalla is a European counterpart, though it is difficult to say whether the American instances had any clearly conscious moral value in view. The Zuñi make a similar discrimination for a different reason, the souls of the members of the Bow priesthood going to the sky-world, but only because of their office as archers and hence as lightning and storm-bringers. A further Zuñi distinction limits entrance to the Dance-House of the Gods, inside a mountain, to initiates in the Kotikili. A moral value is clear enough in the Tlingit conception of the judgement of Nascakiyetl, and in this and other North-West notions it appears that the possibility of rebirth is more or less dependent upon the abode attained, though it may be doubted whether the mode of death is not really the final crux even here, the mutilated and slain finding reincarnation more difficult. One of the most ghastly of North American superstitions is the belief that scalped men lead a shadowy life (ghosts rather than spirits) about the scenes where they met their fate, but this properly belongs to ghost-lore. See Notes 8, 47, 53. *Text references:* Ch. I. iv. — Ch. III. vii (Perrot, *Mémoire*, English translation in Blair, i. 39; *JR* x. 153–55; Rand, Nos. x, xxxv, xlii; Hoffman [b], pp. 118, 206). — Ch. IX. iii, vii (M. C. Stevenson [c], p. 66). — Ch. X. vii. — Ch. XI. iii (Boas [g], xxv. 3); vii (Boas [g], xv. 1; [j], pp. 37–38; Swanton [a], pp. 34–36; [d], p. 81).

11. The Cosmos. — All American tribes recognize a world above the heavens and a world below the earth. Many of them multiply these worlds. Thus the Bella Coola believe in a five-storey universe, with two worlds above and two below our earth. Four worlds above and four below is a recorded Chippewa and Mandan conception, and in the South-West the four-storey underworld is the common idea. It is of extraordinary interest to find the same belief in Greenland. The fact that the earth is divided into quarters, in the Indian's orientations, and that offerings are made to the tutelaries of the quarters in nearly every ritual, may be the analogy which has suggested the multiplication of the upper and under worlds, but it is at least curious that the conception of a storeyed universe should be so definite among the Northern and North-Western Coast peoples, with whom the cult of the Quarters is absent or rare. The notion of a series of upper worlds appears in the rituals of some Plains tribes; thus the Pawnee recognize a "circle" of the Visions (apparently the level of the clouds), a "circle" of the Sun, and the still higher "circle" of Father Heaven; and the Chippewa believe in a series of powers dwelling in successive skyward regions. It is possible that the analogy

of this upper-world series has been symmetrically extended to the world below, and yet it is the four-fold underworld that recurs most definitely. See Notes 6, 10, 31, 66, 68. *Text references:* Ch. I. iv. — Ch. II. v (*45 BBE*, p. 21; Mooney [b], pp. 236–40, 430, note 1). — Ch. V. ix (J. O. Dorsey [d], pp. 520–26; Fletcher and La Flesche, pp. 134–41; cf. J. O. Dorsey [b], [e]). — Ch. VI. ii (Will and Spinden); iii (G. A. Dorsey [e], note 2, states that "Tirawahut" refers to "the entire heavens and everything contained therein"; Tahirussawichi, the Chaui priest quoted in *22 ARBE*, part 2, p. 29, said: "Awahokshu is that place . . . where Tirawa-atius, the mighty power, dwells. Below are the lesser powers, to whom man can appeal directly, whom he can see and hear and feel, and who can come near him. Tirawahut is the great circle in the sky where the lesser powers dwell."). — Ch. VII. iii (Teit [a], p. 19, and Nos. 2, 10, 27, 28; [b], p. 337; Mason, No. 26). — Ch. VIII. ii. — Ch. IX. ii (Cushing [b]; M. C. Stevenson [b], [c]; Fewkes [a], [e]). — Ch. XI. iv (Swanton [a], ch. ii; [e], pp. 451–60; Boas [j], pp. 27–37).

12. Ghosts. — The ghost or wraith of the dead is generally conceived to be different from the soul, and is closely associated with the material remains of the dead. Animated skeletons, talking skulls, and scalped men are forms in which the dead are seen in their former haunts; sometimes shadows and whistling wraiths represent the departed. In a group of curious myths the dead appear as living and beautiful by night, but as skeletons by day. Marriages between the dead and the living, with the special tabu that the offspring shall not touch the earth, occur in several instances, as the Pawnee tale (Ch. VI. v) or the Klickitat story of the girl with the ghost lover (Ch. VII. vi), for which Boas gives a Bella Coola parallel in which the offspring of the marriage is a living head that sinks into the earth so soon as it is inadvertently allowed to touch the ground ([g], xxii. 17). See Notes 8, 20, 53. *Text references:* Ch. I. iv. — Ch. VI. v (G. A. Dorsey [g], Nos. 10, 34; [e], No. 20; Grinnell [c], "The Ghost Wife"). — Ch. VII. vi (see Notes 20, 53 for references). — Ch. VIII. i.

13. Sun and Moon. — The sun is the most universally venerated aboriginal deity of North America; and this is true to such an extent that the Indians have been reasonably designated "Sun-Worshippers." Nevertheless, there are many tribes where the sun-cult is unimportant, but on the other hand, there are well defined regions where it becomes paramount, particularly among the southern agricultural peoples. The moon is regarded as a powerful being, yet quite frequently as a baneful or dangerous one (cf. Note 8). Usually the sun is masculine and the moon feminine, though in a curious exception

(Cherokee, Yuchi) the sun is the woman and the moon the man; in the South-West and North-West both are generally described as masculine. Husband and wife is the usual relation of the pair, and the Tlingit explain the sun's eclipse as due to a visit of wife to husband; but in a myth which is told by both Eskimo and Cherokee, sun and moon are brother and sister, guilty of incest (cf. Note 17). In the South-West, and more or less on the Pacific Coast, the sun and moon are conceived as material objects borne across the sky by carriers, and the yearly variations of the sun's path are explained by mechanical means — poles by which the Sun-Carrier ascends to a sky-bridge, which he crosses and which is as broad as the ecliptic, etc. While the sun is a great deity — "Father Sun" — he is seldom truly supreme; he is the loftiest and most powerful of the intermediaries between man and Father Heaven, and both he and the moon are invariably created beings. Sometimes, however, the sun seems to be regarded as the life of heaven itself, and as its immortal life; this is clearly the meaning of the Modoc myth of Kumush, the creator, who annihilated by fire the beautiful blue man, but could not destroy the golden disk which was his life, and so used it to transform himself into the empyrean (Curtin [b], pp. 39–45). Doublet suns and moons, in the worlds below and above our own, are frequently mentioned; often the sun is supposed to pass to the underworld after the day's journey is completed, in order to return to his starting-point; possibly the notion of an underworld whose days and seasons interchange with ours (a Pacific-Coast notion) is due to the assumption that the sun alternates in the world above and the world below. Among the important sun-myths are: (a) the well-nigh universal story of the hero or heroic brothers whose father is the sun or some celestial person closely akin to the sun (cf. Note 44); (b) the Phaethon myth, common in the North-West, in which the Mink is permitted to carry the sun-disk and, as a consequence, causes a conflagration; (c) the related legend of the creation of the sun, which, until it is properly elevated, overheats the world; (d) traditions of the theft of the sun, which are variants of the Promethean tale of the theft of fire (cf. Note 51). *Text references:* Ch. I. v (Rink, No. 35; Rasmussen, pp. 173–74; Boas [a], pp. 597–98). — Ch. II. vi (*JR* vi. 223; Converse, pp. 48–51; Hoffman [b], p. 209). — Ch. III. i, vi (for the "Ball-Carrier" story, see Schoolcraft [a], part iii, p. 318; Hoffman [b], pp. 223–38). — Ch. IV. ii (Mooney [a], p. 340; [b], pp. 239–49, 256; Lafitau, i. 167–68); iv. — Ch. V. vi (Fletcher, pp. 30, 134–40; for Sun-Dance references see Note 39). — Ch. VI. iii, iv (G. A. Dorsey [e], No. 16; [h], Nos. 14, 15; [a], pp. 212–13; Dorsey and Kroeber, Nos. 134–38; Simms, *FCM* ii, No. 17; Mooney [c], pp. 238–39; Lowie [a], No. 18). — Ch. VII.

iii (Teit [a], No. 8; Lowie [b], No. 8; Powell, p. 24); iv (Powell, pp. 52–56). — Ch. VIII. ii, iii (James Stevenson, pp. 275–76); v (Russell, p. 251; Lumholtz [a], i. 295 ff., 311; [b], pp. 357 ff.). — Ch. IX. iii, iv, vi, vii. — Ch. X. vi (Goddard [c], Nos. 3, 4). — Ch. XI. iv, v (Boas [j], pp. 28–36; [g], v. 2; viii. 2; xv. 1; xviii. 1; xx. 1, 1a; xxii. 1, 19; xxiii. 1, 3, 4; Swanton [a], p. 14. For the Mink cycle: Boas [g], xvii. 1; xviii. 7; xx. 2, 3; xxi. 2; xxii. 1, 2; Boas and Hunt [b], pp. 80–163; Boas [j], p. 95).

14. Stars and Constellations. — No group of myths is more uniform on the North American continent than those relating to constellations; usually they are extremely simple. The Great Bear, Pleiades, and Orion's Belt are the groups most frequently mentioned; and the commonest tale is of a chase in which the pursued runs up into the sky, followed by eternally unsuccessful pursuers. This myth seems quite natural as a description of Ursa Major — the four feet of a fleeing quadruped (usually in America, too, a bear), and three pursuers. Equally obvious is the conception of Pleiades as a group of dancers, or of Corona Borealis as a council circle. Of the stars, Venus, as morning star, which is generally regarded as a young warrior, messenger of the Sun, and the Pole Star, believed by the Pawnee to be the chief of the night skies, are the only ones widely individualized in myth. The Milky Way is universally the Spirit Path. Star-myths are especially abundant and vivid among the Pawnee (cf. Ch. VI. iii). *Text references:* Ch. I. v (Rink, pp. 48, 232; Boas [a], p. 636; Rasmussen, pp. 176–77, 320). — Ch. II. vi (Converse, pp. 53–63; Smith, pp. 80–81; cf. E. G. Squier, *American Review*, new series, ii, 1848, p. 256). — Ch. V. viii (Fletcher, p. 129. G. A. Dorsey [e] states that the Evening Star is of higher rank among the Pawnee. The legend of Poïa has been made the subject of an opera by Arthur Nevin and Randolph Hartley. The version here followed is that of Walter McClintock, *The Old North Trail*, ch. xxxviii. Other versions are Grinnell [a], pp. 93–103; Wissler and Duvall, ii. 4. The story belongs to a wide-spread type; cf. G. A. Dorsey [e], No. 16, and note 117; [f], Nos. 14, 15; Note 36, *infra.* For constellation-myths see Fletcher, p. 234; Lowie [a], p. 177; McClintock, pp. 488–90; J. O. Dorsey [d], p. 517). — Ch. VI. i (Morice, *Transactions of the Canadian Institute*, v. 28–32); iii (G. A. Dorsey [e], No. 1, and Introd.); iv (see Note 13 for references); v (G. A. Dorsey [e], No. 2; [g], No. 35). — Ch. VIII. v (Lumholtz [a], pp. 298, 311, 361, 436). — Ch. IX. iii, vi.

15. Cosmogony. — American cosmogonies ought perhaps to be described as cosmic myths of migration and transformation. In a few instances (notably the Zuñi cosmogony and some Californian legends) there is a true creation *ex nihilo;* but the typical stories

are of sky-world beings who descend to the waters beneath and magically expand a bit of soil into earth, or the characteristically southern tale of an ascent of the First People from an underground abode, followed by a series of adventures and transformations which make the world habitable. The cataclysmic destruction of the first inhabitants by flood, sometimes by fire, is universal in one form or another; it is succeeded by the transformation of the survivors of the antediluvian age into animals or men, by the creation of the present human race, and frequently by a confusion of tongues and a dispersion of peoples. There can be no doubt as to the truly aboriginal character of all these episodes, though in some instances the native stories have clearly been coloured by knowledge of their Biblical analogues. See Notes 6, 11, 31, 40, 49, 57, 70. *Text references:* Ch. I. v. — Ch. III. i (Hewitt [a] gives an Onondaga, a Seneca, and a Mohawk version of the Iroquois genesis, the first of these being the one here mainly followed; other authorities on Iroquoian cosmogony are: Hewitt [b] and "Cosmogonic Gods of the Iroquois," in *Proceedings of the American Association for the Advancement of Science*, 1895; Brébeuf, on the Huron, *JR* x. 127–39; Brinton [a], pp. 53–62; Parkman [a], pp. lxxv–lxxvii; Hale, *JAFL* i. 177–83; Converse, pp. 31–36; Schoolcraft [a], part iii, p. 314; and, for the Cherokee, Mooney [b], pp. 239 ff.); ii (important sources on Algonquian cosmogony are: *JR*, Index, "Manabozho"; Charlevoix, *Journal historique*, Paris, 1840; Perrot, *Mêmoire*, English translation in Blair, i. 23–272; Schoolcraft [a], i.; Brinton [d]; Rand; Hoffman [a], [b]; A. F. Chamberlain, "Nanibozhu amongst the Otchipwe, Mississagas, and other Algonkian Tribes," in *JAFL* iv. 193–213). — Ch. IV. iv (Mooney [b], pp. 239–49; Gatschet [a], [b]; Bushnell [a], [b]). — Ch. V. ix (Fletcher and La Flesche, pp. 63, 570). — Ch. VI. i (Morice, "Three Carrier Myths," in *Transactions of the Canadian Institute*, v.; Lofthouse, "Chipewyan Stories," in ib. x.); ii (Lowie [a], Nos. 1, 2, 22, et al.; Will and Spinden, pp. 138–41; Fletcher and La Flesche; J. O. Dorsey [a]; Eastman [b]; see Mooney [c], p. 152, for a Kiowa instance); iii (G. A. Dorsey [e], No. 1, is the authority chiefly followed here for one of the finest of American cosmogonic myths); vii (G. A. Dorsey [b], pp. 34–49). — Ch. VIII. ii (Matthews [a]); v (Russell, pp. 206–38; cf. Lumholtz [a], pp. 296 ff.; [b], pp. 357 ff.); vi (Bourke [b]; Kroeber [b]; DuBois; James, chh. xii, xiv). — Ch. IX. vi (M. C. Stevenson [b], pp. 26–69; Voth, Nos. 14, 15, 37); vii (M. C. Stevenson [a], [c]; Cushing [b], [c]). — Ch. X. iii. — Ch. XI. vi (see Note 48 for references).

16. Origin of Death. — Stories of the origin of death are found from Greenland to Mexico. What may be termed the Northern type

represents a debate between two demiurgic beings, one arguing for the bestowal of immortal life upon the human race, the other insisting that men must die; sometimes the choice is determined by reason, sometimes by divination maliciously influenced. A South-Western type tells of a first death, caused by witchcraft or malice, which sets the law. On the Pacific Coast the two motives are combined; the first death is followed by a debate as to whether death shall be lasting or temporary; and often a grim reprisal upon the person (usually Coyote) who decrees the permanency of death appears in the fact that it is his child who is the second victim. Other motives are occasionally found. These myths seem to be typically American. *Text references:* Ch. I. v (RASMUSSEN, pp. 99–102; RINK, p. 41). — Ch. III. vii (*JR* vi. 159). — Ch. VI. v (G. A. DORSEY [e], No. 2; [g], No. 35; WISSLER and DUVALL, i. 3, 4; DORSEY and KROEBER, No. 41). — Ch. VII. v (POWELL, pp. 44–45; cf. LOWIE [b], No. 2). — Ch. VIII. ii (MATTHEWS [a], "Origin Myth"); v (GODDARD [a], No. 1); vi (DuBOIS). — Ch. IX. vi. — Ch. X. iii (DIXON [d], Nos. 1, 2); vii (KROEBER [c], Nos. 9, 12, 17, 38; DIXON [b], No. 7; [c], No. 2; FRACHTENBERG [a], No. 5; CURTIN [a], pp. 163–74; [b], pp. 60, 68; GODDARD [b], p. 76). — Ch. XI. vi (BOAS [g], xxiv. 1); vii (BOAS [g], xiii. 2, 6b).

17. MISCEGENATION. — Stories of supernatural and unnatural marriages and sexual unions are very common. Sometimes they are legends of the maid who marries a sky-being and gives birth to a son who becomes a notable hero; sometimes a young man weds a supernatural girl, as the Thunder's Daughter or the Snake Girl, thereby winning secrets and powers which make him a great theurgist; sometimes it is the marriage of the dead and the living; frequently the union of women with animals is the theme, and a story found the length of the continent tells of a girl rendered pregnant by a dog, giving birth to children who become human when she steals their dog disguises. This legend is frequently told with the episode found in the tradition of the incest of sun-brother and moon-sister: the girl is approached by night and succeeds in identifying her lover only by smearing him with paint or ashes. See Notes 13, 32, 50. *Text references:* Ch. I. v (RASMUSSEN, p. 104; BOAS [a], p. 637; RINK, No. 148). — Ch. II. vi (MOONEY [b], pp. 345–47). — Ch. IV. ii (MOONEY [b], p. 256). — Ch. VI. i (MORICE, *Transactions of the Canadian Institute*, v. 28–32). — Ch. IX. vii (M. C. STEVENSON [c], p. 32; CUSHING [b], pp. 399 ff.). — Ch. X. v (DIXON [c], No. 7; [b], Nos. 1, 2; CURTIN [a], "Two Sisters").

18. TRANSMIGRATION. — Belief in the possibility of rebirth is general, although some tribes think that only young children may be reincarnated, and certain of the Californians who practise crema-

tion bury the bodies of children that they may the more easily be reborn. Again, rebirth is apparently easier for souls that have passed to the underworld than for those whose abode is the sky. The Bella Coola allow no reincarnation for those who have died a second death and passed to the lowest underworld. See Notes 10, 20, 46. *Text references:* Ch. I. vi (RASMUSSEN, p. 116). — Ch. V. ii, viii (J. O. DORSEY [d], p. 508). — Ch. XI. iv (BOAS [j], pp. 27–28).

19. CANNIBALS AND MAN-EATERS. — Cannibals occur in many stories. Three forms of anthropophagy, practised until recently by North American tribes, are to be distinguished: (1) the devouring of a portion of the body, especially the heart or blood, of a slain warrior in order to obtain his strength or courage (cf. *JR* i. 268; De Smet, p. 249); (2) ceremonial cannibalism, especially in the North-West, where it is associated with the Cannibal Society; (3) cannibalism for food. This latter form, except under stress of famine, is rare in recent times, although archaeological evidence indicates that it was formerly wide-spread. The ill repute borne by the Tonkawa is an indication of the feeling against the custom, which, on the whole, the cannibal-myths substantiate (cf. Ch. VIII. v). In many legends the anthropophagist's wife appears as a protector of his prospective victim, as in European tales of ogres, and it is interesting to find the "Fe fo fum" episode of English folk-lore recurring in numerous stories. The grisly "cannibal babe" tradition of the Eskimo has a kind of parallel in a Montana tale (Ch. VII. vi); while the obverse motive, of the old female cannibal who lures children to their destruction, is a frequent North-West story. Legends of man-eating bears and lions are to be expected; the man-devouring bird of the Plateau region is more difficult to explain, though the idea may be connected with that of the Thunderbird and the destructiveness of lightning. See Notes 2, 37. *Text references:* Ch. I. vi (RASMUSSEN, p. 186; RINK, No. 39). — Ch. IV. vii. — Ch. VII. iii (TEIT [a], No. 8); vi (O. D. WHEELER, *The Trail of Lewis and Clark*, New York, 1904, ii. 74; cf. McDERMOTT, No. 5, where Coyote takes vengeance on the babe). — Ch. VIII. ii. — Ch. XI. ii (BOAS [f], pp. 372–73; [g], xxii. 5, 6, 7; [j], pp. 83–90; BOAS and HUNT [a]); iii (BOAS [f], pp. 394–466; [g], xv. 9; xvii. 8, 9; xx. 8; SWANTON [a], ch. xi).

20. NAMES AND SOULS. — Ghosts and souls are very generally distinguished. The disembodied soul, or spirit, is mythically conceived as related to fire and wind, and as transiently human in form, sometimes as a manikin. Names also have a kind of personality. Individuals believed to be the reincarnation of one dead are given the same appellation as that borne by him, and Curtin tells a story of a babe that persistently cried until called by the right name

([b], p. 6). A curious custom of renaming a living man after a dead chief, that the character and traits of the departed may not be lost, is described by the Jesuit Fathers (*JR* xxii. 289; xxvi. 155–63). See Notes 12, 18, 53. *Text references:* Ch. I. vi (Stefánsson, pp. 395–400). — Ch. III. v (De Smet, pp. 1047–53). — Ch. V. ii. — Ch. VII. vi (Lowie [b], Nos. 38, 39; Teit [b], pp. 342, 358; [d], p. 611). — Ch. XI. iii (Boas [f], pp. 418 ff.; [j], p. 37); vii (Boas [f], p. 482; [g], xiii. 2, 6; Swanton [a], p. 34).

21. Ordeals. — Ordeals may be classified as follows: (1) initiation trials and tortures, of which flogging and fasting are the commonest methods; (2) trials of a warrior's fortitude, in the forms of torture of captives, expiatory sacrifices and purifications of men setting out on the war-path, and fulfilment of a vow for deliverance from peril or evil; the famous Sun-Dance tortures belong to the latter class; body scarring and the offering of finger-joints are frequent modes of expiation; (3) punishment for crime, especially murder; (4) mourning customs involving mutilation and hardship, particularly severe for widows; (5) duels, especially the magical duels of shamans, which range from satirical song-duels to contests of skill resulting in degradation or even death for the defeated. *Text references:* Ch. I. vi (Rasmussen, p. 312). — Ch. V. vi. — Ch. IX. iv. — Ch. X. vi (Frachtenberg [a], No. 4).

22. Orphans and Poor Boys. — Tales of orphans and poor boys who are neglected and persecuted form a whole body of literature, second in extent only to the "Trickster-Transformer" stories. The return of the hero, after a journey to some beneficent god, who often is his father, and his subsequent elevation to power, as a chief or medicine-man, are recurrent motives. The whole group might be called Whittington stories, but there are many variations. *Text references:* Ch. I. vi. — Ch. IV. vii. — Ch. VI. vii (G. A. Dorsey [e] makes a class of "Boy Hero" stories, many of them tales of orphans). — Ch. VIII. iv.

23. The Five Nations, or tribes of the original Iroquois Confederacy, included the Mohawk, Oneida, Onondaga, Cayuga, and Seneca; later the Tuscarora were admitted, whence the league is also called the Six Nations.

24. Agriculture. — Pumpkins, squash, beans, sweet potatoes, and tobacco are other crops cultivated in various localities by the aborigines. Wild rice and the seeds of grasses were gathered; roots and wild fruits were eaten; in the maple-tree zone maple sugar is a native food, and particularly in the far West acorn meal forms an important article of aboriginal diet. It seems certain that the Algonquians came from the north and learned agriculture of the southern nations, especially the Iroquois. The northern Algonquians —

Montagnais, etc. — practised no agriculture when the Jesuits began missionary work among them, though the cultivation of maize was well established among the New England tribes before the appearance of the Colonists. The introduction of maize among the Chippewa is remembered in the myth of Mondamin (cf. BRINTON [d], ch. vi, and PERROT, *Mémoire*, ch. iv, English translation in BLAIR, i). The Omaha, Navaho, and a number of other tribes among whom agriculture is recent have traditions or myths recording the way in which they first learned it. See Notes 35, 39. *Text references:* Ch. II. i. — Ch. III. ii. — Ch. V. i. — Ch. IX. i.

25. ARESKOUI. — Lafitau, i. 126, 132, 145, discusses Areskoui, or Agriskoue, whom he regards as an American reminiscence of the Greek Ares. This seems to be the primary ground for the assertion that Areskoui is a god of war, though it is to a degree borne out by the nature of the allusions to him in the *Jesuit Relations*, especially Jogues's letter (*JR* xxxix. 219). The members of the Huron mission, who had a better chance to understand this deity, evidently considered him a supreme being, or Great Spirit; cf. with the passage quoted in the text, from *JR* xxxiii. 225, the similar statement in xxxix. 13: "And certainly they have not only the perception of a divinity, but also a name which in their dangers they invoke, without knowing its true significance, — recommending themselves *Ignoto Deo* with these words, *Airsekui Sutanditenr*, the last of which may be translated by *miserere nobis*." Morgan, Appendix B, sect. 62, says: "Areskoui, the God of War, is more evidently a Sun God. Most of the worship now given to the Great Spirit belongs historically to Areskoui." This seems to concede the case; Areskoui is, like Atahocan, a name for the Great Spirit, addressed in times of peril by an epithet, the "Saviour." Cf. Note 6. *Text reference:* Ch. II. ii.

26. OKI. — The Huron Oki is regarded by Brinton ([a], p. 64) as of Algonquian origin. A Powhatan Oke, Okeus, is mentioned by Captain John Smith, and a few other traces of it are found in Algonquian sources. Lafitau, i. 126, calls "Okki" a Huron god, and so it appears in the early *Relations* (*JR* v. 257; viii, 109–10; x. 49, 195), though Nipinoukhe and Pipounoukhe (*JR* v. 173) are Montagnais. It is not certain whether *oki* is a term belonging to the same class as *manito*, or whether it is the proper name of a supreme being, as Lang regarded it (*Myth, Ritual and Religion*, 3d ed., London, 1901, Introd.). *Text reference:* Ch. II. iii.

27. STONES. — Stones are of great importance in both Indian ritual and myth; they are regarded as magically endowed, and a not infrequent notion is that if potent stones be broken they will bleed like flesh. Their principal ceremonial uses are four in number. (1) The

sweat-bath — a universal North American institution, used for healing and purification, and regarded as capable of effecting magical transformations — consists of a small hut, large enough for the body of the patient, which is filled with steam by means of water thrown upon heated stones. (2) Stone fetishes, particularly nodules crudely representing animals, which are sometimes partly shaped by hand, form one of the commonest types of personal "medicine" (cf. especially Cushing [a]). (3) Stones of a special kind are frequently used symbolically. This is particularly true in the South-West, where crystal, turquoise, and black stones are symbols of light, the blue sky, and night. The magic properties of white stones and crystals appear in myths from many quarters: it is with crystal that the Eskimo youth slays the Tunek (see p. 3); a crystal is in the head of the Horned Serpent (cf. Note 50); a suggestion of crystal-gazing is in the Comox myth recorded by Boas ([g], viii. 10), where the serpent gives a transparent stone to a man who thereupon falls as if dead, while the stone leads his soul through all lands. (4) Rocks *in situ* are venerated for various reasons, as seats of power or as natural altars. Mythic themes in which stones are important include: (1) stories of the placing of fire in flint and quartz; (2) stories of "Flint" and the Stone Giants; (3) "Travelling Rock" stories; (4) stories of red-hot rocks hurled by giants — apparently volcanic myths; (5) stories of magic crystals and jewels; (6) cosmogonies with a stone as the earth kernel; and (7) stories of living beings changed into rocks, though sometimes only a part of the body is so transformed. See Notes 31, 32, 37, 38, 62. *Text references:* Ch. II. iii, vii. — Ch. V. ix (FLETCHER and LA FLESCHE, pp. 570–71). — Ch. VI. ii (FLETCHER and LA FLESCHE, pp. 565–71: the name of the Omaha "Pebble Society," *Inkugthi athin*, means literally, "they who have the translucent pebble"); iii (G. A. DORSEY [e], No. 1). — Ch. VII. iii. — Ch. VIII. i, ii, iii. — Ch. IX. iii.

28. KITSHI MANITO. — This term is apparently the original after which the English "Great Spirit" is formed, and Hoffman [a] renders "Kitshi Manido" as "Great Spirit." This is a Chippewa form; the Menominee "Kisha Manido" and "Masha Manido" he translates "Great Mystery" or "Great Unknown." *53 BBE*, p. 143, note, states: "The word *manido* is defined by Baraga as 'spirit, ghost.' The following explanation of the word . . . was given by Rev. J. A. Gilfillan: *Kijie Manido*, literally, 'he who has his origin from no one but himself, the Uncreated God.'" De Smet, *passim*, employs "Great Spirit." The case for a spirit supreme over the evil forces of nature is not so clear as that for the beneficent Great Spirit, although there is some early evidence of Algonquian provenience that points strongly in this direction. Thus Le Jeune in the early

Relation of 1634 writes: "Besides these foundations of things good, they recognize a Manitou, whom we may call the devil. They regard him as the origin of evil; it is true that they do not attribute great malice to the Manitou, but to his wife, who is a real she-devil. The husband does not hate men" (*JR* vi. 175). The wife of Manitou, we are informed, is "the cause of all the diseases which are in the world" (cf. p. 189); and it is possible that she is the Titaness who was cast down from heaven, as the eastern cosmogonies tell, and from whose body both beneficent and maleficent forces arise. Mother Earth is, on the whole, beneficent, although Indian thought fluctuatingly attributes to her the fostering of noxious underworld powers. Bacqueville de la Potherie, *Histoire de l'Amérique septentrionale*, Paris, 1753, i. 121 ff., says of the northern Algonquians, with whom he was associated, that they recognized a Good Spirit, *Quichemanitou*, and an evil, *Matchimanitou*, but the latter is clearly the name for a "medicine spirit," magical rather than evil. The same statement is probably true with regard to the Abnaki Matsi Niouask which Abbé Maurault contrasts with the good Ketsi Niouask (*Histoire des Abenakis*, Quebec, 1866, pp. 18–19); and we may suppose it to have been the original force of the Potawatomi distinction between Kchemnito, "goodness itself," and Mchemnito, "wickedness personified," recorded by De Smet, p. 1079. The devil is less a moral being than a physiological condition, at least in his aboriginal status (cf. the Hadui episode in Iroquoian cosmogony, Hewitt [a], pp. 197–201, 232–36, 333–35). Mitche Manito is described in the Hiawatha myth as a serpent, — a universal symbol. The Menomince have a name "Matshehawaituk" (Hoffman [b], p. 225) for a similar being. See Notes 3, 6. *Text reference:* Ch. II. iv.

29. Human Sacrifice. — Human sacrifice, in one form or another, appears in every part of aboriginal America. It is necessary to distinguish, however, sporadic propitiations from customary and ritualistic offering of human life. The latter, north of Mexico, is rare. (1) The sacrifice of captives taken in war, frequently with burning and other tortures, was partly in the nature of an act of vengeance and a trial of fortitude, partly a propitiation of the Manes of the dead; captives made by a war-party were much more likely to be spared if it had suffered no casualties. The tearing out and eating of the heart of a slain enemy or sacrificed captive was not unusual, the idea being that the eater thus receives the courage of the slain man (cf. *JR* i. 268). The symbolism of the heart as the seat of life and strength occurs in numberless mythic forms and reaches its extreme consequences in the Mexican human sacrifices, the usual form of which consisted in opening the breast and drawing forth the heart of the victim. Possibly the mythic references to this form of offering,

occurring in the South-West (cf. M. C. Stevenson [b], pp. 34, 39, 45, 47), point to a like custom, more or less remote. (2) The sacrifice of children, especially orphans, is not uncommon. A number of instances are mentioned in the Creek migration-legend (cf. Ch. IV. vii); in the cosmogonies of the Pueblo Indians there are references to the sacrifice of children to water monsters, a rite obviously related to the Nahuatlan offering of children to the *tlaloque*, or water-gods; the myth also appears among the Piman-Yuman tribes, and doubtless refers to the same practice. De Smet mentions a Columbia River instance of a child offered to the Manes of one of its companions (De Smet, p. 559). (3) The sacrifice of slaves, especially in the rites of the Cannibal Society, prevailed until recently on the North-West Coast, and is mentioned in the myths of this region. (4) The most notable instance of ritualistic sacrifice is that of the Skidi Pawnee, who formerly offered a female captive to the Morning Star in an annual ceremony for the fertilization of the maize fields. — See Notes 9, 19, 21, 58. *Text references:* Ch. II. iv (*JR* xxxix. 219). — Ch. IV. iv, vii (Gatschet [a]). — Ch. V. i (De Smet, pp. 977–88, gives an account of the sacrifice of a Sioux girl by the Skidi Pawnee). — Ch. VIII. ii, vi (DuBois, p. 184; Bourke [b], p. 188; Russell, pp. 215–17). — Ch. IX. iv, v, vi, vii (M. C. Stevenson [b], pp. 34, 45, 47, 67; [c], pp. 21, 30, 46, 61, 176; Cushing [b], p. 429).

30. The Calumet and Tobacco Rites. — The use of tobacco is of American origin. As smoked in pipes it is North American, cigars and cigarettes being the common forms in Latin portions of the continent. The Navaho, Pueblo, and other South-Western peoples generally employ cigarettes both for smoking and for ritualistic use, though the pipe is not unknown to them. The ritual of the ceremonial pipe, or calumet, is the most important of all North American religious forms, and is certainly ancient, elaborate pipes being among the most interesting objects recovered from prehistoric mounds. The rite is essentially a formal address to the world-powers; its use in councils and other formal meetings naturally made the pipe a symbol of peace, as the tomahawk was a token of war. Cf. Notes 6, 31, 63. *Text references:* Ch. II. iv, v (cf. De Smet, pp. 394, 681, 1008–11, and Index). — Ch. V. iv (Fletcher and La Flesche, p. 599). — Ch. VI. vii. — Ch. VIII. i, v.

31. The World-Quarters and Colour-Symbolism. — No idea more constantly influences Indian rites than that of the fourfold division of the earth's surface, in conjunction with the conception of a world above and a world below. The four quarters, together with the upper and the under worlds, form a sixfold partition of the cosmos, affording a kind of natural classification of the presiding

world-powers, to whom, accordingly, sacrifice is successively made and prayers addressed, as in the calumet ritual. The addition of colour-symbolism, each of the quarters having a colour of its own, forms the basis for a highly complex ritualism; for objects of all kinds — stones, shells, flowers, birds, animals, and maize of different colours — are devoted to the quarter having a colour in some sense analogous. In the South-West the Navaho and Pueblo Indians employ a sixfold colour-symbolism, with a consequent elaboration of the related forms. There is, however, no uniformity in the distribution of the colours to the several regions, the system varying from tribe to tribe, while in some cases two systems are employed by the same tribe (see *30 BBE*, "Color Symbolism," with table). In addition to the Quarters, the Above, and the Below, the Here, or Middle Place, which typifies the centre of the cosmos, is of ceremonial and (especially in the South-West) of mythic importance. As in the Old World, the Middle Place is often termed the "Navel" of the earth. The most usual form of naming the directions is after the prevailing winds, and sometimes seven winds are mentioned for the seven cardinal points (cf. *JR* xxxiii. 227). Settled communities, however, employ names derived from physical characteristics (cf. Cushing [b], p. 356); in the South-West names of directions are apparently related in part to bodily orientation: thus, "East is always 'the before' with the Zuñi" (M. C. Stevenson [b], p. 63). It may be taken as certain that the division of the horizon by four points, naming the directions, is fundamentally based upon the fact that man is a four-square animal: "The earliest orientation in space, among Indo-Germanic peoples," says Schrader (*Indogermanische Altertumskunde*, Strassburg, 1901, p. 371), "arose from the fact that man turned his face to the rising sun and thereupon designated the East as 'the before,' the West as 'the behind,' the South as 'the right,' and the North as 'the left.'" Evidence from Semitic tongues indicates that a similar system prevailed among the early desert dwellers of Arabia. In America orientation to the rising sun is abundantly illustrated in the sun rituals and shrines, and to some degree in burials. Colour-symbolism, too, points in the same direction, the white or red of dawn being the hue ordinarily assigned to the east. See Notes 11, 13, 30, 66, 68. *Text references:* Ch. II. v (De Smet, p. 1083; Converse, p. 38). — Ch. III. ii. — Ch. IV. iv (Gatschet [a], p. 244; Bushnell [a], p. 30; [b], p. 526). — Ch. V. ix (J. O. Dorsey [d], pp. 523–33; McClintock, p. 266). — Ch. VI. vii. — Ch. VIII. i, ii, iii. — Ch. IX. ii (Fewkes [a], [e]; M. C. Stevenson [b], [c]; Cushing [b], pp. 369–70). — Ch. XI. iv.

32. Thunderers. — The well-nigh universal American conception of the thunder is that it is caused by a bird or brood of birds — the

Thunderbirds. Sometimes the Thunderbird is described as huge, carrying a lake of water on his back and flashing lightnings from his eyes; sometimes as small, like some ordinary bird in appearance — even the humming-bird occurring as an analogy. Very often the being is the "medicine" or tutelary of one who has seen him in vision, and Thunderbird effigies are common among the Plains tribes. Almost the only tribal groups unacquainted with the concept are the Iroquois, in the East, whose Dew Eagle is related to the Thunderbird idea, and some of the tribes of the far West and the South-West, such as the Zuñi, who regard the thunder as made by the gaming stones rolled by the celestial Rain-Makers and the lightning as the arrows of celestial Archers. It is notable that a huge man-devouring bird appears in the mythologies of the South-Western peoples, from whose lore the Thunderbird is absent. See Notes 2, 27, 33, 50. *Text references:* Ch. II. vi (Converse, pp. 36–44; *JR* v. 223; x. 45, and note 3; Schoolcraft [b], part iii, p. 322). — Ch. V. ix (De Smet, pp. 936, 945; Fletcher and La Flesche, pp. 122–26). — Ch. VI. iii. The belief that stone axes, arrow-heads, and celts are "thunderstones" or lightning-bolts is world-wide (cf. C. Blinkenberg, *The Thunderweapon in Religion and Folklore*, Cambridge, 1911). The cult of the lightning in almost its Roman form, i. e. the erection of bidentalia, was practised by the Peruvians (Garcilasso de la Vega, *Royal Commentaries*, book ii, ch. i); and a similar suggestion is found in the Struck-by-Lightning Fraternity of the Zuñi (M. C. Stevenson [c]). The Omaha have a "Thunder Society" (Fletcher and La Flesche, p. 133), whose talisman is a black stone — suggestive enough of the black baetyl brought to Rome, 205 b. c., as an image of Rhea-Cybele, or of the hoary sanctity of the Black Stone of Mecca. — Ch. VII. iii, iv (Lowie [b], p. 231; Powell, p. 26). — Ch. VIII. iv (Matthews [a], pp. 265–75; [c], pp. 143–45). — Ch. IX. i, iii (M. C. Stevenson [c], pp. 65, 177, 308, 413). — Ch. X. v (Frachtenberg [a], No. 2); vi (Dixon [c], No. 3; Kroeber [c], p. 186). — Ch. XI. ii (Swanton [e], p. 454; Boas [j], p. 47; [g], *passim*).

33. Rip Van Winkle. — In a note to *Rip Van Winkle*, Irving describes an Indian goddess of the Catskills who presides over the clouds, controls the winds and the rains, and is clearly a meteorological genius. She may be a thunder spirit also, for the incident of the gnomes playing at ninepins, and so producing the thunder, has a parallel in the Zuñi Rain-Makers, who cause the thunder by a similar celestial game with rolling stones. The incident of foreshortened time, years being passed in the illusion of a brief space, occurs in several stories of visits to the Thunder; but this is a common theme in tales of guestship with all kinds of supernatural beings. *Text*

references: Ch. II. vi (Mooney [b], pp. 345–47). — Ch. III. vi. — Ch. IV. v (Mooney [b], p. 324). — Ch. VII. ii (J. H. Williams, *The Mountain that Was God*, Tacoma, 1910).

34. Mother Earth. — The personification of the Earth, as the mother of life and the giver of food, is a feature of the universal mythology of mankind. It prevails everywhere in North America, except among the Eskimo, where the conception is replaced by that of the under-sea woman, Food Dish, and on the North-West Coast, where sea deities again are the important food-givers, and the under-world woman is no more than a subterranean Titaness. In many localities the myth of the marriage of the Sky or Sun with the Earth is clearly expressed, as is to be expected of the most natural of all allegories. The notion that the dead are buried to be born again from the womb of Earth is found in America as in the Old World (cf. A. Dieterich, *Mutter Erde*, Berlin, 1905); and there is more than one trace of the belief in an orifice by which the dead descend into the body of Earth and from which souls ascend to be reborn. De Smet (p. 1378) mentions a cavern in the Yellowstone region which the Indians named "the place of coming-out and going-in of under-ground spirits," and the South-Western notion of the Sipapu is an instance in point; other examples appear in the mythologies of the Creek, Kiowa, and Mandan. In the South-West, where large ground-nesting spiders abound, the Spider Woman seems to be a mythic incarnation of the earth; though elsewhere, very generally, this insect is associated with aerial ascents to and descents from the sky, by means of web-hung baskets, and Spider itself is often masculine. In the Forest and Plains regions the conception of the life of the earth as due to a Titaness, fallen from heaven, is the common one; and the magic Grandmother who appears in so many hero-myths is certainly in some cases a personification of the earth. See Notes 7, 11, 18, 28, 35, 43, 70. *Text references:* Ch. II. vii (Hewitt [a], p. 138). — Ch. V. vii (Fletcher, pp. 31, 190, 721, *et passim;* Fletcher and La Flesche, pp. 376 ff.; cf. Fletcher, "A Study of Omaha Indian Music," in *Archæological and Ethnological Papers*, Peabody Museum, 1893, i; H. B. Alexander, *The Mystery of Life*, Chicago, 1913). — Ch. VI. ii (J. O. Dorsey [d], p. 513). — Ch. VIII. v, vi. — Ch. IX. iii, vii (M. C. Stevenson [b], p. 22; Cushing [b], p. 379; Fewkes [f], p. 688).

35. Corn Spirits. — Spirits of the maize and other cultivated plants are prominent figures in the mythologies of all the agricultural peoples. Ordinarily they are feminine, the Algonquian Mondamin being an exception. Corn, Squash, and Bean form a maiden triad in Iroquois lore, and in the South-West there is a whole group of maiden Corn Spirits. Hopi girls of marriageable age wear their hair in two

whorls at the sides of the head, imitating the squash blossom, which is with them the symbol of fertility. As a rule Corn Spirits are far more vital in ritual than in myth. Ears of maize are important as *sacra* or fetishes in numerous rites, especially in the South-West and among the Pawnee, who show many South-Western affinities; ears and grains of different colours are conspicuous in the symbolism of the world-quarters; blades and stalks are often employed in adorning altars; and corn meal [maize flour] is in constant use in South-Western ceremonial. A similarly ritualistic use is made of other plants. In the South-West the creation of men from ears of maize is a frequent incident. See Notes 7, 24, 31, 34, 39. *Text references:* Ch. II. vii (Converse, pp. 63–66; Smith, p. 52). — Ch. III. i (*JR* x. 139), viii. — Ch. IV. iv (Mooney [b], pp. 242–49). — Ch. V. vii (Fletcher). — Ch. VI. iii (G. A. Dorsey [h], Nos. 3–7; cf. [e], No. 4), vii. — Ch. VIII. i, ii. — Ch. IX. iii, v, vi (Fewkes [b], pp. 299–308; [e], pp. 22, 58, 118; [f], p. 696; M. C. Stevenson [c], pp. 29–32, 48–57; Cushing [b], pp. 391–98, 430–47).

36. Fairies. — The fairy folk of Indian myth are generally diminutive and mischievous. A romantic version of the myth of the marriage of a human hero with a sky-girl is given by Abbé Em. Domenech (*Seven Years' Residence in the Great Deserts of North America*, London, 1860, i. 303 ff.), which he calls the "Legend of the Magic Circle of the Prairies." There are on the prairies, he says, circles denuded of vegetation which some attribute to buffaloes, while others regard them as traces of ancient cabins. The myth tells of a hunter who saw a basket containing singing maidens descend from the sky to such a circle, where the girls danced and played with a brilliant ball. He succeeded in capturing one of the girls, who became his wife; home-sick for the sky-world, she, with their baby, reascended to the heaven during the hunter's absence; but her star-father commanded her to return to earth and bring to the sky her husband, with trophies of every kind of game. All the sky-people chose, each for himself, a trophy; and they were then metamorphosed into the corresponding animals, the hunter, his wife, and son becoming falcons. The dancing and singing sky-girls, on the magic circle, certainly suggest the fairy dances and fairy rings of European folk-lore. *Text references:* Ch. II. vii (Copway; Converse, pp. 101–07; Smith, pp. 65–67; Mooney [b], Nos. 74, 78). — Ch. IV. vi (Mooney [b], pp. 330–35).

37. Great Heads, Cannibal Heads, Pursuing Rocks, etc. — Myths of heads that pursue in order to devour or destroy are found in every part of America. In some instances they have obvious significations, but it is not difficult to surmise that the idea is older than the meanings. Possibly it is connected with the custom of de-

capitation which prevailed in America everywhere before scalping largely displaced it; possibly the tumble-weed of the Plains, in the autumn borne along by the wind like a huge ball, may have something to do with the idea; possibly it was suggested by the analogy of sun and moon, conceived as travelling heads or masks, or by the tornado — (the Iroquois have "Great Head" stories in which the heads are apparently wind-beings). In many examples there is a cosmogonic suggestion in the myths. In Iroquois cosmogony the severed body and head of Ataentsic are transformed into the sun and moon, and there is a Chaui (Pawnee) tale of a rolling head that is split by a hawk and becomes the sun and moon (G. A. Dorsey [g], No. 5). The cosmogonic character of the legend appears also in the Carrier version (Ch. VI. i), though this same tradition as told by the Skidi Pawnee (G. A. Dorsey [e], No. 32) shows no cosmogony. Arapaho stories (Dorsey and Kroeber, Nos. 32–34) are instances in which a travelling rock is substituted for a head; in one instance (ib., No. 5) the pursuer is a wart, and it is interesting to note that "Flint" bears the epithet "Warty" in Seneca cosmogony (Hewitt [a]). Pursuing heads and rocks appear in the far West as well as in the East (examples are McDermott, No. 8, Flathead; Kroeber [a], No. 2, and Mason, Nos. 10, 11, Ute; Matthews [a], sect. 350, Navaho; Goddard [a], No. 10, Apache). Usually they are bogies or monsters — folk-lore beings rather than mythic persons. A curious story found among the Iroquois (Canfield, p. 125, variants of which are very common in the North-West, e. g., Boas [j], p. 30; [g], viii. 18; xvii. 8, 9; xx. 8; xxi. 8) tells of a cannibal head which is transformed into mosquitoes after it has been killed and burnt. One of the most interesting versions is a Californian story preserved by Dixon ([c], No. 14; cf. Curtin [a], "Hitchinna," [b], "Ilyuyu"), which tells of a man who dreams that he eats himself up; afterward he goes to gather pine-nuts, and his son throws one down and wounds him; he licks the blood, likes its taste, and eats all of himself but the head, which bounces about in pursuit of people until it finally leaps into the river. In connexion with head stories it is worth noting that a number of myths relate to a tribal palladium or "medicine" consisting of a skull (e. g. G. A. Dorsey [e], Nos. 1, 12). See Notes 2, 19, 27, 38. *Text references:* Ch. II. vii (Smith, pp. 59–62). — Ch. VI. i (Morice [b]; Lofthouse, pp. 48–51; Lowie [a], No. 22). — Ch. XI. iv.

38. Stone Giants. — Apparently these beings are personifications of implements of stone, especially flint, and they find their best mythic representative in "Flint" of Iroquoian cosmogony. In the far West birds with flint feathers or heroes armoured with flint knives appear. The Chenoo with the icy heart is a familiar concep-

tion in eastern Canada and New England, and may refer to rocky recesses in which cores of ice are preserved through the summer. Like other giants, the Stone Giants are usually cannibals. See Notes 2, 19, 37, 46. *Text references:* Ch. II. vii (SMITH, pp. 62–64; MOONEY [b], Nos. 8, 67, p. 501; LELAND, pp. 233–51; RAND, CONVERSE, etc.). — Ch. III. i, ii. — Ch. IV. vi (BUSHNELL [a]; MOONEY [b]). — Ch. VII. ii (POWELL, pp. 47–51; LOWIE [b], p. 262). — Ch. IX. iii. — Ch. X. v (MERRIAM, pp. 75–82).

39. THE SEASONS. — The seasons that appear in North American myth are almost invariably two, the hot and the cold, summer and winter. Other divisions of the year occur, especially among agricultural tribes (see *30 BBE*, "Calendar"), as governing ritual, but even here the fundamental partition of the year is twofold. What may be called the supernatural division of the year into seasons, in one of which the ancestral gods are present and in the other absent, with a corresponding classification of rites, is found both in the South-West and on the Pacific Coast, and it is in these two regions, likewise, that we meet the interesting suggestion of antipodes — i. e. of underworld seasons alternating with those of the world above. Everywhere the open season — spring to autumn — is the period in which the great invocations of the powers of nature take place in such ceremonies as the Busk (Ch. IV. iii), the Sun-Dance (Ch. V. vi), the Hako (Ch. V. vii), and the Snake-Dance (Ch. IX. v); while rites in honour of the dead or of ancestral and totemic spirits occur (like their classical analogues) in autumn and winter. *Text references:* Ch. II. viii (CONVERSE, pp. 96–100; RAND, Nos. xl, xlvi; SCHOOLCRAFT [b], part iii, p. 324 — obviously the original of the form used by Longfellow, *Hiawatha*, canto ii; *JR* vi. 161–63). — Ch. IV. iii (GATSCHET [a], pp. 179–80; SPECK, *JAFL* xx. 54–56; MACCAULEY, pp. 522–23; *30 BBE* "Busk"); vi (MOONEY [b], p. 322). — Ch. V. ii, vi (*30 BBE*, "Sun Dance"; J. O. DORSEY [d], pp. 449–67; MOONEY [c], pp. 242–44; MCCLINTOCK, chh. xi–xxiii; G. A. DORSEY [a], [b]). — Ch. VI. i (LOFTHOUSE). — Ch. VII. iii (TEIT [a], No. 10; [b], p. 337). — Ch. VIII. iv. — Ch. IX. iv (M. C. STEVENSON [c], pp. 108 ff.; FEWKES [a], pp. 255 ff.; [e], pp. 18 ff.; [f], p. 692). — Ch. X. iv (CURTIN [a], "Olelbis"). — Ch. XI. iii (BOAS [f], pp. 383 ff., 632 ff.).

40. ANIMAL ELDERS. — One of the most distinctive of American mythic ideas is the conception that every species of animal is represented by an Elder Being who is at once the ancestor and protector of its kind. These Elders of the Kinds appear in various *rôles*. Where a food animal is concerned — deer, buffalo, rabbit, seal, etc. — the function of the Elder seems to be to continue the supply of game; he is not offended by the slaughter of his wards provided the tabus are properly observed. Some tribes believe that the bones of deer are

reborn as deer, and so must be preserved, or that the bones of fish returned to the sea will become fish again. Many myths tell of punishment wreaked upon the hunter who continues to slay after his food necessities are satisfied. The Elders of beasts and birds of prey are the usual totems or tutelaries of hunters and warriors; the Elders of snakes, owls, and other uncanny creatures are supposed to give medicine-powers. Divination by animal remains and the use of charms and talismans made of animal parts are universal. Magic animals that have the power of appearing as men and men who can assume animal forms occur along with stories of the swan-shift type, in which the beast- or bird-disguise is stolen or laid aside and human form is retained. Frequently animals assume symbolic *rôles*. Thus the porcupine is an almost universal symbol for the sun, and the mink and red-headed woodpecker appear in a like relation; the bear is frequently an underground genius, and is conceived as a powerful being in the spirit-world; the birds are regarded as intermediaries between man and the powers above; the turkey, in the South and the South-West, is a mythic emblem of fertility, and an interesting episode in the Hako ritual tells how the turkey was replaced by the eagle as the symbolic leader of the rite, on the ground that the fertility of the turkey was offset by its lack of foresight in the protection of its nests (Fletcher, pp. 172–74); the whole Hako Ceremony is dominated by bird-symbolism. Animal-beings are rarely to be regarded as deities in any strict sense. Rather they are powerful genii and intermediaries between men and gods. In the cosmogonic cycles three animals, the hare, the coyote, and the raven, appear as creative agents, but they are beings that belong to the domain of myth rather than to that of religion. Two incidents in which animals conspicuously figure are found the length and breadth of the continent: (1) the diving of the animals after soil from which the earth may be magically created or renewed — most frequently encountered east of the Rocky Mountains, — and (2) the theft of fire — or of the sun or of daylight — by relays of animals who bear afar the brand snatched or stolen from the fire-keepers. The myth of the origin of the animals (Note 41) is almost as ubiquitous. See Notes 3, 4, 5, 9, 13, 18, 46, 47, 48, 50, 52. *Text references:* Ch. II. viii (*JR* vi. 159–61; ix. 123–25; xxxix. 15). — Ch. III. i. — Ch. IV. iv, vi (Mooney [b]). — Ch. V. vii (Fletcher). — Ch. VI. vi (the legend of the Nahurak as here recorded follows a version given by White Eagle — Letekots Taka — a Skidi chief, to Dr. Melvin R. Gilmore, recently of the Nebraska State Historical Society; see also Grinnell [c], pp. 161–70; G. A. Dorsey [g], Nos. 84, 85); vii (Mallery, *10 ARBE*, ch. x). — Ch. VII. iii. — Ch. IX. iii, v. — Ch. X. v (Curtin [a], Introd.; Merriam, Introd.). — Ch. XI. iv.

41. Origin of Animals. — A North American myth found practically throughout the continent tells of the release of the animals from a cave, or chest, or the inside of a cosmic monster, whence they distributed themselves over the earth. This event is sometimes placed in the First Age, as an episode of a creation-story, sometimes it follows the cataclysmic flood or conflagration which ends the primeval period. The people of the First Age are very generally represented as human in form but animal in reality, and a frequent story tells of the transformation of the First People into the animals they really are, as soon as genuine human beings appear. The converse of this recounts how the original animal-beings laid aside their animal masks and became human beings and the ancestors of men at the beginning of the human era. Often both the transformation and the liberation stories appear; in such instances the liberated animals are usually of the food or game varieties. A vast body of traditions and incidents account for the origin of animal traits; and it is these legends which represent what is perhaps the most primitive stratum of Indian mythology. See Notes 36, 40. *Text references:* Ch. II. viii (*JR* x. 137; Hewitt [a], pp. 194–97; 232–41; 302–09). — Ch. III. i. — Ch. IV. iv (Mooney [b], pp. 242–49); v (Mooney [b], pp. 261–311; p. 293, quoted; Bushnell [a], pp. 533–34; [b], p. 32). — Ch. VII. iv (McDermott, No. 2; W. D. Lyman, *The Columbia River*, New York, 1909, pp. 19–21). — Ch. IX. vi. — Ch. X. iv. — Ch. XI. vi.

42. Heaven Tree. — The conception of a great tree in the upper world magically connected with the life of nature occurs in more than one instance. In the Mohawk cosmogony (Hewitt [a], p. 282) it is said to be adorned with blossoms that give light to the people in the sky-world, while in the Olelbis myth (Curtin [a], "Olelbis") the celestial sudatory is built of oak-trees bound together with flowers. The Tlingit regard the Milky Way as the trunk of a celestial tree. In many stories on the Jack-and-the-Beanstalk theme, the hero or heroine ascends to the sky on a rapidly growing tree, sometimes believed to be a replica of a similar tree in the world above. In South-Western genesis-stories the emergence from the underworld is by means of magically growing trees, reeds, sunflowers, and the like. Ascents to and descents from the sky occur with a variety of other methods: the tradition of an upshooting mountain or rock, common in California, is clearly related to the tree conception; the rainbow bridge is a frequent idea, and is sometimes, like the Milky Way, regarded as the Pathway of Souls; in the South-West lightning is conceived as forming a bridge or ladder; and a similar idea in connexion with the fall of Ataentsic is the Fire-Dragon episode; descents and ascents by means of a basket swung from spider-spun filaments

are common in Plains mythology, while magic shells, boats, and baskets, raised to the sky by song or spell, occur east and west; on the West Coast the arrow chain is frequent. The cult use of poles, originating from magically endowed trees, is associated with some of the most picturesque myths and important rites. See Notes 13, 14, 61. *Text references:* Ch. III. i, vi (*JR* xii. 31–37; SCHOOLCRAFT [b], part iii, p. 320; HOFFMAN [b], p. 181). — Ch. IV. iv (GATSCHET [a]). — Ch. VI. iv (see Note 13, for references). — Ch. VII. iii. — Ch. VIII. ii. — Ch. IX. vi. — Ch. X. iii (CURTIN [a], "Olelbis"); vi (POWERS, p. 366).

43. ATAENTSIC. — Spelled also, *JR* viii. 117, Eataentsic. Hewitt ("Cosmogonic Gods of the Iroquois," in *Proceedings of the American Association for the Advancement of Science*, 1895) gives Eyatahentsik, and regards her as goddess of night and earth. She is also named Awenhai ("Mature Flowers"). Cf. *30 BBE*, "Teharonhiawagon," and Lang, *Myth, Ritual and Religion*, 3d ed., London, 1901. See Note 34. *Text reference:* Ch. III. i.

44. HERO BROTHERS. — A common feature of American cosmogonic myths is the association of two kinsmen, usually described as brothers or sometimes as twins. In Iroquoian legend one of the brothers is good, the other evil, and the evil brother is banished to the underworld. In Algonquian tradition (and the same notion is found among Siouan and other Plains tribes), the younger brother is dragged down to the underworld by vengeful monsters. An underworld relative of one of the brothers appears also in the South-West, where the father of the elder is always the Sun, while the younger is sometimes regarded as the son of the Waters, welling up from below. Almost always the elder brother, or first-born in case of twins, is the hero, the doer; while the younger is frequently a magician and clairvoyant. It seems evident that the brothers represent respectively the upper and underworld powers of nature, and it is doubtless for this reason that Flint is described as the favourite of his mother Ataentsic (the Earth) in Iroquois myth. In the South-West Coyote often takes the evil part: thus the maladroit creations assigned to Flint by the Iroquois are there the work of Coyote. Hero brothers occur in other types of myth, and it is interesting to note that the younger brother is the one to whom medicine-powers are ascribed. See Notes 45, 69. *Text references:* Ch. III. i, ii. — Ch. VI. i, iii (G. A. DORSEY [h], No. 1), vii. — Ch. VII. ii, iii. — Ch. VIII. i, ii (MATTHEWS [a]; JAMES STEVENSON, pp. 279–80); iv (MATTHEWS [c], "The Stricken Twins"). — Ch. IX. vi, vii. — Ch. X. iii (FRACHTENBERG [a], No. 1); vi DIXON [d], No. 3; KROEBER [c], p. 186).

45. YOSKEHA AND TAWISCARA. — The names of these twins are variously spelled — as Ioskeha, Iouskeha or Jouskeha, Tawiskara,

Tawiscaron, Tawiskala, etc. Yoskeha, called "Sapling" by the Onondaga and "Maple Sapling" by the Mohawk, has been identified with the sun or light by Brinton ([a], p. 203), though there seems better reason in Hewitt's view that he is "the reproductive, rejuvenating power in nature" ("Cosmogonic Gods of the Iroquois," in *Proceedings of the American Association for the Advancement of Science*, 1895). Tawiscara is rendered by Brinton "the Dark One," and interpreted as "the destructive or Typhonic power." "Flint" is the name given to Tawiscara by the Onondaga; the Mohawk designate him by the Huron name which in their language signifies "flint" or "chert"; while the Seneca know him by the epithet "Warty" (cf. Note 37). He is described as "a marvelously strange personage . . . his flesh is nothing but flint . . . over the top of his head, a sharp comb of flint." Brébeuf's narrative tells how, when Tawiscara was punished by Jouskeha and fled, "from his blood certain stones sprang up, like those we employ in France to fire a gun" (*JR* x. 131). In Cherokee myth Tawiscala appears in association with the Algonquian "Great Rabbit," which would indicate, what is indeed obvious, that Yoskeha and Manabozho are one and the same. Hewitt regards Flint (Tawiscaron, which he interprets as from a root signifying "ice"; see *30 BBE*, "Tawiscaron") as a personification of Winter; while Sapling, whom he identifies with Teharonhiawagon, personifies Summer; but this can be, at best, only in a secondary mode. The name Teharonhiawagon Hewitt interprets as meaning literally "He-is-holding-the-sky-in-two-places," referring to the action of the two hands (*30 BBE*, "Teharonhiawagon"). Other interpretations are: Lafitau, i. 133, Tharonhiaouagon, "il affermit le ciel de toutes parts"; Brinton [a], p. 205, Taronhiawagon, "he who comes from the sky"; Morgan, ii. 234, Tarenyawagon, stating that he was "the sender of dreams"; Hewitt [a], p. 137, Tharonhiawakon, "he grasps the sky," i. e. in memory. Mrs. Smith (p. 52) says that little more is known of this god than that he brought out from Mother Earth the six tribes of the Iroquois. The name is not much used, the cosmogonies preferring an epithet, as Odendonnia ("Sapling"), which is probably also the meaning of Yoskeha. See Notes 38, 44, 47, 69. *Text references:* Ch. III. i. — Ch. IV. vi.

46. Metamorphosis. — Transformations are of course common mythic incidents. They may be classified into (1) phoenix-like periodical rejuvenations, as in the case of Sapling (Yoskeha) in Iroquoian and of Estsanatlehi in Navaho myth; (2) the metamorphosis of the People of the First Age into the animals or human beings of the final period, in which men now live; (3) incidental changes of form, as disguises assumed by magicians or deities, "swan-shift" episodes, were-folk incarnations, all in the general field of folk-tales; (4) reincarnation

or transmigration changes, which may be from human to animal form, as in the Tlingit concept that the wicked are reborn as animals, or the Mohave belief that all the dead are reincarnated in a series of animal forms until they finally disappear; (5) transformations, frequently by way of revenge, wrought by a mythic Transformer or other deity. Especially in the North-West and South-West stone formations are explained as representing transformed giants of earlier times; (6) animal trait stories, in which the distinctive characteristic of an animal kind is held to be the result of some primitive change, usually the consequence of accident or trick, wrought in the body of an ancestral animal. See Notes 3, 5, 18, 35, 40, 41, 43, 48, 62. *Text references:* Ch. III. i (HEWITT [a]). — Ch. IV. iv, v (MOONEY [b], pp. 293, 304, 310–11, 320, 324; BUSHNELL [a], p. 32). — Ch. VII. ii (KROEBER [a], No. 10; MASON, No. 25; POWELL, pp. 47–51); iii (TEIT [a], No. 27). — Ch. VIII. i. — Ch. X. v (CURTIN [a], Introd.; MERRIAM, Introd.). — Ch. XI. vi (BOAS and HUNT [b], p. 28).

47. MANABOZHO AND CHIBIABOS. — These two are the Algonquian equivalents of the Iroquoian Yoskeha and Tawiscara. Manabozho, the Great Hare, is one of the most interesting figures in Indian myth, and probably he owes his importance to a variety of traits: the hare's prolific reproduction and his usefulness as a food animal were the foundation; his speed gave him a symbolic character; and perhaps his habit of changing his coat with the seasons enhanced his reputation as a magician. At all events, in one line of development he becomes the great demiurge, the benefactor of mankind, spirit of life, and intercessor with the Good Spirit; while in another direction he is evolved into the vain, tricky, now stupid, now clever hero of animal tales, whose final incarnation, after his deeds have passed from Indian into negro lore, appears in the "Brer Rabbit" stories of Joel Chandler Harris. In Indian myth the relation between the demiurgic Great Hare and the tricky Master Rabbit varies with tribe and time. The tendency is to anthropomorphize the Great Hare or to assimilate his deeds to an anthropomorphic deity. This has gone farthest with the Iroquois, by whom indeed the conception of a rabbit demiurge may never have been seriously entertained. The Iroquoian Cherokee have many Rabbit stories, but they are folktales rather than myths. Among the Abnaki there seems to be a clear separation between Glooscap, the demiurge, and the Rabbit (cf. Rand, Leland); Glooscap is, however, an obvious doublet of the Hare, having all his tricky and magic character. It is interesting to note that among the Ute, of the western Plateau, where, as in the far North, the rabbit is a valuable food animal, the Rabbit again becomes an important mythic being, though still subordinate to the

Coyote, which effaces him everywhere in the West. Apparently the Coyote or some other Wolf was the original companion or "brother" of the Hare; for in practically every version in which two animals are present as the Hero Brothers, one is a carnivore. In the east it is often the lynx, which, like the wolf, preys upon the rabbit. Sometimes birds replace quadrupeds, as in the Omaha myth of "Haxige" (J. O. Dorsey [a]), where the duck and buzzard appear; but the relation of prey and carnivore is constant. It is at least noteworthy that the food animal should be the eminent hero in Forest Region myth, while the beast of prey takes this *rôle* on the Plains and westward. The Algonquian names and epithets for the Great Hare are many; Messou, Manabush, Minabozho, and Nanaboojoo are mentioned in the text (cf. Note 1). Chibiabos (also Chipiapoos), the companion of Manabozho, almost invariably occurs in the form of a carnivore, as the marten, lynx, or wolf. In the interesting Potawatomi version given by De Smet (pp. 1080–84) two mythic cycles seem to be mingled: Chakekenapok, with whom Nanaboojoo fights, is clearly Flint, the wicked twin of the Iroquoian tale; Chipiapoos, the friendly brother, is Algonquian, and the same being who becomes lord of the ghost-world after being dragged down by the water monsters; Wabasso is clearly another name for the Great Hare, and from the nature of the reference it is plausible to suppose that the Arctic hare is meant — i. e. Nanaboojoo-Wabasso and Chipiapoos-Chakekenapok are in reality only two persons. See Notes 15, 44, 45, 49. *Text reference:* Ch. III. ii (RAND, No. lx; HOFFMAN [b], pp. 87, 113–14; [a], p. 166; for general references, see Note 15).

48. HERO-TRANSFORMER-TRICKSTER. — A being who is at once a demiurge, a magical transformer, and a trickster both clever and gullible is the great personage of North American mythology. In some tribes the heroic character, in some the trickster nature predominates; others recognize a clear distinction between the myths, in which creative acts are ascribed to this being, and the folk-tales or fictions, in which his generally discreditable adventures are narrated. Of the mythic acts the most important ascribed to him are: (1) the setting in order of the shapeless first world, and the conquest of its monstrous beings, who are usually transformed; (2) the prime *rôle* in the theft of fire, the sun, or daylight; (3) the restoration of the world after the flood; and (4) the creation of mankind and the institution of the arts of life. Where these deeds are performed by some other being, only the trickster character remains in a group of fairly constant adventures, nearly all of which have close analogues in European folk-tales. The important hero-tricksters are: (1) the Great Hare, or Master Rabbit, of the eastern part of the continent; (2) Coyote, the chief hero of Plains folk-tales and in the far West

the great demiurge; (3) the Raven, which plays the parts of both demiurge and trickster on the North-West Coast; and (4) "Old Man," who is chiefly important in the general latitude of the Oregon trail, from Siouan to Salish territory. In some instances (as in certain Salish groups) there are a number of hero-trickster characters, Coyote, Raven, Old Man, and the Hero Brothers all being present; such cases seem to be the consequence of indiscriminate borrowing. See Notes 40, 44, 45, 47, 63, 69. *Text references:* Ch. III. ii. — Ch. IV. vi (Mooney [b], pp. 233, 273, quoted). — Ch. VI. vi. — Ch. VII. iii (for references see Note 11); v (Teit [c], p. 621).— Ch. VIII. i, ii, v, vi (Goddard [a], Nos. 15, 16, 23, 33, etc.). — Ch. X. iii, vi (Goddard [b], No. 2; Dixon [b], No. 10). — Ch. XI. vi (Boas [g], esp. xvii–xxv; Swanton [a], pp. 27–28; [b], p. 293; [c], pp. 110–50; [d], pp. 80–88).

49. The Deluge. — The conception of an abyss of waters from which the earth emerges, either as a new creation or as a restoration, is found in every part of the American continent. Not infrequently both the evocation of the world from primeval waters and its subsequent destruction by flood occur in the same myth or cycle, and in many instances what passes for a creation-story is clearly nothing more or less than the post-diluvian renewal of the earth. The same episode of the diving animals is found in connexion, now with the creation, now with the deluge, so that it is difficult to say to which myth it originally belonged. On the whole, it is best developed and most characteristic in the East and North, where its cosmogonic features are also most clearly evolved. The other most familiar deluge motive, the upwelling of a flood because of the wrath of underworld water monsters, is characteristic in the South-West, though it also occurs in the Manabozho stories, generally in conjunction with the diving incident. Physiographic conditions no doubt affect the circumstances of the myth. Thus in the arid South-West the idea of primeval waters is generally absent; the flood is an outpouring of underworld waters, which we may presume is associated with the sudden floodings of the canyons after heavy rains in the mountains; it is curious to find the incidents of the South-Western myth repeated in the North-West (cf. Boas [g], xxiv. 1; Swanton [d], p. 110), although this is not the customary form in that region. Again, in California the notion of a refuge on a mountain-peak is common, and here, too, we find the cataclysm of fire in conjunction with that of water, indicating volcanic forces. Most, if not all, of the incidents of the Noachian deluge are duplicated in one or other of the American deluge-myths — the raft containing the hero and surviving animals, the sending out of a succession of animals to discover soil or vegetation, the landing on a mountain, even the subsequent building of

a ladder to heaven, the confusion of tongues, and the dispersal of mankind. There is no reasonable question but that these incidents are aboriginal and pre-Columbian, although in some instances later coloured by knowledge of the Bible tale; and it is hardly a matter of wonder that the first missionaries were convinced that Indian mythology is only a perverted reminiscence of the events narrated in the Scriptures. See Notes 9, 15, 48, 50, 51. *Text references:* Ch. III. iii (*JR* v. 155–57; vi. 157–59; Hoffman [b], pp. 87–88, 131 ff.; Perrot, *Mémoire*, ch. i, English translation in Blair, i.). — Ch. IV. iv (Bushnell [b]). — Ch. VI. i, ii. — Ch. VII. iii. — Ch. VIII. ii, v, vi. — Ch. IX. vi, vii. — Ch. X. iii (Kroeber [c]; [d], pp. 342–46; Powers, p. 383); iv (Powers, pp. 144, 161, 227, 383; Kroeber [c], pp. 177, 178, 184, 189; Nos. 1, 7, 11, 15, 25, 37; Merriam, pp. 75, 81, 139; Dixon [c], Nos. 1, 2; [d], Nos. 1, 2; Curtin [a]). — Ch. XI. vi (Boas [g], xxiv. 1).

50. The Serpent. — Snakes seem naturally associated with underworld-powers, and are so in many instances, notably the snake rites of the Hopi (Ch. IX. v); but the great mythic serpent of Indian lore is quite as much a sky- as a water-being — probably he is mainly the personified rainbow and lightning and therefore associated with both sky and water. Commonly he is represented as plumed or horned; frequently he carries a crystal in his head; in the North-West the Sisiutl has a serpent head at each end and a human face in the middle. Flying snakes occur in Navaho myth as a *genre;* the Shoshoni regard the rainbow as a great sky-serpent, and the rainbows on the waters of Niagara may be the suggestion which makes this cataract the home of a great reptile. The Sia (M. C. Stevenson [b], p. 69) have a series of cosmic serpents — one for each of the quarters, one for heaven, and one for earth; the heaven-serpent has a crystal body, and it is so brilliant that the eyes cannot rest upon it; the earth-serpent has a mottled body, and is to be identified with the spotted monster which rules the waters beneath the world and, in South-Western myth generally, causes the flood that drives the First People to the upper world. The most frequent identification of the serpent, however, is with lightning. It is partly as connected with the lightning, partly as associated with the underworld-powers, that the snake becomes an emblem of fertility, especially in the South-West. There may be some connexion with the same idea in the frequent myth of the intercourse of a woman with a serpent. In many hero-stories the reptile appears as an antagonist of the Sun or the Moon or of the Hero demiurge. Sometimes he is the husband of Night, and an obvious impersonation of evil. On the Pacific Coast the horned serpent is a magic rather than a cosmic being, though the latter character is by no means absent. Very frequently medicine-powers are ascribed to

snakes, and there are numerous myths of potencies so acquired by visits to the snake-people. In the incident of the hero swallowed by the monster, this being is in many cases a serpent, as in the Iroquois version. E. G. Squier (*American Review*, new series, ii, 1848, pp. 392–98) gives a type of the Manabozho story with the following incidents: (1) the seizing of the "cousin" of Manabozho, as he was crossing the ice, by Meshekenabek, the Great Serpent; (2) Manabozho's transformation of himself into a tree and his shooting of the Serpent; (3) the flood caused by the water serpents, and the flight of men and animals to a high mountain, whence a raft is launched containing the hero and many animals; (4) the diving incident; and (5) Manabozho's remaking of the earth. See Notes 2, 9, 41, 49. *Text references:* Ch. III. iv (HOFFMAN [b], pp. 88–89, 125 ff.; RAND, Nos. 1, xxxiii; MOONEY [b], pp. 320–21). — Ch. IV. vi. — Ch. VI. i (MORICE, *Transactions of the Canadian Institute*, v. 4–10); iv (POWELL, p. 26). — Ch. VII. iv. — Ch. IX. iii (M. C. STEVENSON [c], pp. 94 ff., 179; FEWKES [f], p. 691); v (*30 BBE*, "Snake Dance"; FEWKES [b], [c]; DORSEY and VOTH, especially pp. 255–61; 349–53; VOTH, Nos. 6, 7, 27, 37). — Ch. XI. ii (BOAS [f], p. 371; [g], vi. 5, 5a; viii. 3, 4; xvii. 2; [j], pp. 28, 44, 66).

51. THE THEFT OF FIRE. — The Promethean myth is one of the most universal in America. Sometimes it is the sun that is stolen, sometimes the daylight; but in the great majority of cases it is fire. The legend frequently has a utilitarian turn, describing the kinds of wood in which the fire is deposited. Usually the flame is in the keeping of beings who are obviously celestial, but there are some curious variations, as in the North-West versions which derive fire from the ocean or from ghosts (cf. Boas [g], xvii. 1). It is impossible to believe that the fire-theft stories refer to the actual introduction of fire as a cultural agency; more likely the ritualistic preservation and kindling of fire, with the distribution of the new fire by relays of torch-bearers — rites of which there are traces in both North and South America — constitute the basis of the myth in its commonest form, that is, theft followed by distribution by relays of animals. See Notes 13, 40. *Text references:* Ch. III. v (HOFFMAN [b], pp. 126–27; MOONEY [d], p. 678; DE SMET, pp. 1047–53); vi (HEWITT [a], pp. 201 ff., 317 ff.). — Ch. IV. iv (MOONEY [b], pp. 240–42). — Ch. VII. ii (W. D. LYMAN, *The Columbia River*, New York, 1909, pp. 22–24; cf. EELS, *Annual Report of the Smithsonian Institution*, 1887, part 1); iv (KROEBER [a], No. 1; LOWIE [b], No. 3; PACKARD, No. 1; TEIT [a], Nos. 12, 13; [c], No. 11). — Ch. X. iv, vi (CURTIN [a], p. 365; [b], p. 51; MERRIAM, pp. 33, 35, 43–53, 89, 139; GODDARD [b], No. 12; [c], Nos. 3, 4, 5; FRACHTENBERG [a], No. 4; DIXON [b], No. 3; [c], No. 5; [d], No. 8; KROEBER [c], Nos.

8, 16, 26; [e], No. 17). — Ch. XI. v (BOAS [g], iii. 1, 8; v. 2; viii. 8; xiii. 66).

52. THE BEAR. — It is doubtless the cave-dwelling and hibernating habits of the bear, coupled with his formidable strength, that give him his position as chief of the underworld Manitos. In the Midewiwin the bears are the most important of the malignant Manitos barring the progress of the candidate during his initiation. See Hoffman [a], pp. 167–69, and cf. Note 14. *Text references:* Ch. III. vi. — Ch. X. vi (POWERS, p. 342; DIXON [c], No. 9; GODDARD [c], No. 17; MERRIAM, pp. 103, 111; KROEBER [c], p. 180, No. 10). — Ch. XI. v.

53. RETURN OF THE DEAD. — Stories on the theme of Orpheus and Eurydice are sufficiently frequent to form a class by themselves. In some cases the return of the beloved dead is defeated because of the breaking of a tabu, as in the Greek instance; in others the seeker is given wealth or some other substitute; in still others the dead is returned to life, but usually with an uncanny consequence; altogether ghastly are the stories where the revivification is only apparent, and the seeker awakes to find himself or herself clutching a corpse or skeleton. See Notes 10, 12, 17. *Text references:* Ch. III. vii (*JR* x. 149–53; SMITH, p. 103). — Ch. VI. v (G. A. DORSEY [g], Nos. 10, 34). — Ch. VII. iii, vi (W. D. LYMAN, *The Columbia River*, New York, 1909, pp. 28–31). — Ch. X. vii (KROEBER [c], Nos. 24, 25; POWERS, p. 339). — Ch. XI. vii.

54. HIAWATHA. — For the story of Hiawatha consult *30 BBE*, "Dekanawida," "Hiawatha," "Wathototarho"; Hale, *Iroquois Book of Rites*, a study of the traditions of the League as retained by the Iroquois and reduced to writing in the eighteenth century; Morgan, i. 63–64; Smith; Beauchamp, "Hi-a-wat-ha," in *JAFL* iv; Schoolcraft [a], i.; [b], part iii, pp. 314 ff. *Text reference:* Ch. III. viii.

55. HAIR AND SCALP. — Of the parts of the body, the hair and the heart seem to be particularly associated with the life and strength of the individual. The scalp-lock was a specially dressed wisp or braid of hair, separated out when the boy reached manhood, and it was this that was taken as a trophy from the slain. The custom of scalping seems to have originated in the east and from there to have spread westward, replacing the older practice of decapitation, which, on some parts of the Pacific Coast, was never superseded. Hair-symbolism appears not only in scalping, but in the wide-spread custom of giving a pregnant woman a charm made of the hair of a deceased relative whose rebirth was hoped for (cf. *JR* vi. 207, for an early instance). Hair-combing episodes are frequent in myth, usually with a magic significance. In Iroquois cosmogony Ataentsic combs the hair of her father, apparently to receive his magic power. Hiawatha's combing of the snakes from the hair of Atotarho is perhaps

a symbolic incident. The character of Atotarho's hair may be inferred from Captain John Smith's description of that of the chief priest of the Powhatan: "The ornaments of the chiefe Priest was certain attires for his head made thus. They tooke a dosen or 16 or more snakes, and stuffed them with mosse; and of weesels and other vermine skins, a good many. All these they tie by their tailes, so as all their tailes meete in the toppe of their head, like a great Tassell. Round about this Tassell is as it were a crown of feathers; the skins hang about his head, necke and shoulders, and in a manner cover his face" (*Description of Virginia*, 1612, "Of their Religion"). See Note 37. *Text references:* Ch. III. viii (MORGAN, i. 63). — Ch. V. ix (FLETCHER and LA FLESCHE, pp. 122–26).

56. GAMBLERS. — American Indians are inveterate gamesters, and their myths accordingly abound in stories of gambling contests, in which the magic element is frequently the theme of interest. See Note 21. *Text references:* Ch. IV. vi (MOONEY [b], pp. 311–15). — Ch. VII. iii (TEIT [a], No. 8). — Ch. VIII. ii (MATTHEWS [a], "Origin Myth"); iv (MATTHEWS [a], "The Great Shell of Kintyel"; cf. GODDARD [a], No. 18; RUSSELL, p. 219). — Ch. IX. vi.

57. MIGRATION-MYTHS AND HISTORIES. — Migration-myths and more or less legendary histories are possessed by all the more advanced North American tribes. Such traditions are usually closely interwoven with cosmogonic stories, so that there are formed fairly consistent narratives of events since the "beginning." Chronology is generally vague, though there are some notable attempts at exactitude (see Ch. VI. vii). *Text references:* Ch. IV. vii (GATSCHET [a]; MOONEY [b], pp. 350–97). — Ch. VI. vii (G. A. DORSEY [b], pp. 34 ff.; MALLERY, "Picture Writing of the American Indians," in *10 ARBE*, ch. x; MOONEY [c], pp. 254–64). — Ch. IX. iv (see especially G. P. WINSHIP, "The Coronado Expedition," in *14 ARBE*; cf. Note 67, *infra*).

58. PETALESHARO. — See *30 BBE*, "Petalesharo." The story is told by Thomas M'Kenney, *Memoirs Official and Personal*, New York, 1846, ii. 93 ff., but Dr. Melvin R. Gilmore, recently of the Nebraska State Historical Society, states that the Skidi of today deny its truth; the Morning Star sacrifice lapsed, they say, by common consent. Dr. Gilmore has very kindly given the writer the following data regarding Petalesharo and the Morning Star sacrifice which correct many statements current in government and other publications:

"In the contact of two races of widely variant modes of thought and manners of life there is abundant room for misunderstandings and mistaken ideas to be formed of each by the other, and when one race possesses the art of writing and the other does not, the people with the superior advantage may, without any wrong intention, perpetuate false views and impressions equally with true statements of facts. Thus the misapprehension of one observer is thereafter propagated and confirmed by every writer who deals with the given subject. In such light, I think, is to be regarded the character of Pita Leshara [Petalesharo], and especially one deed commonly ascribed to him in white men's accounts.

"Pita Leshara was chief of the Tshawi [Chaui] tribe of the Pawnee nation. He was a forceful character, wise, brave, and benevolent, and was in the height of his power just at the time that his nation was coming into the closest contact with the white race. Because of his outstanding ability and force of character, and because he was a chief, the whites popularly regarded him as the principal chief of the nation.

"Of the four tribes, originally independent, but in later times confederated into the Pawnee nation, one, the Skidi, possessed the rite of human sacrifice, the offering of certain war captives, provided that at the time of their capture they had been devoted by the consecrational vows of their captors. This ceremony was practised by the Skidi Pawnee until some time after the middle of the nineteenth century. It died out at that time because of the various influences incident to increasing contact with, and more constant propinquity of, the white race. The cessation of this practice occurring contemporaneously with the period of Pita Leshara's public activities, a belief obtained among white people, and crystallized into a dictum, that it was due to a mandate of the chief that the practice of the rite ceased. But the observance of religious ceremonies does not originate nor terminate by mandate.

"By careful inquiry among the old people of the Pawnee I am unable to find any support for either of the statements current among the whites that Pita Leshara was head chief of the nation and that he, by edict, caused the Skidi tribe to abandon their peculiar ritual. The following account will serve as an example of the information on the subject given me very generally by old people now living who were contemporaries of Pita Leshara. My informant in this instance was White Eagle, a chief of the Skidi Pawnee. He was about eighty-three years old at the time he gave me this account in 1914. His father was the last priest, or Ritual Keeper, of the rite of human sacrifice who performed the ceremony, and White Eagle himself, as his father's successor, now has in his keeping the sacred pack pertaining to the sacrifice and described below.

"White Eagle's account follows. I told him the current story, an educated young Skidi named Charles Knifechief being our interpreter. White Eagle listened with attention and at the close he said: 'It is not a true account. Now let me tell you. At one time there was a Skidi chief named Wonderful Sun (Sakuruti Waruksti). This chief ordered the [Skidi] tribe on the buffalo-hunt. So they made ready with tents and equipment. The people went southwest, beyond the Republican River. While they were in that region, they came into the vicinity of a Cheyenne camp. One of the Cheyenne women was gathering wood along the river bottom many miles from camp. Some Pawnees overtook her and made her captive. The Pawnees at this time had finished the hunt and were returning home. They brought the captive Cheyenne woman along. A man of the Skidi declared the woman to be waruksti [a formula of consecration]. They continued on the return journey and camped on the way at Honotato kako [the name of an old village site on the south bank of the Platte River where the Tshawi, Kitkahak [Kitkehahti] and Pitahawirat [Pitahauerat], the other three tribes of the Pawnee nation, had formerly resided]. From this place they travelled along the south bank of the Platte to the ford at Columbus. Before they crossed the river one of the old men of the Skidi, a man named Big Knife (Nitsikuts), went up to this woman and shot her with an arrow. He did so because he thought that the white men at Columbus would take her away from them and send her back to her own people if they learned that the Skidi had a captive. And now this story as I have told it to you is the real truth of the reason that the Skidi Pawnee no longer continued the sacrifice. The captor of the Cheyenne woman was a man named Old Eagle. He pronounced her to be waruksti. Big Knife killed her because she had been made waruksti. The story of Pita Leshara is untrue. If he had interfered, he would have been killed, because he had no authority over the Skidi. He was chief of the Tshawi.'

"The sketch [mentioned below] was made by Charles Knifechief as he sat interpreting for us. He has drawn a Pawnee earth lodge in the distance as seen from the Place of Sacrifice. The door-way of the house opens toward the rising sun. The victim was bound by the hands to the upright posts, standing on the upper of four horizontal bars, the ends of which were bound to the upright posts. White Eagle said that the human sacrifice was not connected with the planting ceremony, but was for atonement, planting being controlled by another Sacred Pack. He declared that he has the Human Sacrifice Pack which he inherited from his father, but he was not instructed in the ritual, so that it is now lost. He said that the body was sacrificed to the birds of the air and to animals, and was left on the scaffold until it was consumed. The victim was put to death by the authorized bowman of the ritual, by shooting with the four sacred arrows. After the archer had thus slain the sacrifice, four men advanced with the four ancient war-clubs from the Sacred Pack and in turn struck the body, after which it was at the will of the populace. The Sacred Pack pertaining to this ritual contains the sacred bow, the four sacred arrows, four sacred war-clubs, and a human skull, the skull of a man who was a chief long ago, distinguished by his great human sympathy."

Despite White Eagle's statement that the sacrifice was not connected with agricultural rites, it may still be noted that neighbouring tribes associated the Pawnee offering of human beings with agriculture. Thus an Omaha narrative (J. O. Dorsey [a], p. 414) declares that the Pawnee "greased their hoes" in the flesh of a victim "as they wished to acquire good crops."

The illustration to which Dr. Gilmore refers, and which is reproduced, through his courtesy, opposite p. 76, is of particular interest since there is, so far as the author knows, no other existing picture of the manner in which the famous sacrifice to the Morning Star was conducted. *Text reference:* Ch. V. i. Cf. De Smet, pp. 977–88.

59. War and War-Gods. — Most North American Indians are courageous warriors, though tribes vary much in their reputations. On the Great Plains the northern Athapascans form an exception, having, as a rule, little inclination for fighting. The Californian tribes, also, were on the whole peaceful, and in the South-West the Pueblo Dwellers, valorous in defence, were little given to forays. The Sun and the Thunder are the war-divinities of the greater part of the continent; in the South-West the war-gods are the twin sons of the Sun. Usually the Indian warrior relied more upon his personal tutelary or Medicine-Spirit — especially the Bear, Wolf, and Eagle — than upon any war-god of a national type. The bearing of palladia into battle was common, however; and the loss of such a treasure was regarded as a great disaster. See Notes 25, 37, 55. *Text references:* Ch. II. ii. — Ch. V. i, ix. — Ch. VIII. ii. — Ch. IX. iii.

60. Feather-Symbolism. — The use of feather-symbols is one of the most characteristic features of Indian dress and rituals. Eagle feathers, denoting war-honours, are in the nature of insignia; but there are many ritualistic uses in which the feathers seem to be primarily symbols of the intermediation between heaven and earth which is assigned to the birds. Feathers thus have a ghostly or spiritual character. Boas records a story in which a house is haunted by feathers and shadows ([g] xxv. 1, 13), and one of the most curious of Plains legends is the Pawnee tale of Ready-to-Give, whom the gods restored to life with feathers in place of brains. In the South-West feathers are attached to prayer-sticks addressed to the celestial powers. Cf. Notes 21, 27, 30, 31, 40, 61. *Text references:* Ch. V. vii (Fletcher, *The Hako*, is perhaps the most important single source on feather-symbolism). — Ch. VI. vi (for stories of Ready-to-Give, G. A.

DORSEY [e], No. 10; [g], Nos. 39–76; GRINNELL [c], pp. 142–60). — Ch. VIII. i, iii. — Ch. IX. iii.

61. SACRED POLES. — The most conspicuous use of sacred poles is in the Sun-Dance rite, where the central object of the Medicine Lodge is a post adorned with emblematic objects, especially a bundle tied transversely so as to give the general effect of a cross. Sacred poles appear as palladia in a number of instances. The Creek migration-legend recounts such a use, and the Omaha tribal legends refer not only to the pillar mentioned in Ch. V. ix, but to another and older sacred post of cedar. In the Hedawichi ceremony of the same tribe a pole made from a felled tree was a symbol of life and strength, and of cosmic organization. The relation of these pillars to the pole employed in the Sun-Dance, all forming a single ritualistic group, seems obvious. The transition from poles to xoana, or crude pillar-like images, is apparent in the wooden statuettes made by the Zuñi and other Pueblo, which are little more than decorated stocks. On the North-West Coast an entirely individual development is found in the carved "totem-poles" and grave memorials carved with totemic figures; but these seem to be heraldic rather than ritualistic in intention. See Notes 4, 42, 65. *Text references:* Ch. IV. vii (GATSCHET [a]). — Ch. V. ix (FLETCHER and LA FLESCHE, pp. 216–60). — Ch. VIII. v (LUMHOLTZ [a]). — Ch. IX. iii. — Ch. XI. i, ii.

62. MAGIC. — Magic is the science of primitive man, his means of controlling the forces of nature. Imitative and sympathetic magic underlie most Indian rites to a degree that frequently makes it impossible to determine where magic coercion of nature gives place, in the mind of the celebrant, to symbolic supplication. Both elements are present in all the important ceremonies, and it is often a matter of interest or prepossession on the part of the reporter as to which — magic or worship — will be emphasized in his record. Magic motives in myth are too numerous to classify, but a few types may be mentioned. (1) Transformations (see Notes 5, 41). (2) Magic increase and replenishment. The idea underlying this form is: Given a little of a substance, it may be magically increased; possibly animal and vegetable multiplication is the analogy which suggests this; at all events it seems less difficult for the primitive mind to imagine continuity and increase than creation *ex nihilo*. Typical notions are the creation of the earth from a kernel of soil, the stretching of the world, the continuous growth of the heaven-reaching tree or rock, the constant replenishment of a vessel of food which, like the widow's cruse, is never exhausted during need, or is emptied only by an orphan after all others have partaken. (3) Songs and spells. The Indian has an inveterate belief in the power of words, and even thoughts, to produce mechanical and organic changes; hence the importance of

song in his rituals, and the tabus which forbid songs to be sung out of season (a hunting song in the closed season, for example). (4) The magic flight. This is an incident that recurs many times: the hero is pursued by a monster; as he flees he creates successive obstacles by means of charms, which the monster in turn overcomes (an example is given Ch. VI. i). The conception of the perilous way to the underworld or spirit-world is related to this idea (see Note 8). (5) Magic use of stones, wands, and other talismans. See Notes 4, 27, 30, 35, 60, 61. *Text references:* Ch. VI. i, vii. — Ch. VII. ii. — Ch. VIII. iii, iv. — Ch. IX. iv. — Ch. X. iv (Goddard [c], Nos. 1, 2).

63. Old Man. — The personage usually called "Old Man" is a distinctly Western figure who seems to be in some instances a personification of the Great Spirit, though for the most part he is clearly a member of the "Trickster-Transformer" group. The Blackfeet and Arapaho, western Algonquians, share this character with their neighbours of Siouan and Salish stocks (cf. De Smet, p. 525; Wissler and Duvall, Nos. 1–23). Old Man is the hero of the raft story and the diving animals in Arapaho myth, their version of which, as given by G. A. Dorsey ([a], pp. 191–212; also, Dorsey and Kroeber, Nos. 1, 2, 3), is one of the best recorded. It is interesting to note in this legend that the raft is made of four sticks — the cruciform symbol of the quarters — and that it supports a calumet, personified as "Flat-pipe," the "Father," and representing the palladium of the tribe. This connects both with the far north and the extreme south, for the story of the raft is known to the Athapascans of the North, while the Navaho and Pueblo traditions of the floating logs and the cruciform symbol are an interesting southern analogue (cf. *8 ARBE*, p. 278; and Chh. VIII. iv; IX. v). The Cheyenne creator, "Great Medicine" (G. A. Dorsey [b], pp. 34–37), is a similar, if not an identical being, personifying the Great Spirit, or Life of the World, as a creative individual. This Cheyenne myth tells of a Paradisic age when men were naked and innocent, amid fields of plenty, followed by a period in which flood, war, and famine ensued upon the gift of understanding. The Crow (Siouan) name for the creator, "Old Man Coyote" (*FCM* ii. 281), is an interesting identification of this character with Coyote. See Notes 6, 48. *Text references:* Ch. VI. ii (J. O. Dorsey [d], p. 513). — Ch. VII. iii, v.

64. Hermaphrodites. — Unsexed beings appear not infrequently, especially in the mythology of the western half of the continent. Matthews ([a], note 30) says: The word (translated "hermaphrodite") "is usually employed to designate that class of men, known perhaps in all wild Indian tribes, who dress as women, and perform the duties usually allotted to women in Indian Camps." The custom is certainly wide-spread. Father Morice describes it among the northern Atha-

pascans; and De Smet (p. 1017) gives a noteworthy instance of the reverse usage: "Among the Crows I saw a warrior who, in consequence of a dream, had put on women's clothing and subjected himself to all the labors and duties of that condition, so humiliating to an Indian. On the other hand there is a woman among the Snakes who once dreamed that she was a man and killed animals in the chase. Upon waking she assumed her husband's garments, took his gun and went out to test the virtue of her dream; she killed a deer. Since that time she has not left off man's costume; she goes on hunts and on the war-path; by some fearless actions she has obtained the title of 'brave' and the privilege of admittance to the council of the chiefs." Perhaps the most interesting case recorded is that of Wewha, a Zuñi man who donned woman's attire, described by Mrs. Stevenson ([c], p. 310) as "undoubtedly the most remarkable member of the tribe . . . the strongest both mentally and physically." The assumption of woman's attire and work by youths reaching puberty is a matter of choice. This choice the boy makes for himself among the Zuñi, and doubtless also in the other Pueblos where the practice exists. "Hermaphrodites" have a certain mythic representation in Zuñi ceremonies, and it is noteworthy that the Zuñi Creator is a bisexed being, "He-She" (M. C. Stevenson [a], pp. 23, 37). Among the tribes of the North-West Coast mythic hermaphrodite dwarfs, life-destroyers, appear as denizens of the moon (Boas [g], xxiii. 3; [j], p. 53). *Text references:* Ch. VIII. ii. — Ch. IX. vii. — Ch. XI. v.

65. Masks and Effigies. — The use of masks in rites intended as dramatic representations of deities finds its highest development in the South-West (among the Navaho and Pueblo tribes) and on the North-West Coast, though it is not limited to these regions. The purpose of the mask is impersonation, but their employment is not on the purely dramatic plane, since they can be worn only by persons qualified by birth or initiation — i. e. the mask is to some extent regarded as an outward expression of an inward character already possessed. In both regions masks are associated with ceremonies in honour of ancestral spirits or clan or society tutelaries rather than concerned with the worship of the greater nature-powers. The use of masks has to a degree affected myth: the Zuñi regard the clouds as masks of the celestial Rain-Makers; the Sun and Moon are masked persons; and in the North-West an interesting mythic incident is the laying aside of animal masks and the consequent conversion of the animal-beings of the First Age into mankind. Wooden images of divine beings also occur in these same regions, and with some ritual use, but on the whole idols are rare in America north of Mexico; objects of especial sanctity are more often in the nature of "Medicine," and even tribal *sacra* have the character of talismans

earlier beings animal or semi-human in form, is usually a rather unimportant theme, with little mythic expansion. Men are made from clay, sticks, feathers, grass, ears of maize, and, in one interesting myth recorded by Curtin, from the bones of the dead. Sometimes they are "earth-born," or issue from a spring or swamp; and in the North-West carved images are vivified to become human ancestors. See Notes 15, 18, 34, 35, 46, 57. *Text references:* Ch. IX. vi. — Ch. X. v (GODDARD [c], p. 185; KROEBER [e], p. 94; CURTIN [b], pp. 39–45). — Ch. XI. ii (BOAS [g], xxii. 1, 2); iv (BOAS [j], pp. 29–32).

BIBLIOGRAPHY

BIBLIOGRAPHY

I. ABBREVIATIONS

AA . . . American Anthropologist.
ARBE . . Annual Report, Bureau of American Ethnology.
BAM. . . Bulletin, American Museum of Natural History.
BBE . . . Bulletin, Bureau of American Ethnology.
FCM . . Anthropological Series, Field Columbian Museum.
JAFL . . Journal of American Folk-Lore.
JR . . . Jesuit Relations, Thwaites edition and translation.
MAM . . Memoirs, American Museum of Natural History.
PAM. . . Anthropological Papers, American Museum of Natural History.
UVC . . . University of California Publications in American Archaeology and Ethnology.

NOTE. — Citation by the author's name refers to the work noted under "General Works" or "Select Literature" (below). Where the same author has several works listed, they are distinguished by letters in the list and correspondingly referred to in the Notes.

II. BIBLIOGRAPHICAL GUIDES

Handbook of American Indians North of Mexico (30 BBE). Especially in part 1 (Washington, 1907), art. "Bureau of American Ethnology"; in part 2 (Washington, 1910), "Bibliography," pp. 1179–1221.

List of Publications of the Bureau of American Ethnology with Index to Authors and Titles (58 BBE). Washington, 1914.

The Literature of American History. A Bibliographical Guide. J. N. Larned, editor. Boston, 1902.

The Basis of American History (vol. ii of *The American Nation*, Hart, editor). By L. Farrand. Especially pp. 272–89. New York, 1904.

Narrative and Critical History of America. By Justin Winsor. Vol. i, *Aboriginal America*, "Bibliographical Appendix." Boston, 1889.

Native Races of the Pacific States of North America. By H. H. Bancroft. Vol. i, "Authorities Quoted." New York, 1875.

Manuel d'archéologie américaine. By H. Beuchat. Paris, 1912.

"Mythology of Indian Stocks North of Mexico," by A. F. Chamberlain, in *JAFL* xviii (1905). Also, same author, "Indians, North American," in *Encyclopaedia Britannica*, 11th ed.

"Ethnology in the Jesuit Relations," by J. D. McGuire, in *AA*, new series, iii (1901). (Guide to the materials in *JR*.)

III. COLLECTIONS AND PERIODICALS

Publications of the Smithsonian Institution, Washington, D. C.:
Contributions to North American Ethnology, vols. i-vii, ix, 1877-93.
Annual Report of the Bureau of American Ethnology, 1881 ff.
Bulletin, Bureau of American Ethnology, 1887 ff.
Report of the United States National Museum, 1884 ff.

Publications of the American Museum of Natural History, New York:
Anthropological Papers, 1907 ff.
Memoirs, 1898 ff.
Bulletin, 1881 ff.

Publications of the American Ethnological Society. F. Boas, editor. Leyden, 1907 ff. (Texts and translations.)

Publications of the Field Columbian Museum. Anthropological Series. Chicago, 1895 ff.

University of California Publications in Archaeology and Ethnology. Berkeley, Cal., 1903 ff.

Memoirs of Canada Department of Mines. Anthropological Series. Ottawa, 1914 ff.

Transactions of the Canadian Institute. Toronto, 1889 ff.

Proceedings and Transactions of the Royal Society of Canada. Montreal, 1st series, 1883-95; 2d series, 1895 ff.

"Ethnological Survey of Canada," in *Reports of the British Association for the Advancement of Science, 1897-1902.* London, 1898-1903.

Comptes rendus du Congrès international des Américanistes. Paris and elsewhere, 1878 ff.

Publications of the Hakluyt Society. Vols. i-lxxix. London, 1847-89.

Publications of the Champlain Society. Toronto, 1907 ff.

Jesuit Relations and Allied Documents. R. Thwaites, editor. Vols. i-lxx. Cincinnati, 1896-1901.

Early Western Travels. R. Thwaites, editor. Vols. i–xxxii. Cleveland, 1904–07.

Voyages, relations et mémoires originaux pour servir à l'histoire de la découverte de l'Amérique. H. Ternaux-Compans, editor. Tomes i–xx. Paris, 1837–41. (Mainly Latin America.)

Library of Aboriginal American Literature. D. Brinton, editor. Vols. i–vi. Philadelphia, 1882–85.

Encyclopaedia of Religion and Ethics. James Hastings, editor. Edinburgh and New York, 1908 ff.

American Anthropologist. Vols. i–xi, Washington, 1888–98; new series, vols. i ff., New York, 1899 ff.

Journal of American Folk-Lore. Boston and New York, 1888 ff.

Memoirs of the American Folk-Lore Society. Boston and New York, 1894 ff.

IV. GENERAL WORKS

(*a*) *Descriptive*

Catlin, George, [a], *Illustrations of the Manners and Customs and Condition of the North American Indians*. 2 vols. 2d ed., London, 1866.

——— [b], *Letters and Notes on the Manners, Customs, and Condition of the North American Indians*. 2 vols. New York and London, 1844.

De Smet, *Life, Letters and Travels of Father Pierre-Jean De Smet, S.J.* Chittendon and Richardson, editors. 4 vols. New York, 1905.

Lafitau, J. F., *Mœurs des sauvages amériquains*. Tomes i–ii. Paris, 1724. (An edition in 4 vols. was also issued simultaneously.)

Schoolcraft, H. R., [a], *Algic Researches*. New York, 1839.

——— [b], *Historical and Statistical Information Respecting the History, Condition and Prospects of the Indian Tribes of the United States*. Parts i–iv. Philadelphia, 1851–57.

(*b*) *Critical*

Brinton, D. G., [a], *Myths of the New World*. 3d ed., Philadelphia, 1896.

——— [b], *American Hero Myths*. Philadelphia, 1882.

——— [c], *Essays of an Americanist*. Philadelphia, 1890.

Lowie, Robert H., "The Test-Theme in North American Mythology," in *JAFL* xxi (1908).

POWELL, J. W., "Sketch of the Mythology of the North American Indians," in *1 ARBE* (1881).

RADIN, PAUL, *Literary Aspects of North American Mythology* (*Museum Bulletin No. 16, Canada Department of Mines*). Ottawa, 1915.

V. SELECT AUTHORITIES

CHAPTER I

AMUNDSEN, R., *The Northwest Passage*. London, 1908.

BOAS, F., [a], "The Central Eskimo," in *6 ARBE* (1888).

——— [b], "The Eskimo of Baffin Land and Hudson Bay," in *BAM* xv (1901).

——— [c], "Eskimo Tales and Songs," in *JAFL* ii, vii, x (1889–97).

GOSLING, W. G., *Labrador*. London, 1910.

MURDOCH, JOHN, "Ethnological Results of the Point Barrow Expedition," in *9 ARBE* (1892).

NANSEN, F., *Eskimo Life*. 2d ed., London, 1894.

NELSON, E. W., "The Eskimo about Bering Strait," in *18 ARBE* (1899).

PEARY, R., *The Conquest of the Pole*. New York, 1911.

RASMUSSEN, KNUD, *The People of the Polar North*. London, 1908.

RINK, H., *Tales and Traditions of the Eskimo*. London, 1875.

STEFÁNSSON, V., *My Life with the Eskimo*. New York, 1913.

THALBITZER, WILLIAM, [a], "The Heathen Priests of East Greenland," in *15 Internat. Amerikanisten-Kongress*. Vienna, 1910.

——— [b], "Eskimo," in *Handbook of American Indian Languages* (*40 BBE*, part 1). Washington, 1911. (Bibliography of Eskimo literature.)

CHAPTERS II–III

(*a*) *Algonquian Tribes*

BARBEAU, C. M., *Huron and Wyandot Mythology* (*Memoirs of Canada Department of Mines. Anthropological Series*, No. 11). Ottawa, 1915.

BLAIR, E. H., *Indian Tribes of the Upper Mississippi and the Great Lakes Regions*. 2 vols. Cleveland, 1911. (Early documents.)

BRINTON, D. G., [d], *The Lenâpé and their Legends* (*Library of Aboriginal American Literature*, v). Philadelphia, 1885.

COPWAY, GEORGE, *The Ojibway Nation*. London, 1850.

Dixon, R. B., [a], "The Mythology of the Central and Eastern Algonkins," in *JAFL* xxii (1909).

Heckewelder, John G. E., *Account of the Indian Nations.* Philadelphia, 1819. (Hiawatha legend.)

Hoffman, W. J., [a], "The Midewiwin or Grand Medicine Society of the Ojibwa," in 7 *ARBE* (1891).

Jones, William, *Fox Texts* (*Publications of the American Ethnological Society*, i). Leyden, 1907.

JR. Especially Le Jeune's "Relations."

Leland, Charles G., *The Algonquin Legends of New England.* Boston, 1884.

Mechling, W. H., *Malecite Tales* (*Memoirs of Canada Department of Mines. Anthropological Series*, No. iv). Ottawa, 1914.

Owen, Mary A., *Folklore of the Musquakie Indians.* London, 1904.

Parkman, Francis, [a], *The Jesuits in North America.* Boston, 1867.

——— [b], *History of the Conspiracy of Pontiac.* Boston, 1868.

Radin, Paul, [a], "Winnebago Tales," in *JAFL* xxii (1909).

——— [b], *Some Myths and Tales of the Ojibwa of Southeastern Ontario* (*Memoirs of Canada Department of Mines. Anthropological Series*, No. 2). Ottawa, 1914.

Rand, S. T., *Legends of the Micmacs.* New York and London, 1894.

Speck, F. G., *Myths and Folk-lore of the Timiskaming Algonquin and Timagami Ojibwa* (*Memoirs of Canada Department of Mines. Anthropological Series*, No. 9). Ottawa, 1915.

(*b*) *Iroquoian Tribes*

Canfield, William W., *The Legends of the Iroquois.* New York, 1912.

Colden, Cadwallader, *The History of the Five Nations of Canada.* 2 vols. New York, 1902.

Converse, Harriet M., "Myths and Legends of the New York State Iroquois," in *Bulletin 125, New York State Museum.* Albany, 1908.

Hale, Horatio, *The Iroquois Book of Rites* (*Library of Aboriginal American Literature*, ii). Philadelphia, 1883.

Hewitt, J. N. B., [a], "Iroquoian Cosmology," in *21 ARBE* (1903).

——— [b], artt. "Hiawatha," "Tawiscaron," "Tarenyawagon," in *30 BBE.*

JR. Especially Brébeuf's "Relation" from the Huron Mission and Jogues' Letter from the Iroquois country.

MORGAN, L. H., *League of the Iroquois.* H. M. Lloyd, editor. 2 vols., New York, 1901.

SMITH, ERMINNIE A., "Myths of the Iroquois," in *2 ARBE* (1883).

CHAPTER IV

(*a*) *Iroquoian Tribes*

MOONEY, JAMES, [a], "Sacred Formulas of the Cherokee," in *7 ARBE* (1891).

——— [b], "Myths of the Cherokee," in *19 ARBE*, part I (1900).

ROYCE, CHARLES C., "The Cherokee Nation of Indians," in *5 ARBE* (1887).

(*b*) *Muskhogean Tribes*

BUSHNELL, D. I., [a], "The Choctaw of Bayou Lacomb, Louisiana," in *48 BBE* (1911).

——— [b], "Myths of the Louisiana Choctaw," in *AA*, new series, xii (1910).

GATSCHET, A. S., [a], *A Migration Legend of the Creek Indians* (*Library of Aboriginal American Literature*, iv). Philadelphia, 1884.

MACCAULEY, CLAY, "The Seminole Indians of Florida," in *5 ARBE* (1887).

SPECK, F. G., "Notes on Chickasaw Ethnology and Folklore," in *JAFL* xx (1907).

(*c*) *Uchean Stock*

GATSCHET, A. S., [b], "Some Mythic Stories of the Yuchi Indians," in *AA* vi (1893).

CHAPTERS V–VI

(*a*) *Northern Athapascan*

JETTÉ, P. J., [a], "On the Superstitions of the Ten'a Indians," in *Anthropos*, vii (1912).

——— [b], artt. in *Journal of the Anthropological Institute of Great Britain and Ireland*, xxxviii–xxxix (1908–09). (Texts and myths.)

LOFTHOUSE, Bishop, "Chipewyan Stories," in *Transactions of the Canadian Institute*, vol. x, part I (1913).

MORICE, A. G., [a], "The Great Déné Race," in *Anthropos*, i–v (1906–10).

MORICE, A. G., [b], artt. in *Transactions of the Canadian Institute*, *Proceedings and Transactions of the Royal Society of Canada*, *Comptes rendus du Congrès international des Américanistes.*

PETITOT, ÉMILE, *Traditions indiennes du Canada nord-ouest.* Alençon, 1887.

(*b*) *Algonquian and Kiowan*

DORSEY, G. A., [a], "The Arapaho Sun Dance," in *FCM* iv (1903).

——— [b], "The Cheyenne," in *FCM* ix (1905).

DORSEY and KROEBER, "Traditions of the Arapaho," in *FCM* v (1903).

GRINNELL, GEORGE B., [a], *Blackfoot Lodge Tales.* New York, 1892.

MCCLINTOCK, WALTER, *The Old North Trail.* New York, 1910.

MOONEY, JAMES, [c], "Calendar History of the Kiowa Indians," in *17 ARBE*, part 1 (1898).

WISSLER and DUVALL, "Mythology of the Blackfoot Indians," in *PAM* ii (1909).

(*c*) *Siouan Tribes*

DORSEY, G. A., [c], "Traditions of the Osage," in *FCM* vii (1904).

DORSEY, J. OWEN, [a], "Dhegiha Texts," in *Contributions to North American Ethnology*, vi (1890).

——— [b], "Omaha Sociology," in *3 ARBE* (1883).

——— [c], "Osage Traditions," in *6 ARBE* (1888).

——— [d], "A Study of Siouan Cults," in *11 ARBE* (1894).

——— [e], "Siouan Sociology," in *15 ARBE* (1897).

EASTMAN, CHARLES A., [a], *The Soul of the Indian.* Boston, 1911.

——— [b], *Indian Boyhood.* New York, 1902.

FLETCHER, ALICE C., and LA FLESCHE, F., "The Omaha Tribe," in *27 ARBE* (1911).

LOWIE, ROBERT H., [a], "The Assiniboine," in *PAM* iv (1910).

MOONEY, JAMES, [d], "The Ghost-Dance Religion," in *14 ARBE*, part 2 (1896).

WILL and SPINDEN, "The Mandan Indians," in *Peabody Museum Papers*, iii. Cambridge, 1906.

(*d*) *Caddoan Tribes*

DORSEY, G. A., [d], *Mythology of the Wichita.* Washington, 1904.

——— [e], *Traditions of the Skidi Pawnee.* Boston and New York, 1904.

DORSEY, G. A., [f], *Traditions of the Caddo.* Washington, 1905.

——— [g], *The Pawnee, Mythology,* part i. Washington, 1906.

——— [h], *Traditions of the Arikara.* Washington, 1904.

FLETCHER, ALICE C., "The Hako: a Pawnee Ceremonial," in *22 ARBE*, part 2 (1903).

GRINNELL, GEORGE B., [b], *The Story of the Indian.* New York, 1898.

——— [c], *Pawnee Hero Stories and Folk-Tales.* New York, 1909.

CHAPTER VII

(*a*) *Salishan Tribes*

FARRAND, L., "Traditions of the Quinault Indians," in *MAM* iv (1909).

McDERMOTT, LOUISA, "Folklore of the Flathead Indians of Idaho," in *JAFL* xiv (1901).

TEIT, JAMES, [a], *Traditions of the Thompson River Indians of British Columbia* (*Memoirs of the American Folk-Lore Society*, vi). Boston and New York, 1898.

——— [b], "The Thompson River Indians of British Columbia," in *MAM* ii (1900).

——— [c], "The Lillooet," in *MAM* iv (1909).

——— [d], "The Shuswap," in *MAM* iv (1909).

(*b*) *Shahaptian Tribes*

PACKARD, R. L., "Notes on the Mythology and Religion of the Nez Percés," in *JAFL* iv (1891).

SPINDEN, H. J., [a], "Myths of the Nez Percé Indians," in *JAFL* xxi (1908).

——— [b], "The Nez Percé Indians," in *Memoirs of the American Anthropological Association*, ii (1908).

(*c*) *Shoshonean Tribes*

KROEBER, A. L., [a], "Ute Tales," in *JAFL* xiv (1901).

LOWIE, ROBERT H., [b], "The Northern Shoshone," in *PAM* ii (1908).

MASON, J. A., "Myths of the Uintah Utes," in *JAFL* xxiii (1910).

MOONEY, JAMES, [d], "The Ghost-Dance Religion," in *14 ARBE*, part 2 (1896).

POWELL, J. W., "Sketch of the Mythology of the North American Indians," in *1 ARBE* (1881).

SAPIR, EDWARD, "Song Recitative in Paiute Mythology," in *JAFL* xxiii (1910).

CHAPTER VIII

(a) Southern Athapascans

BOURKE, JOHN G., [a], "The Medicine Men of the Apache," in *9 ARBE* (1892).

GODDARD, P. E., [a], "Jicarilla Apache Texts," in *PAM* viii (1911).

MATTHEWS, WASHINGTON, [a], *Navaho Legends* (*Memoirs of the American Folk-Lore Society*, v). Boston and New York, 1897.

——— [b], "The Mountain Chant: a Navajo Ceremony," in *5 ARBE* (1887).

——— [c], "The Night Chant: a Navaho Ceremony," in *MAM* vi (1902)

STEVENSON, JAMES, "Ceremonial of Hasjelti Dailjis and Mythical Sand-Painting of the Navajo Indians," in *8 ARBE* (1891).

(b) Piman and Yuman Tribes

BOURKE, JOHN G., [b], "Cosmogony and Theogony of the Mojave Indians," in *JAFL* ii (1889).

DUBOIS, C. G., "The Mythology of the Diegueños," in *JAFL* xiv (1901).

JAMES, GEORGE W., *The Indians of the Painted Desert Region.* Boston, 1904.

KROEBER, A. L., [b], "Preliminary Sketch of the Mohave Indians," in *AA*, new series, iv (1902).

LUMHOLTZ, CARL, [a], *Unknown Mexico.* 2 vols. New York, 1902.

——— [b], *New Trails in Mexico.* New York, 1912.

RUSSELL, FRANK, "The Pima Indians," in *26 ARBE* (1908).

CHAPTER IX

CUSHING, F. H., [a], "Zuñi Fetiches," in *2 ARBE* (1883).

——— [b], "Outlines of Zuñi Creation Myths," in *13 ARBE* (1896).

——— [c], *Zuñi Folk Tales.* New York, 1901.

DORSEY, G. A., [i], *Indians of the Southwest.* Published by Atchison, Topeka & Santa Fe Railroad, 1903. (Bibliography.)

DORSEY and VOTH, "The Stanley McCormick Hopi Expedition," in *FCM* iii (1901–03).

FEWKES, J. W., [a], "Tusayan Katcinas," in *15 ARBE* (1897).
——— [b], "Tusayan Snake Ceremonies," in *16 ARBE* (1897).
——— [c], "Tusayan Flute and Snake Ceremonies," in *19 ARBE* (1900).
——— [d], "Tusayan Migration Traditions," in *19 ARBE* (1900).
——— [e], "Hopi Katcinas," in *21 ARBE* (1903).
——— [f], "The Tusayan Ritual: a Study of the Influence of Environment on Aboriginal Cults," in *Annual Report of the Smithsonian Institution*, 1896.
LUMMIS, CHARLES F., *Pueblo Indian Folk Stories*. New York, 1910.
STEVENSON, MATILDA COXE, [a], "The Religious Life of the Zuñi Child," in *5 ARBE* (1887).
——— [b], "The Sia," in *11 ARBE* (1894).
——— [c], "The Zuñi Indians," in *23 ARBE* (1904).
VOTH, H. R., "The Traditions of the Hopi," in *FCM* viii (1905).

CHAPTER X

(*a*) *Californian Tribes*

BANCROFT, HUBERT HOWE, *The Native Races of the Pacific States of North America*, iii, "Myths and Languages"; also, "Authorities Quoted," i, for bibliography. New York, 1875.
CURTIN, JEREMIAH, [a], *Creation Myths of Primitive America*. Boston, 1912.
DIXON, R. B., [b], "Shasta Myths," in *JAFL* xxiii (1910).
——— [c], "Maidu Myths," in *BAM* xvii (1902–07).
——— [d], *Maidu Texts* (*Publications of the American Ethnological Society*, iv). Leyden, 1912.
GODDARD, P. E., [b], "Hupa Texts," in *UVC* i (1904).
——— [c], "Kato Texts," in *UVC* v (1907–10).
KROEBER, A. L., [c], "Indian Myths of South Central California," in *UVC* iv (1905).
——— [d], "The Religion of the Indians of California," in *UVC* iv (1905).
——— [e], "Wishosk Myths," in *JAFL* xviii (1905).
MERRIAM, C. HART, *The Dawn of the World: Myths and Weird Tales Told by the Mewan Indians of California*. Cleveland, 1910.
POWERS, STEPHEN, "Tribes of California," in *Contributions to North American Ethnology*, iii (1877).

(b) Oregonian Tribes

Boas, F., [d], "Chinook Texts," in *20 BBE* (1894).

——— [e], "Kathlamet Texts," in *26 BBE* (1901).

Curtin, Jeremiah, [b], *Myths of the Modocs.* Boston, 1912.

Frachtenberg, L. J., [a], *Coos Texts* (*Columbia University Contributions to Anthropology*, i). New York, 1913.

——— [b], *Lower Umpqua Texts* (*Columbia University Contributions to Anthropology*, iv). New York, 1914.

Gatschet, A. S., [c], "Oregonian Folk-Lore," in *JAFL* iv (1891).

——— [d], "The Klamath Indians of Southwestern Oregon," in *Contributions to North American Ethnology*, ii (1891).

Sapir, Edward, *Wishram Texts* (*Publications of the American Ethnological Society*, ii). Leyden, 1909.

Chapter XI

Boas, F., [f], "The Kwakiutl Indians," in *Report of the United States National Museum*, 1895.

——— [g], *Indianische Sagen von der Nord-Pacifischen Küste.* Berlin, 1895. (Reprinted from *Zeitschrift für Ethnologie*, xxiii–xxvii.)

——— [h], "Tshimshian Texts," in *27 BBE* (1902).

——— [i], *Tshimshian Texts* (*Publications of the American Ethnological Society*, iii). Leyden, 1912.

——— [j], "The Mythology of the Bella Coola Indians," in *MAM* ii (1900).

——— [k], "The Kwakiutl of Vancouver Island," in *MAM* viii (1909).

——— [l], "Tshimshian Mythology," in *31 ARBE* (announced).

Boas, F., and Hunt, G., [a], "Kwakiutl Texts," in *MAM* v (1905).

——— [b], "Kwakiutl Texts. Second Series," in *MAM* xiv (1908).

Johnson, E. Pauline, *Legends of Vancouver.* 8th ed., Vancouver, 1913.

Jones, L. F., *A Study of the Tlingits of Alaska.* New York, 1914.

Swanton, John E., [a], "Contributions to the Ethnology of the Haida," in *MAM* viii (1909).

——— [b], "Haida Texts," in *MAM* xiv (1908).

——— [c], "Haida Texts and Myths," in *29 BBE* (1905).

——— [d], "Tlingit Myths and Texts," in *39 BBE* (1909).

——— [e], "The Tlingit Indians," in *26 ARBE* (1908).